Canadian Craft and Museum Practice 1900–1950

Sandra Flood

Mercury Series
Canadian Centre for Folk Culture Studies
Paper 74

Published by
Canadian Museum of Civilization

© Canadian Museum of Civilization 2001

CANADIAN CATALOGUING IN PUBLICATION DATA

Flood, Sandra
Canadian craft and museum practice, 1900-1950

(Mercury series, ISSN 0316-1854)
(Paper/Canadian Centre for Folk Culture Studies, ISSN 0317-2244; no. 74)
Includes an abstract in French.
Includes bibliographical references.
ISBN 0-660-17838-9

1. Handicraft — Canada — History — 20th century.
2. Museums — Acquisitions — Canada — History — 20th century.
3. Museums and women — Canada — History — 20th century.
I. Canadian Museum of Civilization.
II. Canadian Centre for Folk Culture Studies.
III. Title.
IV. Series.
V. Series: Paper (Canadian Centre for Folk Culture Studies) ; 74

TT26.F56 2000 745.5'0971'075 C00-901338-5

PRINTED IN CANADA

Published by
Canadian Museum of Civilization
100 Laurier Street
P.O. Box 3100, Station B
Hull, Quebec
J8X 4H2

Senior production officer: Deborah Brownrigg
Cover design: Roger Langlois Design

Front cover: "The Singers", stoneware, ca 1945, by Dora Wechsler, Ontario, CMC 94-589. (Photo by Harry Foster)

Back cover: Doukhobor woman (Mrs. Wasyl Bludoff) spinning at the Saskatoon Arts and Crafts Society demonstration (University of Saskatchewan, June 1925) S-2480 Saskatchewan Archives Board.

OBJECT OF THE MERCURY SERIES

The Mercury Series is designed to permit the rapid dissemination of information pertaining to the disciplines in which the Canadian Museum of Civilization is active. Considered an important reference by the scientific community, the Mercury Series comprises over three hundred specialized publications on Canada's history and prehistory.

Because of its specialized audience, the series consists largely of monographs published in the language of the author.

Titles in the Mercury Series can be obtained by calling 1-800-555-5621;
by e-mail to <publications@civilization.ca>;
by Internet to
<http://www.cyberboutique.civilization.ca>;
or by writing to:

Mail Order Services
Canadian Museum of Civilization
100 Laurier Street
P.O. Box 3100, Station B
Hull, Quebec J8X 4H2

BUT DE LA COLLECTION MERCURE

La collection Mercure vise à diffuser rapidement le résultat de travaux dans les disciplines qui relèvent des sphères d'activités du Musée canadien des civilisations. Considérée comme un apport important dans la communauté scientifique, la collection Mercure présente plus de trois cents publications spécialisées portant sur l'héritage canadien préhistorique et historique.

Comme la collection s'adresse à un public spécialisé, celle-ci est constituée essentiellement de monographies publiées dans la langue des auteurs.

Vous pouvez vous procurer les titres parus dans la collection Mercure par téléphone,
en appelant au 1 800 555-5621,
par courriel, en adressant votre demande à
<publications@civilisations.ca>, par Internet, à
<http://www.cyberboutique.civilisations.ca> ou par la poste, en écrivant au :

Service des commandes postales
Musée canadien des civilisations
100, rue Laurier
C.P. 3100, succursale B
Hull (Québec) J8X 4H2

Canadä

Abstract

This research looks at the relationship between the craft community, as an integral part of Canadian culture, and the museum community from 1900 to 1950. The relationship is examined primarily in terms of the recognition of craft by museums as arbiters of cultural value and custodians of national material culture.

Contemporaneous publications about craft are analyzed for location, authorship, geographical and craft media coverage, and key issues in craft discourse. In contrast to the limited focus of the publications, the survey of handcraft production uncovers a diverse range of craft makers and production circumstances. These include production to generate income, as part of the domestic economy, as a leisure activity, as therapy, and for community and national purposes. The composition and activities of a variety of craft organizations – including the national Canadian Handicrafts Guild – are documented, and a detailed account of the Saskatoon Arts and Crafts Society is given. The interactions of these organizations with related organizations and government departments, the subsequent involvement of governments in craft marketing and education, and the consequences for the development and perception of craft are explored. A survey of formal craft education through selected institutions and their programs, and the activities of studio craftspeople as a self-defined subgroup, completes this first overview of Canadian craft. The historiography and the survey of craft activity indicate that women were highly involved in writing, production, organizations – including marketing, exhibiting, promotion, collecting and education – and in formal craft education.

The multiplicity of community-embedded handcraft practices is contrasted with the more constricted activity of the small museum community. This is done through an account of the development of Canadian museums and of craft collecting by museums and by craft organizations in relation to museums. Craft organizations were the primary collectors of craft. Because of a number of factors, including gender (male dominated), history and focus, and disciplinary constraints, museums were unwilling to accommodate craft, with the consequent loss of early collections and devaluation of a major component of Canadian culture.

Résumé

Cet ouvrage est le fruit d'une recherche qui examine le rapport entre la communauté des artisanes et des artisans, comme partie intégrante de la culture canadienne, et la communauté muséale, de 1900 à 1950. On y étudie la relation principalement en termes de reconnaissance, par les musées, de cette communauté comme dépositaire de la valeur culturelle et gardienne de la culture matérielle nationale.

Des publications contemporaines touchant ce sujet sont analysées au regard des lieux, des auteurs, de la couverture médiatique géographique et de celle du milieu ainsi que des principaux thèmes du discours artisanal. Par opposition à l'objet limité des publications, l'étude de la production artisanale révèle tout un éventail d'artisans et de situations de production. Celles-ci comprennent la production comme moyen de générer des revenus, comme partie de l'économie familiale, comme activité de loisir et comme thérapie, dans un idéal communautaire et national. On y recense la composition et les activités de diverses associations d'artisanat — notamment la Corporation canadienne de l'artisanat — et on y donne un compte rendu détaillé de l'Arts and Crafts Society de Saskatoon. On y explore l'interaction de ces organismes et des organismes et ministères apparentés du gouvernement, l'implication ultérieure des gouvernements dans la commercialisation de l'artisanat et la formation qui s'y rattache de même que les répercussions sur le développement de l'artisanat et la perception qu'on en a. Une étude sur l'enseignement structuré de l'artisanat, réalisée par le truchement des programmes offerts dans des établissements choisis et des activités menées par des artisanes et des artisans en atelier, à titre de sous-groupe qui s'est lui-même défini, complète ce premier survol de l'artisanat canadien. L'historiographie et l'étude de l'activité artisanale indiquent que les femmes s'engagent très fortement dans la rédaction, la production, l'organisation — y compris la commercialisation, les expositions, la promotion, la cueillette et l'éducation — et l'enseignement structuré de l'artisanat.

La multiplicité des pratiques artisanales communautaires contraste avec l'activité plus restreinte de la communauté des petits musées. On le voit par l'exposé de l'évolution des musées canadiens et de la cueillette de pièces d'artisanat qu'effectuent les musées par rapport à celle que font les associations d'artisanat. Celles-ci ont été les premières à recueillir des pièces d'artisanat. En raison de certains facteurs, notamment le sexe (dominés par les hommes), l'histoire, l'orientation et les contraintes relatives à la discipline, les musées ont été réticents à accueillir l'artisanat dans leurs murs, avec pour résultat la perte des anciennes collections et la dévalorisation d'un élément essentiel de la culture canadienne.

Dedication

This research was, from its beginning,
with his consent and ongoing encouragement,
dedicated to my youngest son who faced death with great courage.

Magnus William Flood
1965-1997

Contents

CHAPTER 1 Introduction.. 1
Research resources and methods.. 1
Definitions... 3
    Craft.. 3
        Craft defined within art history... 4
        Craft defined by media and museum practice.................................. 4
        Craft defined as practice.. 5
        Historical practice.. 6
        Craft defined within folklore... 8
        Craft defined as handmade.. 9
        Thesis definition of craft and craftspeople.. 9
    Ethno-cultural parameters.. 10
    Time frame.. 11
Context... 12
    The land... 12
    The geopolitical entity.. 13
    Settlement.. 14
        Atlantic Canada... 15
        Central Canada.. 16
        The Prairies... 17
        British Columbia... 19
Craft at the end of the nineteenth century.. 20

CHAPTER 2 Historiography: "A new and fresh utterance"............................ 23
Introduction... 23
Historiography.. 25
    Publications.. 27
    Key Issues... 31
        Loss of skills.. 32
        National economy... 32
        Industrial design.. 32
        Craft:Machine... 34
        Rural life... 36
        National art.. 41
        Racial unity.. 45
        Universality... 48
        Art:Craft.. 49
Summary.. 53

CHAPTER 3 Crafts: "An important activity of Canadian Citizens" ... 57
Sources of information ... 57
Craft Production ... 62
    Crafts for a living ... 63
        Textiles ... 63
        Pottery ... 64
        Woodwork ... 68
        Metalwork ... 75
        Glass ... 78
    The Domestic Economy ... 81
        Textiles: Weaving, spinning, knitting, recycled products ... 81
        Basketry ... 86
        Furniture ... 88
    Leisure activities ... 90
        Woodwork ... 92
    General craft education and therapy ... 93
        Pottery ... 93
        Occupational therapy ... 96
    Community projects ... 98
        Quilts ... 98
        Churches ... 99
    National projects ... 100
        The war effort ... 100
Summary ... 101
    Range of activity ... 101
    The 'usual' ... 102

CHAPTER 4 Organized crafts: "Where crafts flourish there will be found a happy and contented people" ... 104
Craft cottage industries ... 104
    Individual initiatives ... 105
        Bell, Fairchild, Burke NS 1922 ... 105
        Charlotte County Cottage Crafts NB 1914 ... 108
        Romanchych AB 1928 ... 110
        Murray Tweeds BC 1932 ... 111
        Canada Homespun Reg'd PQ 1929-1960 ... 112
        Gaelic College Highland Home Crafts 1944 ... 112
    Missionary organizations ... 114
        Bissel Institute AB 1930s ... 114
        Grenfell Medical Mission NFD 1905 ... 114

NONIA NFD 1920	116
Star of the Sea Handicrafts NS 1938	118
Summary	118
Craft organizations	119
Saskatoon Arts and Crafts Society SK 1924-1956	119
Canadian Handicrafts Guild 1906-1974	130
Government intervention	140
Governments and rural women, and related ventures	140
Federal Department of Agriculture and CHG	140
Provincial Departments of Agriculture and the Women's Institutes	141
La société d'enseignement postscolaire MB	147
Searle Grain Company weaving program MB, SK, AB	148
Jubilee Guilds NFD	150
Governments and rural men	152
Governments, reconstruction and marketing	153
Federal government: initiatives	153
Federal government: reports	154
Provincial government initiatives PQ, NS, NB	158
Summary	164
CHAPTER 5 Studio crafts: "not only a craft but a *major* art"	167
Academic craft education	167
Owens Art Museum/Mount Allison University NB	169
Victoria School of Art/Nova Scotia College of Art NS	174
Ontario School of Art/Ontario College of Art ON	181
Winnipeg School of Art	186
Alberta Provincial Institute of Technology and Art AB	189
Vancouver School of Art BC	194
L'École du Meuble PQ	203
Summary	208
Studio craftspeople	211
Database	211
Class and education	214
Income generation	217
Selfconcept	221
Studios	221
Exhibitions	227
Associations	234
Canadian craft	239
Summary	241

CHAPTER 6 Museums and craft collections: "A courageous but precarious existance"

Introduction	244
Canadian museums to 1932	245
Central Canada: Montreal Museum of Fine Arts and the CHG collection	247
Collections at l'École des Arts Domestique and l'École du Meuble	249
Central Canada: National Museum of Canada and Marius Barbeau	251
Western Canada: Saskatoon collections and the Ukrainian Museum of Canada	260
University (Folk) Museum, Saskatoon 1910/17-1941	260
Saskatoon Arts and Crafts Society Collection 1925-[?]	262
The Museum of the Ukrainian Women's Association of Canada 1941	264
Western Canada: CHG Collections	268
Canadian Handicrafts Guild: Albert Branch	268
Canadian Handicrafts Guild: Manitoba Branch 1932	269
Eastern Canada: New Brunswick Museum	270
The Royal Commission on Arts, Letters and Sciences 1949-51	273
Canadian Museums 1932-1951	273
Craft and Museums	275
Summary	280
Discussion	284
Museums and Craft	284
Applied Arts	285
Anthropology	287
Gendered museums	289
CHAPTER 7 conclusion	291
The thesis	291
The context	291
The communities	291
The relationship between the communities	292
The shared understanding of craft	292
- through publications	292
- through activity	293
Extent of recognition of contemporary craft activity by museums	294
- effect on the public concept of craft	294
- effect on the craft community	295
Final comments	295
APPENDIX 1	296
APPENDIX 1:2a-e	298

APPENDIX 1:3	303
APPENDIX 2a-h	304
BIBLIOGRAPHY	312

Acknowledgements

This book is the text of a doctoral thesis submitted to the University of Manchester, England in 1998, with the exception of Chapter 2 which has been updated. Errors in presentation or interpretation are my own.

I thank the Department of History of Art, Manchester University for supporting this research, through their consent and through the financial support of Manchester University Studentships, and the Canadian Museum of Civilization, Hull, Quebec for work space, access to all facilities, to their ever helpful and expert staff, and other support through my status as an Associate Researcher.

I also gratefully acknowledge a grant from the Saskatchewan Arts Board, and The Sheila Hugh Mackay Foundation Inc., New Brunswick.

I thank my thesis Supervisors for their unstinting support:
Ian Wolfenden, Program Director, Art Gallery and Museum Studies, Manchester University and Dr. Stephen Inglis, Director General of Research and Collections, Canadian Museum of Civilization.

The following have provided me with otherwise unobtainable information or have gone beyond the call of duty or friendship to help, please accept my grateful thanks:
Cheryl Avery USK.A; Anne Barros ON; Elizabeth Bell BC; Ruth Bitner SWDM SK; Lynn Brockington VAG.A BC; Ronald Burke USA; Mary Burnett PEI; Cindy Campbell NGC.A; Joan Champ SK; Joyce Chown NS; Michael Clark ECIAD.L BC; Stan Clarke BC; Gail Crawford ON; Althea Douglas ON; Autumn Downey CHG:NWT; Beth Greenhorn ON; Marie Elwood NS; Cheryl Ennals UMA.A NB; Rose Marie Fedorak UMC SK; Winifred Fox NS/ON; Fredette Frame NB; George & Molly Fry, NB; Margaret Gaunt CGMB; Paula Gustafson BC; Tanya Harrod UK; Anne Hart CNS MUL NFD; Ruth Horlick SK; Tam Irving BC; Regina Landwehr Surrey Archives BC; Peter Laroque NBM; Gloria Lesser PQ; Betty Lord NS: Colleen Lynch NFD/NB; Tom McFall AB; Kathleen MacKenzie UStFX.A NS; Ellen McLeod ON; Claudine Majzels UW MB; John Massier KCA ON; Kevin Rice CCAGM PEI; Scott Robson NSM; Gail Rogers BC; Megan Rogers, MBFS NS; Heather Ross PNE BC; Joan Seidl VM BC; Elsa Shamus BC; Catherine Shields WAG MB; Judith Silverthorne SK; Ruth Stanton & daughter BC; Mark Vajcner UAB.A; Judy Villett AB; Madeleine Walker SK; Roberta York MB.

Abbreviations

Abbreviations are given in brackets after the full name on the first occasion it occurs. The abbreviations listed below are those used throughout the text.
provinces: these are also used in combination with abbreviations for branches of national organizations eg. Canadian Handicraft Guild Ontario Branch - CHG:ON

BC	British Columbia	NB	New Brunswick
AB	Alberta	NS	Nova Scotia
SK	Saskatchewan	PEI	Prince Edward Island
MB	Manitoba	NFD	Newfoundland and Labrador
ON	Ontario	NWT	NorthWest Territories
PQ	Quebec	YK	Yukon Territory

nb: '.A' after an institution indicates the archives of that institution

AC	Artists in Canada: A Union List of Artists
AGO	Art Gallery of Toronto/later Art Gallery of Ontario
CdF	Cercles des Fermières
CGJ	Canadian Geographic Journal
CGMB	Craft Guild of Manitoba
CGP	Canadian Guild of Potters, Toronto
CHG	Canadian Handicraft Guild
CNE	Canadian National Exhibition, Toronto
CNR	Canadian National Railway
CTS	Central Technical School, Toronto
CPR	Canadian Pacific Railway
CSL	Canadian Steamship Lines
EdAD	École des arts domestiques, Quebec
EdBA	École des beaux-arts
EdM	École du meuble, Montreal
NCW/LCW	National Council of Women/Local Council of Women
MAG	Metal Arts Guild
MBCM	Manitoba Craft Museum, Winnipeg
MMFA	(Art Association of Montreal gallery) Montreal Museum of Fine Arts
NAC	National Archives Canada, Ottawa
NBM	New Brunswick Museum, Saint John
NGC	National Gallery Canada, Ottawa
NMC/CMC	National Museums of Canada/later Canadian Museum of Civilization
NSCA	Nova Scotia College of Art, Halifax
NSM	Nova Scotia Museum

OCA	Ontario College of Art, Toronto
PAM	Provincial Archives of Manitoba
PEI:PE	PEI:Provincial Exhibition
PITA	Provincial Institute Technology and Art Alberta, Calgary
PNE	Pacific National Exhibition, Vancouver
SACS	Saskatoon Arts and Crafts Society
SKAB	Saskatchewan Archives Board (Saskatoon branch unless noted)
SPLm LHR	Saskatoon Public Library, main branch Local History Room
UAB	University of Alberta, Edmonton
UMA	University of Mount Allison, NB
USK	University of Saskatchewan, Saskatoon
UWAC	Ukrainian Women's Association of Canada
UWAC:UMC	UWAC:Ukrainian Museum of Canada, Saskatoon
VAG	Vancouver Art Gallery
WAAC	Women's Art Association Canada
WAG	Winnipeg Art Gallery
WI	Women's Institute (national FWIC)
WSA	Winnipeg School of Art
WWI	First World War
WWII	Second World War

CHAPTER 1
INTRODUCTION

This thesis examines the relationship between two communities, the museum community and the craft community, in the context of Canada from 1900 to 1950. It is generally presumed that museum collections act as the collective memory in relation to a nation's material culture and certainly assign cultural and economic value to practice. The thesis examines museum practice and craft production and craft organizations' activities to determine:
1. the degree of shared understanding of 'craft' and
2. the degree of recognition of contemporary Canadian craft activity by museums with its consequent effect on the development of a concept of contemporary craft in Canada.

There are no scholarly or popular histories of twentieth century Canadian craft activity, thus in order to assess museum response to craft production the thesis first surveys Canadian craft practice. The extent and variety of craft production described in chapters 3 to 5 is contrasted with the apparently limited interest of museums, chapter 6.

In examining craft activity in the period 1900 to 1950, this thesis also challenges the current craft community mythology that "nothing happened here in craft until the late 1960s, early 70s."[1]

Research Resources and Methods

Relevant published material on Canadian twentieth-century craft activity and production is sparse, localized, uneven, and content is restricted largely to region, medium and/or maker. There are no surveys from which to identify potential source material. The library classification system has over 34 categories and sub-categories under which craft information might be found, despite there being a library classification 'handicrafts'. This makes searches very time consuming and unpredictable in their outcome.[2] Information has been gleaned from scholarly publications, not necessarily directly about craft, including books and articles; publications relating to craft written for the general public, collectors and the craft community, which included books, booklets, magazine and newspaper articles, promotional material, exhibition lists, catalogues and

---

[1] A senior member of the BC craft community, during discussion, Canadian Craft Museum, Vancouver, 21 October 1996

[2] In addition, titles of books become less and less indicative of contents and with the imposition of a minimum inter-library loan fee of $10 by libraries speculative reading costs mount up.

government papers; and publications written for the general public including documentary and autobiographical or biographical material and fiction from the period or relating to the period. Current scholarly material, including several pre-publication manuscripts and theses, provided a 'snowball effect' through bibliographies and footnotes, however "more popular writings tend to omit footnotes or reviews of related literature."[3]

The problem of classification also applies to archives listings and to directories of other potential sources of information such as that of Canadian doctoral and masters' theses. Moreover much archival material relating to craft is listed under organizations, personal names or other unrelated headings requiring prior knowledge of these as a source. Archival material was mainly traced through references in popular publications. I made a number of brief visits to do research in provincial or organizations' archives, libraries or museums in the Halifax area NS, Saint John and Fredericton NB, Vancouver BC, Saskatoon SK, Montreal PQ and Winnipeg MB, and to meet senior craftspeople, curators, archivists, historians, collectors and others associated with the craft community. These visits also bought more vividly to life the particularities of different parts of the country, which was relevant to the contextualization of the information I was examining. Correspondence and conversations with senior craftspeople, curators, archivists, contacts in the craft community and others provided more information. In Ottawa I had access to the facilities of the National Gallery of Canada (NGC), the Canadian Museum of Civilization (CMC) and the National Archives Canada (NAC).

A search of the Artists in Canada (AC) database through the Canadian Heritage Information Network (CHIN) by media[4] provided limited information about individual craftspeople and, although some new names were found, there were notable makers missing. CHIN the computer collections classification system used by all major Canadian museums and galleries,[5] was accessed for information about products as indicators of activity in general and of named makers. Its use for searches is limited as its current lexicon does not have a definition 'handicraft', 'craft' or 'handmade', data is not consistent and may be determined by the type of museum and

---

[3] Janet C. Mainzer 'The Relation between the Crafts and the Fine Arts in the United States from 1876 to 1980' Ph.D. thesis (New York 1988) p.23-24 discusses the same problem in her area of research.

[4] The search was done first by computer through the CHIN database identifying media, makers, period active in chronological order, then by manually searching the makers files at NGC. Files contained newspaper clippings, less frequently cv.s, very occasionally catalogues, rarely bibliographies. The files of craftspeople who were also painters tended to concentrate on their fine art rather than their craft activities. Moreover the Directory is heavily predicated in favour of fine arts.

[5] A few provinces have a different system equivalent to CHIN for their provincial museums. CHIN as a collections management tool for Canadian museums was dismantled in March 1998, it is currently available as a subset of artifact collections data to contributing museums through Internet.

Introduction

department under whose aegis the artifact is,[6] and certain data such as donors is not available outside the museum of origin although collections staff at various museums responded to specific requests for information.

I read widely in material culture, folk culture, anthropology, art history, history and contemporary literature not only because they provided craft-related information but also to provide ways of contextualizing and constructing a craft history.

Museums offered hardly more published material than craft history. There are two overviews (Miers and Markham 1932; Key 1973) but published information about specific museums and their historical practices is limited. Although museums and collections generally have archival material relating to their development, time and distance limited on-site research.[7]

Typically for a survey thesis, as an initial foray into new territory and possibly a new discipline, it was difficult to make systematic searches and to build on previous authorities. The questions asked were the most basic: What activity went on, where, and who was involved. I first looked at contemporary textual material where it was available. Where I have not found contemporary material I have used later texts critically. I have also given primacy to original material, particularly the voices of makers and others within the craft community and museums. Particular resources, such as exhibition lists, and the ways I used them are described at the beginning of relevant chapters or sections.

Wherever possible I have looked at craft work from the period, in part as evidence of craft activity, types of activity and standards, also as evidence of collecting practices by museums and others. Much of this work was in public collections, but I was also fortunate to see craft works in private hands. I also looked at a wide range of illustrations and photographs for evidence of craft works and activity.

Definitions

Craft

The definition of craft is at the crux of much that concerns this thesis in relating a history both of craft and museum practice. The concept 'craft' is that evolving out of Western cultural history.

---

[6] Even within a museum there is variation, thus the Canadian Museum of Civilization data for a thrown stoneware plate gives 'Department - Folk; Category - Art Objects; Sub-category - Original Art; Group - Craft', for a thrown bowl in the same Department - Folk, the category is Packages and Containers.

[7] I spent a brief time doing research at New Brunswick Museum (NBM), Vancouver Art Gallery (VAG), Ukrainian Women's Association of Canada: Ukrainian Museum of Canada (UWAC:UMC), and University of Saskatchewan Archives (USK.A) on the defunct University Folk Museum; also I visited with staff at Nova Scotia Museum (NSM) and Manitoba Craft Museum (MBCM). I had access to archives and museum staff in all departments at CMC.

In the twentieth century the finer definitions of craft have varied, changing with time and depending on the purposes of the group using the word, although these definitions are frequently not articulated.

During the writing of my Master's dissertation I realised that the assumption of knowing what craft is is so deeply rooted that neither I in my questionnaire nor the museums in their policies had seen a need to define it. This was also characteristic of a very wide range of the literature. Rosalind Krauss, in a discussion of the ways in which, "categories like sculpture and painting have been kneaded and stretched and twisted in an extraordinary demonstration of elasticity, a display of the way in which a cultural term can be extended to include just about anything" suggests that we do in fact know what sculpture is, "It is a historically bounded category, with its own set of rules which are not open to very much change", and that this applies to other visual arts too.[8] However as I argued in my dissertation, "where something is not defined, we are unable to question decisions surrounding it, or ask what is excluded or why."[9]

Craft defined within art history
Janet Kardon, director of the American Craft Museum,[10] attempts to define craft by asking the following questions:
> "Is it different from other visual expressions, and if so, what are the differences? What is unique to craft, and how is it similar to other art forms? Where does it converge or diverge from the history of painting, sculpture, architecture, design, and the decorative arts? Who are its leading figures? What are the seminal works? What have been the critical issues? What are its primary documents?"

In doing so she clearly locates craft within the parameters of the fine arts and fine art historiography.

Craft defined by media and museum practice
In line with museum practice, Kardon then defines craft first by material, "one of the five craft materials, or disciplines, that have delineated the field - clay, fiber, glass, metal, or wood. Material has been so strong a determinant that each medium has attracted its own artists, writers, societies, publications, schools, collectors, exhibitions, and even museums", and second by technique, "the handmaiden of material".

She further defines craft through function (or utility) or reference to function; modest scale which

---

[8] A.Barnett 'A Stitch Out of Time' *Women's Art Magazine* (U.K.1993) p.11

[9] S.Flood 'Contemporary Craft Collecting in Museums' M.A. dissertation (Manchester: 1993) p.33

[10] J.Kardon ed. *The Ideal Home: The History of Twentieth Century American Craft 1900-1920* (New York 1993) p.24

Introduction

has "relegated craft to the domain of the merely decorative"; decoration which "often draw[s] on the aesthetic traditions of painting"; and tactility. Further refinements are formal training for the maker and innovation, "increasingly in this century" seen as a critical attribute of craft. The last of Kardon's attributes is spirituality, "the act of making a craft object often resonates with a spiritual aura that can bestow a vestige of spirituality upon the object itself"[11] which firmly moves craft into the fine art bailiwick. Michael Owen Jones defines fine arts as "allegedly genteel in nature, befitting the upper classes, serving primarily an aesthetic function, and tending to refine or elevate the mind."[12]

My M.A. research into museum craft collections and collecting policies concurs with Kardon's observation, the primary basis of designation for craft, albeit often by inference and default, is by material - glass, wood, etc. - or by product - furniture, ceramics, textiles, etc. A second level of criteria relates to technical excellence and skilled use of material, 'virtuosity'. The etymology of craft indicates that the transference of meaning to 'skill, art, occupation' takes place only in English.[13] In Old English, *craeft* meant 'skill, art; ability in planning or constructing; ingenuity, dexterity; an art, trade or profession requiring special skill or knowledge'. From Middle English on, 'craftsman' designated "a person who practices a handicraft, an artisan" or until late in the nineteenth century, "a person who cultivates one of the fine arts" i.e. an artist. 'Aesthetic excellence' was mentioned only once in the ten British craft collections policies I looked at. Innovation and designation of maker as an 'artist craftsperson' or 'professional' or 'acclaimed' were additional criteria in those policies.

Craft defined as practice

Noris Ioannou also cites media, plus form, function, ornament and technical proficiency but argues that these are "notions that may be reduced to: the artefact itself, the making of the artefact, and the *individual/social elements generally associated with the range of activity which could be referred to as craft.*" [my emphasis] Of contemporary craft, he says that this is an activity "manifested in a wide variety of practices and expressions" mirrored in the variety of titles appropriated by craftspeople, the diversity of creative work from "functional/domestic to gallery sculptural-decorative", and the range of models of practice or production, citing handmade to CADCAM, one-off to serially produced, traditional to innovative, one person studio to co-operative workshop.[14] Craft he defines "as a creative process that encompasses many ways of

---

[11] Kardon 1993 p.25

[12] M.O.Jones *The Handmade Object and Its Maker* (California 1978) p.16

[13] *The New Shorter Oxford English Dictionary* (Oxford 1993)

[14] N.Ioannou *Craft in Society: An Anthology of Perspectives* (Australia 1992) p.19

material manipulation, expression, communication, and social functioning."[15] Ioannou moves craft beyond the object and the fine arts. He maintains that craft can be examined within an interdisciplinary approach, which includes cultural anthropology, social history, material culture, ethnography and textual criticism, as well as art history and theory.

Ioannou, by implication, refers to the 'professional', those who conceive of themselves as craftspeople.[16] Pamela Johnson extends the constituency to "a wide range of practices that include a huge amateur sector, the country crafts, a concern with tradition, contemporary applied art which is innovatory and allied to style and fashion, interiors, architecture, the theatre and there is expressive work that articulates ideas, deals in metaphor, attempts to produce meaning using craft materials." Within this mixed and ill-defined group, however, her concern is with the post-war 'professionalised' craft producer involved with decorative and applied arts[17] and with expressive work in which the maker uses "what are thought of as craft materials...to create metaphor, express emotions or ideas, to pose questions, make a narrative, challenge perceptions."[18] Both position craft activity in relation to fine arts by default or association. Within the current craft establishment, writing reflects a narrow concentration on 'professional' activity and fine craft.

Historical practice
What Ioannou and Johnson infer about the diversity of makers, intent, practice and production models is true historically. Within the Western tradition, makers worked as a member of a guild, a religious community, in a small workshop including early industrial manufactures with division of labour requiring highly skilled, specialist and often guarded craft knowledge,[19] or as an outworker.[20] Craftspeople have worked for a patron or employer exclusively, for patrons by

---

[15] Ioannou 1992 p.26

[16] This is one of the definitions in the UNESCO recommendations concerning the Status of the Artist, Belgrade 1980 quoted *Saskatchewan Municipal Government Visual Arts and Crafts Economic Impact Assessment Final Report* 1996 p.2-3, "any person who creates or gives creative expression to, or re-creates works of art, who considers his/her artistic creation to be an essential part of his/her life, who contributes in this way to the development of art and culture and who is or asks to be recognized as an artist, whether or not he/she is bound by any relations of employment or association."

[17] *Crafts* calls itself "the decorative and applied arts magazine", a museum category full of confusion, so it may not be surprising that as Johnson says, "the crafts still do not have an established or easily recognisable position within contemporary culture."

[18] P.Johnson 'Naming of Parts' *Crafts* May 1995 pp.44-45

[19] R.L.Blaszezyk 'The Aesthetic Moment' *Winterthur Portfolio* 1994 p.123

[20] L.Green 'Ayrshire Whitework' *Piecework* March 1995 p.38

Introduction

commission and for the general market. They have included housewives, domestic servants and children working within the domestic economy. All social classes have produced craft as a leisure activity. Thus craft makers have come from a wide variety of situations which have affected process, control and intent.

Makers have worked alone, co-operatively or as one in a production sequence. They have had total control over design and production, control mainly over production (for example working to a design made by a painter for a tapestry or as an outworker producing lace), or have contributed to both. Design sources have included patterns and iconography in the public domain selected and arranged to personal taste or the work of a designer (which could be the maker). Work has ranged from being totally defined by another to the most personal meditation. All of these may fall along a continuum from the conservative to the innovative. In addition products may be one of a kind, one of a series, or a typical piece from a large number of similar pieces.

The standard of work from both working and leisure craftspeople has ranged from the crude to the refined, from the technically complex to the technically simple, from the decoratively ornate to plain; these have frequently had little bearing on the attributed aesthetic or social power of the work which relate to contemporary or cultural response. However, historically and ethnographically craft has had its own critical parameters which have included levels of skill and appropriate form and iconography.[21]

Craft works have since time immemorial covered the full continuum from the primarily decorative to the primarily functional. Craft objects, both decorated and plain, have carried meaning and metaphor intended by the artist or attributed by the community or individual.[22] Craft objects are enmeshed in a web of concepts and conventions which determines for what it is used, where, how and by whom. They can carry the same level of religious, political, moral and social propaganda and commentary as paintings, indeed craft often deals with issues not dealt with by the fine arts.[23]

---

[21] R.Parker *The Subversive Stitch: Embroidery and the Making of the Feminine* (New York 1989) pp.120-22 ref. appropriate distribution of embroidered flowers for a 18th century gown; J.C.Berlo *The Early Years Native American Art History* (UBC 1992) p.171 Karok baskets

[22] Csikszentmihaly and Rochberg-Halton *The Meaning of Things* (Cambridge 1981)

[23] S.Flood *Made for a Cause* catalogue (Saskatchewan 1994) For example, the Bayeux Tapestry c1070 like a lot of other historical embroideries was made to be hung on a wall like a painting. Its subject matter was a series of scenes carefully selected to illustrate and justify the right of William I to the English throne. Paintings are as frequently about status and decoration as ideas and are closely linked to decorative arts/crafts through iconography.

Craft defined within folklore
David S. Hults as a folklorist, citing Glassie, draws attention to other parameters, those of the constituency for which the work is made, patronage and the position of the artist within that constituency, transmission of skills and rate of change. Using these he defines three strands of craft: elite, popular and folk.[24]

Elite craft Hults sees as being driven by difference and competition, innovation is valued therefore change is accelerated. Transmission of skills is through academic institutions, and the audience frequently needs someone with formal training to mediate between the object and the viewer. The involvement of the art market, wealthy patrons, and more recently institutions and funding bodies as active generators and supporters distinguishes elite (or fine) craft.

Popular craft is that of mass production and the mass media, a commercial enterprise in which kits, patterns and how-to-do-it magazines and books are sold to the maker. Hults sees popular craft skills as transmitted through formal mechanisms, tied to rapidly changing fashions (although in my opinion some of these may be surprisingly conservative or nostalgic), and operating on the principle of the common denominator, reinforcing and spreading the dominant culture through wide spread access and frequent exposure. The completed popular craft object is not generally made for sale and is probably classwise the most widespread.

Folk craft Hults sees as being transmitted informally within a group which can be identified as peer, regional, ethnic, religious, occupational or national. It tends to be the most conservative because it functions within a group-sanctioned tradition but change does take place. The object has a cultural significance clear to those within the group which reinforces group solidarity. This significance is not necessarily open to interpretation by outsiders and thus flags a distinctive group. Folk craft produces work both for sale through its constituency market, work to commission and work for personal or group use.

What is not discussed is the hierarchical, class and financial structures implicit in the designations elite, popular, folk. Nor am I happy with the rural connotations of folk. Jones argues convincingly that "criteria usually employed to distinguish folk...art... from other kinds of behaviours are not consistent or mutually exclusive; several qualities such as the degree of originality or conservatism, the range of skills and imagination claimed to differentiate the folk...artist from the elite (or "sophisticated") artist are obviously disconfirmed by research of individuals making and doing things."[25] Jones' argument is that the categories are a product of the elite and are not productive in investigating modes of behaviour. Hults sees the three categories as a continuum,

---

[24] D.Hults 'Australian Craft: Within a Folkloric Context' in Ioannou 1992

[25] Jones p.7

Introduction

highly fluid and influencing and imitating each other, which suggests both that the categories are not substantial and that craft activity is more complex than categorization would suggest. Hults, Jones and others emphasize the context of the activity as well as the object.

Craft defined as handmade
Although it has not been mentioned in any of the above definitions of craft, the opposition of contemporary craft, the handmade, to industrial mass production seems to remain central, and is attributed to the writings of Ruskin and Morris at the end of the nineteenth century. As with 'aesthetics', only one British collection's policy mentioned 'handmade'. The opposition of craft to industrial seems not only defined by hand skills but also by the scale of production. The scale of craft production is small, one maker or a small team; the one-off object, a series, or small batch production; the production of the unique or of replicated objects in which slight variation is both expected and acceptable, in which the mark of the maker may be seen, and above all, the possibility of intervention and change at any point in production remains. This is opposed to the industrial where exact and mass duplication of an object takes place, the precise specifications of the object being predetermined, and the designer is separated from an increasingly deskilled maker. The Old English definition of *craeft* does seem to hint at distinctiveness as well as skill.[26] Historically and today, craft and industry form another continuum also highly fluid, influencing and imitating each other.

Thesis definition of craft
In the definitions above, once beyond the limited, market driven concerns of much fine art history, craft is situated in a wider constituency. It is a basic premise of this thesis that craft activity cannot be divorced from the activities and experiences of the wider community.

As the history of twentieth century Canadian craft activity is largely uncharted territory, I have chosen to interpret craft practice as widely as possible. I have not included craft production in which the object is entirely utilitarian with no variable or decorative component.[27] In line with the predominant definition by media, I have included the production of objects made in glass, metal, wood, fibre and clay, although this is not exclusive where materials have been used in a craft tradition, for example leather. Effective use of media presumes a level of technical proficiency and knowledge of materials although not necessarily at a virtuosi level. Small scale production forms another parameter of my definition of craft.

---

[26] *Gage Canadian Dictionary*

[27] Even within this definition craft includes a huge number of categories of objects. Certain categories which have become part of current 'studio craft' practice, such as musical instruments and toys, have been excluded because they do not appear as part of 'craft' practice in the period.

I have not used the terms 'amateur' as opposed to 'professional'. Amateur, presuming a lack of academic training and/or a part-time or secondary commitment, is problematic and predicated on a particular social and historical stance. Its use is class (upper and middle) and frequently gender (female) specific. The latter is illustrated in C.R.Ashbee's outcry against amateurs and what he saw as their underpriced competition. Referring to them collectively as 'Dear Emily' he says, "the output of the amateur, which is in bulk an output of very second rate work...has absorbed a large part of the skilled craftsman's market in many directions",[28] thus positioning women with the derogatory "Dear Emily", "amateur" and "very second rate work" against "skilled" and "crafts*man*".

The epithet is often wrong, for example Lucie-Smith refers to the socially prominent women leading the Arts and Crafts movement as amateurs, in fact most had academic art or craft training and, like William Morris and other male entrepreneurs, when they moved into new media they learnt from skilled artisans.[29] Primary responsibility for domestic commitments, particularly child rearing, interrupted or restricted the time available to many women. This was particularly onerous in the first half of the twentieth century when even critically acclaimed women painters were regarded as merely talented amateurs, if they were acknowledged at all.[30] Additionally if professional implies that craft production provides a financial return, much women's work which had an unacknowledged economic value would be discounted.

The soubriquet amateur (or worse, hobbyist) or professional is not necessarily relevant in relation to the quality of the finished product. Where craft is made purely for the maker's enjoyment I have referred to it as leisure craft.

I use 'tradition' in the sense of procedures or styles established over a period, as opposed to more ephemeral 'fashion'. Tradition is neither static nor necessarily of particularly long duration. I use 'artisan' for skilled craftspeople who make all or part of their living working in an established craft tradition, independently or in small manufactures and who learned their skills through apprenticeship or from other artisans.

Ethno-cultural parameters

'Ethnic' refers to groups distinguished by national or cultural characteristics, customs and

---

[28] E.Lucie-Smith *The Story of Craft: The Craftsman's Role in Society* (Oxford 1981) p.268 This is a reoccurring theme, "Under-the-counter hobbyists and nonprofessional craftspersons damage the industry. Church craft sales have wiped out the market." *Saskatchewan Municipal Government Visual Arts and Crafts Economic Impact Assessment, Final Report* 1996 Appendix 3

[29] Kardon 1993 p.40

[30] P.Blanchard *The Life of Emily Carr* (Washington 1987) p.177

Introduction

language, it is not pejorative and does not refer only to minority groups. The dominant culture in twentieth-century Canada has been European, from 1900 to 1950 British, and because the concept 'craft' as defined is European, I have not looked at the work of indigenous peoples. Some of the activities and organisations described in this thesis have extended to or been paralleled by First Peoples (Native Americans). First Peoples have produced and are producing fine craft work, which has influenced and been influenced by European practice, however inclusion of First Nations work could introduce other parameters and make this overview considerably more complex.

Immigrant groups until the late twentieth century were predominantly of European origin. However particularly on the Pacific coast, but in Western Canada generally, there were small groups of Chinese-Canadians. Used as cheap labour in building the Canadian Pacific Railway (CPR) and in mining, the population in British Columbia had climbed to nearly 40,000 by 1921. Mainly single men - a unique entry tax raised to $100 in 1901 and $500 in 1904 enforced the gender imbalance - they were the most highly discriminated against of all ethnic groups. On the west coast, Japanese-Canadians formed substantial communities prior to the Second World War (WWII). Early in the war they were deprived of their property and dispersed inland across the country. Afro-Canadians were also a very small group early in the century, unlike the situation in the United States. Distinctive work for these groups has not been identified by the literature and they are for the purposes of this thesis considered only where they are part of the dominant culture. By 1951, these groups formed 0.2%, 0.15% and 0.1% of a population of just over 14 million.

Canadian is not used in the sense of chauvinistic nationalism - Maple Leaf craft - although that Canadian craft should reflect a distinct Canadian culture has at various times been an issue. I wish to consider a particular arbitrary geopolitical entity which, for reasons of history, geography and peoples, has produced a milieu different from its powerful neighbour to the south and to the dominant colonising country, Britain.

Anglophone and francophone have been used to designate groups speaking the two official languages. Canadians of many ethnic groups and mother tongues customarily speak either, therefore language does not imply ancestry. Francophones of French ancestry live as variously named groups in many parts of Canada outside Quebec, for example Acadians in New Brunswick, although 'French Canadian' in many texts, such as those of Marius Barbeau, refers exclusively to Québécois.

Time frame
The dates 1900 to 1950 were chosen as the first half of an eventual survey of the whole century. In this sense the dates are arbitrary, the Canadian Handicraft Guild (CHG) was not incorporated until 1906, the first identified if brief overview of 'Canadian' craft was published in 1904, the first

major Canadian museums survey was completed in 1932. However the Women's Art Association Canada (WAAC), the precursor of CHG, had been active for twenty years by 1906[31] working towards a national organization for promoting, reviving, exhibiting and, above all, marketing crafts.

In another sense, the dates at a national level and within the museum and craft communities have an internal logic. The Canadian Handicraft Guild, operating from the early years of the century, drew attention to the production of the craft community in general and organized a range of activities on a scale not attempted in any country before. Run by women, who were administrators, albeit voluntary, rather than craft makers, it was an organization typical of this period. The Royal Commission on Arts, Letters and Sciences 1949-1951 comes at the end of the period. Submissions to the Commission and its Report give an official view of the state of the museum and craft communities. The Commission also marks changes, including a swing toward government cultural patronage (albeit at arms length) and a move by craftspeople, along with other artists, to organize themselves. It also marks closure of five decades of social upheaval, economic instability and nation building and the start of five decades of unprecedented stability and affluence.

The Context

Craft activity and museum practice are inseparable from the wider context. The Canadian milieu presented a unique situation defined by the land itself and by its settlement and creation as a national entity within the twentieth century.

The Land

Canadian histories always begin with geography because of the size of the country and because the geography of this northern continental land-mass determined population distribution in the twentieth century.

With the dissolution of the USSR, Canada became the largest nation state, encompassing 9,970,610 square kilometres. The TransCanada highway now runs east-west for 7699 kilometres from St. John's, Newfoundland (NFD) to Victoria, Vancouver Island, through five and a half time zones.

The physical configuration of the land tends to run north-south. On the Atlantic coast the northern reaches of the Appalachian mountains peter out through the Atlantic provinces of New Brunswick, Nova Scotia, Prince Edward Island and Newfoundland. Sandwiched between them and the dominant feature of the Canadian land mass, the Canadian Shield, the St. Lawrence River

---

[31] n/a *Industrial Canada* VII:8:647 March 1907

Introduction

lowlands drain the Great Lakes. The Canadian Shield, precambrian rock pitted with lakes and bogs, and forested where there is thin soil cover, sweeps south from Baffin Island, girdles Hudsons Bay covering almost all of Quebec and Ontario, and rises through the northern areas of Manitoba and Saskatchewan to cover two thirds of the Northwest Territories. Thus much of Canada through latitude or terrain is not suitable for farming, or offers a scant living at best. To the west and south of the Shield the interior plain runs through the Prairie provinces up to the MacKenzie Delta on the Arctic Ocean. Between the interior plain and the Pacific rise the northern ranks of the American cordillera, from the western border of Alberta through British Columbia and Yukon Territory. To the north is the High Arctic. To the south is the national border which parallels the east-west thrust of water routes, forests, soils and climate. In this vast land most Canadians live within a few hundred kilometres of this border.

The Geopolitical Entity

The earliest European intrusion followed by settlement came along the east coast and followed the St. Lawrence River into the Great Lakes area. Confederation in 1867 was not the establishment of modern Canada but merely the joining under a federal umbrella of the four original colonies: Nova Scotia and New Brunswick with a largely Canadian-born population engaged in agriculture, fishing and a booming shipbuilding and manufacturing economy; Canada East (southern Quebec), formerly New France, British by conquest but still predominately francophone and Catholic, and boasting the major mercantile cities of Quebec City and Montreal; and Canada West (southern Ontario),[32] the new west, largely immigrant and rural. This uneasy alliance, which the British North America Act had transformed into the Dominion of Canada under financial and political coercion from the British government, was held together by the promise of an expanded railway system and, particularly in Central Canada, by the commercial possibilities of the western hinterland, Prince Rupert's Land.[33]

In 1869, the Hudson's Bay Company's title to Prince Rupert's Land (or the Northwest Territories)[34] was transferred to the Dominion of Canada. In 1870 the fifth province, Manitoba, then a small area of a hundred square miles centred on the predominately Métis[35] fur trading settlement of the Red River Colony, joined the Dominion. On the Pacific coast the two bankrupt colonies of Vancouver Island and British Columbia reluctantly amalgamated in 1866 and, with generous financial grants and the promise of a transcontinental railway, became the sixth province

---

[32] The two latter were referred to as Lower Canada and Upper Canada, later jointly as Central Canada.

[33] Much of the information for this chapter came from Conrad et al Volume 1 and Finkel et al Volume 2 *The History of the Canadian Peoples* (Toronto 1993) and wide reading of Canadian history over many years.

[34] At that time the Northwest Territories included the entire west and north of Canada.

[35] People of French or British and Amerindian parentage forming a distinct cultural group.

in 1871.[36] The same lures enticed Prince Edward Island, the smallest of the Maritime[37] provinces into the Dominion in 1873. The island of Newfoundland, the remaining British Atlantic colony did not become part of Canada until 1949, (however for the purposes of this thesis it will be treated as part of Canada from 1900 on.)

By 1882 the prairies had been surveyed and divided into the districts of Saskatchewan, Assiniboia, Alberta and Athabaska. In 1905, with redrawn boundaries extending from the 49th to the 60th parallel, these became incorporated into the provinces of Alberta and Saskatchewan. Manitoba had its boundaries redrawn and extended likewise in 1912. The transCanada railway was completed by the CPR in 1886 and by 1891 the Dominion had over 20,000 kilometres of railway track.

Thus not until the early twentieth century did the country achieve a cohesive form with the major internal boundaries laid out, and with a transportation system covering the southern, most populated part of the country. Politically there was constant tension between provincial and federal governments, between regionalism and nationhood. This was complicated by historical precedent, shifting population and ethnic balances, and the size of the country. These in turn had particular effects on the practice of craft and museum history, both nationally and by region.

Settlement
Five years prior to Confederation, the population of Canada was 3,230,000 with barely 140,000 people outside the four federating colonies.[38] In 1871 the population of the Northwest was less than half that of PEI, the smallest province, and 1% of the Canadian population.[39] By 1901 there were 5,371,000 Canadian residents,[40] 88% were of British or French descent, 6.25% of German descent, and Dutch, Scandinavians, Russians, Jews and peoples from the Austrian Empire formed 2.24%. The following decade saw a population increase equivalent to that of the previous four

---

[36] Finkel p.38

[37] The Maritimes refers to the provinces of Nova Scotia, New Brunswick and Prince Edward Island; Atlantic Canada refers to the Maritimes and Newfoundland with Labrador

[38] Finkel p.28
1861 census: ON 1,396,091; PQ 1,111,566; NS 330,857; NB 252,047 = 3,090,579
p.33 MB <12,000 (9840 Métis, 1500 whites), BC 10,500 (8576 whites, 1549 Chinese, 462 blacks)

[39] Canadian population 3,689,000; PEI 94,021 (Finkel p.40); MB 25,000, Northwest 18,000 (G.Friesen *The Canadian Prairies: A History* (Toronto 1987) p.512)

[40] *Canada Year Book 1994* p.113

decades,[41] to 7,207,000. Between 1901 and 1921, the decades of major immigration to the Prairies, the Prairie population rose from 7.8% to 22.3% of the Canadian population and contained 54% of foreign born Canadians,[42] marking a major change in regional and ethnic population balances. By 1951 the Canadian population was 11,506,655.[43]

The geographic and ethno-cultural distribution of the population, settlement patterns and chronology, and population, power and wealth concentrations divided the country into distinct regions which were reflected in the craft and museum communities.

Atlantic Canada

In the Maritimes the descendants of the original French settlers, francophone Catholic Acadians were by 1900 a poor but fast increasing minority with a distinct identity. The dominant population was of British ancestry, English, Loyalists,[44] Irish and Scots, the latter the largest ethnic group in Nova Scotia. This ethnic mix changed little during the period as the economy stagnated and living standards dropped behind the rest of the country, emigration became a dominant trend and the great wave of New Canadians[45] bypassed the Maritimes on their way west. Areas retained distinct ethnic identities and, to varying degrees, retained traditional skills, techniques and products modified by time and circumstances. These were to provide a reservoir of knowledge and the impetus for a revival or reinvention of 'traditional' techniques and motifs.

The nineteenth century boom in manufacturing and ship building was over by 1900. The early establishment and prosperity of Maritime cities had led to the founding of a number of universities and art schools with craft programs, and museums. Outside the urban areas, agriculture, lumber and fishing brought a scant living.[46] The First World War (WWI) gave a brief boost to the economy but through the 1920s, fishing and farming were crippled by falling prices. Atrophy in the railways affected coal, iron and steel bringing industrial Cape Breton, NS, to the brink of civil war. The provinces were responsible for social policies and through the 1920s the poor were left to help themselves. In good years average incomes in the Maritimes barely reached

---

[41] During those four decades, emigration from Canada was substantially higher than immigration. Natural increase was always a considerably higher factor in population increase than immigration.

[42] Finkel p.216

[43] Finkel p.415

[44] Loyalists were mainly New Englanders of British origin (but also included people of African ancestry and others) who fled to the British Canadian colonies from the American Revolution.

[45] Usually applied to immigrants not speaking French or English.

[46] Finkel p.80

the level of the wealthiest provinces at the worst of the Depression. This deepening economic crisis stimulated craft cottage industry initiatives.

Newfoundland and the neighbouring mainland Labrador, a British colony until 1949, had a grossly unstable economy dependant on fishing and the limited production of domestic goods. As in the Maritimes, the fisheries were run by a handful of merchants through the truck system where credit was advanced for gear and sustenance against a monopoly on the catch, keeping communities in poverty and debt. The seasonal, often migratory, activities of sealing and fishing provided a poor living even in good times. The harsh environment encouraged little more than subsistence farming. French, Irish Catholics, Scots, New Englanders and English had settled in fairly distinct areas. Most people lived in small, isolated communities. The gross poverty attracted the intervention of 'outsiders' to initiate craft cottage industries.

Central Canada
Throughout the period more than half the Dominion's population lived in Central Canada and although that proportion fell from 75% in 1891 to 60% in 1921, it was rising by 1950. The centres of wealth and manufacturing had moved from the Maritimes to Montreal by 1900, which in turn was superseded over the next fifty years by the growth of manufacturing conurbations along Lakes Ontario and Erie centred on Toronto. In both major cities, wealth and manufacturing were controlled by an Anglo-Canadian elite. Quebec and Ontario however remained distinct societies.

Quebec, the original *Canada*, by 1900 had been in existence for almost 300 years. With more than threequarters of the population francophone and Catholic, Quebec maintained a separate cultural continuity. Quebec's population was polarized between a predominantly rural population mainly living on small and often marginal farms and its fast growing cities, particularly Montreal. There was constant emigration, to the West but principally to northern and eastern Ontario and to Quebec's cities.

Montreal, long Canada's largest mercantile city, became a major national transportation and banking centre. There was an impressive increase in manufacturing, including a strong textile and clothing industry which employed women, many as outworkers and formed a background to studio and rural textile production and promotion. For urban workers, francophone or anglophone, employment was sporadic, wages were meagre and, as in other Canadian cities well into the century, living conditions were grim with polluted water supplies, slum housing, poor diets and high infant mortality. Against this background the propaganda emanating from the Catholic church, Quebec politicians and the media, aimed at deterring the flow of rural populations to the cities is not altogether surprising. It led to initiatives in craft education, production and promotion.

Introduction

The Quebec government's priority to 1936 was economic development and private enterprise, before 1920 public health and welfare took less than 10% of government expenditure. To some extent, government inertia in social and nursing services and education was counterbalanced by the activity of a large population of nuns. The convents in all the francophone areas of Canada also seemed to have been a reservoir of ecclesiastical craft skills and to have eagerly participated in the acquisition and dissemination of craft techniques particularly through the provincial government sponsored weaving revival.

An old established and wealthy city, rivalling Boston, Montreal had a well-developed cultural infrastructure which benefitted from the new infusion of corporate and personal wealth and the location of corporate headquarters in the first decades of the twentieth century. This is reflected in the large number of museums, the activity of craft patrons and the anglophone interest in Québécois crafts, which was later overtaken by educated Québécois' reappraisal of their heritage.

Ontario, the most recently settled of the confederated colonies, had a population predominantly British-born or Loyalist, protestant and anglophone, and was generally more prosperous than Quebec. Central Canada received some western and southern Europeans throughout the period.

An economy based on commercial agriculture was superseded by manufacturing of consumer goods and by 1901 Ontario produced half the gross value of Canadian manufactures. The second industrial phase from 1900 on was in capital goods, machinery and equipment, and in new technologies. This concentration on manufacturing seems to have absorbed skilled Canadian-born and immigrant craft workers and to have equated industrial production with modernity in the public mind. Industrial growth, general prosperity, and comparatively high urbanization largely obviated the need for cottage industry programs experienced in other parts of Canada. In the literature activity appears concentrated in the greater Toronto area.

By 1900 the second largest city in the Dominion, Toronto's growing population and wealth would challenge Montreal for supremacy, and gave rise to corporate cultural patronage, major education institutions teaching craft programs, museums, and a concentration of studio craftspeople with associated activities. Ottawa the national capital, distanced on the Ontario/Quebec border from the economic and industrial metropoli of Montreal and Toronto, retained the psychological and financial advantage of being the nation's capital, which included the location of national institutions and the determination of federal cultural policies which, as in other areas, were perceived as favouring central Canada by the Maritimes and the West.

The Prairies
Under the Dominion Survey, 1871, the entire western part of Canada, starting from the baseline of the Fort Gary (Winnipeg) meridian and the 49th parallel, was surveyed and divided into basic units of a square mile, 640 acres. This unit was divided into quarter sections of 120 acres which

formed a homestead. The imposition of this extraordinary grid over a vast and varied landscape and the policies that went with it deeply affected settlement patterns. Fiftysix million acres were available for homesteading, approximately 60 million acres of prairie lands were available for sale.

Homesteading meant that people were widely scattered, particularly before the advent of the automobile, in contrast to the village-centred life of Europe. Land quality varied and many quarters were not suitable for farming. Although to prove-up[47] on a homestead only required a $10 deposit and a residence of three years, a substantial financial investment was needed to purchase equipment, animals, and supplies to survive the pioneering years and frequent years of crop failure or low prices. Under these conditions community, isolation, subsistence or commercial agriculture, and permanence all affected the continued production of craft.

The peopling of the West introduced a previously unknown diversity into the culture of the Dominion that was not experienced in eastern Canada until after WWII. By 1900, Manitoba was largely settled, first by Anglo-Ontarians, British and block settlements of Russian Mennonite, Icelandic and Jewish agricultural communities whose basic unit was the village not the homestead.[48] A second wave maintained the dominance of Anglo-Canadians and British but included large groups of northern and western Europeans settling in defined areas.

Major immigration into Saskatchewan and Alberta followed, between 1897 and 1913, and was composed almost equally of British, Canadians, Americans, eastern and western Europeans, with a sprinkling of other nationalities. With a hiatus during WWI the second major influx in the 1920s was ethnically an extension of the first. The population rose from 400,000 in 1901 to 1,654,000 in 1931. By 1931 the population of the three prairie provinces was 2,354,000.[49]

Friesen suggests that,
> "To a degree that is difficult to imagine today, these ethnic[50] people lived in discrete blocks...Some of the nearly exclusive enclaves included up to thirty towns and villages within a single district. The enclaves were isolated from each other and, to a remarkable degree, from the larger prairie community. They retained such localisms as ... dialect, customs, and traditions peculiar to their home

---

[47] To forfill the requirements to gain legal title

[48] None of these communities as such was long lived.

[49] Friesen pp.511, 512

[50] Friesen uses 'ethnic' in the Canadian sense of people not of British or French ancestry.

districts."[51]

As late as 1951 in the three prairie provinces nearly a third of the population had a mother tongue other than English or French.[52] However Friesen also suggests that many immigrant groups assimilated quickly to Anglo-Canadian norms voluntarily and with few apparent reservations, they did not abandon language and culture but "wished to be seen as good citizens and to conform to the conventions of their new home."[53] He also points out that,

> "Canadians in the West, exposed to the same environmental influences as American frontiersmen, demonstrably possessed very different ideas about politics and society.[54]

Saskatchewan quickly became the most populous and powerful, the people were the most diverse in background, but the one crop economy was tied to the vagaries of the international markets and unpredictable growing conditions. In 1928-9 Saskatchewan enjoyed the fifth largest average annual per capita income of $478, by 1933 in the depth of the Depression and drought years it had fallen 72% to $135, the lowest in the country. Both Saskatchewan and Manitoba (with the Maritimes) were slow growth provinces by 1950. Alberta grew more slowly on a broader economic base which included, as well as grain growing, ranching and mining, and by 1947 with the discovery of oil, it was set to join the fastest growing provinces of Ontario, Quebec and British Columbia.

British Columbia

British Columbia, to the far west, developed yet another distinctive population profile and economy. Settled by Americans, British and eastern Canadians, British Columbia also attracted a small European and Asian population reflected in Vancouver's population in 1911 which was 73.7% Anglo-Canadian, 11.5% European and 6.1% Asian.

Mining, lumber, scattered agricultural and ranching settlements in the interior valleys such as the Okanagan Valley, which became a major fruit growing area, and the rapid growth of the salmon canning industry supported an economy largely dependant on exports to Pacific Rim markets and Britain. British Columbia boasted the highest average per capita income in 1928-9 of $594 and managed to maintain that position in 1933 despite a 47% drop to $314. As in Ontario, the buoyant economy supported a cultural infrastructure in the major cities and obviated the need for cottage industry programs.

---

[51] Friesen p.272

[52] Of which some would be Aboriginal languages

[53] Friesen p.261

[54] Friesen p.171

Finkel et al argue that many characteristics of the pre-industrial economy still survived and "that the Canada of 1919 was more like the Canada of 1867 than superficial evidence would suggest",[55] in addition in the interwar period "it is likely that more than half of the Canadian people were never anything but poor."[56] Despite the settling of the agricultural West, in all areas the population drift to urban areas accelerated throughout the period. As wealth and people increasingly congregated in the cities, the disparity between the countryside and the cities, the affluent and the poor was exacerbated. The poor economic environment, in combination with an unsettled, diverse and thinly scattered population, impacted directly on craft maker, craft production and type of consumer, it also impacted on museum development through the level of community support and public spending priorities.

Craft at the end of the nineteenth century

The state of Canadian craft activity at the end of the nineteenth century reflected diminished artisan activity, the impact of British influence and imports, the rising profile of women in initiating and organizing cultural activity, and the effect of the Arts and Crafts movement on education, organizational philosophy and style.

Ian McKay, referring specifically to Nova Scotia, but describing a situation prevalent in eastern and central Canada argues that,
> "Industrial capitalism marginalized many urban crafts; others it destroyed entirely...The pattern of Craft disorganization was probably no less pronounced in rural areas. High levels of out-migration, the extensive penetration of the countryside by urban manufactures and merchant credit...the instability of occupational categories outside the cities meant that 'old ways' of making things were under severe pressure from the mid-nineteenth century on."[57]

Descriptive accounts of objects and makers in the late 1800s, written about synchronologically and uncontextualized, are not seen as being overtaken by new technologies, materials and fashions but as being overwhelmed by "the late 19th century storm of factory-made goods which were grotesque and unbeautiful."[58] Huia Ryder reflects Britain's New Imperialism and the

---

[55] Finkel p.203

[56] Finkel quoting Michiel Horn p.429

[57] Ian McKay *The Quest of the Folk: antimodernism and cultural selection in twentieth-century Nova Scotia* (Montreal 1994) p.155

[58] H.Ryder in R.Tweedie et al *Arts in New Brunswick* (NB 1967) p.261

corresponding need to export more manufactured goods[59] in linking the accelerating trend towards factory-made articles to "close economic and patriotic bonds" with England. British goods flooded the market affecting Canadian craft production particularly in the fast growing cities of the west such as Vancouver which had not had time to establish its own workshops and market niche,

> "For a rapidly growing town it was more natural to depend on pattern books for building, and to fill houses with readily available imported furnishings, than to develop local production...Arts & Crafts style furnishings were imported... English and American "art" pottery and ceramic tiles, and hand-made "art" glass products were shipped here."[60]

However by 1950 Finkel et al argue that Canada had achieved independent nationhood, and Britain had been replaced by the United States as the major trading partner and cultural influence.

Against the domination of imported goods ran national and local commercial competitiveness and cultural aspirations. Industries' need for staff with design and related skills ensured limited support for public art and technical school training. In Canada, as in Britain, this hastened the erosion of skilled craft labour but allowed access for a new group, women. Craft education through teaching studios, private schools and colleges, and designing for industry became acceptable areas of activity for women at the end of the nineteenth century.[61] The foundations were laid for some of the most influential craft schools during this period through the direct involvement of women. Women were also active in exhibiting, organizing exhibitions and in promoting the sale of work through organizations such as the Women's Art Association of Canada started in 1887 in Toronto by Mary Ella Dignam to serve women artists.[62] In 1894 the WAAC:Montreal Branch, the forerunner of the Canadian Handicraft Guild, was formed by Alice

---

[59] P.Johnson *The Offshore Islanders: A History of the English People* (1992) p.334

[60] M.Shaw-Rimmington *'The Arts and Crafts Tradition in Vancouver'* catalogue (Vancouver 1986) p.7

[61] For example Mary Martha (May) Phillips 1856-1937 (co-founder of WAAC:Montreal Branch and CHG) in 1892 with Harriette J. MacDonnell reorganised the Victoria School of Art, Montreal to teach fine arts, design and china painting and in 1897 became principal of the School of Art and Applied Design, Montreal, where programs included wood carving, ceramic art, pyrography and principles of design for application to manufacturing and crafts. Phillips was educated in the 1880s at Art Association of Montreal School, and Art Students League, New York.

[62] WAAC Toronto, founded 1887, had at various times 20 branches: 11 ON, 3 MB, 3 SK, 1 PQ, 1 NB, 1 AB. Ten were founded in the 19th century but branches continued to be founded until 1951. The majority were relatively short term, between 3 and 25 years, in 1989 four Ontario branches were still in existence, 2 having celebrated their centenary.
Allison Thompson 'A Worthy Place in the Art of Our Country: The Women's Art Association of Canada 1887-1987' MA dissertation (Ottawa 1989) p.202

Peck[63] and May Phillips with nineteen others. Societies such as these and the Arts and Crafts Society, Toronto,[64] founded in 1902/3 by Mabel Adamson[65] were inspired by the Arts and Crafts movement.

In North America, the Arts and Crafts movement with its mix of new design ideas, socialism and re-evaluation of craft emphasizing the equality of artist and craftsman, the elevating potency of making and the importance of the domestic interior swept through elements of the middle and upper classes. Canadians, given their constant contacts and rivalries with the United States, watched and learnt from stylistic, manufacturing,[66] educational and organizational developments particularly in Boston, Detroit, Chicago and Cincinnati. The British-Canadian art community closely followed developments in Britain through visits to the 'mother country', magazines such as *The Studio*, *The Builder* and *The Art Journal*, the immigration of trained practitioners and *aficionados*, and the importation of Arts and Crafts objects.

---

[63] Mrs Mary Alice Skelton Peck 1855-1943 Education: England, France possibly Sorbonne; European travel 1871, 1875-6. Widowed 1903, writer, teacher, weaver, bookbinder with own handpress. WWI worked in a private hospital London UK.

[64] Arts and Crafts Society of Canada, later Canadian Society of Applied Art. The membership, which included Alice Peck and Percy Nobbs, came from several cities; the aims were the encouragement of original design and its individual expression.

[65] Mabel Cawthra Adamson (Mrs Agar Adamson) 1871-1943 Studied enamelling and metal work at C.R.Ashbee's Guild of Handicraft, Chipping Camden, UK 1903-3; also an embroiderer, and later a potter; with husband set up Canadian branch of W & E Thornton-Smith & Co., interior decorators; founded Arts and Crafts Society of Canada; involved with executive Handicrafts Association of Canada:ON, Canadian Guild of Potters.

[66] Ontario furniture was built copying Gustav Stickley's "Mission Style" Shaw-Rimmington p.7

CHAPTER 2
HISTORIOGRAPHY: "A NEW AND FRESH UTTERANCE"[1]

This chapter looks at writing about Canadian craft in relation to my construction of a pan-Canadian history and as a textual support for craft collections. An analysis of texts in the period 1900 to 1950 covers the nature of the publications, types of author, national coverage, content and key issues, gaps and emphases. Ideas specific to the discourse on craft, as compared to fine art, are identified.

Introduction

The literature on the twentieth century craft movement in other countries is limited. In 1992, Grace Cochrane with the support of the Australian Craft Council produced the pioneering, comprehensive overview, *The Craft Movement in Australia: A History*.[2] Tanya Harrod is currently (1997) writing a account of the British craft movement with the partial support of the British Craft Council.[3] Kardon in 1994 described *The History of Twentieth-Century American Craft: A Centenary Project* as "the American Craft Museum's decadelong pioneering effort to organize a major exhibition series and compile a multi-volume history. At its culmination near the end of this century, the museum will have produced the first historical overview of the American craft movement."[4]

Kardon says, "It was apparent that the leading figures, the issues and the aesthetic development of craft in the century often have remained in discrete and unrelated clusters of information, separated by divisions of medium, region, or ethnicity, awaiting basic research, analysis, and compilation."[5] Furthermore, "Most texts focus on the marketplace and anecdotal commentary,

---

[1] W.Colgate *Canadian Art: its origin and development* (Toronto 1926) p.243

[2] G.Cochrane *The Craft Movement in Australia: A History* (New South Wales 1992)

[3] Tanya Harrod letter 20 June 1996 "My book has been partly funded by a grant from the Crafts Council to the publishers."

[4] J.Kardon ed. *Revivals! Diverse Traditions 1920-1945* (New York 1994) p.19
Kardon left ACM in 1997 and this program of publications and exhibitions is currently suspended, with 3 volumes bringing the history to 1945.

[5] Kardon 1994 p.22

offering minimal descriptions of artists or their objects... since scholarship is often in the formative stages and not properly co-ordinated, the available information is disparate and uneven" and must often rely on "clusters of memory systems rather than actual texts."[6] This is an accurate description of current Canadian historiography, which is compounded by not having a powerful, well-funded national craft organization,[7] or national magazine, as in Britain, Australia and the United States, the latter also having an associated major craft museum.[8]

Disparate and uneven information is not restricted to craft in Canada, related disciplines such as folklore and material culture have similar problems. Carpenter in 1979 comments "Canadian folklore studies are subdivided into encapsulated areas associated with delimited and identifiable entities usually regional and often ethnic within the country. Few all-Canadian studies or scholars exist."[9] In addition, she adds that interest had been in limited genres, and that "Canadian work has been extraordinarily selective in the peoples and traditions considered...Native people...compose only a small percentage of the nation's population (less than 2% in 1971). The materials concerned with the traditions of this minority have nonetheless vastly overshadowed anything associated with the larger populace other than French Canada."[10] Pocius in 1991 sees little change, "Canada is called a community of communities, a country of regions, and it is fair to say that many of these regions are more interested in self-definition than anything that could be considered pan-Canadian. Publications and exhibits focus on the range and characteristics of objects or traditions found locally. The researcher becomes the expert on a particular locality, and rarely sees any need to relate his or her work to neighbouring traditions...may be interested strictly in the artifacts within a certain political boundary or those things belonging to a particular ethnic or cultural group."[11]

---

[6] Kardon 1994 p.25

[7] By April 1996 the Canadian Craft Council no longer had any government funding or offices.

[8] "The American Craft Museum which for over 30 years had been a major program of the American Craft Council, became an independent, nonprofit organization in 1990, legally separated from the Council. From this point, the Museum began to form its own membership base distinct from that of the Council...Both organizations agreed to have an affiliate relationship...The American Craft Museum chose to end this affiliate status on January 1, 1997. Effective that date, benefits are no longer shared between the Museum and the Council." insert *American Craft* 57:1 February/March 1997

[9] C.H.Carpenter *Many Voices: A Study of Folklore Activities in Canada and their Role in Canadian Culture* (Ottawa 1979) p.65

[10] Carpenter p.21

[11] G.L.Pocius *Living in a Material World: Canadian and American Approaches to Material Culture* (Newfoundland 1991) p.243

Historiography: "A New and Fresh Utterance"

A concentration on minorities, on specific media, and on particular regions characterizes research into Canadian craft. The focus tends to be on object collection and description, by type or place, a connoiseurial approach concentrating on named makers, style and period, historical rather than contemporary, with minimal information about technique and little wider contextualization or interpretation. This militates against the construction of a coherent overview of national activity.

Even this limited research did not start until relatively late. Lesser[12] notes that in francophone Quebec, distinguished by being the longest settled area of Canada, scholarly interest in their material heritage, which became for political reasons an area of intensive research, did not begin until the 1920s and 1930s when it was primarily focussed on the period encompassing the French Regime to pre-Confederation (1600-1867). Marius Barbeau, ethnologist at the Museum of Man,[13] influenced by Franz Boas, is credited with initiating scholarly research and was the most prestigious and prolifically published writer on "Canadian craft", ie. Québécois craft, for more than a decade. During the same period, Jean-Marie Gauvreau, director of l'École du Meuble, with aid from the Quebec Ministry of Trade and Commerce prepared an inventory of Quebec craftspeople, information which was published in journal articles and as *Artisans du Québec* in 1940.

Historiography

The earliest published accounts of pan-Canadian activity in the twentieth century that I have identified are two articles attributed[14] to Alice Peck, one of the cofounders of CHG, in *The Argus*[15] 1904 and *Industrial Canada*[16] 1907.[17] A booklet *The Arts and Crafts of Canada* by William Carless published in 1925 furnishes the next comprehensive overview.[18] Carless was a professor in the department of Architecture at McGill University, Montreal who with colleague

---

[12] G.Lesser *École du Meuble 1930-1950* catalogue (Montreal 1989) p.107

[13] See chapter 6 for a critique of this attribution and discussion of Barbeau's work

[14] Neither article has authorship

[15] n/a [attributed to Alice Peck] 'The Canadian Handicraft' *The Argus* 1904 pp.15,16

[16] n/a 'Canadian Industries in the Home' *Industrial Canada* 1907

[17] These are, I suspect, only two of a number of articles written by Peck throughout her association with WAAC:Montreal Branch from its establishment in 1894 and its Home and Handicrafts Committee, and then with CHG.

[18] W.Carless *The Arts and Crafts of Canada* (Montreal 1925)

Ramsey Traquair[19] and Barbeau were doing pioneering research on Quebec architecture.[20] The booklet was the fourth in a series on Art and Architecture published by the University. The contents were reprinted, with additions, from articles in *The Family Herald and Weekly Star*.[21] Over the next 40 years, punctuated only by the publication in 1943 of Mary Graham Bonner's *Made in Canada*[22] and in 1967 of *A Heritage of Canadian Handicrafts* edited by H. Gordon Green[23], articles[24] in journals and newspapers are the main sources of published information on craft activity. Newspapers, through journalists and occasionally members of craft organizations, seemed to have consistently covered local activity, however the information remained, with the exception of national newspapers, mainly in the originating community.

An analysis was done of 92 published texts circulated nationally or within a major constituency rather than locally.[25] The questions covered the nature of the publications, audience, authors, national and regional cover, and content, Appendix 1:1. From this original group of publications a selection was made of 32 texts by 28 authors, reflecting a wide-ranging approach to craft, from which key issues were isolated, Appendix 1:2a-e. These key issues and their number of references were grouped under a hierarchy of national (29), societal (24) and personal benefits (58), with attributes of craft (130) as a distinct but connected cluster. Charting these themes shows ranking and interconnections, Appendix 1:3.

---

[19] Traquair's mother, Phoebe Anna Traquair was a leading member of the Edinburgh Arts and Crafts movement, a painter, muralist, embroiderer, enamellist and designer. She corresponded with Percy Nobbs, also in the McGill Architecture department. Traquair's sister Hilda (Mrs John? Napier), who emigrated to Canada, worked with her mother on embroideries, as did her daughter (or niece) Mrs Margaret Bartholomew. Traquair published on the origins of hooked rugs.

[20] Montreal: McGill University Publications Series XIII (Art and Architecture) Carless *Architecture of French Canada* #3 1925; Traquair #1 1925, #5 1926; Traquair and Barbeau #13, #14 1926, #22, #29 1929.

[21] *The Family Herald and Weekly Star* Montreal 1 and 8 April 1925

[22] M.G.Bonner *Made in Canada* (New York 1943)

[23] H.G.Green *A Heritage of Canadian Handicrafts* (Toronto 1967)

[24] Articles, particularly those by academics, tended to be repeated in different journals under different titles, and to turn up as chapters in books. For example, Barbeau's 'Isle aux Coudres' published in *Canadian Geographic Journal (CGJ)* April 1936 appears in his book, *Kingdom of Saguenay* of the same year, as the chapter 'Bright Yarn on the Loom.' Wilfrid Bovey's *Canadian Handicrafts Survey of Domestic Art and Craft in Canadian Intellectual and Economic Life* 1938 is printed as 'Canadian Handicrafts' in *The Canadian Banker* 1939.

[25] In one sense this is a random selection, however despite this being an incomplete list, critical reading and comparison of the texts leads me to believe the results are valid.

Historiography: "A New and Fresh Utterance"

Publications - Appendix 1:1

The 92 publications included 11 books, 4 booklets, 2 government reports, an instruction manual and 74 articles. The government reports were included because their committee and consultative process involved many major agents from craft organizations and therefore act as a voice for ideas in circulation in a sector of the craft community;[26] despite the number of people actually involved, authorship for each report is attributed to one person.[27] The manual is included because of its introductory historical overview.

Only half of the books were specifically about craft activity or craftspeople, of these one was a book for children and four were in French. Two books were Quebec travelogues and three were art histories. As art histories rarely mentioned craft, these are exceptions. F.B.Housser[28] 1926 quotes Arthur Lismer on craft. William Colgate[29] 1943 locates handicrafts in a chapter with murals and portraiture in which craft becomes part of a polemic about taste, industrial design and education; three craftspeople are mentioned in detail - Douglas Duncan, a Toronto bookbinder, and Erica and Kjeld Deichmann, potters from Sussex, NB. D.G.W.McRae[30] 1944 gives craft one page of text but five pages of pictures of contemporary work principally from Quebec and Ontario. A children's reader,[31] contains a story about a real craftsman, John A. Petrik; another story entitled 'Never worked and never will' concerns a woodcarver.

Of the 74 articles, 5 were scholarly papers, 50 were in journals appealing to particular interest groups, such as *Canadian Geographic Journal* (15) and after 1943, *Canadian Art* (7), business/professional in specialist journals or current affairs magazines (13), arts (5), education

---

[26] Quotations in the discussion have occasionally been taken from the 'Handicrafts' section of the *Report of the Royal Commission on Arts, Letters and Sciences* (pp.235-238) although it was not included in the analysis as, despite evidence from 44 societies or individuals, the Massey Commission makes it clear that in an investigation of Canadian 'Arts' it had not expected to deal with 'handicrafts', and its interest was clearly elsewhere. It is quoted as a reflection of an aspect of government which was to later affect the craft community. There are also a few quotations from other texts outside the analysis which elucidate the idea under discussion.

[27] The 1941 Russell Report committee included 12 men and 1 woman (from Indian Affairs). The 1944 Russell Report committee included 17 men and 3 women. 'Visitors' included 8 men and 10 women including Vaughan, Bovey, Crowell, and Gibbon. 'Correspondents' included 10 men, 2 named women. It is noticeable that a higher proportion of women exists among the 'Visitors'. The proportions are 3:1 men:women. Bouchard and Barbeau were on both committees. The Reports are discussed in chapter 4

[28] F.B.Housser *A Canadian Art Movement* (Toronto 1926)

[29] Colgate *Canadian Art: its origin and development* (Toronto 1943)

[30] D.G.W.McRae *The Arts and Crafts of Canada* (Toronto 1944)

[31] B. McLeod 'Petrik the Potter' in *Gay Adventurers* (Toronto: Macmillan 1944)

(1) and women (9); 10 were in magazines of general interest and 9 in major newspapers (4 Montreal based, 2 Toronto based, and 3 in Western Canada, the latter dealing with western Canadian activity and aimed at rural audiences.)

There are 60 authors, Barbeau dominates with 13 publications. The authors range from architects, artists and government employees (3 in craft departments, 2 in agricultural departments, one in overseas trade) to journalists. Two were museums employees, Barbeau and Ruth Home, Royal Ontario Museum. Thirteen come from craft organizations (4 from CHG) and only 8 I know to be craftspeople. Possibly only one author was primarily a craftsperson.[32] The principal actor is therefore mediated predominantly through an educated, middle or upper class (which may or may not reflect the social situation of the craftsperson), non-participant viewpoint. Exceptionally the voice of the maker is heard through quotations. The material is written from different degrees of involvement with craft, with different goals and foci, for different audiences even though the tone of all the publications, including academic and government documents, is popular and easily accessible to a general audience. The publications almost never appear aimed specifically at craftspeople.

The gender of the writers is 28 male[33] to 29 female, 2 are unknown. All the scholarly articles and books, except a book for children, were written by men. Article authors are 20 men to 28 women which, given the contemporary predominance of male scholars and journalists, would indicate that craft was seen as a women's interest area and was an area in which women were highly active.

'Content' indicates the main focus of the publication and excludes overlap. Five texts were general (usually travelogues) rather than craft focused. Twentysix texts dealt with a specific article, technique or medium such as hooked rugs (6), Assomption sashes (2) weaving (10), wood carving (2), pottery (5), needlework, fine and base metalsmithing, and printed textiles. Nine dealt with named craftspeople: a book details major Québécois studios and craftspeople c.1940. Twentynine were surveys of activity, 13 covering Canada (2 were government reports), 10 covering Quebec, and one each for Central Canada, Eastern Canada, New Brunswick, the Prairie provinces, Saskatchewan and British Columbia. Although organizations were often mentioned in surveys, only 10 texts concentrated on particular organizations, the national organization CHG (4), its Ontario branch (2) and small marketing/production organizations in Nova Scotia, New Brunswick, Saskatchewan and British Columbia. Three articles focussed on formal craft education, through a national survey, Vancouver programs and l'École du Meuble, Montreal. Although the role of craft was under continual discussion, in the late 1940s articles discussing the role of craft in the

---

[32] My knowledge of these authors is incomplete but other than those identified, none has been cross-referenced through my database of craftspeople.

[33] See note above on gender bias in Russell report committees 1941, 1944.

post-war world proliferate.

Geographically, 28 articles are national[34] in scope but 18 were written after 1942. Provincially, 29 publications concern Quebec; 4 are in French, of which 3 are amongst the 13 authored by Barbeau. In comparison, 9 articles concern Ontario. One concerns Central Canada and 2 Eastern Canada. Six texts feature the Atlantic provinces, Nova Scotia 3, New Brunswick 2 and Newfoundland, at that time not a part of Canada, 1. Twelve texts cover the West[35] - Western Canada 1, the Prairie provinces 2,[36] Manitoba 1, Saskatchewan 1, Alberta 2, and British Columbia 5. In the light of further research, this provides an inaccurate and inadequate overview. This kind of regional imbalance also occurs in art histories. As late as 1943, Colgate in *Canadian Art* allots fine art in 'Central Canada', in this case southern Ontario, seven of seventeen chapters, Quebec gets two, Nova Scotia one but the chapter on the Maritimes continues the saga of Nova Scotia artists and devotes a paltry four pages to New Brunswick artists. The "North West"[37] and British Columbia share one chapter.

With few exceptions, the writing reflects an extraordinarily centralist and arbitrary view. Until WWII this is in part due to a relatively small, predominantly anglophone circle centred in Montreal who with Marius Barbeau in Ottawa dominated the field. Situated in Montreal were McGill University (Traquair, Percy Nobbs,[38] Carless - all architects, and later I.H.Crowell), and the headquarters of the CHG (Peck, Wilfrid Bovey, John Murray Gibbon), the *CGJ*[39] and the CPR (Gibbon). Barbeau, as the recognised expert and high profile promoter, appears a common link with, for example, E.-Z. Massicotte, Carless,[40] Georges Bouchard[41] and Gibbon. Housser,

---

[34] Where texts are to do with general topics such as planning and are not obviously aimed at a particular region or organization, I have considered them national in scope.

[35] Four were published by a prairie based company or publisher.

[36] These cover the same activity

[37] The "North West" ceased to be the North West in 1905 with the creation of the provinces of Saskatchewan and Alberta.

[38] Nobbs was knowledgeable about "the Old Crafts of Britain". Peck *Sketch of the Activities of the Canadian Handicrafts Guild* (booklet n/p 1929) p.13

[39] *CGJ* had branch offices in Toronto, Winnipeg, Calgary and Vancouver.

[40] Carless returned to England in 1929 and was unable to give a repeat to the Ottawa Arts Club of earlier talks, in Quebec and Montreal, on "Canadian Handicrafts." CMC.A Barbeau correspondence, Barbeau to Carless 19 March 1929; Carless to Barbeau 21 March 1929

[41] Bouchard and Barbeau sat on the two Russell committees 1941, 1944

1926, writing principally about the new, quintessential Canadian painters, the Group of Seven, quotes Lismer and A.Y.Jackson who accompanied Barbeau on the first of his craft-collecting forays to Île d'Orlèans and Île aux Coudres in 1925. Lismer, formerly principal of the Nova Scotia School of Art and in 1925 vice-principal of the Ontario College of Art, was involved with craft education. Bonner, 1943, a professional writer, who grew up in Halifax, NS and lived in New York, leaned heavily on information from Barbeau, who she contacted through Paul Standard of the CPR. The CPR was a major supporter of Canadian craft through their publicist, Gibbon who organized a number of Folk Festivals across Canada, the Quebec festivals with Barbeau, and through sales outlets in its hotels.

Thus common background, social and professional contacts and location affect the earliest overviews. None can be called a rigorous survey. They use easily accessible information, quoting the same ideas and small number of makers and organizations. A very limited range of traditional textiles from Quebec and the Maritimes, weaving and hooked rugs, receive primary coverage. The Prairie provinces *per se* are not referred to except through the craft activity of 'New Canadians', non-anglophone immigrants. Typically, Colgate mentions British Columbia only once, referring in passing to a named craftswoman[42] and "handicraft groups that are springing up on every side, but more particularly in the provinces of British Columbia, Quebec, New Brunswick and Nova Scotia."[43] Surveys from CHG written by Peck, who with other founding members before WWI travelled across the country and were responsible for making the organization truly national, and Bovey cover the widest ground geographically and by media.

A thorough survey of national craft activity was not achieved until 1943/44 when *CGJ*[44] published a national overview in eight articles, mainly written by members of CHG.[45] The Guild's attempt to publish a book, *Crafts in Canada*, through the Canadian publisher Dent and Sons started in 1926 but was eventually frustrated in 1933 by the disparaging suggestion that, despite their unrivalled knowledge and experience, they publish it as a children's text book.[46] In 1937,

---

[42] Lilias Farley educated at the Vancouver School of Art, sculptor in clay and wood, commended for textile designs at the British Empire Industrial Art Exhibition 1930

[43] Colgate p.244

[44] At that time Barbeau was on the board of both CHG and *CGJ*.

[45] Ellen M.E.McLeod 'Enterprising women and the Early Years of the Canadian Handicraft Guild 1905-1936' M.A.dissertation (Ottawa 1994) p.175 McLeod says that CHG members contributed articles on handicrafts to a series in the *Family Herald and Weekly Star*, to *Macleans* and *Canadian Home and Gardens* in 1927.

[46] McLeod pp.11, 33-34, 17-8. McLeod suggests that the book arose in part from the lectures on craft organized by CHG at McGill University 1926/7 and given by members of foreign consulates (possibly 7 of the 24 writers were associated with the talks) and the "inferior Canadian handicrafts exhibit at the 1927 Imperial Institute Exhibit in

Historiography: "A New and Fresh Utterance"

Georges Bouchard, founder of the Cercles des Fermières and a listed contributor to CHG's unpublished book,[47] wrote,

> "[E]xperts in the different phases of handicrafts should cooperate to produce in one volume a comprehensive survey of the entire subject in Canada. Hitherto there has been no attempt to treat the subject as a whole. A first-rate account of these matters would be most interesting and would reveal to the public treasures of an astonishing nature."[48]

In 1929 a 22 page booklet *Sketch of the Activities of the Canadian Handicraft Guild and of the Dawn of the Handicraft Movement in the Dominion* written by Peck detailed the history of CHG, and in 1934 a shorter history by Peck was published in *CGJ*. *Canadian Handicrafts: Survey of Domestic Art and Craft in Canadian Intellectual and Economic Life*, a 16 page booklet written by a former CHG president (1931-1935), Wilfrid Bovey, was published in 1938. Bonner's *Made in Canada* was one in a series of 'Books for Young People' published by the American company Borzoi and is a superficial, romantic account. Green's *A Heritage of Canadian Handicrafts* 1967 was written as a Centennial project by members of the Women's Institute.[49] There is no book on pan-Canadian craft written from within the craft community.

Key Issues - Appendix 1:2a-e, Appendix 1:3

Carless, in 1925, raised ideas[50] which continued to reoccur throughout the period. They are also ideas which are specific to the discourse on craft and distinguish it from fine art. These ideas cover: concerns about skills and traditions and their loss; the contribution of craft production to the national economy; the contribution of craft to industry through the improvement of design;[51] the benefits of craft as an occupation; handcraft as embracing a universal, participatory community; and craftspeople's role in the establishment and constitution of a distinctive, inclusive Canadian culture, embracing the multicultural nature of the population rather than reflecting only

---

England." The book was to consist of 24 articles covering the crafts of First Nations (5), the two dominant cultures and other European and Eastern European cultures, and a chapter on CHG. Spinning, weaving, ceinture flechée, quilts and Italian lace and embroidery were also covered. McLeod Appendix D p.185 As early as 1929 Dent & Sons requested a second school edition for a juvenile audience. In February 1933 Dent terminated the project.

[47] "'The Spinner'. 1800 words. Photograph" McLeod p.185

[48] Georges Bouchard 'The Renaissance of Rustic Arts' *Scientific Agriculture* 1937 p.15

[49] I recognize only one writer, Geneva Lent, as an active craftswomen although other writers may have been. See chapter 4 on the Women's Institutes and craft.

[50] He covers 20 of 25 categories identified.

[51] This was common ground for art and craft.

the dominant 'founding nations', the French and the British. The link between craft and rural life is developed. Also the changing location of craft in relation to fine art is constantly alluded to, implicitly and explicitly.

These themes are presented as Canadian, societal and personal issues, and in relation to particular definitions of craft (Appendix 1:3.) They reoccur singly or in combination from all sources and are embedded in the activity of craft organizations and later, government. It is hard to know whether they generated, shaped or simply described activity.

Loss of skills
The loss of skills and traditions was a concern which up to WWII was directly (15)[52] or indirectly alluded to by almost every writer. It was pivotal to activity and ideas.
> [W]e buy things rather than make them...We lose that *skill of hand* which should be *common in every civilized community*, and with it a *source of occupation*..."[53]

> "In 1896 many of the cottage industries in the eastern provinces of Canada were in a very languishing condition and in some districts they were already becoming extinct. In the west except among the Indian tribes they were non-existent or merely appeared in widely separated localities."[54]

National economy
At a national level, key issues are almost equally divided between the national economy (14) and a national art (15). However the economy at all levels, against a background of the settlement of the bulk of Canada's agricultural land, the Depression, the prairie Drought, the continuing economic crisis in the Maritimes and a world war, looms large both in the explicit connections and in their number and complexity. Craft is linked in three ways with the national economy, through the critique of industrial working conditions, product design and consumer preference initiated by William Morris and others shown in references to craft and industrial production (13), through the potential role of the craftsperson as industrial designer (5), and through the link with rural life (15).

Industrial design
The craftsperson as industrial designer has the fewest explicit references in this period. Typical of implicit references is the way Carless links instruction in design and craftworking with "more

---

[52] Numbers in brackets refer to direct references in articles, there are considerably more indirect allusions eg. Carless alludes to but does not directly discuss the role craftspeople might play in industrial design.

[53] Carless p.4

[54] M.A.Peck 'Handicrafts from Coast to Coast' *CGJ* 1934 p.201

Historiography: "A New and Fresh Utterance" 33

individual output of artistic work" and with the separation of designer and maker "which is only advantageous from the standpoint of commercial distribution,"[55] the inference being that the trained designer/maker would be a better production designer because of his knowledge of making, techniques and materials. Arthur Lismer c.1926 wrote "articles for a business man's magazine urging Canadian manufacturers to originate new designs in textiles, pottery, furniture and other manufactured products" advocating that manufacturers, salesmen, retailers and advertisers get together with artists.[56] There is a gap until the increased importance of Canadian manufactures and craft production during WWII, with planning for their continuation in the post-war period, resulted in the Interdepartmental Committee on Canadian Handcrafts, 1944. The fifth of seven findings states, "that <u>standards for industrial production</u> of useful and decorative commodities may be greatly improved through encouraging closer co-operation with craft designers and craft specialists (makers of original models for mass production)."[57] There was only one representative from the Board of Trade on the Committee and no manufacturers. Colgate suggests that, "One of the chief obstacles to progress in the past has been the lack of contact and mutual sympathy and understanding between the artist and the manufacturer."[58] He points out that chemists, accountants, lawyers and engineers "have established themselves in the great task of production" but not artists, who could produce designs both simple, for ease of machine production and cost reduction, and visually attractive "so that delight in them as well as demand for them may increase."[59]

In general, writing about how the designer/craftsperson fitted into the industrial scene was vague, "[A] long term policy planned to provide for the gradual merging of fine handicraft into fine machine art"[60] or "Through advance experimental production by specially trained craftsmen many new industries may be established."[61] These industries, with an eye on Scandinavian successes, were "domestic linens, fine tweeds, crystal, metal and clay products."[62] Remarks about the

---

[55] Carless p.18

[56] Housser p.174 Lismer appears to use 'artist' in its most general sense, in the context including craftspeople.

[57] D.H.Russell *Review Statement outlining the Work and Recommendations of the Provisional Interdepartmental Committee on Canadian Hand Arts and Crafts* (Ottawa 1944) p.4

[58] Colgate p.246

[59] Colgate p.246

[60] E.W. Wood 'A National Program for the Arts in Canada' *Canadian Art (CA)* 1944 p.93

[61] N.E.Vaughan 'The Future of Handicraft in Canada' *Public Affairs* 1943 p.10

[62] Vaughan p.10

designer/craftsperson and industry seems to reflect both industry's lack of recognition of the importance of the designer and to have been superseded by designer/craftspeople's own activity in finding small-scale production niches.

Craft:Machine
Carless, 1925, critiques industrial products,
> "Often there is only *bad workmanship and poor design* [in department store furniture]; and pervading it all the *unmistakable mark of commercialized machine production*...how seldom is there any evidence of the workman himself - of the *human touch* which should be apparent in every *work of art* and which tells us that *pleasure and interest were found in the making*,"

identifying attributes of craft such as the mark of the 'human hand' (13), 'skill' (15) and superior 'quality' (21), which has the highest ranking. These are directly linked with the handcraft:machine dialectic. 'Originality' (10), 'ingenuity' (4), and 'patience' (as opposed to the speed of machine production and equated with quality or "fine workmanship") (4) are inferred links. Colgate's critique, 1943, is more sweeping,
> "every sort of commodity produced by the average mind and bought by the common average public [also by "many who have had had superior opportunities" he later admits] is too often vulgar to the last degree,"[63]

indicting, in best Arts and Crafts fashion, both industrial design and the consumer.

Bouchard, 1937, and Sr. Anselm, 1942, position craft in the competition with manufactured products,
> "In the early days home industries were productive of articles of mere utility (i.e. linen for sacks, cheap home spun) as well as of articles of ornamentation...We are concerned at present with the beautiful rather than the useful only, because mass production has discouraged the producer of cheap articles."[64]

> "What we should encourage is not a cheap type of handwork that can undersell machine products, but rather a superior type of work that will command a higher price than machine products and be worth it."[65]

According to Anselm, this superior handwork has a distinctive character, better workmanship and better quality materials, and appeals because it is an interesting product of good quality, "not because it is 'the thing' to use handicrafts". In this there appears little move away from the

---

[63] Colgate p.242-3

[64] Bouchard p.14

[65] M.Anselm 'Handcraft for Commercial Purposes: its Possibilities and Dangers' *Maritime Art* 1942 p.154

original Arts and Crafts position.

The critique of industrial working conditions is also explicit and implicit in the writing. Location, independence, childcare and health are part of the dialectic,
> "It is difficult for the city dweller to visualize this industry [home weaving in the Laurentians], which requires no factories, no stated hours of work...The baby sleeps peacefully in its cradle, lulled by the soft rhythmic clatter of the loom, and if he wakens, mother and grandmother and big sister are right there...In summer the machines [looms] may be moved outdoors...and the family works in the healthiest surroundings. In Winter the warm attic accommodates the home industry."[66]

> "Handloom weaving also is superior to machine weaving if judged by the effect it is likely to have on the worker. The hand weaver is employed in a pleasant, ingenious occupation which exercises all her faculties, while the attendant on a power-loom is engaged in a monotonous toil in which intense watchfulness only is required[67]...The operation of the hand-loom calls for quite a great deal of energy and skill."[68]

Given conditions in many Canadian cities and factories, the critique has a sound basis, however it glosses over the economic exigencies and political, sectarian and ethnic agendas, discussed in chapter 4, which linked the national economy, rural life and the personal economic benefits of craft.

Bovey elaborates "independence" to make it the definition of a craftsperson, in contrast to the industrial worker,
> "the handicraftsman obtains his own materials, chooses his own design, completes the job from start to finish and finds a market."[69]

He admits that independence is relative giving as an example that a weaver must consider what materials are economically available, time and cost of making and design in relation to consumers' purse and preference, and available marketing outlets.

---

[66] A.MacKay 'French-Canadian Handicrafts' *CGJ* 1930 p.28

[67] H.Turcot *The French-Canadian Homespun Industry* (Ottawa 1928) p.10

[68] Turcot p.13

[69] W.Bovey *Canadian Handicrafts Survey of Domestic Art and Craft in Canadian Intellectual and Economic Life* (Montreal 1938) p.5

Rural life

In almost all of the texts examined, apart from the national surveys in the 1940s, craft production and craftspeople are located in the countryside.[70] This polarization was fuelled by the nostalgia of the urban, middle-class 'tourist' reflected in writing exhibiting, to a greater or lesser degree, a 'rural romanticism' and by the initiation of 'folk culture' studies, the discovery of the exotic, transient, rural 'other', whose main proponent was Barbeau.[71] It was also fuelled by the reality of a rural population tied into seasonal work and market uncertainty and by governments intent on land settlement. Lismer comments on the latter in 1925,

> "In very many instances these immigrants [from Europe] have some form of expression other than the business of agriculture. There must be among them leaders, workers in metal and wood, potters and stone-cutters...In our policy of Canadianization, in thinking only in terms of agricultural development, we do not seek to preserve these talents..."[72]

Peck recalls CHG's universal commitment at the beginning of the century,

> "to reviving and making profitable all such crafts as could be carried on in cottage or castle, *in town* or in the remotest part of the country."[73] [my italics]

However by 1938 a president of CHG, despite providing contrary evidence,

> "Toronto[74] has many outstanding craftsmen, as have other cities[75]...It would, of course, be absurd to suggest that all the tweeds and other "peasant" materials and articles which modern Canada uses for clothes and curtains and ornaments are country-made. Beautiful woven stuffs are produced in more than one Canadian city. Charming iron work is wrought by modern architect-craftsmen...Skilful potters are at work in town as well as by country streams."

---

[70] This is not true of local newspaper accounts, particularly those relating to formally trained craftspeople.

[71] Barbeau is explicit about this polarization in his account of the first Canadian Folk Song and Handicraft Festival, Quebec City, "It appeared that town and country folk did not easily meet on common ground. They found themselves at variance as to ways and means in foods, in songs, in dress, and in craftsmanship, and both groups were equally honest and determined." Elsewhere he contrasts "habitant stock" with "bourgeois class", information gained by word of mouth with information from books, and housewives with trained professionals, suggesting that class and formal education were at least as potent forces. Barbeau 1948 p.128-130

[72] Housser p.173-4

[73] Peck 1934 p.202

[74] The whole sentence reads, "If one had to pick the most notable Ontario craftwork it would be in metals - Toronto has many outstanding craftsmen, as have other cities; but there is also much excellent work in pottery and woodcarving." He characteristically conflates Ontario with Toronto.

[75] Bovey 1938 p.12

linked craft firmly to rural life,

> "It is not surprising that on the whole we look to the country rather than to the city for our craftsmen and women. To say that handicraft cannot thrive in cities would be...wrong...but handicrafts...thrive better in country air. There are economic reasons, but...the art of which handicrafts are an expression is essentially part of Canadian rural life. The independence of the handicraft worker is the independence of the farmer; the scenes that the rug-maker depicts are country scenes; the tweeds from the weaver's loom exude country air."[76]

Bovey, by highlighting hooked rugs and handweaving, chooses those crafts most closely associated with rural Quebec and the Maritimes and most heavily promoted through marketing agencies.

Carless, 1925, identified Canadian art and craft roots through "art traditions which have grown up in this country in the past" and those "which are continually being brought in by immigrants."[77] The "past" was that of Eastern Canada but, in fact, the cluster of anglophone authors and organizations in Montreal and Barbeau's work led to a concentration on the rural heritage of francophone Quebec. MacKay's explanation is a contemporary mixture of naivety, condescension and half-truth,

> It is curious that in their peaceful, white homes along the St. Lawrence River, there has survived so strongly an occupation essential to pioneer Canada...Today, many of the original pioneer homes of Quebec's sister province, Ontario, have electric power for all kinds of modern household equipment. The people wear 'store' clothes, and the household linen and woollens come from great manufacturing houses. They tour in their motor cars and come home to the radio which links them closely with all the outer world. They are not isolated. Many of their sons do not remain on the farms. Daughters seek occupation and education in the larger cities. Father and mother look forward to retiring to town or village life.
>
> Not so in rural Quebec, where farming is an hereditary calling, and where the struggle with nature remains primitive...Modern conveniences are not regarded as essential or even particularly desirable. Here is a people content with a simple life, grateful for health, and faithful to the religion which is their strongest guide.
>
> The peaceful monotony of the spindle and the loom is a natural pursuit for these

---

[76] Bovey 1938 p.9

[77] Carless p.45

people whose hands are never idle."[78]

The increasing manufacturing and agricultural wealth and urbanisation of Ontario, the source and expression of 'modernity', seems to have overridden recognition of Ontario's traditional craft activity[79] indicated throughout southern Ontario on Peck's 1910 map and the note in 1934 that "Today, a similar map would show heavy representations of crafts-workers in all Provinces."[80] Bovey's (and others) "independence of the farmer", reflects the years of economic-crisis driven activity described in chapter 4. The country scenes depicted by rug makers and the tweeds that "exude country air", a continuous leit-motif, are part tourist marketing ploy, "spreading the gospel of rustic beauty among the consumers as well as among the producers.",[81] and part rural romanticism, which itself was compounded of nostalgia and exploration of a vast, diverse landscape.

The tone of rural romanticism in MacKay's quotation above meets its apogee in Cunningham's article 'Among the Cottage Crafters' published in *Canadian Home Journal* March 1933,
> "Beauty of sunset and dawn, of the high rolling hills, of the sweeping ocean, of the brown face, the bright eye, the cheery heart and voice, the warm welcome by the blazing hearth; this is the land where lives the girl who is sitting by the fire with her knitting, the little kitten who plays with the yarn, the yellow bird in his cage above; this is the land where dwell the people who weave and spin and sew, finding the only true and lasting beauty in life, expressing it not in symphonies or epics of the brush or pen, but by the magic of faery looms, making it live in patterns of sunset and sea and sky and field and forest. Here is the true soul of our land, the finding of beauty at one's own doorstep, the making of beautiful things by the skilful, loving toil of strong brown fingers."[82]

The vocabulary of rural romanticism includes: quaint, usually in conjunction with 'old'; 'honest' in conjunction with work, products or 'folk'; looms and other equipment are 'ancient'; colours are

---

[78] MacKay pp.31-34

[79] Kaija Sanelma Harris says of her mother-in-law's family that like many moderately affluent Americans (and Canadians) they had a cottage in the Muskoka (a region of lakes north of Toronto) to which, in the period between the wars and immediately after, women and children went for the whole Summer. Through that period Mrs Harris senior remembers considerable craft production in the region which was patronised by Summer visitors, paralleling similar activity in Quebec, New Brunswick and Nova Scotia. Personal communication 27 March 1997

[80] Peck 1934 p.206.

[81] Bouchard p.15

[82] L.A.Cunningham 'Among the Cottage Crafters' *Canadian Home Journal* 1933 p.8

bright and gay; towns, which teem with dirt and squalor, "the smoke and film of modernity, of hurried commerce", are happily distant. Makers are anonymous,[83] shy, depreciating of their work, invariably happy and contented,[84] have creative ability and skills but latent and undirected (or misdirected into copying contemporary designs from catalogues or magazines), and don't have 'nerves', complexes or repressions. Moreover there is always a 'grandmother' or old man to pass on 'forgotten' skills.

Rural romanticism permeated not only journalist's writing but that of scientists, such as Barbeau, and government officials, such as Bouchard. Bouchard, by 1941 Assistant Deputy Minister of Agriculture, referring to "the tenderness of their rustic hearts and the candour of their ingenuous souls," acknowledges the official agenda, that young farm women should be "kept from the lure of idle dreams, the seduction of the catalogues and the attraction of big centres", and his tone, "would you blame me for speaking sentimentally of what is left of a glorious and peaceful past."[85] This fed into government activity and official attitudes.

The triangle of 'national economy', 'rural life' and 'personal economic benefits' became linked through the latter with another personal benefit of craftmaking, 'emotional well-being' (12) and to a lesser extent 'mental' (10) and 'physical' (9) well-being. The revival of crafts was originally pursued by the CHG in "the belief that the country would become happier, healthier and wealthier."[86] Carless, 1925, remarks that the making of beautiful and useful things has mental, physical and financial benefits, "...particularly for people living in remote districts who are haunted by loneliness and inactivity."[87] Lismer, 1926, expands this latter,

> "'Art' he says, 'is a way of life...It is a necessity.' There is no domain of life from which he would banish it. Down on the Isle aux Coudres and Isle D'Orleans he found habitant women making hook-mats, homespuns and catalognes, not as articles of service but for the fun of doing them. The women stow their mats and catalognes away in cupboards by hundreds without using them. Lismer claims they are creations of necessity and that the making of them helps these women to live contentedly their remote isolated lives without sinking down beneath the weight

---

[83] Cunningham mentions 7 specific craftspeople but names none of them. He does however name "the little girl, Frances Wren" and Helen Mowat. Barbeau may name craftspeople in the text but they are often not named in accompanying photographs eg. "A typical old woman..." *CGJ* April 1936 p.203. This photographic anonymity is typical of craftspeople and their work throughout this period.

[84] Cunningham uses cheerful or happy at least 10 times.

[85] Bouchard p.5

[86] Peck 1934 p.202

[87] Carless p.4

of drudgery as so many women do on the prairies who have no creative outlet."[88]
Bovey, 1938, also argues the economic concomitants of craft,

> "While handicrafts have an artistic and intellectual side, they also have an economic value greater for the average person than other expressions of art which are often economically valueless."[89]

Thus through official and media writing, the low price paid for craftwork became justified by such intangibles as good use of time and job satisfaction,

> "The prices are rather low in comparison with the quality of the goods produced [Québécois handweaving], but this industry is remunerative in this sense that the work is performed in the long winter season in the course of which nothing else could readily be done, the utilization of spare time meaning, after all, double saving."[90]

So caught up were the government in the extraordinary felicity of craft not only having economic value but educational, social, cultural, aesthetic, philosophic and therapeutic values,[91] that they were unable "to separate completely the purely economic benefits of handcraft practices from the many other benefits."[92]

> "The *privilege* of being able to work at a craft provides the worker with the undeniably real and well-earned feelings of satisfaction and contentment...the more or less abstract feelings of general contentment make quite unnecessary and, indeed, undesired, countless services and possessions which others feel so all-

---

[88] Housser p.173 Hayward gives a similar example, "[M]adame had a let-in cupboard stacked high and pressed in to the very top full of her handiwork in rugs and quilts and carpets." Allen Eaton *Handicrafts of the Southern Highlands* (New York 1937) gives several examples from cash-poor Appalachian communities: in a remote North Carolina location, three cupboards full of "kivers" (coverlets) and patchwork quilts were to be passed on to the maker's children, the maker would not sell one even though with no money for taxes she might lose the farm (p.111); 22 quilts and woven mountain coverlets piled high from a low shelf to the ceiling made for two sons upon their eventual marriages (p.129); "the light of my candle revealed the whole sleeping apartment floor covered with beautiful patchwork quilts and, neatly hanging from the roof beams the entire length of the room and on both sides of my bed, were coverlets and quilts to afford additional protection from any drafts, or rain, or snow..." (p.130) Textiles in this context seem to represent family wealth and prestige rather than the arbitrary accumulation suggested by Lismer and Hayward.
The basis for Lismer's final remark is not well-founded as my research shows, and does not take into consideration the difference between settled communities and disrupted pioneering communities.

[89] Bovey 1938 p.3

[90] Turcot p.11

[91] D.H.Russell *Composite Report to the Minister of Agriculture concerning some values to be derived from the development of a National Handicraft Programme* (Ottawa 1941) n/p 'Comment

[92] Russell 1944 p.27

important in order to secure and keep a place in society."[93] [my italics]

Thirteen writers in my analysis saw use as integral to the craft object, implicit in the range of objects discussed was usage in practice or by reference, only two articles deal with purely decorative objects in craft media. Carless argues for,

> "those familiar objects of every day use...works of art which are a part of our daily habits and customs...those arts and crafts whose object it is to provide us with home furnishings."[94]

Rugs were "practical, and at the same time they satisfied a desire for self-expression,"[95] they show "human endeavour for comfort and artistic expression."[96] By the middle of WWII, the utility of craftmaking dominated the writing. Craft products fitted into current fashion trends and replaced imports,[97] reinforcing craft's economic potential in the domestic economy and seasonal economy of cash-poor rural communities;[98] craftmaking fulfilled a therapeutic use in the rehabilitation of mental and physical disabilities,[99] in primary and secondary education and as a productive leisure activity,[100] all were aspects of personal benefits of craft, economic (21), physical (9), emotional (12), spiritual (6) and mental (10). In the eyes of many writers, craftspeople had primarily become the rural disadvantaged (however gift-wrapped in rural romanticism they were) and "homemakers". Women were seen as forming the majority of craftmakers.

National art
Craft as a component in the development of a distinctively Canadian national art (15) is a constant theme throughout the period. It is linked with culture (3) as a societal benefit and with social and cultural issues such as traditions and skills loss (15), which are in turn linked with racial harmony (5) and universality (10). It is also linked with the art:craft dialectic (8), and

---

[93] Russell 1941 n/p 'Comment' This echoes MacKay's contrast between conditions in Ontario and Quebec above.

[94] Carless p.3

[95] O.A.Beriau 'The Handicraft Renaissance in Quebec' *CGJ* 1933(b) p.143

[96] Peck 1934 p.206

[97] Bovey 1938 pp.2, 9

[98] Bovey 1938 p.14-16, Russell 1944 p.4 Findings 2, 3, p.28 'Home conservation', 'Economic-interest fields' 1, 2, 6, 7, 8; 'Major Social and Cultural Values', 'Social and cultural-interest fields 1, 2

[99] Russell 1944 p.29 'Economic interest fields' 9, 'Social and cultural-interest fields' 3

[100] Bovey 1938 p.3

thence to 'art' as an attribute of craft (10). The changing definition of craft in relation to its attributed constituency and to art complicates the analysis. It is also linked to the economy, through the marketing of characteristic regional and national crafts within and outside Canada.

Almost more important in a national art context than in the economic context, the concern with skills and traditions and their loss reflected a particular Canadian experience, that of the immediate encounter with and accommodation of pre-existing Native populations and, viewed from Central Canada, an ongoing influx of 'foreigners', European (and other) peoples, and the concurrent need to create a stabilized, civilized nation. In the ensuing shake-down, craft was seen as having a unique and perhaps pivotal position in constructing a national image, in nation building and in providing a common meeting ground between the component ethnic groups.

The interest in the development of a national art expressed fledgling Canada's need for recognition as a country abroad and the search for a national identity at home. Peck starts her 1934 article on CHG, "When the arts and crafts of a country gain recognition that country takes a new position in the respect of the world."[101] She enumerates some of the international exhibitions to which the Guild sent craftwork, with the result that "Canada gradually gained a reputation for her minor crafts."[102] The place of craft in this development of national prestige was that, "No nation began with fine buildings, great sculptures, noble paintings. They all began with lowly crafts" and thus in the revival and encouragement of crafts, "an art-foundation was being laid for Canada."[103]

Lismer and Carless both saw craft as an essential component in nation building. For Lismer it was 'permanency',
> "Immigrants have some form of expression other than the business of agriculture...leaders, workers in metal and wood, potters and stone-cutters...we do not seek to preserve these talents for the upbuilding of a permanent quality in our nation, and yet these forms of expression are of the very heart of permanency."[104]

For Carless, it was a 'civilized nation' and,
> "Every civilized nation of today has taken steps to preserve whatever arts and crafts it possesses, not only because of their value as historical and artistic records, but from an economic and industrial point of view as well. Keeping alive those art traditions which have grown up in this country in the past...[and] those also

---

[101] Peck 1934 p.204

[102] Peck 1934 p.208

[103] Peck 1934 p.212

[104] Housser p.174

which are continually being brought in by immigrants...is an essential part of the fabric which some day may go to make up a distinctively Canadian art."[105]

Carless saw a "distinctively Canadian art" as a "series of national arts and crafts, characteristic, not of a small portion of it as in the past, but of every province and locality in its wide expanse."[106] He suggests two impediments to a national craft, "There are many crafts being practised in Canada...which, owing either to their late introduction or other causes, follow along the lines typical of modern work and show no characteristics which attach them to the place of their manufacture"[107] and "To what extent such different traditions...may fuse and produce an original growth, only time will show."[108]

Colgate, 1943, had other doubts, speaking from an anglo-Canadian standpoint,
> "[If] there is any one thing which the average Canadian mind needs it is an awakening of the artistic sense. Beauty of form and colour are not with us a daily necessity...the artistic feeling, which is so evident in the Oriental, the European, the Indian tribes of our West Coast and in nearly all savage races, is a thing unknown to us as a nation."[109]

He gives as examples Czechoslovakian garments, a Swedish glass dish and Chinese earthenware "costing but a few cents", all have been "given a beauty, a finish...no matter how insignificant its value...In our desire to express utility with economy...we have overlaid any aesthetic tendencies that survived puritanism."[110]
> "[I]t is hard to see how the artistic sense is to be awakened to such an extent that it will find a spontaneous, national expression; but with all our lack, we have, as a nation, a quick imitative spirit, a genuine desire for self-cultivation, an eagerness to appropriate that which appeals to us as best, and these qualities may, in time, help us to assimilate the art of older countries and give it a new and a fresh utterance."[111]

A CHG exhibition in Toronto in 1942 did cause some hope,

---

[105] Carless p.4-5

[106] Carless p.5

[107] He gives as an example lacemaking.

[108] Carless p.17

[109] Colgate p.242

[110] Colgate p.242-3

[111] Colgate p.243

"Visitors to the exhibition discovered with surprise what a varied wealth of artistic talent and original craftsmanship exists in this Dominion."[112]

What form the "fresh utterance" was to take was not clear and from the writers' point of view was not in the hands of the makers. Cunningham wrote,

"Here is the true soul of our land, the finding of beauty at one's own doorstep...Simple, beautiful designs and motifs, the country-dance, the fair, the little boys skating on a pond...In the cloth...one sees the stripes of the rainbow, the colours of the sunset[113]...It wasn't easy at first. To go to a country lass and tell her to throw aside the neat, ordered pattern from which she worked, and to use a design borrowed from the sunset."[114]

Ringland suggests, again from an anglo-Canadian stance,

"In a young country it is continually necessary to warn the craft workers against the imitation of exotic foreign models and designs. Surely we have plenty of typical Canadian motifs such as the beaver, the pine tree and cone, the maple leaf, the apple and the characteristic Indian designs to develop distinctive decorative themes of our own. The naive, unsophisticated designs of the hooked rugs of Quebec and the Maritimes have shown what can be done when originality has its fling without regard for any stilted, stylized art forms."[115]

In Quebec,

"Examples of the finest old work were secured and given as patterns to the most capable women. Canadian artists were employed to create suitable Canadian motifs."[116]

There are continuous complaints by writers of craftspeople being seduced by motifs found in magazines, catalogues and pattern books. In Quebec,

"[I]t was found that many of the oldest patterns, embodying real beauty and local symbolism, were all but extinguished, and the farm women were showing a regrettable tendency to find designs in the more inferior forms of mail-order advertising."[117]

---

[112] Colgate p.284

[113] Cunningham p.8

[114] Cunningham p.40d

[115] M.C.Ringland 'Encouraging Canadian Handicrafts' *Echoes* 1932 p.16

[116] MacKay p.28

[117] MacKay p.28

At mid-century Bell, writing about the Contemporary Canadian Arts Exhibition, complains about European influences,

> "[C]rafts which will only be appropriate and fresh if they smack of a Canadian environment. As it is, our crafts tend too much to be a meaningless reproduction of what used to go on in Europe."[118]

Suggesting that, in his eyes at least, Canadian craft had yet to find a distinctive voice. Although the Massey Commission was set up, in part, to find ways of counteracting American influence on Canadian culture,[119] there is no indication that American influence is an issue in the texts analyzed. However Beriau in 1943 wrote,

> "The various races composing our great Dominion will bring their contribution so that all the groups, working together on a common ground of interest and understanding, will help to create a truly Canadian *popular* art, which will give to the people of other countries the impression of a human and spiritual reality: "THE LIVING SOUL OF CANADA".[120] [my italics]

Racial unity

This debate on what constituted Canadian art was conducted from a Central and largely anglo-Canadian position, however, as Carless had written in 1925 (and Beriau says above), the genesis of a national art was to be found in an accommodation between established and incoming peoples,

> "It is indeed a matter of national importance...[K]eeping alive those art traditions which have grown up in this country in the past...[and] those which are continually being brought in by immigrants...is an essential part of the fabric which some day may go to make up a distinctively Canadian art."

The preservation of immigrant traditions historiographically in the analyzed texts was a very poor second to activity in Quebec, meriting little published writing and having nobody of Barbeau's authority as publicist. Although it gave rise to much activity, predominantly through women's organizations, in collecting, recording, marketing, exhibiting and teaching, there are no more than fleeting references until the national overviews in the 1940s. At this time formally trained immigrant craftspeople, predominantly Northern Europeans, also began to be mentioned as they took a major part in teaching and production development, and in exhibiting. The contribution of skilled immigrant artisans is ignored during the period. Western Canadian community papers, which are not included in this analysis, carried articles about craftspeople of European extraction

---

[118] A.Bell 'An Exhibition of Contemporary Canadian Arts' *CA* 1950 p.155

[119] V.Massey et al *Report:National Development in the Arts, Letters and Sciences* (Ottawa 1951) pp.13,14

[120] O.A.Beriau 'Home Weaving in Canada' *CGJ* 1943 p.29 This article was not part of the analysis.

throughout the period as, increasingly, did local papers in metropolitan areas of Central Canada. The tone of the writing from Western Canada is, in general, straightforward reporting, often appreciative, and there is no trace of the rural romanticism found in Eastern Canada.

The idea of craft as a common meeting ground between various ethnic groups, 'racial unity' (5), first seems to appear in Western Canada. The primacy of British culture in the Dominion was more easily taken for granted in Central Canada than in the West. Of 31 photographs accompanying Peck's 1934 article on the history of the national handcraft organization, only two show work which is not Native, or franco- or anglo-Canadian.[121] Mention is made in the text of European immigrant work, significantly with reference to the New Canadian Handicraft Festivals, which took place throughout the West between 1928 and 1933,

> "what is not so generally understood is that it was also of real cultural and historical value to the country. At the Festivals one could envisage the extraordinary growth of the population and observe the types of men and women who were to influence the people of the Dominion, and one could make a rough estimate as to what kind of influence that would be."[122]

Clara Holmes, a Winnipeg journalist, started (and finished) a 1928 article headed 'Saskatchewan treasures an inheritance of talent and skill' with a brief blast of jingoism[123] which indicates something of the ethnic accommodation in process,

> "He would be an un-British Britisher who would deny the stranger of another race, choosing Canada as home, the homely pleasure of fashioning with his hands the crafts that are for him tradition."[124]

The article is otherwise a straightforward account of the craft production of immigrants of European origin and the work of the Saskatoon Arts and Crafts Society. Vivian Morton, a member of the Society later wrote,

> "besides the practical aspect of providing a market for work, a common interest in handicrafts often proved to be the first meeting place towards understanding and

---

[121] Peck 1934 p.208 work of immigrant children taught through CHG, probably resident in Montreal; p.210 weaving "by a Norwegian living in Canada..."

[122] Peck 1934 p.213

[123] Articles on racial issues in the West up to the 1940s could be hair-raisingly racist by today's standards, however articles on craft, many of which were written by craft community organizers, and archival material show a more generous accommodation. Many craft organizations from early on had members from various ethnic groups and looked with interest and admiration at the work of other cultures.

[124] C.L.Holmes 'Old Crafts in a New Land' *The Country Guide* 1928 p.4

the realisation that many and varied gifts were being pooled in our Canadian life."[125]

But in 1943, Gibbon could still write of a craft "bound up with the history of Canada, and to-day ...practised by some three million Canadians",

"Needlework provides many points of contact between *the two major racial groups*, the French and the Anglo-Canadians, *not to mention* the Indians and the new Canadians of European extraction."[126] [my italics]

By 1944 the Federal Government was acknowledging the changed population dynamics[127] in Findings 6 and 7 of the Interdepartmental Committee,

"that a national-scale encouragement of useful creative talents offers a common denominator of interest to all Canadians which may be considered independent of: provincial, economic, social, racial and political differences"

"that such a non-contentious subject offers unique opportunities for developing a nationally appreciated and internationally distinctive Canadian home culture"[128]

This theme re-occurs in the Recommendations,

"there is an important national need to continue the study...The invariably ready agreement concerning the values of this study, and the spontaneous offers of co-operation, indicate an unusual national-scale interest -- which is, perhaps, possible only when a subject is of such a common-denominator and non-contentious nature."[129]

Craft is perceived as also being independent of religious differences. The report concludes,

"It is vital, consequently, that widespread attention be focussed on matters of common interests, if we are to enjoy a harmonious blending of interests leading to a real national feeling for Canadian culture."[130]

---

[125] SKAB SACS B88-D Dissolution of Society V.Morton letter 31 May 1957. Although this was written much later, other material in the SACS archives support the statement.

[126] J.M.Gibbon 'Canada's Million and More Needlecraft Workers' *CGJ* 1943b p.144 Gibbon gives several pages of text to describing European needlework traditions found in Canada, however the 15 photographs of work show only 4 from outside Central Canada, of which 2 are anglo-Canadian

[127] It was also acknowledging a legacy from the Depression of popular political activism, social disruption and government ethnic discrimination which gave the government cause for unease.

[128] Russell 1944 p.4

[129] Russell 1944 p.5

[130] Russell 1944 p.30

The Massey Report, 1951, also commented on the theme in section 7 (of 8) under 'Handicrafts', "this matter is also of national concern since it clearly affects the lives of so many of our fellow Canadian citizens. Various organizations appearing before us on this matter have suggested that handicrafts and handicrafts exhibits and demonstrations can and do exert an important influence on our national unity."[131]

To support this contention, the section quotes from briefs presented by CHG:MB, and from CHG:HQ,

"Handicrafts - the practical arts, like other forms of art, can be a great force in the integration of a national culture in society in fostering mutual appreciation, co-operation and unity of spirit between widely diverse age groups, social groups and newly arrived racial groups."[132]

Universality

'Universality' (11), the belief that the making of things is a "natural tendency" and that "anyone, whose eyes, hand and brain are trained to work in unison" could produce a piece of craftsmanship,[133] and the reality of the numbers of people producing handwork, which left the Massey Commission in no doubt "that handicrafts are an important activity of Canadian citizens,"[134] is a theme throughout the period. It became, as indicated in the quotations above, a part of the social and cultural aspects of craft, and loosely related to issues of 'racial unity'.

A careful reading of the texts shows that 'universality' is, in part, a chimera assembled from the writers' concentration on the general rather than the particular, the association of crafts with anonymous, reified makers, with domestic makers and use, and with the pioneer, and therefore rural, myth of self-sufficiency. Within the "many homes in the valley of the St. Lawrence," "most of the work [weaving] is done by women", "[t]he nature of the work is so deeply suited to the country and to the women who live upon it." However amongst the weavers there were, in fact, degrees of expertise, "finer" and "finest".[135] Writers also perceived handcraft as having an expanding constituency, in general education (from kindergarten to college), occupational therapy, and adult and children's leisure activities.

By the time it had reached the Interdepartmental Committee in 1944, 'universality' had expanded

---

[131] Massey p.237

[132] Massey p.237

[133] Carless p.4

[134] Massey p.235

[135] MacKay p.27

Historiography: "A New and Fresh Utterance"

to become "all Canadians", "our rural and urban populations"[136] but it had also narrowed to an reiterated attachment to low income families[137] and homemakers.[138] The Massey Commission, 1951, viewing the universality of makers along a different continuum, appeared confused,

> "the term [handicrafts] is employed in Canada rather loosely to include the work of highly-skilled full-time professionals (notably in metal crafts, ceramics and textiles), of skilled amateurs who augment their normal income by part-time handicrafts, of invalids who find a therapeutic value in such work, of Indians or Eskimos, of cellar-workshop hobbyists who work for their own and their friends' pleasure, of employees in small 'handicraft industries', of part-time workers who make at home to a fixed design what are essentially mass-produced goods for commercial markets, and no doubt of still other groups such as housewives who take pleasure in weaving their own curtains, or their husbands who under-take to make new rungs for the wobbly windsor chair, or to fashion built-in cupboards for the kitchen."[139]

Their definition of craft described product and maker without including technical and material knowledge and skill as parameters. More importantly, they appear to be imposing a hierarchy based on income generation, formal education and ethnicity.

Art:Craft

Carless started his 1925 article,

> "If art is to mean anything to us at all it must be through the medium of things which have a real significance in our lives, and to most of us it will be through those familiar objects of everyday use which surround us in the home. It is there, if anywhere, that art can become truly intimate and human: the statues and paintings in our museums, admirable though they may be, stand aloof in comparison to works of art which are a part of our daily habits and customs."[140]

He identifies craft as art, and situates it within the art:craft dialectic, giving it primacy as the truly intimate, significant and human art. Twentyfive years later the Massey Report, as an investigation into the state of Canadian 'Arts', appeared bemused at the inclusion of craft,

> "to none of us...did it occur that we should be receiving submissions on heraldry, chess, numismatics, mediaeval studies, town-planning, folklore, zoological gardens

---

[136] Russell 1944 pp.4,5

[137] Russell 1944 pp.4, 28, 29

[138] Russell 1944 p.30

[139] Massey p.235

[140] Carless p.3

and *handicrafts*."[141] [my italics]

The art:craft dialectic which started at least as far back as the Italian Renaissance was deeply entrenched in a European hierarchical art history. Fine art traditionally heads the hierarchy with, by the nineteenth century, craft arguing its position in relation to fine art.[142] The art:craft dialectic (8), in this analysis, concerns the changing relationship of craft to art identified through common and distinguishing attributes, positions in a hierarchy, constituencies and foci. I have situated it as a subset of the cultural context (3),[143] connected with 'national art' and 'attributes of craft', particularly that of 'art' (10) but also with such attributes as 'beauty' (17), 'originality' (10) and 'personal expression' (12).

Janet Mainzer, in an analysis of 40 American texts on the relationship between craft and art, written between 1880 and 1980 and almost entirely from the craft viewpoint, identified as common attributes and key words: ideas (5), emotion (5), imagination (5), creativity (6), self-expression (7), "one art" (13), and beauty (14). Bracketed numbers indicate how many of 19 authors between 1900 and 1950 raised the topic.[144] Between 1880 and 1898, beauty is cited an average of 16 times each by 6 authors, between 1900 and 1950 it is cited an average of 4 times each by 19 authors, after 1950 about once by less than half the authors. Mainzer says that her authors,
> "almost uniformly take the position that neither the utilitarian purpose of an object nor the (traditional craft) medium from which it is made is a legitimate criterion for distinguishing craft from art."[145]

In my analysis of Canadian texts 'ideas', in the sense of conceptual craft (none) or work indicating a scholarly knowledge of the field (rare), was not an issue. 'Emotion' is seen as a personal benefit of craftmaking and much more heavily stressed than Mainzer indicates. 'Imagination' seems to be supersede 'ingenuity' (its situation in the text indicates the change is nuance rather than substance), in the same way 'creativity' seems to be used as a synonym for and in addition to 'personal expression' and 'originality' from the 1940s on, neither 'imagination'

---

[141] Massey p.235

[142] Mainzer p.261 Mainzer notes she "found very few writers who took the trouble to argue craft is not art."

[143] The use of 'cultural', usually linked with social, occurs only in the government reports authored by Russell and an article by Vaughan which refers to the reports

[144] Mainzer pp.616-620 Mainzer also has 3 subcategories of beauty including "beauty: transcendent value implied"; and 2 subcategories on craft and moral education.

[145] Mainzer p.310

or 'creativity' were mapped in my analysis. "One art", craft as art and equal with fine art seems a higher profile issue in Mainzer, and beauty is primary in both. 'Originality' is not identified by Mainzer although it would seem to be a shared attribute.

By default, evidence of the human 'hand', 'skill', 'usefulness', 'quality', 'patience' and 'technical knowledge' (indicated by accounts of production processes) become associated with craft. Colgate says of Douglas Duncan of Toronto, "one of the very few bookbinders in Canada who regard the binding of fine books as an art",
> "In all he does he reveals the trained hand, patient skill and the aesthetic judgement of a true craftsman."[146]

Bovey does point out that listening to,
> "Clarence Gagnon [painter] describing the purely technical side of his work...the enthusiasm of Robert Pilot over the etcher's skill, it is evident that the most outstanding among our artists honour the excellence of their craft as well as the beauty of the result."[147]

'Hand', 'skill' and 'quality' are particularly associated with the craft:machine dialectic.

Craft products or makers are constantly positioned in relation to fine art throughout these texts. So although Carless gives craft the paramount position and maintains that,
> "From the remotest ages of our civilization the torch has been handed on by the skill of the craftsman"[148]

he still positions craft in relation to the "aloof" statues and paintings in museums. Likewise Turcot, 1928, talking of "the beauty of French-Canadian homespun...and its honest and homely workmanship" argues,
> "For art it is, and an art worthy to be ranked beside that of the carver in wood or stone."[149]

Peck, 1934, gives craft primacy in the sense of 'founding' but, surprisingly in view of her Arts and Crafts background and the energy she put into promoting craft, places it low in an evolutionary hierarchy,
> "No nation began with *fine buildings, great sculptures, noble paintings*. They all began with the *lowly crafts*...these were the founders from whose efforts art finally

---

[146] Colgate p.246

[147] Bovey 1938 p.7

[148] Carless p.18

[149] Turcot pp.5, 17

reached the heavens and has strewn the earth with beauty."[150] [my italics]

Crafts, for Peck, were "the minor arts." By 1938, Bovey was on the defensive over whether craft was art at all. Defining handcraft as,

> "handicraft art, the thrill of independent creation, the love of beauty, the appreciation of line and form, the vision which it needs, the skill to which it bears witness."[151]

He says,

> "Handicraft as we are employing the word implies a true manifestation of art. At first blush the average person thinks that handicrafts are so low in the artistic scale as to be scarcely art at all."

Having argued that the hooked rug or batik picture are "a real picture, suitable to the medium used", he qualifies his position,

> "This must not be taken to mean that the work of the painter is not a higher manifestation of art but each creator *feels* and each expresses his feelings."[152]

Elizabeth Wyn Wood wrote in 1945,

> "we have...a few, perhaps less than a hundred, ceramists to whom pottery is *a very high art*...Zema Haworth, teaching ceramics, and Peter Haworth, directing the department [at the Central Technical School], have consistently maintained the principle that pottery is not only a craft but a *major art*."[153]

Peck also located craft beyond art in a wider context,

> "Handicrafts show the human endeavour for comfort and artistic expression in relation to the resources, climate and scenery of various localities in addition to reflecting to some degree, social conditions and ideas."[154]

This is the most sophisticated definition of craft in this literature. Although resources, locale and social conditions and ideas were recognised implicitly, and explicitly to a limited degree, as underlying craft production, the same analysis was not applied to fine art which continued to be uncritically accepted as the pinnacle.

Not only was there an external hierarchy against which craft positioned itself but an internal hierarchy. Barbeau refers to,

---

[150] Peck 1934 p.201

[151] Bovey 1938 p.9

[152] Bovey 1938 p.7

[153] E.W.Wood 'Canadian Handicrafts' *CA* 1945 p.191

[154] Peck 1934 p.204

> "a bed-spread of *paresseuse boutonnue* which was a work of art unsurpassed in its kind...the Pednaud bedspread was too complex and artful to be an improvised piece of craftsmanship. It surely...went back to some noted prototype."[155]

Barbeau's proposed prototype,

> "the twisted knot of the *paresseuse boutonnue* is derived from tapestry-making presumably as it was taught by the Ursulines in Quebec."[156]

The context intimates that the contemporary work despite being "one of the finest decorated textiles in existence"[157] was itself in a hierarchy, that of descent from tapestry, an elite craft form implicitly defined by cost, consumer and display location, and the Ursulines, an elite defined by religious and educator status and acknowledged skill in work again implicity defined by cost, location and form, with the additional cachet of resting "upon old French traditions". Barbeau also describes a rocking chair, which "had character as a work of art"[158], was made by a "skilled joiner", "a folk artists [sic] unsurpassed among his kind"[159] and was linked through ancestry to the Church and to an architect in the early eighteenth century,

> "The talent in carving here goes back to *high professional standards.*"[160]

Barbeau positions elite craft against folk craft, the "professional",

> "architects in those days were also wood carvers, Jean must have been a practising craftsman with apprentices."

against the "folk artist", the formally trained against the informally trained, the urban against the rural (and isolated),

> "The arts of carving and tapestry-making must have been handed down from that time to the later generation that moved out of town to the north-east coast and Isle-aux-Coudres."[161]

Ringland in 1932 had written,

> "It is often difficult...to convince the modest worker that her ideas have value...

---

[155] M.Barbeau 'Isle aux Coudres' *CGJ* 1936c pp.202, 203

[156] Barbeau 1936c p.206

[157] Barbeau 1936c p.204

[158] Barbeau 1936c p.201

[159] Barbeau 1936c p.202

[160] Barbeau 1936c p.206

[161] Barbeau 1936c p.206

The same reluctance to experiment in design is not found among the Studio Crafts[162] as these represent quite a different type of work as well as of worker from what we have come to think of as home industries or peasant crafts. They include many fascinating types of work such as...pottery, pewter, batiks, block-printing, wood-carving, leather and metal working, all of which give ample scope for self-expression and originality. They also provide...articles which may be used...in interior decoration."[163]

Thus Ringland like Barbeau delineates a hierarchy in which studio crafts are defined by a maker the social equal of the writer, specific media and techniques commonly taught through formal craft programs, and innovation. Her 'peasant' craftspeople were by implication rural, not trained artists, worked on a part-time basis usually combined with housework and thus were predominantly women, and were likely to be poor.[164] The clientele also appears different, 'Studio Craftspeople' are allied with 'interior decoration', 'peasant' craftspeople were allied with philanthropy and tourism. Predominantly these texts deal with the 'lowly crafts' in more senses than one, with 'home art industries', 'home industries', 'home crafts', 'cottage industries', 'cottage craft', 'peasant crafts', 'rural art', 'rustic arts', 'peasant art', 'popular art', 'manual arts'.[165]

Summary

Substantial published material on Canadian craft activity in the period 1900 to 1950 is limited. The number of articles and the extent of their circulation is difficult to access or assess for the first decades, which undoubtedly relates to the early and uneven state of Canada's development. Nor is it surprising that most of the publications in this analysis emanate from Central Canada, primarily Montreal as the principal city in Canada and the headquarters of organizations (particularly CHG:HQ), publishers, universities and corporations which became involved with craft activity and writing. This in combination with Barbeau's ethnological work on the rural culture of French Quebec contributed to an imbalance of material dealing with Quebec throughout the period. This imbalance is only partially moderated by pan-Canadian overviews, which until 1944 either referred to the work of CHG or were written by members of the Guild. The two

---

[162] The capitalization of one and not the other is in itself indication of hierarchy.

[163] Ringland pp.24-25

[164] Ringland begins her article with the story/example of a rug maker, "Away down in a little Nova Scotia village...She was no artist but with infinite care and patience she had sketched the design...she hurried through her housework to spend a few happy hours at this pleasant task...the fishing season so poor and her husband out of work" The rug was bought by a "prominent Toronto business man who, learning it was made in the little village near where he had spent his boyhood, gladly purchased the rug for his den." Ringland p.16

[165] Used by Carless 1925, Peck 1934, Gibbon 1943, Peck, Cunningham 1933, Ringland 1932/Gibbon, Beriau 1933, Bouchard 1937, Beriau, Beriau 1943, Ringland.

Historiography: "A New and Fresh Utterance"

major sources of information were Barbeau on French Quebec, who Wood in 1945 described as "our greatest writer on the crafts",[166] and CHG on Canadian activity. They are associated with at least 35 of the 92 texts and influenced many more.

Although there were constant references to the work of New Canadians it was rarely detailed. Given the proportion of Europeans in the population by mid-century, particularly the prominence of formally-trained craftspeople, Bell's (and others) complaints about European influences are ingenuous. References to craft production in Ontario, the wealthiest and most populated province, are minimal and, apart from the map accompanying Peck's 1934 article, are centred on Toronto. Nor are the traditional techniques of the dominant society, the English, discussed. This suggests that many writers were aligned with the governing and social elite, who saw Canada as a British Dominion remaining firmly within the English cultural orbit.

This writing about craft production and activity was by people who were not making a living from craft production, some had art and craft training but for the most part they were government officials, academics, journalists, volunteer administrators of craft organizations and teachers. They had education, income, institutional or government connections, middle to high social status and influence in contrast to the sector of the craft community they mainly wrote about. Nor was the audience for whom they wrote the producing craft community, in particular that section of the community most written about, isolated francophone and other rural communities. The writing seems aimed at a fairly wide generalist audience. The distance - physical, social and experiential - between the writers (and their perceived audience) and craftspeople led, particularly during the 1930s, to a vein of 'rural romantic' writing which fed into government attitudes to the disadvantage of craftspeople and craft. The historiography shows that craftmakers, with very rare exceptions, did not write about the craft community, much less about their experience or philosophy as craftspeople.

A relatively high proportion of women wrote about craft suggesting that it was seen as a women's interest. However despite the number of women with expertise in craftmaking and long organizational involvement, which included collecting, no academic papers by women on craft have been noted and the only book authored by a woman was for children. In the texts, women are also seen as forming a majority of craftworkers, linking craft with domestic production and rural subsistence economies. The heavy involvement of women in craft marketing and exhibiting organizations and government involvement with rural women's organisations, both generating much writing, furthered the impression that craft was predominantly a women's activity. Gender bias during the period constrained and devalued women's contribution to the domestic and market economy, their abilities, interests and activities, and by association demoted their craft production in an art hierarchy. Not only was craft in this writing associated with women but with "peasants"

---

[166] Wood 1945 p.225

- francophone Québécois and "foreigners", "new citizens" - a mass of voiceless craftspeople deemed uneducated, unsophisticated, poor. By the middle of the century in official eyes craft had become established as "Canadian home culture". However "nationally appreciated and internationally distinctive", it was to be "useful", "characteristic", "non-contentious", "the arts and crafts of our homemakers."[167]

A major emphasis in the writing was on the utility of craft, product and process, at all levels national, societal and personal. The personal benefits of craftmaking were constantly stressed and were referred to more frequently than national or social benefits (58:29:24), although personal benefits also fed into both. Foremost were the economic benefits (21) but emotional (12), mental (10), physical (9) and spiritual (6) benefits received significant attention. The writing was underlaid by and largely described rural economic crisis-driven activity. Articles on craft (and intervention from outside the community) increased during the Depression and WWII charting mounting rural poverty during the former and shortage of consumer goods during the latter. Marketing crafts to tourists as an answer to rural poverty was a topic throughout the period.

In craft media, the emphasis was overwhelmingly on traditional woven textiles and hooked rugs. Embroidery, lacemaking, quilting, knitting and tapestry were given a passing mention, other needlecrafts and textile construction were neglected. Woodcarving, pottery and furniture-making came into Barbeau's sphere of interest, but in general crafts associated with men, with skilled artisans, with formally trained craftspeople, or predominantly urban or 'architectural', as opposed to 'domestic', crafts were enumerated rather than discussed. Furniture-making, wood-turning, woodcarving, pottery, metal-smithing in base and precious metals, leatherwork and book-binding were mentioned; hot glass, stained glass and lampwork were not. No medium was described with the thoroughness of farm weaving.

In relation to the construction of a history of pan-Canadian craft, this contemporary literature presents problems. The geographic and media coverage is inadequate and geographically unbalanced, as is the acknowledgement of all the craft community in its diversity. Its importance is that it reflects the views, at first and second hand, of an influential sector concerned with craft organizations, marketing and promotion, and with a national museum, both of which were linked to government. In the following chapters I will address these gaps and emphases through an exploration of the range of production circumstances and products in chapter 3, through an account of craft organizations, organizations involved with craft production and government involvement with craft in chapter 4, and through an account of academic craft education and the activity of studio craftspeople in chapter 5.

---

[167] Russell 1944 pp.4, 30

CHAPTER 3
CRAFTS:"AN IMPORTANT ACTIVITY OF CANADIAN CITIZENS"[1]

In response to the gaps and emphases identified in the historiography, in this chapter I want to construct from the available evidence a sketch of craft activity in the first half of the twentieth century. These activities engender, overlap and stand apart from work organised, exhibited or marketed through craft and other organizations and that of academically trained or studio craftspeople discussed in the following chapters. The division of activity into these chapters and the categories used are 'working containers' to organize complex material in order to pursue one of a number of possible threads of enquiry. Within this sketch, I want to identify the range of activity and to locate the 'usual'.

Sources of information

The historiography suggests that museums, organizations and government departments within the period had specific foci and as such have limited usefulness as sources of information. In the latter half of the century, craft organizations, dealers, collectors and museum curators noting the demise of particular craftspeople or interested in historical or ethnic craft traditions broadened the picture of production between 1900 and 1950.

Newspapers and magazines provide a contemporary source of information about craft activity.[2] Newspapers seem to reflect a relatively high level of craft activity amongst women. Craft-related articles cover local events and personalities, fashion, interior decorating, home economics, travel or general interest. Newspapers offered kits or patterns particularly in stitchery. Numerous advertisements indicated available materials, techniques and products such as, "The Canadian Spool Cotton Company, Makers of Coats' and Clarks' Cord Spool Cotton" and Regent Wools patterns, knitting needles and thread for hand-knit ladies' jacket and skirt sets.[3] They could also reflect the perception of craft in the wider society, as in the Province of Quebec Tourist and

---

[1] Massey p.235

[2] Newspapers were also a way for craft organizations to disseminate information about their activities. "The [CHG] prize lists have always been advertised in numberless newspapers in every Province, and in this way the news permeated to even very remote corners of the Dominion." M.A.Peck *Sketch of the Activities of the Canadian Handicraft Guild* (Montreal? 1929) p.6

[3] *The Country Guide and NorWest Farmer* April 1937 p.46

Publicity Bureau war-time advertisement,
> "from Handicrafts/ to Warcrafts/ French-Canadian women and girls have long been noted for their skill in handicrafts, at the spinning-wheel and the loom. Today, thousands of them are applying this adroitness in many an arsenal and war factory. Their trained fingers move with lightning speed at tasks now far removed from the arts of the distaff with a skill inherited from generations of handicraft mothers..."[4]

Newspapers also ran children's sections which usually included crafts, gender biased and often requiring considerable skill and application. For boys these included horncraft and macrame (belts).[5]

Not only newspapers and farm weeklies but magazines carried craft articles on a regular basis and provide an indication of the level and type of activity. In a 1943 survey of needlecrafts, Gibbon lists 11 publications including *National Home Monthly*,[6] *Canadian Home Journal* and *Chatelaine*.[7] Magazines devoted to particular crafts, the majority published outside Canada, were instructional with little background information about design or technique origins in the early part of the century, the frequently mundane designs ranged from Arts and Crafts style to mainstream European. By 1930, *Needlecraft* (U.S.A) included articles on Russian historical crafts, Swiss needlework and Norwegian tapestry weaving, *Ladies Home Journal* (U.S.A) covered Norwegian embroideries and *The Modern Priscilla* (U.S.A) published Helen Mowat of Charlotte County Crafts, New Brunswick on hooked rugs.[8] These are of interest because they reflect the diversity of cultural traditions from which active craftspeople came and to which craftspeople and the general public were increasingly exposed in North America. A 1912 *Modern Priscilla* included basketry (based on Amerindian patterns), metal craft, tooled and dyed leather work, china

---

[4] *CGJ* May 1944 p.1 Curiously, the handicrafts pictures show a *man* making snowshoe frames and an elderly women at a spinning wheel.

[5] *The Country Guide and NorWest Farmer* December 1937; October 1937

[6] c.1943 Mrs Mary Sieburth "prominent among the craft workers in Vancouver" contributed articles on knitting to *National Home Monthly* (Winnipeg) and *Women's Home Companion* (New York). She also did a manual on knitting for the Canadian Legion Educational Services. SKAB SACS File typescript J. Murray Gibbon 'Notes on Canadian Handicraft...'

[7] Gibbon 1943a p.153 The others are: *Country Guide, Farmer's Magazine, Canadian Countryman, Farmer's Advocate, Saskatchewan Farmer, Montreal Family Herald and Weekly Star, Winnipeg Free Press Prairie Farmer, Western Producer* with a combined circulation of nearly two million

[8] USK.A J.E.Murray Collection magazine cuttings: *Needlecraft Magazine* 1930 'A Peep into Russia's Past, Reveals Her Excellence in All Handicrafts', 'Industrious Needlewomen of Switzerland', 'Norwegian Tapestry Weaving Old and New' June 1930; *Modern Priscilla* n/d 'In Quest of the Hooked Rug' by Helen Mowat; *Ladies Home Journal* 'Norwegian Embroideries'

Crafts: "An Important Activity of Canadian Citizens"

painting, and stencilling as well as various needle techniques.[9]

Exhibition lists provide another source of information.[10] Although I have only looked at a very limited number of these,[11] Appendix 2a-h, they provide information on participants, range of activity, shifts in interest and comparison of activities in different areas of the country.

Vancouver's Opening Exhibition 1910[12] (PNE:1910) included crafts under 'Fine Arts', 'Household Arts' and 'Women's Work'.[13] As the two latter suggest, craft categories at industrial and/or agricultural exhibitions were aimed predominantly at women. The earliest prize lists from the Prince Edward Island Provincial Exhibition (PEI:PE) are divided into 'Woolen and cotton goods (handmade)' and 'Industrial: Ladies Fancy Work', the prize recipients are exclusively female[14] until 1950.[15] However PNE:1910's 'Fine Arts' class included wood carving, furniture, pottery and glass blowing which suggests some male entrants. There is no indication whether any of the

---

[9] *The Modern Priscilla* February 1912 (Boston 1912)

[10] Mary Burnett personal correspondence, 8 November 1996, said,
"The finest weaving declined around the end of the 19th century, but handspinning and plainer weaving persisted in many rural homes [in P.E.I.] until the end of the first World War, when they largely died out...there were always exceptions, some lovely coverlets were woven after 1900, and an Acadian woman was still weaving blankets for people from their own handspun until 1940."
However on 3 December 1996, Burnett wrote,
"This has certainly been an eye opener for me and I'm very grateful to you for causing me to do [research into provincial exhibition prize lists.] It was a great surprise to find linen tablecloth and draft weaving classes still having entries in 1939."

[11] Prize lists from the Prince Edward Island provincial exhibition (PEI:PE) for 1900, 1910, 1920, 1930, 1930, 1939 ("the regular provincial exhibition...was cancelled this year because of the withdrawal of the federal government grant and the similar cancellation of exhibitions in other provinces." Mary Burnett letter 3 December 1996), 1950, 1951 ("It seemed as though the hooked mat results were not published for 1950" ibid), P.E.I.: The Charlottetown Guardian 27 September 1900, 1 October 1900; 22,23 September 1910; 13 November 1920; 16, 18 September 1930; 17, 26 August 1939; 17 August 1950; 15 August 1951 xeroxes from Mary Burnett.
In Saskatchewan, 'Ladies' Work' categories from Watson Agricultural Society Second Annual Fair 1908, Watson A.S. 1910, Foam Lake 1937 provided by Ruth Bitner, Nokomis Agricultural Fair 1927, all SK:WDM.A
PNE:1910 Wilks C. *The Early Years* Vancouver: PNE 1994.

[12] Later the Pacific National Exhibition (PNE)

[13] Wilks p.n/p

[14] The information I received from PEI and Saskatchewan included only women's and youth categories; it is not clear whether these are all the craft classes, or whether it reflected the contributor's interest or conception of 'craft' as women's activity.

[15] 1950, 1951 Fred House and Sylvain Gallant from the Provincial Sanatorium

entrants were production craftspeople, although the 1900 PEI:PE list suggests the likelihood[16] as do categories such as glass blowing at PNE:1910.[17] PEI:PE's 'Woolen and cotton goods (handmade)', comprising plain and fancy weaving, knitting and rug making, show that winners were mainly from the country in contrast to the 'Ladies fancy work' classes where the majority of winners were from Charlottetown. These lists also show makers winning in a number of categories, and names reappearing through the first three decades suggesting a small number of highly skilled craftswomen. There are occasionally winners from outside the province. In 1920, locally from New Brunswick and Nova Scotia and from Regina, SK; in 1930, from Edmonton, AB, Vancouver, BC and Ontario when Mrs A.G.Savage of Listowel, ON took 11 prizes; her name appears in the 1939 lists, with one Saskatchewan and three Manitoba entrants.[18] In 1950 and 1951, under the auspices of the Women's Institute, these classes had only provincial winners.

Handwork classes in the PEI:PE and Saskatchewan lists are predominantly textiles. 'Crochet and knitting' and 'embroidery' had consistently the greatest number of classes, which increased until 1939. 'Embroidery' had a higher average number of classes. In PEI:PE 1939 'embroidery' classes reached a high (40) and 'knitting and crochet' a low (10), by 1950/51 the position had reversed. At PNE:1910, under Women's Work 'embroidery', there were an astonishing 35 categories for lace. Knitting, plain and fancy, in silk, cotton and wool, was predominately garments and bedspreads. Mary Burnett's comment that in PEI, "Unquestionably the major decorative (albeit still utilitarian) crafts 1900-1950 were quilting and mat hooking"[19] is not reflected in the exhibition classes, there were only five categories of quilt making in all, averaging two a year, and until PEI:PE 1939 a maximum of four categories of mat hooking. In 1939 there were 19 categories mainly rugs,[20] by 1951 it had fallen to 12 categories. PNE:1910 unexpectedly[21] had 12 classes for rugs. Wilks comments that "quilting was a minor craft in early Fairs." Although

---

[16] There are two divisions of textiles: 'Woolen and cotton goods (handmade)' and 'Ladies' fancy work, embroidery etc'. The first with prizes for "7 1/2 Yards Black Cloth, all wool, full dressed", "Twenty yards carpet, cotton warp, woolen filling" etc. could suggest production work; the second division includes "Best collection of Ladies' Work of various kinds, not less than 5 pieces of different designs, *professional or amateur*. Best collection, do. *amateurs only*." [my italics] Charlottetown: Guardian 27 September 1900 p.21

[17] G. Stevens *Canadian Glass 1825-1925* (Toronto:1967) p.xiv Stevens notes only The Crystal Glass Company, New Westminister 1907-1908

[18] It is possible that outside entrants were Islanders who had moved away or there may have been a number of craftswomen who competed across the country, this would be consistent with sales and exhibition networks, see chapter 5 *'Studio craftspeople:Self concept'*.

[19] Burnett personal correspondence, 8 November 1996

[20] This probably reflects the height of the commercial popularity of hooked rugs, see chapter 4

[21] 'Unexpectedly' because Eastern Canada is projected as the hooked rug production area.

there were consistently more categories of stitchery, it was constantly overlooked by collectors and the literature. Weaving which attracted considerable official interest was represented in PNE:1910[22] and PEI:PE.[23] In the latter, "10 yards twilled flannel", blankets, draft weaving and linen weaving classes continued to 1939. Of 261 classes noted in these exhibitions, 182 are specific objects of which 56 are garments, the remainder being household accessories. In the textile classes, approximately sixty techniques were stipulated.

'Girl's' classes were limited versions of 'Ladies' but 'Children's' categories also included, for example, "Reed work, boys or girls, 'teen age'; article made from lumber 'teen age', article made from wood, boys 12 years and under."[24] Other categories included, at PNE:1910 in the 'Fine Arts' class, wood carving, basket making, bead work, furniture, pottery, glass blowing and decoration on china; at Nokomis 1927, gesso work, wax work and leather work.

At PNE:1910, first prize for an embroidered shirtwaist was $3.00, second $2.00, third $1.00. Watson and Foam Lake Agricultural Societies' shows, over 30 years, awarded $1.00 for first prize in most categories. Nokomis 1927 ranged from $2.00 for knitted, crocheted or embroidered bedspreads or a "Child's knitted dress or suit" to $1.00 for lesser items. At the Alberta Provincial Exhibition, Edmonton, 1906, prizes for quilts were $2.00 and $1.00 and for a collection of Battenburg lace $3.00. Villett says, "Best cured ham, or best fowl prizes were also $3.00. Wheat was $15.00, Best Bull $35.00"[25] At Nokomis the best pint sealer of raspberries got the same prize as a quilt, two heads of lettuce or six stalks of rhubarb won $1.00, "Butter, 5 lbs in crock or tub" won $5.00. Children's category prizes were often the same as women's. The level of awards in

---

[22] *The Daily Province* 16 August 1910 "charming examples of hand weaving" quoted Wilks n/p. Unfortunately Wilks does not give more details.

[23] The reason why weaving did not occur in the Saskatchewan lists may be because those areas did not have ethnic groups involved in weaving or because "around Buchanan the [Doukhobor] women do not enter the Doukhobor drawnthread work and the typical things partly because the prize lists oftimes do not include them but have crocheting etc. and partly because they are ashamed of their own things." Vivian Morton to A.S.Morton 21 June 1926, SKAB Vivian Morton Papers A699 file 6
brought to my attention by Joan Champ

[24] Nokomis 1927; also rope splicing, knots, milking stool and bird house, Foam Lake 1937.

[25] J.Villett 'Women's Work: A History of Quilts in Agricultural Fairs' lecture notes Calgary 1990 p.2

craft exhibitions was consistently low,[26] they did not reflect the economic value of the skills, materials, time and knowledge involved. It is difficult to tell how much this undervaluation was gender biased as gardens, fowls and food production were also women's responsibilities.

Craft production

Craft production took place for a number of reasons. The first three categories cover crafts produced to make a living on a full-time, part-time or cyclical basis by craftspeople who sold usually within their immediate or regional community; crafts made as part of the domestic economy; and for leisure. These have a long history although the constituencies, products and media change. In a sense these were situations generated and controlled by the craftsperson and mark a personal decision to create. The next two categories cover craft in the public education system and as occupational therapy. They were directly related to two twentieth century developments, namely the continued expansion of universal education and its accompanying educational philosophies, and the extension of medical care challenged by the aftermath of two world wars. The situation in both was educational but outside the art school system. These activities were linked to leisure and to gainful occupation. The final two groups, craft as a community or national endeavour, were socially cohesive activities. There was no personal economic benefit neither were they in the proper sense a leisure activity because the product was restricted to that required by the situation.

Production, such as textiles or furniture making may be covered in more than one category. Furniture, for example, is discussed as an artisan activity and as part of the domestic economy. Where I use examples unless I indicate otherwise I assume that similar activity was going on across the country. The examples are the tip of an iceberg which would repay further exploration.

---

[26] It seems that CHG may have paid higher awards, "sent some fine embroidery to the prize competition and had received $52.00 [for sales] and a prize of $10.00." Peck 1934 p.212
Peck 1929 pp.8,9 Gives a donors list for prizes for the 1908 CHG annual exhibition and indicates what part of the country objects and award winners came from. The relative values of the awards reflect particular interests and availability, locations may indicate contact.
For prizes: for "good weaving" $100;
pottery, embroidery, metal-work, lace-making, wood-carving, each $50;
book-binding, leather-work each $25;
sewing and knitting $21.
Awards for hooked rugs - NS, NB, PEI.;
lace - "(English, Irish, Belgian, Swedish, Russian)" all provinces;
woven materials - "All the Eastern Provinces and Saskatchewan";
embroideries - all provinces;
leather-work - PQ, ON, NB, BC;
stencils - PQ, ON, MB;
metal work - PQ, ON, SK, "(with competition from other provinces)";
pottery - PQ, ON (At a later date Man. [MB] and Labrador competed)."

Crafts for a living

Traditional artisan crafts, transmitted by apprenticeship[27] or within the family or group, were seen by the literature as declining in Eastern Canada throughout the nineteenth century[28] and lingering on into the first decades of the twentieth century before becoming a rarity or disappearing. Some became reinvigorated and transformed, at least temporarily. Many were associated with remote and usually poor rural areas.

Textiles

Florence Mackley and Dorothy Burnham (both weavers) agree that there were a number of artisan weavers operating in Cape Breton well into the twentieth century. Mrs John Munro of Margaree Harbour, Cape Breton, "the last traditional professional coverlet weaver in Canada" according to Burnham, made her last coverlets in the mid-1960s.[29] Alex MacLeod, Baddeck, a production weaver who died in 1944, taught his daughter-in-law, Elizabeth MacLeod who became the weaving assistant at the Gaelic College in Cape Breton, in the process transferring traditional skills through a formal system. Artisan weavers also continued in Prince Edward Island into the twentieth century.[30] Burnham suggests that in Ontario some artisan weavers stayed in business by weaving rag rugs, citing Addie Mick, who was taught by her mother a weaver from Ireland, and who worked from 1880 until the 1950s.[31] NMC anthropologist Marius Barbeau's research in the 1920s found women artisan weavers active in eastern Quebec.[32]

In the ethnically more complex and unstable conditions of the west, where weaving continued it was traditionally done for home or community consumption and it is hard to tell whether some of these weavers were specialists. There are references to independent weavers making a living

---

[27] P.N.Moogk 'In the Darkness of a Basement: Craftsmen's Associations in Early French Canada' *Canadian Historical Review* LVII:4 (Toronto 1976) Moogk suggests that the European tradition of craft 'guilds' or trade associations quickly broke down as a result of greater social and occupational mobility, "part of a classic New World phenomenon", as a result apprenticeships were much shorter, journeymen were not common, craft businesses were family affairs, the children frequently choose other occupations. Although this relates to a particular history and cultural group, this phenomenon may have been widespread.

[28] Tweedie pp.233-258
The 1851 census for NB shows 52 carding and weaving mills, 5454 looms in use and production of 622,237 yards of homespun cloth. Assuming one weaver to a loom, with a population of 193,800 only 3% of the population was weaving which seems low.

[29] D.K.Burnham *The Comfortable Arts: Weaving in Canada* (Ottawa 1981) p155

[30] Burnham p.156. These almost certainly are among the prize winners at PEI:PE.

[31] Burnham p.125

[32] Chapters 4, 6

from their work but current information is insufficient to decide whether by training and product they are continuing an artisan tradition within a changing marketing situation or had academic training. An example is Mrs Bergklint, Cloverdale, BC, of Swedish extraction and,

> "very knowledgable about the Swedish handcraft movement and industry, produced handwoven pillow cases, runners...using traditional and modern adaptions."[33]

Murray Tweeds, Vancouver Island, in the early 1930s apparently had no problem in finding about eight artisan weavers, and "there are weavers there not connected with this industry" including one man who had the specialist skills to weave pure camel hair.[34]

In 1923, Mrs De Backer gave a talk to the Saskatoon Arts and Crafts Society (SACS). She had spent four years in Brussels learning the lace making trade and remained with the same firm for 13 years designing for them in Brussels and Paris before coming to Saskatchewan c1918. Amongst examples of laces she showed were "designs of the various provinces" made by her mother, "the Queen lace maker", and her sisters.[35] Earlier in Eastern Canada, an Irish immigrant lace maker who had made the flounces for the wedding-dress of Queen Alexandra, had a lace handkerchief included amongst specimens of each craft practised in Canada presented to Queen Mary.[36] Carless in 1925 mentions,

> "we shall find lace makers in every part of the Dominion producing good examples in the various well-known styles, such as English thread, Honiton, Irish crochet, Carrickmacross, Limerick, Rose point, Italian point, and various Russian and other foreign laces."[37]

How many of these lace makers came from European lace production areas is not indicated. Whether and how craftswomen such as Mrs De Baker continued to ply and sell their craft is not known.

Pottery
Despite overwhelming competition from British manufacturers, a number of small potteries in Eastern Canada also continued into the twentieth century producing mainly inexpensive domestic earthenware and stoneware such as jugs, crocks and milk pans, but some, generally run by expatriate British potters, also produced transfer-decorated teapots and table ware. Pottery could

---

[33] SKAB SACS B88-B2 letter 6 December 1936

[34] Mrs W.Garland 'Murray Tweeds' *Family Herald and Weekly Star*, 24 December 1941 p.41

[35] SKAB SACS B88-A Minute book 1, March 1925

[36] Peck 1934 caption p.202

[37] Carless p.17

Crafts: "An Important Activity of Canadian Citizens"

be wheelthrown, slab moulded or slip cast. In Nova Scotia, Marie Elwood cites James Prescott and Sons established in 1888 as continuing in business until the late 1930s.[38] Like the Foley Pottery, Saint John, NB, they responded to current fashions such as that for terra cotta wall plaques and garden ornaments during the 1920s. It seems that a line of Art pottery was considered and at the Foley Pottery experiments were certainly made in that direction. Many of these potters, as in other artisan crafts,[39] made experimental or unique pieces as demonstrations of skill or for pleasure.[40]

In the 1930s Alice Hagen, a noted china painter, learnt to throw at the Prescott factory at Halifax from Charles Prescott, "the last 'commercial thrower' and owner of the Prescott factory". Hagen then set up her own pottery studio at Mahone Bay. These potteries were often important to the early studio potters providing clay, expertise and kiln space. Foley Pottery supplied clay for a time to Erika and Kjeld Deichmann, NB,[41] and Lloyd Shaw, owner of the brickworks and clay pit at Lantz, NS, invited the Lorenzens[42] to work there in 1949. Mabel Adamson fired in the Sovereign Pottery kilns, Hamilton, in the 1930s, as did a number of other Toronto studio potters including Nunzia D'Angelo.

Barbeau records potters peddling their wares through eastern Quebec as late as 1936. For example, while his uncle and son continued at the pottery, *le vieux* Joseph Drolet travelled with bowls, milk pans, platters, and butter crocks which frequently were bartered for goods, meat, bacon, flour, eggs, "whatever was offered, rarely money; at Petite-Rivières maple sugar; at Île aux Coudres fish." Such peddlers would have a regular route along which there were houses where they could expect to get a meal or even stay overnight.[43] These small potteries were not

---

[38] M.Elwood *Potters of Our Past* exhibition leaflet (NS 1996)

[39] E.Cooper *People's Art: Working Class Art from 1750 to the Present Day* (Edinburgh 1994) pp.31-79; I have come across few Canadian examples identified as such, E.Arthur *Iron: cast and wrought iron in Canada from the seventeenth century to the present* (Toronto 1982) p.130 shows a cast-iron galleon 13x11in., "workmen in the Fleury Plough Company modelled and cast toys." n/d possibly early 20th century

[40] Examples are Foley pottery at NBM; the work of Odilon and Gustav Delisle, Bassin noted in Marius Barbeau *Maitres artisans de chez nous* (Montreal 1942a) p.139

[41] Chapter 5, *Studio craftspeople: income generation*

[42] Ernst Lorenzen b.Denmark d.1990; wife Alma Lorenzen b.1918, NB; education: Mount Saint Bernard College, NS, design and painting. Both self-taught in pottery, started 1944; Ernst threw and tended electric kiln, Alma made small sculptures and decorated. Ernst built foot-powered, then motor-powered wheel, kilns; experimented with clays, glazes. First studio in house, Dieppe nr Moncton, NB, by the move to Lanz, NS, in 1949, they were already full-time potters

[43] Barbeau 1942a pp.115,6 [my translation]

necessarily initiated by artisan potters, Barbeau records an engineer, a farmer who did an apprenticeship at Howisons, Cap Rouge one of the major industrial potteries, and Napoléon Tremblay, "a brilliant classical student who preferred business to a profession and became a craftsman."[44]

The large clay deposits on the Saskatchewan/Alberta border which gave rise to the industrial potteries centred on Medicine Hat, Alberta from the beginning of the century must have attracted artisan potters. In Saskatchewan, three[45] artisan potters are named, all attached to the Ukrainian community. Steve Bugera "migrated to Benito, MB, then moved across the border to Aaran, SK. Little is known about his work."[46] Peter Rupchan and Nick Sarota apprenticed in pottery manufactures in the Ukraine before coming to homestead, Sarota in the Vonda area c1902-1929, Rupchan in six locations north of Yorkton c1902-1944. Sarota recognised the possibilities of reddish clay near the farm and built a 4 by 3.5 foot kiln in a loghouse to produce unglazed wares such as bowls, jugs and poppyseed mortars.[47] Like Sarota, Rupchan found and prepared his own clays and glazes, built his own kickwheels and primitive kilns and by 1914 was making simple but well-thrown kitchen ware. These relatively fragile, low-fired pots were peddled over an area of about 120 square miles by cart or sleigh. The demands of homesteading periodically forced Rupchan to abandon pottery but by 1928[48] he had attracted the attention of several patrons including SACS and Professor W.G. Worcester of the University of Saskatchewan Department of Ceramic Engineering who was "able to render considerable assistance to him in the matter of small equipment and glaze formulas."[49]

This University department (1921-1952), the first in Canada, was interested in industrial applications but had a variable speed wheel and a kiln, and employed William Phipps, an English-trained master mould-maker, who also threw "beautiful hand-turned pottery...He was a Master and a real artist."[50] Worcester, as a leisure activity, experimented with glazes and clay

---

[44] Barbeau 1942a p.139 Tremblay soon moved on to other ventures.

[45] J.Silverthorne *Made in Saskatchewan: Peter Rupchan* (Saskatoon 1991) pp.67, 81. Current accounts suggest there were more, and R.M.Bozak, London ON writing to Mohyla Institute Saskatoon 3 June 1972 refers to 'Safruk' also UWAC:UMC has a 'Rupchan' pot with a stamp 'SE' (none of Rupchan's pots are stamped.)

[46] Silverthorne p.84

[47] Wayne Morgan 'Early Saskatchewan Pottery' *The Craft Factor* 2:1 p.17

[48] Holmes 1928 p.4

[49] USK.A W.G.Worcestor [sic] papers II Correspondence with D.E.Snodgrass 18 April 1934

[50] Silverthorne p.85

bodies. His son, J. Cameron Worcester, probably learned from Phipps and ran a pottery in Saskatoon, Canadian Clay Craft Studios c1938-1941,[51] producing art ware, souvenirs and special order products such as beersteins and ash trays which sold from Toronto to Vancouver. He specialized in hand-turned[52] pottery, making his own glazes.

Axel Ebring, born in Sweden into a family of potters, homesteaded in the Terrace area of BC in the 1920s where he established a pottery using local clay, building his own kick-wheel and wood-fired kiln. In 1939, Ebring moved his pottery to Vernon, perhaps encouraged by "Mrs. Middleton and other Vernon women seriously interested in the arts."[53]

> "He dug his own clay from a clay bank right next to his studio, he threw functional earthenware on a rickety wooden wheel, glazed it with a raw lead glaze and fired it in a wood fired kiln using pine slabs from the local sawmill. The pots were marked 'Vernon' on the bottom."[54]

Ebring made a range of glazed dishes, jugs, large bowls, candleholders, vases, and later when he had arthritic hands, figures, which were bought at the studio by people from Vancouver to Calgary. Several people spent time with him learning to throw.[55]

It is certain that many more artisan potters came to the West than had the opportunity to use their skills and it is to be assumed that there were other isolated potters working in the rural west for varying periods, however unless their work attracted the attention of middle-class patrons or lasted long enough to become of historical interest no note of them remains. Judith Silverthorne suggests that within his own family and community Rupchan's pots were not particularly valued, their father's eccentric vocation caused the younger children to be ridiculed by classmates[56], and that there was a hiatus of about thirty years before his work re-attracted recognition.

Worcester commented, in 1939,
> "...as far as the writer knows...no kilns suitable for a small pottery on the market

---

[51] Silverthorne suggests that the Canadian Clay Craft Shop was reopened under the Saskatchewan Arts Board in the 1950s, and that it was acquired by Folmer Hansen and David Ross, potters, in 1961.

[52] I have assumed that 'hand-turned' is an alternative term for 'hand-thrown' from the context. 'Turning' is today used for the trimming of shapes with tools when the clay is leather-hard.

[53] B.Kingsmill *A Catalogue of British Columbian Potters* (1977) p.3

[54] Stan Clarke, potter, Surrey, BC letter 10 February 1996

[55] S.Inglis 'A Company of Travellers: Some Early Studio Potters in Canada' in Mayer C. ed. *The Potter's Art: Contributions to the Study of the Koerner Collection of European Ceramics* (Vancouver 1997) p.175

[56] Silverthorne p.71

in Canada. Most studios either purchase the kiln from the U.S.A. or construct rather a simple type of their own."

Further,

"In Eastern Canada, there are a fairly good number of small art potteries producing ware for the tourist trade. In addition, there are three or four small potteries in B.C."[57]

Lesser notes the start of a number of

"studios, without historical precedent in Quebec, where artists ran small, independent ceramic industries"[58]

in the late 1930s and mid-1940s. These were students of Pierre Normandeau,[59] a Canadian who trained at l'École Nationale de Céramique de Sèvres, Paris, and from 1935 taught the ceramics program at l'École des Beaux-Arts (and later when it moved to l'École du Meuble.) His main goal was "to form craftsmen capable of turning out articles for domestic use or in the fabrication of molds for mass-produced items."[60] In 1935 Normandeau had toured Quebec with Barbeau in an unsuccessful search for a distinctive Quebec pottery tradition. In 'art pottery' despite academic training the link with artisan methods and traditions was still remarkably close, the difference between artisan potters and the 'artists' was principally in the type of clientele, which in turn affected product and marketing.

In 1946, David Lambert set up a small production pottery in Vancouver, pots were made on the jigger or on the wheel and then passed to a decorator. Lambert employed apprentices, some of whom may have had no previous experience with clay, or

"highly skilled potters and decorators, mainly European immigrants who where looking for a job...Lambert usually decorated pieces made by others. While the production of pots was going on, Lambert was also making, buying and selling materials, kilns and equipment and establishing retail outlets for his pottery."[61]

Woodwork

As with pottery, so with furniture making, mass production situated predominantly in central

---

[57] USK.A W.G.Worcestor [sic] papers II correspondence Worcester to Kenneth E. Smith, Ceramic Art Department, H.Sophie Newcombe Memorial College, New Orleans 30 May 1939

[58] Lesser 1989 p.63

[59] Pierre-Aime Normandeau 1906-1965

[60] Lesser 1989 p.61

[61] Elsa Shamis 'David Lambert, Vancouver's First Potter' 1984
Despite the title Shamis says "At that time none of the few studio potteries in town were similar to Lambert's enterprise"

Canada must have absorbed skilled artisans.[62] There were also smaller workshops or factories producing 'art furniture' or custom built furnishings for residences or public buildings. Elizabeth Collard notes,

> "furniture in Victorian and Edwardian Montreal was often of local manufacture...Under the seductive heading of "art furniture", cabinetmakers advertised everything from Japanese to Egyptian styles and from Eastlake to so-called Queen Anne. Owen McGarvey, who flattered himself in print on the "art workmanship" of his factory's products, made ebonized cabinets into which Minton tiles were set. William Coysh provided customers with screens whose glass panels they could paint artistically with flowers."[63]

Working within the Arts and Crafts Movement the Bromsgrove Guild (Canada) workshop in Montreal,[64] 1911-1938, employed woodworkers, carvers and cabinet makers. Commissions from architects such as Edward and William Maxwell included carved woodwork, handwrought ironwork and furniture. The "emphasis was on craftsmanship and on the need for a close relationship between the designer and craftsman",[65]

> "For the Art Association gallery [MMFA 1912], the Maxwells were fortunate in being able to rely on the Bromsgrove Guild of craftsmen to follow their design specifications. The Guild's men also contributed their knowledge of materials and their technical skills to the outcome of the work."[66]

How much design input craftsmen had is unacknowledged although one of the carvers was Elzéar Soucy,[67] a sculptor in his own right and later a professor at l'École du Meuble. The Artist's Workshop, a co-operative studio and showroom set up by a group of woodworkers and metalsmiths, including Gert Lamartine, a furniture maker and designer, was producing avant garde work during the mid 1930s.[68]

---

[62] Virginia Wright *Modern Furniture in Canada 1920 to 1970* (Toronto 1997) "Ontario's industry had been established and sustained by skilled immigrant German cabinet-makers" whereas Quebec produced more low-priced furniture relying on semi-skilled labour. p.134

[63] Elizabeth Collard in *The End of an Era: Montreal 1880-1914* (Montreal 1977) p.16

[64] The original Bromsgrove Guild in Birmingham, England, established 1897, was a loose association of artists connected with Birmingham School of Art working under the influence of the Arts and Crafts movement.

[65] Rosalind M. Pepall *Building a Beaux-Arts Museum* (Montreal 1986) p.76

[66] Pepall 1986 p.82

[67] Pepall 1986 p.140

[68] Wright 1997 p.42

The Arts and Crafts movement inspired Rosa Breithaupt Hewetson Clark to set up the Guild of All Crafts[69] (1932-1941) at Scarborough near Toronto, which employed woodcarver Dane Aage Madsen, furniture maker and restorer, Herman Reidl from Austria, and from England, Fred Mildred, woodturner and Frank Carrington,[70] furniture maker.[71] In Vancouver, where the Arts and Crafts tradition remained strong into the 1940s, furniture makers included John Allen c1921 and Lawrence Thomas c1913-1943, and George Gibson a gifted woodcarver and wood-inlay artist.[72]

In rural Eastern Canada, an established population eased the continuation of isolated pockets of craftspeople into the twentieth century. Barbeau refers to Joseph Mailloux and his three brothers of Cap-au-Corbeau, who made country hardwood chairs[73] and "other fine examples of cabinet-making."[74]

Newfoundland did not have a widespread cash economy until the construction of American Armed Forces bases during WWII and the introduction of industries after Confederation in 1949. Most rural Newfoundlanders eked out a living, bartering goods and services, and few could afford the luxury of imported mass-produced furniture. Even so in the last quarter of the nineteenth century and into the twentieth several small furniture factories operated in St. John's and several of the larger outport[75] communities. They included, at Harbour Grace, Francis Cody, and Alexander and Edward Parsons whose furniture factory was carried on by Edward's son Reuben, and Henry William Winter (active 1890-1935) at Clarke's Beach. Winter was a self-taught commercial furniture maker, who with the help of only one employee and using simple hand tools and foot or dog powered lathes and jig saw, "mass-produced large quantities of furniture and sold it over a wide area of rural Newfoundland."[76] Peddle suggests that
> "many of the outport pieces were...built by tradesmen other than formally trained

---

[69] Also known as the 'Guild of All Arts'

[70] After the demise of the Guild, Carrington set up his own furniture workshop and later taught at Ontario College of Art (OCA) and was on the Board of CHG:ON

[71] G.Crawford ms (Toronto 1998/9)

[72] Shaw-Rimmington pp.8,10,12

[73] 'Country furniture' particularly chair making obviously continued. Photographs show wooden ladder-back or other tall back chairs with turned or spoke-shaved legs and woven seats for sale at CHG:HQ 1934 (Peck 1934 p.202) and at The Trading Post, Andover, NB c1940 (McAnn 1940 p.134)

[74] Barbeau 1936c pp.201-206

[75] small fishing villages

[76] W.E.Peddle *The Traditional Furniture of Outport Newfoundland* (St. John's NFD 1983) p.89

Crafts: "An Important Activity of Canadian Citizens"

> furniture makers...a carpenter, cooper, wheelwright or even an ordinary man who was adept at working with wood was called upon to produce household furnishing for a fisherman who lacked either the time or the skill."[77]

He also suggests (but gives no examples) that a

> "piece of furniture might be the product of several people...a skilful lathe owner would be called upon to produce legs, rungs, spindles and various turned decorations such as pilasters and bosses, while a talented carver or grainer would also be employed."[78]

Furniture was made from local woods, pine, birch, spruce, tamarack and fir.

For the artisan furniture-maker trying to establish himself in the prairie West there were a number of problems. Traditional furniture woods other than birch did not grow locally. The pattern of homestead settlement spread the population thinly over a vast area in terms of horse transport[79]. As the century progressed and farms became bigger this was exacerbated. Increasing settlement was matched by the extension of the railway network and population centres were situated on the rail line making access to manufactured goods from Central Canada and beyond relatively easy. In turn this facilitated the mail-order business. The Timothy Eaton Company built a huge department store in Winnipeg about 1905 and soon after established a catalogue mail-order business.

> "The town carpenters made some very fine pieces of furniture, but they couldn't compete with the sideboards and the tables and chairs that Eaton's could ship out from their factory in Hamilton or wherever it was...even with freight, Eaton's could do it cheaper."[80]

These craftsmen included Stark, a German blacksmith and cabinet-maker who came to Regina in 1910 and worked there as a cabinet-maker, "There are still [c1978] lots of pieces around that people can point at and say, "Old man Stark made that."[81]

Under these circumstances furniture makers tended to diversify, combining furniture making with carpentry, homesteading and other work, often on a seasonal basis working on buildings in the

---

[77] Peddle p.26

[78] Peddle p.31

[79] Dayton Duncan *Miles from Nowhere: Tales from America's Contemporary Frontier* (London 1993) p.162 discusses the 'team haul' principle calculating that homestead = 160 acres, each family approximately 5 members = rural density of 20 people a sq.mile, a town would have more than 4000 patrons in a 10 mile radius that is within a half-days haul. When farm size increases to a section, 640 acres the number of people drops by three quarters.

[80] Barry Broadfoot *The Pioneer Years 1895-1914* (Toronto 1976) p.281

[81] Broadfoot 1976 p.165

summer and making furniture in the winter. Judith Silverthorne identified 120 woodworkers making furniture and smaller items in Saskatchewan between 1870-1945[82] and suggests that there may be a significant number undiscovered.[83] These makers were most productive between 1900 and 1930.[84] Her findings show that most woodworkers lived in the parkland area which runs diagonally across the province and in pockets of treed areas such as the Qu'Appelle valley giving them access to local woods such as pine, spruce, birch, aspen poplar and Manitoba maple, or in communities situated on the railway with access to commercial woods. While some were self-taught, many appear to have been artisans, some with formal craft qualifications.[85] A few, such as Olaf Pearson, set up businesses on their farms; fewer, including Joachim Pilon, had a commercial establishment in a town; most, even where there were other makers in the area, were individualists making and selling work locally.

Four examples suggest the range of artisan activity. Florian Teodor (Ralph) Samuels (1891-1960) born in Bukovyna of Romanian parents, came to the Canora area in 1905 and constructed buildings, furniture and church furnishings including, in 1926, a tabernacle in the form of the Greek Orthodox church at Isinger. Joachim Pilon, born 1864 in Quebec, built houses for employees of the Pullman Cars Company in Chicago. In 1911 he moved to Melville and bought a blacksmith shop where he built sleighs, cutters and wagons. The renovated shop had a second storey wood-finishing and painting area.[86] Pilon's sons worked with him and he also had some employees. By 1920 he had moved into building houses, furniture, violins and coffins. He made a wide range of furniture using diamond willow and other local woods, wood provided by customers and imported lumber.

Olaf Linius Pearson trained as a carpenter in Sweden and took up a homestead in the Broadview area c1897. Pearson worked on rail track maintenance and building construction but eventually abandoned these for fine woodworking. From his shop he worked full-time making church and domestic furniture, woodworking tools and small wares such as bowls and boxes, hand carved

---

[82] J.Silverthorne 'Prairie Harvest: Saskatchewan Woodworkers and Furniture Makers, 1870-1930' ms 1996 p.24 also the related concurrent exhibitions 'Early Saskatchewan Woodworkers: works from 1890 to 1940' at the Saskatchewan Craft Gallery and the Mendel Art Gallery, December 1997

[83] Silverthorne quotes Linday Anderson, a furniture collector, as saying that British/English-speaking immigrants made virtually nothing and "Although several predominant craftspeople existed in Manitoba, Alberta never saw much in the way of crafts."

[84] Silverthorne fax 6 August 1997

[85] Possibly 20%. Silverthorne fax 6 August 1997

[86] Silverthorne describes him as "mostly self-taught", but says that he learned wood finishing and appears to have done some finishing work inside the cars in Chicago.

Crafts: "An Important Activity of Canadian Citizens"

or painted with traditional Swedish designs. He also made grave markers. He worked to commission, on consignment and for his own pleasure. His early work is in pine but later he used birch, maple from the Qu'Appelle valley and recycled wood. He also made the metal parts for his tools, hinges and other small hardware.

David Caldwell, originally from Britain, came to the Neeb area in 1931 and responded to the shortage of large wood by using willow twigs, of which there was a plentiful supply, to make furniture. Although he was only in the area for seven years his furniture "was found in the homes of nearly every homesteader in the Neeb area."[87] He is the only example of a twig or willow furniture maker Silverthorne found. 'Rustic' furniture[88] is primarily associated with Eastern Canada's summer camp and cottage areas, with public park and garden furnishings, and with National Parks such as Jasper and Banff. Producers ranged from manufacturers to contracted or self-employed individuals.[89]

The very strong impression given by the published material is that a clientele for craft furniture-making did not survive beyond the first decades of the twentieth century either in rural communities, ethnic communities[90] or those middle-class groups which might be expected to have an interest in the handcrafted for reasons of prestige or philosophy. However in 1958 there were two small firms[91] in Winnipeg still making custom designed, fine quality furniture with carved

---

[87] Silverthorne 'Early Saskatchewan Woodworkers: works from 1890 to 1940' exhibition photo and biographical information file.
Caldwell was 60 when he came to Neeb and left in 1938, he used only a jackknife, a draw knife and a saw and hammer for building. Silverthorne fax 6 August 1997

[88] S.I.Posen 'Reminiscent of a Tree: A Canadian Rustic Album' ms (CMC 1997)
Posen defines 'rustic furniture' as made from branches or twigs (or horn), formed or as found, peeled or bark-on, stick or bentwood, decoration included applied bark, twig mosaic, attached twig decoration, chip carving and painting p.14

[89] Woven willow and straw furniture are discussed under Domestic Economy.

[90] I.Camb 'Fachwerk and Brettstuhl: The Rejection of Traditional Folk Culture' in *Perspectives on American Folk Art* (New York 1980) pp.172-176; R.K.Janzen and Janzen *Mennonite Furniture: A Migrant Tradition (1766-1910)* (Pennsylvania 1991) limit the Mennonite (one of a number of Anabaptist groups of Dutch/German origin who migrated from Eastern Europe to the North American Plains 1870s-1920s) tradition from 1766 to 1910. "The manufacturing of [this furniture tradition's basic set of a dozen or so functional types and features] ceased rather abruptly a generation after the immigrants came to the Plains and was replaced by mass-produced American furniture." p.12

[91] These were: Villarbiotto Brothers est.c1920, owned by Peter d.1947 and Orest Villarbiotto b.1879, born and trained in Italy, Orest did a woodcarving apprenticeship with a Paris firm; employees Carlo Fusetti b.1901, woodcarver, born and apprenticed in Turate, Italy, Karl Bundt b.1902, who later became a partner, cabinetmaker born and trained Germany; and Cramer's est.c1923 by Philip Cramer d.c1958, apprenticed cabinetmaking Liverpool

decoration in traditional styles for Winnipeg's upper middle class, churches and government buildings.

Despite the demise of the era of large wood sculpture for ship's figure heads, shop signs including standing figures and, in Quebec, decorating the inside and outside of churches, carving, sometimes described as whittling, of small scale wood sculpture and reliefs continued to provide an income for some. Two outstanding examples, Medard Bourgault and W. Garstang, emphasize the difficulty of categorizing work, both fit more nearly into a studio craft tradition in terms of artistry and relation to fine art traditions although neither had a formal art education.

Médard Bourgault,[92] St-Jean-Port-Joli, PQ, was encouraged by Marius Barbeau to become a full-time sculptor.[93] Bourgault's father was a furniture maker with experience in ship building, a maternal uncle had trained in the carving workshops of the Quevillon family at Isle-Jesus near Montreal. Bourgault spent some years as a sailor before returning to work in his father's workshop in the early 1920s. In 1931 he invited his brother Jean-Julien, a furniture maker in Quebec City, to join him in opening a woodcarving studio as by that time he had more work than he could manage alone. His sculptures and reliefs frequently portrayed local country people and occupations. Patrons such as Barbeau, George Bouchard and Adelard Godbout both members of the Quebec government, and Wilfrid Bovey of CHG ensured numerous commissions. By 1935 Médard had moved from small pieces to monumental religious sculptures commissioned for major churches. In 1932 another brother André joined the studio, as did his sister Yvonne, a nephew and later his son Raymond. In 1935 André opened his own studio where he produced series of small sculptures commissioned through CHG and for several years exclusively for Mr. Henderson of Bathurst, NB who sold to clients in the Gaspé region. André was joined by two nephews.

> "Over long years of unremitting labour and constant application he [Médard Bourgault] has built up a large connection and trained a new generation of carvers in wood."[94]

W. Garstang Hodgson a rancher of Dorothy, AB, also turned the hobby of whittling into a vocation in the late 1920s, spurred by poor cattle prices.

UK, son Lou taught woodcarving, cabinetmaking by father.

[92] Médard Bourgault (1898-?), c1918 first wood carving experiments, 1927 visit by Barbeau. Father, Magloire Bourgault b.1863. Médard's studio: brothers Jean-Julien b.1910, André b.1915, sister Yvonne, son Raymond b.1924; nephew Alphonse Toussaint b.1918. Andre's studio: nephews Antonio Bourgault and Léon Toussaint.

[93] J.H.Dunn 'The Wood-Carver of St-Jean-Port-Joli' *CGJ* 65:6:234 December 1952 pp.234-241
J-M Gavreau *Artisans du Quebec* (Montreal? 1940) pp.93-140

[94] Dunn p.237

"Self-taught, using unconventional materials [juniper roots] and unorthodox tools which he designed and made, Hodgson has produced imaginative wood sculpture that is quite distinct from the work of other artists. Yet...he is familiar with the sculpture of today and yesterday [through his early life in England and education in a Yorkshire monastery and]...the books of Eric Gill, Epstein and other eminent sculptors."

"The gnarled streaked wood lends itself to fantastic shapes, to symbolic forms, to flowing lines and swirls. Most of Hodgson's subjects are feminine figures."[95]

Hodgson's work was widely exhibited and marketed, the SACS file 17 February 1944 notes, "no juniper root figurines available for purchase in Canada as a buyer had agreed to take his entire output intending to ship them to France after the war."[96]

Metalwork

Metalsmiths too diversified and skills such as tinsmithing were retained and put to other uses. Honorè Foisy, advertising as a "plumber and general tinsmith" (amongst other skills), with the help of four members of his family,[97] sheathed his house in Lower Town, Ottawa between 1902 and 1916 with a fantastic baroque facade of thin tin, folded and beaten, butt soldered, showing "extraordinarily high craftsmanship" and "originality of design."[98] Weather cocks and weather vanes in three-dimensional forms of hammered and soldered tin or copper also gave scope to the tinsmith.[99] Eric Arthur shows two beautiful three-dimensional sprays of twigs, leaves with, in one a thistle head, in the other a rose. Captioned "typical work by a whitesmith in Dundas, ON, in 1932 showing great delicacy of detail and expression" he gives neither maker, dimensions, material nor purpose.[100]

---

[95] L.Harrington 'Sculptor of Wood - W.G.Hodgson' *CGJ* 39:5 1949

[96] SPL:MB LHR SACS Minutes, Documents LH8542 p.15

[97] brother Jean-Baptist Foisy, uncle David Larose, cousin Napolèon Gariépy, nephew René Richard

[98] Lambert, Barbara 'A wonderfully-accurate restoration' Ottawa:*The Saturday Citizen* 8 September 1973 About 1973 the facade of the house was hung on the blank side of a building in Tin House Square, Lower Town where the plaque says 'galvanised iron', however the article says "paper thin tin." Patterned pressed tin sheeting, was a common sheathing material for house interiors and exteriors c1890-1935 and easily obtainable through hardware catalogues.

[99] CMC collection, which includes a splendid weathercock made by "a talented [but even at this late date anonymous] Longueuil tinsmith" in early 1970s

[100] Arthur p.21 The photo credit is Olive Newcombe.

Percy Nobbs, in a 1944 article covering "far less than one per cent of what has been done",[101] notes Paul Beau,[102] Herman Sontheim[103] from Switzerland[104] and Jack Hedges from England, all working in Montreal in the early decades of the century, the latter two worked primarily on major church commissions (the ones illustrated all designed by Nobbs.)

> "After these came many skilled artificers in metals from Middle Europe, many of them Jews, who found a market for their talents in Toronto and Winnipeg as well as in Montreal."[105]

Nobbs thought there was relatively little activity in the Maritimes and Eastern Quebec, and that in Ontario,

> "there are relatively few craftsmen who work from their own designs...More numerous are the very expert metal artificers...who carry out work designed by architects."

Frederick Flatman was an independent designer/maker who had become a master ironworker at the Woolwich Arsenal, England. He came to Hamilton, ON, in 1910 and turned to blacksmithing and shoeing horses to make a living. George Hendrie provided a shop and forge. As the Hendrie business changed from horse-drawn to motorized vehicles, Flatman turned to truck repairs. Throughout the period he made and sold decorative wrought iron objects including large entrance gates for a private house and ornamental screen doors.[106]

Kenneth Noxon did train as an architect but became a designer and ironworker employing "eight or nine families of craftsmen" in his forges in Toronto. Known as The Metalsmiths (or The Iron Workers[107]), from the 1920s on, Noxon's forges produced chairs, tables, plant-stands, fire-screens,

---

[101] P.Nobbs 'Metal Crafts in Canada' *CGJ* 28:5:212 May 1944

[102] Beau is discussed in detail in chapter 5, 'studio craftspeople'

[103] Herman Sontheim 1877-1958 b.Switzerland; trained as a cabinetmaker; 1891 travelled through Europe; went to Maine, USA mid 1890s worked as a blacksmith. In 1900 to Montreal, learned metalworking at John Watson and Son Ltd. 1928 Watson absorbed by Robert Mitchell Ltd, St Laurent. Sontheim worked for over 20 years as superintendent and general co-ordinator of the Iron and Bronze section. 1952 responsible, with designer-architect Ernest Cormier, for 7 nickel silver doors at the Entry to the United Nations General Assembly Building, NY. Made ornamental gates, balconies, plaques, stairways including that for the Supreme Court Building, Ottawa.

[104] Nobbs says Bavaria but Deborah Woodward in a detailed article 'Death reveals artistic metals genius' newspaper clipping Sontheim file, Artists in Canada (AC), NGC, says Disenhoffen, Switzerland.

[105] Nobbs 1944 p.214

[106] Arthur pp.80-1

[107] *Canadian Art* 11:5:190

Crafts: "An Important Activity of Canadian Citizens"

fireplace equipment, light fixtures, weather vanes and hardware of all types. Pieces in wrought iron, cane and glass were advertised by Eaton's store and work could be purchased or ordered at Metalsmiths' outlet on Yonge Street.[108] Also in Ontario, the Guild of All Crafts, Scarborough, recruited A.E.Freeman, a wrought iron smith in 1923, who when the Guild disbanded in 1941 after nearly a decade of production, set up his own business in Toronto. Keith Heartwell and his nephew and apprentice Fraser Heartwell were also producing metalwork through the Guild of All Crafts.

In Western Canada, Nobbs mentions a predominantly Scandinavian group of designer/makers in Winnipeg which included Gustav Roos,[109] Eric Bergman,[110] Henry Seeholzer and Percy Marsh. Also in the west, people of Icelandic extraction presented intricate metalwork at the New Canadian Folk Song and Handicrafts Festival, Winnipeg 1928.[111] It was probable that country blacksmiths with metalworking shops, like the fictional Arne Arnesson, made decorative ironwork,

> "In Hanbury that year [Saskatchewan 1924] there was a craze for fancy metal gates...The gates would have the homeowner's initials worked into them at the top, surrounded by metal shapes, hearts, butterflies, ovals, scrolls."[112]

They would also have made the wrought-iron grave markers in communities where these were traditional.[113]

Given the vogue for wrought-iron balustrades, verandas and stairways in Quebec city houses, there must have been many small *ferronnerie d'art* in production although Nobbs suggests there was something of a revival in wrought iron work associated with architectural fashions, exterior

---

[108] Wright 1997 p.42
Wright comments that over the period from the mid 1920s to 1960s, Metalsmiths moved from "an entirely craft based method of production to a combination of industrial processes and handwork." p.166

[109] Nobbs 1944 (picture) p.223 Roos was a prize recipient at the New Canadian Folk Song and Handicrafts Festival, Winnipeg 1928; later Mrs Roos, a weaver, taught at CHG:MB

[110] Nobbs 1944 (picture) p.224 shows a hall lamp in wrought iron designed by Bergman, made by Louis Wielander. Eric Bergman (if it is the same person) was better known as a fine artist. He was associated with CHG:MB as a designer and was on the Board. Mrs Bergman in 1943 was running the CHG:MB shop.

[111] USK.A J.E.Murray File newspaper cutting 20 June 1928 'Picturesque Scene Marks First Western Canadian Handicrafts Exhibition' The article suggests that the work was done in Canada not brought from Iceland.

[112] Hugh Hood *Be Sure to Close Your Eyes* (Ontario 1993) p.57

[113] M.S.Bird *A Splendid Harvest: Germanic Folk and Decorative Arts in Canada* (Ontario 1981) p.221 shows a gravemarker in the Roman Catholic cemetery Bruno, SK, 1920 which resembles similar ones in Alsatian- and German-Canadian cemeteries in Southern Ontario.

and interior, after WWI. As well as The Artists' Workshop in Montreal, five McGill University architecture graduates in 1933 set up a design company called The Iron Cat[114] which produced decorative metal works such as candlesticks and sconces.[115] Huges and Jean-Camille Lebrun, designer/makers were running a small forge at Trois Rivières, Quebec around the same period.

In 1951 *Mayfair* magazine could still say, "In almost every city there's a leading jeweler who'll take your order for custom-made flatware or holloware"[116] indicating that precious metalsmiths and jewellers continued to practice their craft throughout the period. Ryder says of New Brunswick that established family firms continued "making large quantities of silver and jewellery until well after the first quarter of the twentieth century."[117] Steve Deverz, Hungarian born and educated in Budapest as silversmith, by 1938 was working in Saskatoon where he talked about his craft, showed "several beautiful pieces worked in silver and gold", and demonstrated his skills to SACS. Many also must have worked under the auspices of national companies such as Henry Birks and Sons Ltd. who employed Carl Poul Petersen[118] as their master goldsmith when he arrived in Montreal from Denmark in 1929.

Glass
Despite competition from firms in Britain[119] and the United States, stained glass windows were designed and produced in the major cities, by firms such as the Robert McCausland Company, Toronto, established 1856 and still extant in 1960.[120] Old established Central Canadian firms such as McCausland and Luxfor Studios, Toronto, tended to dominate the national market hampering the development of local studios but there were a few art glass designers, painters and glaziers

---

[114] Wright 1997 p.42

[115] Bovey 1938 p.8

[116] n/a 'Canadian Metalsmith Creates Unique Beauty' *Mayfair* p.55

[117] Tweedie p.257

[118] Carl Poul Petersen (1895-1977) b.Copenhagen; apprenticed George Jensen, silversmith c1910-1915, also studied fine arts possibly at the Royal Danish Academy of Fine Arts in Copenhagen. Emigrated to Canada 1922, master goldsmith Henry Birks and Sons Ltd. 1922-1937, 1939; independent studio 1937-1939, 1944-1979 with 3 sons as C.P.Petersen and Sons.
G.Lesser 'Carl Poul Petersen: Master Danish-Canadian Silversmith' *Material History Review 43* 1996

[119] A.Hamilton *Manitoban Stained Glass* (Winnipeg 1970) p.78 In Winnipeg and no doubt elsewhere stained glass for Anglican church windows continued to be imported from William Morris Company, and others, until 1955.

[120] Robert McCausland Ltd *On the Making of Stained Glass Windows* (Toronto 1912) pp.13-14 McCausland had shipped stained glass by "rail, steamer, and 'Red River cart'" to Fort Garry (later Winnipeg MB) in 1870 and to Yukon Territory in 1901.

in Winnipeg from 1899 on and in Vancouver, the first local art glass firm, Henry Bloomfield and Sons,[121] specializing in leaded glass for public and private buildings started in New Westminster in 1890 but moved to Vancouver in 1898. Over the next decade they were joined by a number of similar firms primarily employing immigrant craftsmen from Europe and Britain.[122]

Of the 33 Canadian nineteenth century glass factories Gerald Stevens documented, 17 continued into the twentieth century by which time they were rapidly becoming fully mechanized.[123] Only four survived beyond 1925.[124] Stevens says that, "During the period 1875-1915 glass-makers used every technique but the pure mechanical" and referring to The Burlington Glass Works 1875-1909, glass

> "was produced and shaped by blowpipe and punty, by blowing it in a mould, by pressing or by casting, and was decorated by means of acid, cutting, sandblasting and paint...the Burlington works experimented in every known coloration of glass. Some of the master craftsmen imported sticks of special glass for making paperweights and other whimseys..."[125]

He adds,

> "In this glass house were trained many of the artisans whose mastery of the medium was transmitted to present day Canadian glass workers."

Glass blowers apprenticed in Canada and came from England, France, Scandinavia, the United States and elsewhere. Skilled workers tended to move between Canada and the States and across the country as work or the company demanded. This was a craft which did seem to run in families and which had craft associations such as the Glass Blowers Association.[126] Young boys were employed but,

> "The Canadian apprentice was a man who had worked in a glass house for a

---

[121] James Bloomfield (Blomfield) 1872-1951 Educated: 1887-9 Calgary (painting); 1895-1902 Manchester, London, Chicago, New Orleans, Antwerp (art glass); 1903-5 Art Students League, NY. Commissions: decorative paintings Government House, Parliament Buildings, Victoria; windows Parliament Buildings and Christ Church Cathedral, Victoria BC. Also made a number of illuminated addresses for visiting dignitaries and an illuminated *Proverbs* decorated with religious symbols and Canadian wild flowers. Charles Bloomfield fl.1892-1925 glazier/designer.

[122] R.D.Watt *Rainbows on our walls: art and stained glass in Vancouver 1890-1940* (Vancouver c1980)

[123] Stevens 1967 p.xiv
NS 2, ON 5, PQ 6, MB 2, AB 1, BC 1

[124] Stevens 1967 p.xiv Four (PQ 2, ON 1, AB 1) have no end date so were still running in 1967.

[125] G.Stevens *Early Canadian Glass* (Toronto 1960) p.32

[126] Stevens 1960 pp.86-7

sufficient number of years to learn the basic techniques. When he had arrived at an age and a knowledge warranting further training he was apprenticed and after a period usually of four to five years he became a fully qualified glass blower, with the prestige and high rates of pay demanded by expert craftsmen."[127]

The glass blowers in their lunch breaks and at weekends made whimseys, off-hand (free-blown) forms, as a demonstration of their skills. These included paperweights, drapes (triple lengths of glass links joined by decorative finials), hats, walking sticks, witch balls, rolling pins, pipes, birds and animals. Just prior to the closing of the Humphreys Glass Works, Moncton NB, 1920, each of the glass blowers participating in a Labour Day Parade carried a glass cane.[128]

Glass stainers, cutters and decorators, and lampworkers were skilled artisans using glass products. Stevens refers to Stephen Cusac, a glass stainer, who visited the Humphreys glass factory in Moncton c1920.[129] Lampworkers shaped, bent, expanded and contracted glass tubes and sticks to produce castles, ships, animals, baskets, vases, watch chains and so on. Requiring limited equipment lampworkers worked in shops, basements, country fairs and amusement parks. Glass houses in Hamilton, Toronto, Montreal and elsewhere had produced

> "a large amount of non-commercial lampwork and when the Burlington Glass Works closed in 1909, many of the glass blowers, being 'the aristocracy of labour', refused jobs operating the new automatic machines and set up independent lampwork workshops."[130]

It is possible that lampwork is referred to as 'glass blowing' in PNE:1910.

The O.H.Johns Glass Company, Toronto, 1945, was a family business, including sons and daughters, who worked in a "glass blowing factory by day."

> "Nights, saturdays, holidays their relaxation is their art - glass blowing in their home studio. For two generations they have turned out all manner of glass ware ranging...from animals, stemware, bottles and bowls to hospital, laboratory and factory equipment, fireproof cooking-ware and neon tubing."[131]

Oscar Hugo Jahns (later Johns) was born and served his glass apprenticeship in Germany. He moved to Michigan, USA in 1890 and, unable to find work, joined a road show. Jahns moved

---

[127] Stevens 1960 p.149

[128] Stevens 1967 p.67

[129] Stevens 1967 p.67

[130] Stevens 1967 p.247

[131] *CA* 11:5:225

to Canada and was associated with Beaver Flint Glass in 1897, joined Richards Glass Company in 1912 and in 1928, with his son, also O.H.Johns, established his own company.[132]

The Domestic Economy

The 'domestic economy' covers the production of skilled craftspeople who made things for their own use, and occasionally for sale or barter within their community. These were frequently made from necessity, however intricately constructed and decorated. This work is also for the most part the work of thousands of anonymous and unacknowledged craftswomen and men. As with artisan production, the maker's attitudes to the work often appeared to be ambivalent, particularly where there was industrial competition. Peck speaking of CHG's activities in reviving Quebec crafts wrote "women, who now began to take a pride in work that had been held in rather low esteem."[133]

Much of this work is associated in Eastern Canada with poorer, remote rural areas, in the West it is associated with homesteading, in all areas the Depression caused a partial revival of hand production, which in its organised forms will be discussed in the next chapter. Handcraft in the domestic economy hides a complex interaction of fashion, technological innovation particularly affecting entertainment and communications, women's social and legal status and societal perceptions of appropriate behaviour, played out against wider economic, political and national activity.

Textiles: weaving, spinning, knitting, recycled products

Textiles present a major area, largely because women were the primary textile makers and played a primary part in homemaking and the domestic craft economy. Parallel with artisan weaving in Eastern Canada, domestic weaving continued from the nineteenth century into the twentieth virtually unchanged in many rural areas. Commercially processed fibres and fibres raised, processed, and spun in the household, continued to be woven into household linens, sheets, towels, pillowcases, and even farm sacks, into blankets, carpets, mats, coverlets, and clothing fabrics.

In the West, Burnham says that,
"there was plain utilitarian weaving done in a scattered way but weaving of a high

---

[132] Stevens 1967 p.248

[133] Peck 1934 p.204
Behm and Leitch in 1981 speaking of interviews with Saskatchewan "craft workers", spinners and weavers, say, "These people were often ashamed of their skills, believing that we and others find them 'old-fashioned' or 'clumsy'. Many spoke to us reluctantly of what was for most a great pleasure, needing first to be convinced of the sincerity of our interest." Behm, D. and K. Leitch 'Spinning and Weaving on the Prairies' *The Craft Factor* Summer 1987 p.8 based on their unpublished research, and recorded interviews deposited at SKAB:Regina.

order occurred among two groups, the Ukrainians and the Doukhobors."[134]
Lazarowich confirms that Ukrainian women from a rural background where textile production, including growing and preparing fibres, was part of their traditional work, continued to weave utilitarian and decorative textiles for personal consumption during the settlement period (until about 1920) in the three prairie provinces. Equipment not brought from the Ukraine was manufactured by the husband or a neighbour. She suggests that the most active group was in north-eastern Alberta, where weaving continued into the 1940s in response to the Depression when traditional decorative weavings were made for sale. Interestingly, she identifies within a characteristic continuation of nineteenth century designs a "similarity in the choice and sequencing of patterns, and colors [that] produce a distinctive regional style, characteristic to this group of weavers."[135] Because weaving skills were traditionally only passed from the mother to the eldest daughter, Lazarowich contends that "home weaving in the traditional style was prematurely halted with the onset of WWII and the need to produce other items for the war effort"[136] and by the continuing shift of population from country to town. In general by the 1940s isolation was no longer so great because of better roads, vehicles, radios and publications in Ukrainian and English, with the result that although weavers continued to use traditional techniques they modified size, shape, colours and patterns, combining elements of old world patterns and contemporary designs.

Burnham also says that for the most part those that came from the British Isles and Ontario or who had come from Europe with a sojourn in the United States had abandoned their weaving skills, however newspaper exhibition reviews[137] suggest that there was rather more than "plain utilitarian weaving done in a scattered way" throughout the period. The depression certainly stimulated spinning and weaving through the 1930s, not only for want of money to buy clothing and bedding but because the wool market had suffered a severe slump and it was more economic to home process than sell wool. The shortage of imported fabrics during the war supported the revival into the 1940s.

Burnham cites research which indicated that in the West,
"a great deal more handspinning was done than had been realized. It was found that Ukrainians, Germans, Austrians, Poles, Rumanians, Russians, Scandinavians

---

[134] Burnham 1981 p.202

[135] L.A.Lazarowich *A Social History of Ukrainian Cottage Weaving in Alberta 1900-1940* (Manitoba 1983) p.85

[136] Lazarowich p.68

[137] SKAB SACS file B88-4-H, newspaper cuttings c1928, 15 December 1939, c.March 1945. Many newspaper cuttings have the newspaper name and date trimmed off, where they are attached to minutes the dates of the minutes have been given, otherwise the author has used her knowledge of events to give an approximate date.

Crafts: "An Important Activity of Canadian Citizens"

and French spun particularly for knitting yarns and the same was true among the Hutterite, Doukhobor, and Mennonite settlements. The same study indicates that, although there was considerable use of spinning wheels, many simpler methods were used...spinning was widely practised among western settlers, except those of English-speaking origin."[138]

Lazarowich, referring to Ukrainian women in north-eastern Alberta, says that although both spinning wheel and spindle were used in the Ukraine, few wheels were brought to Canada and a limited number were home made. "A significant number of weavers said they used the drop spindle and continued that practice in preference to the wheel well into the 1930s."[139] Later, these Alberta weavers used spinning wheels and drum carders from a Ukrainian manufacturer at Sifton, MB. Behm and Leitch record that spinning bees were held in the Prince Albert area of Saskatchewan between 1912 and 1920. "The bee would last all day, with the women in the area bringing their wheels and spinning for the hostess."[140]

Across Canada on range land, sheep were part of small, mixed operations, and like other agricultural produce wool was subject to fluctuating markets. Before 1914 the wool market was not organized,

> "[M]y wife had too much wool and the store wouldn't even take it in storage. I said that we might as well burn it, what use was it to us? She said she'd give it to a Norwegian family that lived over by the lake. I drove over with these bags of wool and gave them to the woman. She took these bags of wool and made them into yarn and about a month later, one Sunday, she and her husband drove over and they gave us two lovely wool sweaters. Knitted."[141]

By 1918 the Canadian Co-operative Wool Growers handled the bulk of the market, in 1920, 5.1 million kilos of shorn wool was produced, reaching a high of 7 million in 1945. In 1918, the average price per kilo for clean shorn wool was $1.36, by 1932 it was $0.11.[142]

Knitting has attracted remarkably little research until very recently, perhaps for the same reason that SACS did not find knitting, crocheting and tatting marketable, "so many people do similar

---

[138] Burnham 1981 p.202

[139] Lazarowich p.78

[140] Behm and Leitch pp.8,9

[141] Broadfoot 1976 p.170

[142] S.A.Scott *Canada Knits: Craft and Comfort in a Northern Land* (Toronto 1990) p.68

work."[143] As indicated by the agricultural exhibition lists, knitting, and other 'needle' textile construction such as crochet, were major areas of activity. They provided essential clothing for Canadian winters, household items and decorative trimmings. In an early Manitoba log cabin hung "hand-knit lace curtains, brought from Ontario."[144] SACS's first exhibition in 1923, contained some "very prosaic stockings, woolly-warm and beautifully made withal. For the latter the yarn was carded and spun by hand."[145] Burnham collected (and exhibited in an exhibition that "has the word 'ART' in its title")

> "a pair of worn and darned 'Long Johns'...a rare example of skilled craftsmanship and a unique survival...Care has also been taken to shape the garment well, with careful attention to detail, and the knitting is expert."[146]

They were made about 1900 in a Newfoundland outport, of handspun wool.

Shirley Scott suggests that Canada, in particular eastern Canada, was part of the 'North Atlantic knitting culture' with roots in Western Europe, Scandinavia and the Baltic. Janetta Dexter describes distinctive mitts designed to meet the requirements of the user's trade, for example fishing, made with a separate first finger or shaped to protect the parts of the hand at risk. Double knit, felting or raw wool worked into the back of the knit ensured warmth. Patterns in traditional motifs bear names echoing patchwork, 'flying geese' and 'partridge feet'.[147] Work socks, buskins (gaiters), tams and toques, and working sweaters, related to the British gansey with a circular construction and simple shaping, were standard work gear. Many pairs of socks and mittens would be worn out in a season.

The number of commercial yarn producers,[148] pattern books and advertising suggest that this was not just a rural phenomenon but a part of the domestic economy for many urban women. Knitting required no dedicated space or special equipment, and was portable. Making family clothing

---

[143] SKAB SACS B88-B Committee Reports 1922-42 Work Committee 1st annual report 1923 These figures compare with a production low of 1.2 million in 1976, price of $1.78 in 1977.

[144] Nellie McClung *Clearing in the West* (Toronto 1976) pp.166,67

[145] SKAB SACS file B88-4-H newspaper cutting

[146] Burnham 1981 p.107 (one of the few knitted articles in the NMC collection)

[147] J.Dexter *Traditional Nova Scotian Double-Knitting Patterns* (NS n/d) suggests that in the 1970s in Nova Scotia these patterns were still quite local.

[148] eg. Aked and Co. Ltd. Toronto was formed 1918 to produce fancy knitting yarns, acquired by Patons and Baldwins 1928; Briggs and Little, New Brunswick 1857 to present; Spinrite Yarns originally Perfect Knitting Mills 1913 Listowel ON, expanded 1916, sold 1931 Maitland Spinning Mills Ltd, 1952 bought by David Hay formerly head dyer 1926-1948; White Buffalo Mills, Brandon MB ?date began producing White Buffalo unspun yarn

demonstrated a satisfying combination of skill, aesthetic expression and economy. In the 1920s knitting designs more closely reflected clothing fashions and in the 1930s women were knitting 'tailored' suits and dresses with knitted gores, darts and trims, a major investment of time and expertise and an economic way of remaining fashionable.

As early as 1924, W.J.Mather of Winthrope, SK, wrote, "One [Ruthenian] family have started with an auto-knitter and I believe are finding it pays well"[149] and in 1938 SACS did consider for marketing, "hand knit mitts, Norwegian style and some machine knit articles" made by a recent immigrant from Norway.[150] In 1947 another Norwegian immigrant was paying the rent by, "knitting and making quilts and I think I made about thirty dollars a month on them..."[151]

Recycling of materials was long a part of the domestic economy.
> "Two long widths of rag carpet in bright stripes with orange warp...the good mats, one hooked and one braided...patchwork cushions, crazy pattern of silks and satins, and two log cabins, one of 'stuff' pieces, the other one of prints...a quilt,"[152]

all reflect various recycling techniques. The contribution to the domestic economy could be more than thrift,
> We were poor off as mice in a stone church... Neighbors would give my wife old clothes, scraps and such, and she'd dye them, making pretty colors, and make comforters and rugs and trade them in the store and get a little trading out of that."[153]

Chiasson lists five Acadian rug types using recycled materials: *defaisures* of recycled knitted garments, cut in two inch strips, sewn down in close rows on jute canvas and frayed to give a "velvety texture"; braided; *catalognes* woven with rag weft; rosette with diminishing circles sewn to jute; and *breillons*, hooked rugs using fabrics other than wool.[154] Chiasson also adds,
> "Sometimes the most beautiful ones were set aside for special occasions...for special holidays or when they received important visitors...as a gesture to

---

[149] SKAB SACS B88-E(1) Correspondence 1922-24 W.J.Mather to Professor Morton 20 June 1924

[150] SKAB SACS B88-B2 Minute book 2 p.138 2 May 1938

[151] Broadfoot 1976 p.220

[152] Nellie McClung pp.166-67

[153] Broadfoot 1976 p.126 Probably trading them for food and store goods.

[154] A.Chiasson *The History of Cheticamp Hooked Rugs and Their Artisans* (NS 1988) p.7

demonstrate their faith, some people donated their rugs to the church."[155]

He gives no indication whether this was historic or contemporary practice (although there are similar accounts in other areas[156]), in other words whether it was a reflection of outside value or of the community or individual values, however it does suggest that self-selection was going on for quality and design and there were canons of criticism, if not articulated, and a recognised social function.

Hooked rugs attracted the interest of collectors early in the twentieth century,[157] but patchwork and quilted bed covers did not until considerably later. Quiltmaking in the early twentieth century, Weizman, and Robson and MacDonald suggest, became predominantly a group activity. There are occasional references to quilted clothing, including a pieced jacket made about 1900 and quilted jackets to wear under coats.[158]

Basketry

Basket making in connection with specific trades carried on into the twentieth century. It is possible that itinerant artisan basket makers continued to make a living at their trade on the prairies but in the continuous cycle of settlement problems and crop failure - "Froze out, hailed out, burned out, rusted out, and the grasshoppers ate the halters off the teams and the catalogue in the privy"[159] - supplementary trades provided welcome income. In Saskatchewan, Mr. Schreiber of Tisdale "sat on people's doorsteps and made split willow baskets to order" during the late 1920s.[160] The depression exacerbated the problems of survival. Widowed, with three children and no relief or farming equipment, a homesteader recalls,

---

[155] Chiasson p.18

[156] Hayward 'Rug Hunting in Habitant Quebec' *Toronto Star* 30 June 1928 "the great parlour...The floor was painted in that rich pumpkin-yellow so much in vogue among the habitants. Upon this, laid a foot apart, were six strips of homewoven rag carpet, and upon these were set with a mathematical exactitude...twenty...of the most beautiful hooked rugs..."They were all made by a woman now dead. She made them one at a time...they are not alike, each one is different, but she make them to harmonize in ze colors...she was a fine rugmaker.I pay very dear..I pay two hun're dollars for the rugs."
In Newfoundland a maker said in 1980, "It was not uncommon for a home to have thirty to forty hooked mats in daily use at the peak of the popularity. Floors would be 'covered right over,' 'right tight together.'" C.Lynch 'A Handle on the Past: A Compilation of Research on Craft Design in Newfoundland and Labrador' (Newfoundland 1994) p.14

[157] see chapters 4 and 6 'Marius Barbeau'

[158] S.Robson and S.MacDonald *Old Nova Scotian Quilts* (NS 1995) p.99

[159] Barry Broadfoot *Ten Lost Years 1929-1939* (ON 1975) p.46

[160] *The Craft Factor* 4:4 1979 p.15

"A man named Mr. Wood said I should make willow baskets and sell them...The kids went out along the Red Deer River [Alberta] and cut willows and I learned the ropes and I soon was making very good baskets. Like Indian baskets, with designs. I tried to sell some in Red Deer but others had taken this Mr. Wood's advice and nobody wanted these fine baskets so...my brother got a ride...to Calgary...I think he had a load of about 60. That was our whole winter's work...We were asking 50 cents each and in two days of door-to-door, he sold two. I stored them away...I made another 35 or 40 the next winter just to keep busy...Ten years later, this would be about 1945, I took them into the Bay [national store originally the Hudson's Bay Company]...the man said he would give me one dollar each...what one hundred dollars would have done in 1934...it would have [kept] that little family alive for nearly a year."[161]

Woven willow furniture[162] and woven straw furniture[163] were made in Saskatchewan in the late 1970s and 1980s and it would be surprising, given the style of these pieces, the local availability of materials and the widespread domestic use of wicker furniture in the early part of the century if there were not makers producing such furniture for their own use or sale. Jugo-Slavs at the 1928 Winnipeg New Canadian Handicraft Festival showed willow furniture, "some of it had been fatally embellished, but some had not and was good."[164] Brantford Willow Works, an Ontario manufacturer illustrated "'Wrought Willow' Art Furniture" in a 1909 *Canada-West Advertiser*.[165] Wheat weavings in the form of small sculptures of, for example, 'Cart and Horses',[166] and possibly wheat mosaics, brought Mr.A.R.Rhodes to the attention of SACS, "English...in the King's Guards in his youth...an excellent craftsman with wheat straw...recently in a very destitute condition."[167]

---

[161] Broadfoot 1975 p.32

[162] Stefan Horpynka, red willow table chairs and picnic basket illustrated in *The Craft Factor* August 1978 p.8; 'Stefan Horpynka: Master Willow Weaver' Kristina Komendant *The Craft Factor* Summer 1994 p.11

[163] Reinhold Adams, Yorkton, straw furniture including various side tables, plant stands and lamp stand at what appears to be a market booth *The Craft Factor* September 1980 p.14

[164] USK.A J.E.Murray Collection newspaper clipping 'The Future For Handicrafts' n/d

[165] *Canada-West Advertiser* April 1909 p.cxciii

[166] c.1920s Saskatchewan Western Development Museum, Saskatoon

[167] SKAB SACS B88 Correspondence 15 June 1939

Furniture
In general, the advent of industrial mass-produced furniture and the means to acquire it, seem to have spelled the demise of artisan furniture making and of furniture making as part of the domestic economy. Where money was not available as in Newfoundland,

> "the majority of outport pieces were either homemade or built by tradesmen other than formally trained furniture makers... Consequently, the form, design and decoration of rural Newfoundland furniture was influenced less by the conventional guidelines followed by formally trained furniture makers or factories than by the skill, ingenuity and imagination of the individual makers."[168]

However commercial furniture was influential. Rural makers generally duplicated the methods of furniture construction practiced by professional furniture makers. Local woods (pine, spruce, fir, tamarack and birch), boards from demolished houses and outbuildings, parts of older furniture such as legs, rungs and spindles, and boards from packing cases were used in furniture which was,

> "usually painted to resemble the woods - mahogany, rosewood, walnut or oak - used in commercially produced furniture...[although] most graining was done...for decorative effect, and seldom resembled any known wood. By the beginning of the twentieth century many items were profusely decorated...early folk forms were decorated with late factory inspired fretwork and turnery. In others, the styles were factory-inspired but the decorations were traditional...some pieces displayed, sometimes along with traditional and factory influences, design elements and embellishments that originated with the maker."[169]

All types of furniture were made, often modified to fit a particular dwelling.

Amongst a number of makers, Peddle notes the furniture of Billy Wheeler in the early twentieth century. Much of it was tailor-made for his house in Keels, where it remains in its original setting used by his son John who "may not consider his father's furniture of particular significance."[170] It includes a parlour couch, a shallow bedroom commode "probably made more for relieving the starkness of tiny bedrooms than for providing storage space for clothing...Sarah Devereaux explained: "You never had nothing to put in them anyway"[171], a rocking chair, sideboard, and a shaving mirror. Hand carved motifs on the furniture were mirrored in the carving on a door and door frame, and a decorative staircase balustrade. Wheeler also made some pieces for other

---

[168] Peddle p.26

[169] Peddle pp.31,32

[170] Peddle p.91

[171] Peddle p.112

Crafts: "An Important Activity of Canadian Citizens"

people, "You'd give him a couple of sticks of tobacco, or you'd haul a load of wood for him. You'd try to pay him back some way or another."[172]

Although all Peddle's named furniture makers are men, and he implies that furniture making as part of the domestic economy ceased when rural Newfoundland moved to a cash society, Elizabeth Gale (1911-) suggests at least a limited continuation of that tradition. Living and raising a family in an isolated outport, Gale

> "made all the furniture she was unable to purchase. Completely self-taught, Elizabeth carefully studied items in the Eaton's catalogue, and developed her own designs. With a small array of tools consisting of an axe, a pocketknife and a saw, she made washstands, bureaus, couches, barrel chairs and picture frames...She decorated her furniture with intricately carved designs inspired by embroidery patterns and stained them with tobacco or coffee. Within a few years...she was supplying furniture to communities along the base of the Great Northern Peninsula."[173]

Among other tasks she also spun wool, hooked rugs and made clothes. Gale has continued furniture making throughout her life.

The other area of recorded activity is on the Prairies. As with other craftspeople it is probable that carpenters and furniture makers came to the west to homestead and produced furniture for personal use. However attention has focussed on particular groups, mainly from rural Eastern Europe, a number of whom for religious reasons were conservative, self-contained and had identifiable craft traditions. Silverthorne says that part of the Doukhobor doctrine was,

> "that 'all men should work in wood,' and they were continually apprenticing the next generation of men, However, even though they worked communally, many individuals of note emerged, such as Bludoff and Popov from the Veregin region."[174]

Among the Mennonites who moved into Saskatchewan around 1903, individuals, like Neustaeter of Schoenfeld, had their own business within each community.[175]

Examples of furniture range,

> "from the crude and improvised to the spectacularly artful. Furniture with an

---

[172] Fred Devereaux, Duntara quoted Peddle p.82

[173] *Herstory* calendar (Regina 1997) p.62

[174] Silverthorne 'Early Saskatchewan Woodworkers: works from 1890 to 1940' exhibition, Saskatoon December 1996 'Doukhobor' information sheet

[175] Silverthorne 1997 p.14

identifiable ethnic character was only made and valued for a short period of time,
and then often only by the first generation."[176]

Aspen poplar, birch, spruce, construction grade spruce, fir tongue and groove, and salvaged crate boards were used. Shape and construction had classic community characteristics or were copied from mail-order catalogues. The pieces were painted in ethnically distinctive colour combinations or wood grained.

Leisure activities

Newspaper accounts of local exhibitions and archives such as SACS's frequently lack detailed information about makers, which makes it difficult to assess what are truly leisure crafts.[177] This assessment is doubly complicated as married women were precluded from employment in many occupations using academic craft training, for example teaching, until well into the 1950s and much women's production was automatically labelled 'amateur' or 'leisure'. As indicators I have looked at the motives and economic position of the maker where possible, and also at the degree of decorativeness as opposed to utility although decoration is an integral part of many crafts of necessity. Interior decor and fashion in this period dictated the extensive use of trimmings and decorative pieces. These display a high level of intricacy and craft technique whether commercially replicated by machine or handwork, or home produced.

The Canadian winter divided the rural year decisively providing an involuntary leisure for some,
"Finished with all work yet last week. Now just waiting for the cold winter in which we always have our long rest. Just all we do is cook eat and sleep. So I hope to get work for the whole winter cause I like working embroidering...I wish I could have some now cause its so lonely with out work the day seems so long"
wrote Mary Kabatoff in 1938.[178]

As the century progressed the increase in automobiles and the creation and improvement of road networks decreased isolation in rural communities and changed social patterns. Cars and radio also enhanced contact between urban and rural areas, and in the 1940s there was a major migration from the countryside to the cities. These and other factors influenced the availability of leisure and its use, which in turn affected craft. Lazarowich suggests that in the 1920s among Ukrainians in Alberta the weaving of traditional textiles started to be replaced by embroidery and *pysanky* (egg painting) because of a Canadianization of lifestyle, also neither demanded dedicated

---

[176] T.McFall 'Prairie Folk Furniture' *The Craft Factor* Winter 1989/90 p.23

[177] As was common in these exhibitions, some works were historical but many were made by contemporary, and often named makers, and could be on loan or for sale; newspaper accounts are frequently unclear about categories.

[178] SKAB SACS B88-B2 letter 11 October 1938 included in year end report 31 October 1938. This letter was in fact seeking paid work.

Crafts: "An Important Activity of Canadian Citizens"

loom space or the physical effort of weaving.

The energetic promotion of needle crafts through publications indicates one widespread leisure occupation, traditionally done by women, of all classes and nationalities, rural and urban. The first exhibition of the Arts and Crafts committee of the Local Council of Women in Saskatoon, 1922, contained loaned works of the "most exquisite needlework" by people of at least nine nationalities.[179] The intent of the committee was "to represent the arts and crafts produced in Saskatchewan...[and] that the finished articles be typical of the peoples...who are living in this middle west locality."[180] Also exhibited were weaving (mats, bedspreads, tapestries and throws), knitting and crochet. The 1927 Nokomis Agricultural Fair prize list has under 'Ladies Fancy Work' 61 categories of which at least 35 could be considered leisure activities,[181] moreover there seems little distinctively rural about the range of crafts. Craftspeople continued to practice heritage craft skills as a leisure activity, a Norwegian immigrant Rosa Peterson demonstrated bobbin lace, which she had learned as a child, to a SACS meeting in 1930.[182]

Amongst its other activities SACS, from its inception in 1922, organized exhibitions and demonstrations of a wide range of crafts. Many of these demonstrations were by craftspeople, predominantly women, who had academic training and some of whom probably practiced their craft to generate income. While these demonstrations promoted appreciation rather than taught skills, undoubtedly part of the audience were also practitioners at some level and this became a way of disseminating new skills and ideas. By 1935, even a small centre like Saskatoon had three societies fostering 'art appreciation'.

> "Bridge and badminton have not been the only means of diversion for Saskatoon women this past Winter according to the needlework and handicraft display which opened yesterday in the Spanish Room of the Hudson's Bay [department store]."[183]

Mixed with "valuable antiques" seem to have been contemporary work: wrought iron ornaments, rag rugs, brass and copper ware, woven rugs, bags and scarfs, tooled leather book covers, jars and vases made from Saskatchewan clay, embroidered pictures and maps, batik silks, patch-work quilts, carved and burnt wood trays and plaques, and hand-painted china. By 1950,

---

[179] Japanese, Chinese (both of which also exhibited crocheted pieces), Greek Norwegian, Icelandic, English, Ukrainian, Hungarian, Austrian

[180] SKAB SACS B88-4-H newspaper clipping n/d c1922/23

[181] Appendix 2

[182] SKAB SACS B88-B2 Report Program Committee 1930/31

[183] SPL(main) LHR Art file newspaper clipping 13 April 1935

"Hundreds of residents of this city have taken up hobbies realizing not only their beneficial effect upon health but also their value in the making of handmade articles fit to adorn the home."[184]

Similar societies and activities were found in all areas of the country and had a long history. Predominantly instigated and sustained by women, they included organisations such as the WAAC and more local, independent organizations, often named Arts and Crafts societies. These tended to be part of informal local or provincial networks. Although these groups have been critiqued by Tippet, Wetherell and Kmet and others as being controlled by an Ontario-British elite, exponents of the dominant culture, and while that may be true of Eastern Canada, Vancouver and Victoria, and possibly parts of the prairies, a close reading of SACS archives suggests a less clear-cut scenario both in membership, dynamics and activities. The dynamics seem to relate to class and education more than ethnicity.

Woodwork
Ethnology, folk and tramp art collections contain numerous small decorative articles and sculptures of wood, for example boxes for trinkets or sewing or pencils, corner shelves and book shelves, plant stands, picture frames and trays. Most of these because of scale, intricacy and the context of the maker, I assume to be made during leisure. For the prairie region many of these have been collected from distinct ethnic groups and were made primarily in the early part of the century. Ukrainian pieces include such things as a carved and painted fretwork lamp shelf and picture frame, an ornate wall shelf possibly made for a church to support a statue, a coat rack where the pegs are carved bird heads, and a chandelier made of turned threaded balls.[185] Peter Hofer the carpenter at Rosebud Hutterite Colony, AB, made small decorative chests with painted designs and lettering in a Germanic tradition c1950.[186] A series of photographs c1924 shows the work of Thore Thorson, a logger, one of group of Norwegian settlers at Bella Coola, BC. They include carved picture frames, salad servers, boxes and shelves and carved bent wood boxes in traditional Norwegian designs, the painting done by Magnus Thorson.[187]

It would be surprising if there were not urban woodworkers producing smaller household objects

---

[184] SPL(main) LHR Art File newspaper clipping 20 April 1950

[185] Michael Rowan *Ukrainian Pioneer Furniture* UWAC:UMC Ontario Branch 1992 p.10,11,19,22,18

[186] M.Einarsson, H.B.Taylor *Just for Nice: German-Canadian Folk Art* (Ottawa/Hull 1993) p.27, illustration, also of work by John Waldner, Hutterville Colony AB p.47, and Jake Wollman, Leask Colony SK child's horse p.73

[187] CMC photo file Harlan I Smith series 62214-18, 62220, 62222

Crafts: "An Important Activity of Canadian Citizens"

and possibly even furniture as furniture-making books and articles were available.[188] A 1912 Manitoba Society of Arts and Crafts and Western Art Association First Exhibition list records wood mosaic work, wood carving, burnt relief work and chip carving done by both men and women.

General craft education and therapy

Although the materials and tools for needle and wood working crafts could be home produced, they were mostly directly or indirectly of commercial origin. Apart from looms and some woodworking machinery which required dedicated space, many of the crafts were portable and had minimal requirements. The skills were predominantly informally learned.

Pottery

Pottery, like smithing, in European societies seems to have remained a specialist craft thus its appearance as a leisure activity indicates different parameters. China painting (mainly overglaze painting) became fashionable as a leisure activity in the late nineteenth century and continued into the twentieth. Closely allied with painting in skills, it required access to ceramic blanks, china paints and a kiln. The production of pots demanded more specialised equipment and dedicated facilities as well as specialist teachers. Occasionally these were local artisans such as Axel Ebring, more frequently art school graduates. Access to pottery, was often through evening classes or summer schools for teachers such as those c1920 in Victoria, BC.[189] In 1920 the Art Department of Vancouver Education Board also ordered clay presumably for use in its public schools.

As with china painting, the early references are to women practitioners, a point noted by MacLean's Magazine in 1927, "This craft remains, as it was since its beginning, entirely in the hands of the women of British Columbia."[190] 'Ceramics' was taught and exhibited prior to 1900, however it is not clear whether this meant china painting, thrown pottery or slipware. The 1903 exhibition of the Arts and Crafts Society, Toronto contained 'pottery'. The 1908 CHG Annual exhibition lists pottery from Quebec and Ontario, and later from Manitoba and Newfoundland.[191] The Vancouver's Opening Exhibition 1910 (PNE:1910) had both 'pottery' and 'painting on china'

---

[188] For example Popular Mechanics Company *Mission Furniture: How to Make It* Parts I,II & III (originally published 1909, 1910, 1912) (new York 1980); 'Homemade Furniture:An Oak Table of Good Lines and Proportion' *Canadian Thresherman and Farmer* December 1919 p.62

[189] see chapter 5 Craft Education, VSA

[190] N.De Bertrand Lugrin 'Women Potters and Indian Themes' *MacLean's Magazine* 15 March 1927 p.79
In 1900, the U.S. had 3 college ceramics programs, one of which was Sophie Newcombe Memorial College for Women, New Orleans

[191] Peck 1929 pp.8, 9

in its Fine Arts class. In 1912, "Mrs Barber [F.R.S.A., UK]...fired the first clay in Saskatchewan...and has her own kiln. She is particularly expert at enamelling clay with her own original designs"[192] and Margaret McDonald exhibited 'pottery', as opposed to china painting which was also exhibited, at the Manitoba Society of Arts and Crafts.[193] By 1919 Medalta Pottery, Medicine Hat, AB, provided, as a public service, technical information and clay to schools and colleges over a wide area of the country. The first SACS exhibition, 1922, included a pottery display with pieces done by local school children. The level of activity indicates an early and fairly extensive interest in ceramics in all its various forms despite technological restrictions.

In Victoria, BC, in the early 1920s, Emily Carr was digging local red clay from the coastal cliffs, hand modelling dishes, lamp holders, smaller vessels and ornaments which were decorated with West Coast Native motifs and, unglazed, were fired in kilns she had built, first in her house basement which nearly set her house on fire, "the kiln hadn't been built properly in the first place anyway and she wanted to build another one".[194] Carr writes,

> "With the help of a chimney sweep I built a brick kiln in my back yard...The kiln was a crude thing, no drafts, no dampers, no thermometer - one door for all purposes...A firing took from twelve to fourteen hours; every moment of it was agony, suspense, sweat. The small kiln room grew stifling, my bones shook, anticipating a visit from police, fire chief, or insurance man. The roof caught fire. The floor caught fire. I kept the hose attached to the kitchen tap and the roof of the kiln-shed soaked."[195]

---

[192] SKAB SACS 'Notes on Canadian Handicraft made during a trip to Western Canada - Summer of 1943' J. Murray Gibbon p.8

[193] WAG Carnegie Library 'Manitoba Society of Arts and Crafts and Western Art Association First Exhibition' exhibitors list 1912

[194] Blanchard pp.160-161,243 It cannot be described as a leisure activity for Carr but was a money making strategy, however she is not recorded as having any training in pottery although she had extensive art training. She produced pottery from the early 1920s to c1931, which was sold through the CHG:Montreal, NGC, and shops in Banff, Vancouver and Victoria, and through a show case and 'pottery evenings' at her studio.

[195] Emily Carr *The Complete Writings of Emily Carr* (Vancouver 1997) p.439
Carr says "I made hundreds and hundreds of stupid objects, the kind that tourists pick up - I could bake as many as five hundred small pieces at one firing...Because my stuff sold, other potters followed my lead and, knowing nothing of Indian art, falsified it...I loved handling the smooth clay." Carr signed her work 'Klee Wyck', 1996 fine auction estimates for two "stupid objects" painted with an eagle motif and owl/bear motif were $10,000-12,000.

Also in Victoria, Mrs Margaret Grute,[196] a graduate of Goldsmith's College, London, attended the Summer school for teachers referred to above in 1923 and ran a pottery school in Victoria from 1927 with a "large following."[197] "She uses the potter's wheel and her work is always glazed."[198] As a result of all this activity,

> "It is expected that the Government will start work shortly on a large community kiln where the women can fire more ambitious pieces than they have been able to handle heretofore: urns, fountain decorations, bird baths and other things, suitable for gardens."[199]

These hardly sound like the work of dilettantes. Even in the interior of the province, three members of the Summerland Art League, in 1922, were using local clay for modelling and for bowls, jugs and vases.[200] As in other crafts, for many women 'leisure activities' may have covered a serious pursuit.

It is possible that scattered activity of this kind was going on across the country, dependant on enthusiasm and access to the growing number of graduates of art school pottery programs, many of whom were women, who worked as public school teachers or occupational therapists or who wished to carry on with their craft. Although the University of Saskatchewan had a Ceramic Engineering department from 1921, pottery was taught in the school system, and small clay industries were located on major clay deposits in the southern part of the province, clay does not show up as a widespread leisure activity until the mid-1930s when evening classes in throwing and clay modelling were offered at the Saskatoon Technical School by Cameron Worcester. His "semi-commercial art pottery", Canada Claycraft Company, also supplied clay, and may have fired work for local potters. Work from Saskatchewan potters was shown to the Canadian Potter's Association[201] in 1937, who responded "we were very interested...and thought some of it very good."[202] The WAAC:Regina were considering pottery classes in 1936 but were hampered by lack

---

[196] Margaret Grute mrs b.Queenstown Ireland. Educated: Cork School of Art; Goldsmiths College, London; 1923 Victoria Summer School (pottery). Qualified as an Art Teacher, worked as a designer for Liberty's of London. Emigrated to Victoria on marriage.

[197] see chapter 5 Craft Education, VSA

[198] De Bertrand Lugrin p.79

[199] De Bertrand Lugrin p.79 The government appears to have been interested in "affording employment for hundreds of women."

[200] Green pp.220-1

[201] presumably this is the Canadian Guild of Potters (CGP) started in Toronto in 1936

[202] USK.A W.G.Worcestor [sic] papers correspondence Helen Turner, Toronto to W.G.Worcester, 15 October 1937

of a kiln.[203] A 1935 travelling exhibition of crafts in Alberta sponsored jointly by CHG, University of Alberta Extension Division and the Carnegie Foundation contained "earthenware, from local clay" and "in the immediate postwar period, the most popular handicrafts were various needlework crafts, weaving, and ceramics."[204]

Pottery as a leisure activity charts a growing formalization of leisure crafts requiring trained teachers, classes, a set location and usually fees. Whether 'leisure' pottery attracted a particular section of society can only be hypothesized in a fluid social situation; disposable income was not necessarily a condition, classes in many crafts were offered for philanthropic reasons. Metalsmithing skills, for simple jewellery, decorative panels and hollow-ware, were taught in the same way, as were skills which traditionally had been informally transmitted such as basketry, woodworking, weaving, leatherwork and needlework. Throughout the period, the productive use of leisure was seen as a moral good, "the devil finds mischief for idle hands."[205] Handcraft was also seen as having physical and mental benefits. Thus handcraft skills found a growing place in school curricula and in occupational therapy. The formalization of leisure activities implies the presence of institutional structures ranging from those directly involved with craft education and promotion such as art schools and craft organizations to those indirectly involved through the promotion of the moral and physical welfare of particular groups through rehabilitation, improvement of domestic skills, and retention of a viable rural population, to name a few aims.[206]

Occupational therapy
At the first SACS exhibition, 1922,
> "Probably the most interesting part of the exhibit is that to which the inmates of the North Battleford asylum[207] have contributed. It is almost unbelievable that people handicapped as they are can turn out such splendid work."[208]

---

[203] USK.A W.G.Worcestor [sic] papers correspondence 27 October 1936.

[204] D.Wetherell *Useful Pleasures: The Shaping of Leisure in Alberta 1896-1945* (Regina 1990) p.63 This statement has no references.

[205] as my grandmother born in the 1880s frequently used to say

[206] Some of these are discussed in chapters 4, 5

[207] The Provincial Mental Hospital, North Battleford, opened 1914,"is noted for its progressive methods, particularly in its adoption of occupational therapy on a generous scale. In this it did pioneer work." In 1937, Miss Hazel Jacques, who joined the hospital in 1919 was made director of occupational therapy for the province. In 1939 "About ninety [women] are learning the hooking of rugs, embroidery, knitting and needlepoint." 'Prairie Provinces Have Fewest Cases Of Mental Illness' *The Daily Colonist* Victoria 26 March 1939

[208] SKAB SACS B88-4-H newspaper clipping 'Throngs attend arts and crafts exhibition organised by L.C.W. n/d probably 1922 as the official report is dated 30 January 1923

This ranged from small furniture to baskets in reed and wickerwork, objects in brass and copper including a "huge" umbrella stand, an "ornate tea kettle", candlesticks and "tiny" vases, woven rugs, inlaid and carved woodwork and a wooden cradle.

Although this report suggests a degree of individuality in the work, in general it has been assumed that, as in other kinds of popular art, the levels of creativity were low. However in learning any skill, creativity initially is secondary. Occupational therapy in hospitals used craft techniques to improve muscle function and co-ordination as well as to divert, therefore the end product was not judged necessarily by craft standards. Occupational therapy was started in the Vancouver General Hospital in 1931 through funding and volunteer support from the Junior League. The Occupational Therapist instructed patients and Junior League volunteers who became aides. In 1943 patients were doing

> "leatherwork, bookbinding, needlework, knitting, raffia, woodwork, glove-making etc., under the direction of three professional instructors, assisted by a corps of volunteers. According to the last report, twenty-five patients earn regular monthly salaries in the workshop, eleven do piecework in their homes and an average of fifty-two patients per month receive instruction in the Tuberculosis Pavilion and the Wards of the General Hospital."[209]

At a time when there were no government sickness benefits or financial resource for industrial accidents such acquisition of skills and financial return were important.[210]

Two major wars provided a new constituency for crafts. May Phillips, co-founder of CHG, became a volunteer when the Red Cross was organised in Canada in 1909. From 1914 to 1918 she supervised all branches outside Montreal and instituted the Junior Red Cross. Alice Peck, another CHG co-founder, c1917 initiated a veteran's self-help project, Undermount Industries, in her large house where approximately 25 disabled veterans were taught weaving or bookbinding, Peck's areas of expertise.[211] The Guild's interest continued during WWII. Gibbon, CHG President, reporting on a trip to Western Canada in 1943 constantly refers to craft education projects for the

---

[209] SKAB SACS J. Murray Gibbon 'Notes on Canadian Handicraft 1943' p.3

[210] Peck 1934 p.203 caption "A returned soldier...Unable to carry on at his former work, he was taught book-binding and now holds a good position and is able to support his family happily." (Possibly this is the same man who became chief book-binder for the University of McGill 'Cottage Industries of Canadian-Born and Immigrant Settlers' *Family Herald and Weekly Star, Montreal* 26 October 1927 p.31) p.205 caption "A train-coupler paralysed in a railway accident in 1901, this man was a burden to a very poor family. He was taught basket weaving...Later he supported the family..."

[211] Peck had her own handpress. It may be one of Peck's protegees shown demonstrating book-binding at a 1927 exhibition Peck 1934 1934 p.203

armed forces including prisoners of war and to occupational therapy programs.[212]

> "Many demobilized soldiers after the last war [WWI] took up various forms of knitting, needlework, tapestry and other forms of work."[213]

Gibbon refers to Geneva Lent, Calgary, who was writing a manual on needlework for a series co-ordinated by Dr Ivan Crowell at Macdonald College, McGill University for the Canadian Legion Educational Services (who also provided funds for instructors on bases) and Y.M.C.A. War Services.

> "Her instruction is based on Cross stitch, illustrated with designs suited to male taste - such as cowboys, bucking bronchos, animals, Indians..."

These instructional pamphlets covering a wide range of crafts became an inexpensive series of about fifty titles issued by McGill University Adult Education Service in 1944/5, various supplies and tools could be purchased in kit form from MacDonald College Handicrafts Store. Lent also referred to 'Occupational Parcels' containing materials and instructions for rug-making, slipper making, basketry, bookbinding, raffia, tapestry and cross stitch which were "in great demand in internment camps."[214]

In 1945, the Vancouver Art Gallery presented a "large and varied exhibition" of work from 11 stations and convalescent hospitals under Western Air Command, notable exhibits were an inlaid wood table, bowls and lampstands in both turned and inlaid wood, fine tooled leather travelling and hand bags and a "hand-hammered kettle of original design".[215] The exposure to crafts through recreational activities for the armed forces and occupational therapy for the psychologically and physically injured from both wars may have been a passing encounter for most, but for some it became a vocation.

Community projects
Quilts
Quilts seem to hold a particular place in the history of craft community projects. Various accounts of quilting in the twentieth century underline the social nature of the activity,

> "Many of the quilts we have documented were done as group efforts, through 'quilting bees' or through group affiliations, such as Ladies' Aids of churches,

---

[212] SKAB SACS 'Notes on Canadian Handicraft 1943' J. Murray Gibbon

[213] Searle Grain Co Ltd (Weaving Dept.) circular 11 September 1942 quoted J.A.Hoskins 'Weaving Education in Manitoba in the 1940s' (Manitoba 1982) The Company was proposing that demobilized soldiers might want to take up weaving for the same reasons.

[214] SKAB SACS J. Murray Gibbon 'Notes on Canadian Handicraft 1943' p.2

[215] VAG.A 'Air Force Art, Crafts Display Proving Popular at Gallery' *Province* Vancouver 21 March 1945

Women's Institutes and Handicraft Guilds."[216]
Women's needles must have funded many hospitals and churches in the early years on the Prairies and, as in other parts of the country, provided goods and money toward charitable causes. An Alberta quilt catalogue shows photographs of quilt-making members of the Balmoral District Ladies Hospital Aid c1910, and a sale of quilts and other embroidered goods by the Ladies Aid of a church at Sedgewick c1911/12, the money from which would go to buy church furnishings and a new church building.[217] For a small sum individuals could have their name embroidered on a quilt and the quilt might then be auctioned. The proceeds from a 1910 signature quilt in Medicine Hat museum went to the Brotherhood of Locomotive Engineers No.472.[218] Signature quilts were made as a tribute to a local midwife and as a farewell gift for parish minister. "The signature quilt made [to be raffled] by the Finnish Women's Sewing Association of the Dunblane, Macrorie, and Birsay districts of Saskatchewan in 1928 reflects the Finnish heritage of the community."[219] During the Depression quilts were sent from Nova Scotia, which has a particularly strong record of quiltmaking for charitable causes, to the Prairies and in 1950, "thousands of quilts went to flood victims in Manitoba."[220]

Churches

The church, as part of the community, also elicited the work of local craftspeople where traditionally the building was decorated and the priests robed. Predominantly in the francophone parts of Canada, the Catholic church had an illustrious history of support for craftwork, through the activity and training of nuns, the employment of skilled artisans such as woodcarvers and smiths, and through the contributions of the congregation, such as Chaisson's examples of hooked rugs made for particular areas of the church. On the prairies, the Ukrainian Orthodox community, and others, recreated the churches of their homeland. Much of the work, for lack of money to pay professional church artists, was done by skilled craftspeople within the community including the carving and painting of iconostasis (decorative partitions) with their richly decorated Royal Doors, chandeliers, processional crosses and standards, and the embroidering of altar cloths, church banners, and *rushnyky* for draping above icons.[221]

---

[216] S.Morton Weizman, E.Eliot-Los *Alberta Quilts* (Edmonton 1984) p.9

[217] Morton Weizman pp.7,8

[218] Morton Weizman p.10

[219] R.Bitner 'Prairie Patchwork' *The Craft Factor* Summer 1993 p.11

[220] Robson p.24

[221] Stepovyk in R.Klymasz *'Art and Ethnicity'* (Ottawa/Hull 1991) particularly processional standard 1915 p.43, iconostasis by Pavlo Zabolotnyi c1930, and Royal Doors 1911 p.41

National projects
The War Effort

Two world wars created what Donna Fallis describes as "an amazing social and economic phenomenon...one of the largest and most productive knitting industries in North America, albeit volunteer."[222] From 1914 to 1918 the Canadian Red Cross (whose branches outside Montreal were supervised by May Phillips a co-founder of CHG) was the major promoter and organizer of knitting for the war effort. Knitters worked individually but mainly through various established national and local women's organizations such as the Women's Institutes and the Imperial Order of the Daughters of the Empire, and through groups specifically set up for the purpose. These included people of many ethnic origins. The co-ordination of producing groups and the organization of distribution of supplies and information, inspection, collection and warehousing of products and their dispatch to distributing organizations involved much hard work but apparently posed little problem for women already running national networks.

Initially the garments the Red Cross accepted were of various types and quality, and included pure wool socks, sleeveless sweaters, balaclava caps, scarves, mitts and gloves and cotton yarn washcloths. The Red Cross and women's magazines published patterns. By 1917 the production of garments had become tightly controlled as a wool shortage became acute. Articles needed were determined by the Canadian War Contingent Association and the military. Wool supplies could be obtained from the Red Cross, yarn weight, needle size, preparation of wool, dyes and patterns were specified, and only those garments which met their standards were accepted. This was not necessarily well received by the knitters,

> "I'll never forget what I called The Great Kitchener Toe Controversy. It was a way of knitting socks of soldiers just so...I've got these two old biddie aunts, and Uncle Bert, a coal miner. They'd knit, all three of them...so when the wool and the instructions came from the Red Cross, they just ignored the details, just went ahead like they had for 50 years or so...I think Aunt Bessie had about 10 pairs sent back. No Kitchener Toe...With a note, a firm little note. Rip them out and do them over. Well, by God, war was declared...There were articles in the paper and people got talking about the Kitchener Toe. It was quite a fight...finally after a few months it all died down...the old biddies decided that if they were to win the war they'd better do it the right way."[223]

'Soldiers' Comfort Kits' provided items that soldiers, sailors and prisoners of war would otherwise have gone without and also included knitted garments. Apart from knitted garments, sewn garments, blankets, quilts, bandages, and other 'comforts' were produced for service people, prisoners, casualties and refugees.

---

[222] D.Fallis 'World War I Knitting' *Alberta Museums Review* Fall 1984

[223] Barry Broadfoot *Six War Years 1939-1945* (Toronto 1974) p.359

Crafts: "An Important Activity of Canadian Citizens"

As in WWI so in WWII, women through their organizations and the Red Cross went into production. In 1940, the Red Cross Association in the small agricultural community of Findlater, SK,

> "sent to headquarters during the year: $290 cash, 45 pairs of socks, 25 suits of pyjamas, 20 hospital gowns, six pneumonia jackets, two sweaters and 18 triangular blankets. Six quilts and three wool blankets were also donated for the refugees."[224]

During the last four years of the war 25,149 quilts handmade in Nova Scotia were shipped overseas.[225] Hand knitting had not diminished either, in 1941 over a million handknitted articles were made for the Canadian Forces. As well as blankets, quilts, afghans, bed covers and lap robes issued to the British Forces and Merchant Marine, they received 369,438 knitted articles including 116,877 pairs of socks, 4,751 pairs of seamen's stockings and 72,110 sweaters. British and Canadian Forces received 120,247 quilts.[226] In addition to work made for fundraising, hospitals, for bombed-out British citizens and refugee Europeans, this adds up to an impressive contribution to the war effort. As in WWI, children were involved too, through Junior Red Cross and other organizations. "And all across our Dominion thousands of boys and girls are doing all they can." In a Manitoba school boys and girls gave up their recesses to carve brooches and other wooden articles, and make lapel posies of felt flowers to raise money. "The boys can knit as well as the girls and have completed several lovely afghans."[227] In Nova Scotia,

> "These energetic Juniors also made a quilt of flour and feed bags with a picture of their school, and appliqued designs, mottos and names. Their teacher...adds, 'Every block is a work of art.' They raised $10.10 on the names."[228]

Summary

The range of activity

This brief overview indicates that, despite an industrialized society, handcraft activity continued to be widespread through all levels of society, in all parts of the country and in a wide range of media throughout the period. Particularly notable is the very large variety of textile techniques identified through women's entries at industrial/agricultural exhibitions. Nineteenth century artisan

---

[224] *Country Guide and Nor-West Farmer* March 1941

[225] Robson p.24

[226] Gibbon 1943a p.155

[227] *Country Guide* September 1943

[228] *Junior Red Cross Newsletter*, Nova Scotia, October 1943 (Hebbville School, Lunenburg Co.) quoted Robson p.24

skills continued to move into predominantly domestic production as in textiles, or were transferred to contemporary trades and to leisure or intermittent activity, for example blacksmiths turned to agricultural machinery and car repair yet continued to make decorative wrought iron on commission. Historically, capricious fashions have involved changing materials, patterns and techniques combined with on-going technical innovation and surely meant that small craft businesses have always had to adapt to survive and must have been in a constant state of flux or demise, thus some of the changes taking place during this period may appear more radical than they were.

The imposition of universal education continued to seemingly change the social status of the craft artisan, and introduced craft activities into child education, increasingly formalized leisure activities, occupational therapy and popular general and specialist publications.

The 'usual'
The 'usual' included a wide range of products for commercial, economic, domestic, leisure, community and national purposes which included work from the decorated but predominantly functional to the mainly decorative. The 'usual' was integral to its communities. Despite (or because of) acting as social signifiers, which included status, ethnicity, affluence or its lack, and industriousness, crafted objects particularly where they were the work of craftswomen were undervalued, most obviously economically.

Because of the nature of the makers and their communities, it is unlikely that anything was recorded of this aspect of life and attitudes. In the absence of evidence to the contrary craft works appear to have been for the community the 'usual', the expected, and appear divorced from the craft criteria operating within the community of makers, namely knowledge of materials, techniques, form and motifs, skill and artistic effect. In Canada, the communities in which these objects were made and used ranged from established communities, sometimes isolated, communities in transition, to families, groups or communities re-establishing or discarding traditional lifestyles within a foreign land, surrounded by unfamiliar communities, and with a dominant culture itself moving, often unconsciously, away from its origins. This also led to a reappraisal of the 'usual' within the community and outside.

Many of these objects because they were an integral part of personal, domestic and community life were used to destruction or discarded as fashions changed. This combined with the ambivalence or apparent lack of community esteem for handcrafts, demonstrated particularly through the cultural currency of attributed economic value, had repercussions for its entry into museums.

Crafts: "An Important Activity of Canadian Citizens"

Research by museum staff[229] did contribute to this overview. But it was research published almost entirely from 1970 on. It was based on works assembled for temporary exhibits or related to their museum's permanent collections or in pursuit of specialist interest. Such research is generally circumscribed by the museum's regional mandate, by the arbitrary nature of collections and by continuing historical museum interests. Both collections and publications are inadequate as a gauge of the variety and range of craft activities in this period.

Areas in which craft activity might be expected from the literature of other countries, particularly urban popular, craft industries workers' own work and much women's domestic production have not attracted the interest of collectors and a material record or literature does not appear to exist.

---

[229] Mackley, Burnham, Barbeau, Elwood, Peddle, Rowan, Einarsson, Klymasz, Morton Weizman, Robson and MacDonald.

CHAPTER 4
ORGANIZED CRAFT:
"WHERE CRAFTS FLOURISH THERE WILL BE FOUND A HAPPY AND CONTENTED PEOPLE"[1]

This chapter looks at the organizational activity which generated or affected a substantial part of the literature reviewed in the historiography. It looks at intersection of craftspeople and two powerful networks, women's organizations and government departments, through the first half of the twentieth century. The intersection of women's organizations (or women organizers) and craftspeople gave rise to a number of organizations devoted to promoting, perpetuating, exhibiting and marketing handcrafts. These organizations predominantly drew on reservoirs of traditional skills among rural women in depressed economic circumstances. Government interest initially worked through federal and provincial departments of agriculture. The net effect was the development of small-scale craft industries through private initiatives or later, government intervention.

Craft cottage industries

A complex combination of a counter-assessment of the colonial and industrial experience, a search for national identity and cultural roots, ideas emanating from the new studies of anthropology and folkculture, and nineteenth-century philanthropy, voiced through people such as William Morris, gave rise in the last two decades of the nineteenth century to a number of experiments in craft-based cottage industries in Eire, England and the United States.[2] These were distinguished by being private ventures, frequently initiated and run by educated or affluent women as self-help projects for the impoverished: middle-class women, working-class rural and urban people, and in North America, immigrants and Aboriginal Peoples. They drew on and 'revitalized' selected traditional skills, and reworked historical motifs and techniques felt to be of national significance. Canada was not isolated from this movement.

---

[1] Peck 1929 p.10

[2] eg. Eire: 1884 Donegal Industrial Fund, 1892 Clare Embroidery, Ennis; England: 1884 Home Arts and Crafts Industries Association, 1885 Langdale Linen Industry; U.S.A: 1889 Hull House, Chicago, 1896 Deerfield, Mass. Lady Aberdeen founded the Irish Industries Association c.1886, organised exhibitions of lace and opened a store in Dublin, 'The Irish Lace Depot' while her husband was Lord Lieutenant of Ireland. *Piecework* July 1997 5:4:44. Lady Aberdeen came to Canada when her husband became Governor-General (1893-1898) and continued to be an active patron of the arts and women's organizations.

Canadian experience in craft-based home industries reflected specifically Canadian circumstances, agendas and products. They ranged from individual efforts, which varied in scale and duration, to regional, provincial and national networks sustained through organizations and in some cases through government. To varying degrees, privately sponsored craft industries, organizations and government intersected through marketing and exhibiting networks and funding or support in kind. In the first half of the century, this aspect of the craft community seems a small world.

Intent and scale define these home industry initiatives. The intent being to provide or develop organized employment or marketing opportunities for a number of local craftspeople or to train local people in craft skills. Craftspeople worked at home or on site. This contrasts with the activity of Mrs MacFarlane, an American whose husband managed the gypsum mine at Cheticamp, NS, from 1923 to 1939, "a woman of taste, an artist who devoted a lot of her time to fancy work"[3] became interested in the hooked rugs made locally. She designed and hooked them herself with the help of local women, using local hand-spun wool, and also hired local women to make carpets,[4] but only for her personal use.

In some cases it may be a matter of rhetoric which distinguishes the work of factory workers or outworkers using craft skills and 'home' industries.[5] In 1892 the Montreal[6] clothing manufacturer, H. Storey Company had only 130 of its 1530 employees working on the premises. The remainder, all women, were scattered throughout the city and surrounding countryside doing piecework for a pittance in their 'spare time' at home.[7]

Individual initiatives
Bell, Fairchild, Burke Nova Scotia 1922
In 1894, Mrs Mabel (Alexander Graham) Bell, an American who had a summer residence in Baddeck, Cape Breton Island started five sewing schools for local women and young girls. In response to the economic situation she also tried to establish a lace industry.[8] Thread and cloth were bought at wholesale prices and patterns were supplied to local women who worked under

---

[3] Chiasson p.48

[4] McKay p.203 She paid 50 cents for a nine hour day.

[5] see Eileen Boris 'Crafts Shop or Sweatshop? The Uses and Abuses of Craftsmanship in Twentieth Century America' *Journal of Design History* 2:2:175-92 1989 for an excellent account of the thin line between cottage industries and factory out-work, and the response of makers.

[6] Montreal and Quebec were major textile manufacturing areas.

[7] Finkel p.205

[8] This does not appear to have been a local tradition

Bell's instruction. Aimed at tourists, the project failed because tourists were infrequent and machine-made lace was much cheaper.

Bell's daughter Marion Fairchild first invited Lillian Burke to Baddeck in 1914. After war-service as an occupational therapist, Burke, an American art teacher trained in a range of craft techniques, came back in 1922 to investigate the possibility of establishing cottage industries for rural women in the area. By 1924, Fairchild and her sister had formed Cape Breton Home Industries (CBHI), which was managed by Burke, who received 10% of the sales income. Summer sales of handcrafts were held at the Baddeck Library. Alice Peck of CHG visited the Bell family in 1927, CBHI became a branch of CHG[9] and Peck purchased and advance-ordered hooked rugs, weaving, blacksmithing and furniture for the Montreal CHG shop. In that year Lillian Burke became involved with hooked rug making at Cheticamp, an Acadian village on the north east coast of Cape Breton.

Nova Scotia hooked rugs had already attracted the attention of collectors. Pedlars moved into Cape Breton around 1920 and bartered for considerable profit.[10] Seven ten foot square rugs for a cheap winter coat[11] hardly seems a fair exchange however these pedlars broke the monopoly of the local company store[12] and provided cash or goods at a time of economic crisis. Trading through pedlars had finished by WWII.

Burke was not satisfied with the volume of rug sales at Baddeck which she attributed to the colours used and poor workmanship. Baddeck craftswomen resisted changing from their traditional patterns in vivid colours.[13] Craftswomen at Cheticamp were more receptive to Burke's advice.[14] The style of rugs changed totally. Burke introduced a new type of dye, dye fixative (from vinegar to the more dangerous sulphuric acid) and dyeing technique. She insisted on pale,

---

[9] Marion, Mrs David Fairchild was a CHG vice-president 1943

[10] As they did throughout the Maritimes and Quebec, looking not only for rugs but other antiques mainly to feed the American "folk" market.

[11] Chiasson p.39

[12] Chiasson p.11

[13] Dunn p.234 describes Quebec hooked rugs "their bright magenta, orange, scarlet and cobalt colours echo the reds, purples and yellows of zinnias"; "Newfoundland mats were boldly drawn and used strong colour combinations." Lynch 1980 p.1

[14] Baddeck was predominantly protestant/Presbyterian. Marie Elwood personal communication 26 February 1997 Elwood suggests this may have made the Baddeck women less amenable to change dictated by an 'outsider', who was besides Catholic and francophone, which made Burke more acceptable to the Acadian community.

soft colours on fine quality wool rather than rags. Initially small rugs designed and stamped[15] by Burke were completed to her precise directions under the supervision of a Cheticamp woman, Mme Doucet. They were forwarded to Baddeck and sold, on sale or return, through the shop run by Fairchild and Burke. Doucet also got ten percent of sales.

Mme Willie Aucoin, another Cheticamp woman, replaced Doucet in 1932. By this time Burke who wintered in New York had opened a studio and gallery there to display the rugs. Interior designers ordered large carpets, and for these a square foot prototype was made, sometimes several, which Burke retained but did not pay for. Burke would send money to cover dyes and wool with commissions. Rugs were paid for by the square foot on receipt and approval (not always forthcoming) of the finished work, a time lag of six months to a year was normal for payment. Where a group of women worked on a large commission the money was apportioned according to the number of hours or days each had spent. In the 1920s Christie-Anne Poirier was paid $1 a square foot (a special price for exceptionally fine work) for a 114 square foot rug portraying a map of the world. It was sold to Henry Ford, the car manufacturer, for $4000. Compared to the makers, Burke made a very substantial income. Anselme Chiasson points out that the business developed during the economic depression when money was scarce and the proceeds from rug-making were an "unexpected windfall. The village became a veritable 'workshop' where men as well as women...whole families, almost everybody was involved with rug-making."[16] In 1930, prices for rugs averaged $4 to $12, they normally ranged from $50 to less than $1; fishermen got $1 for 100lbs of cod. Cheticamp rugs brought $14,000 a year into the community, although it was noted that "the women who made them receive far less than the lowest paid factory worker."[17]

Knowledge of Burke's profits combined with the growing influence of the Antigonish Movement, a Catholic co-operative initiative, in 1936-7 caused a majority of makers to demand higher pay from Burke. Burke refused and took legal action contending the rugs made in Cheticamp were the result of her artistic work and consequently her property. She lost. Despite the tight control exercised by Burke, some makers had designed their own rugs and had sold through other outlets. The makers now organized themselves. New markets came through increased tourist activity with the opening of the Cabot Trail, a tourist route, in 1936 and the first bus tour specifically to

---

[15] 'Stamping' is drawing out the design, often using stencils, on the fabric to be hooked.

[16] Chiasson p.77

[17] Soeur Anselm, quoted Jim Lotz *Head, Heart and Hands: Craftspeople in Nova Scotia* (Halifax 1986) p.15

Cheticamp in 1940. A local woman was the first to open a rug boutique in the village in 1939.[18] The initiative of a Cheticamp man living in Montreal lead to the Canada Steamship Lines (CSL) selling rugs through their tourist facilities and buying them for their ships' salons, also to CHG selling and exhibiting work through their national and international network.

In Cheticamp the stimulus of outsider demands for 'high quality' work, which involved a different dyeing technique and blending of colours within the design, a change to wool from rags and precise hooking, combined with financial reward and widespread recognition seems to have released a surge of creativity and technical tour de force in the community. Rugs became much larger, mimicking manufactured carpets. They also moved from the floor to the wall as the pictorial element became dominant and more complex, challenging and demonstrating the technical and artistic expertise of the maker. These wall-hangings reproduced a range of painterly styles. Smaller rugs, 'pictures' and furniture mats were aimed at a range of tourists' purses. Cheticamp is a particular example of the organized hooked rug cottage industry which sprang up in many areas, particularly in the Maritimes and Quebec.

Charlotte County Cottage Crafts NB 1914
Grace Helen Mowat (1875-1964) was a native of New Brunswick. She was educated at the Women's Art School, Cooper Union, New York and taught at Halifax Ladies College. In 1914, she returned to the family farm at St. Andrews. Situated near the American border, St. Andrews was a fashionable Summer resort for wealthy Americans and Canadians. For local people it was an area of impoverished farms and ill-paid seasonal work in primary industries. Mowat, with a limited capital of $10, started Charlotte County Cottage Crafts.

Initially she too interested the women in making hooked rugs, using her designs, for which she found markets. However there seems to have been a tradition of weaving in the area[19] and that soon became the principal product. "The women mostly do the weaving, though the menfolk know much about it and are, some of them, highly skilled."[20] For the most part makers worked at home, but certain activities such as fulling were done at a central workshop. The intervention of an academically trained artist in this case is presented as less rigid and rigorous than Burke's,

---

[18] Eleven boutiques have operated during the intervening years, usually run by women rug makers. In 1988 many people still made hooked rugs and the sale of rugs and other local handcrafts gave Cheticamp an annual revenue of half a million dollars.

[19] St. Andrew's had/has other weaving companies. *Blue Book New Brunswick* 1954 mentions Boyd K. Merrill of St. Andrew's Woolens, who had been weaving since 1925, production manager since 1945, producing "fine tweeds in plain shades, checks and tartans."

[20] Cunningham p.8

Organized craft

being a local woman must have engendered some constraints. "They have guidance, kindly criticism, expert advice from their friend and leader...[but] workers have arrived at a high degree of skill and dexterity."[21] The focus appeared to be on the creativity of the makers not purely on their technical skill at reproduction, and on developing a distinctively local product using local materials,

> "The work of the Cottage Craft is open to anyone in Charlotte County who is capable of doing *good reliable and artistic* work in weaving, rug making, embroidery, vegetable dyeing, or any other hand-made work, providing it is *sufficiently original and well executed* to meet the demands of the market...The chief object of the Cottage Craft is to establish a *native Art* that will be *the original expression of the people*, and to adapt the natural beauty of the country homes and their familiar surroundings to decorative *designs done on native material...The work requires not only skilled workmanship, but it means the patient working out of an original idea till it develops into an artistic production.*"[22] [my emphases]

It appears that workers bore development costs. There is no indication of whether Mowat took a percentage of sales, presumably it was not a totally philanthropic venture.

Yarn was from local sheep, hand and mill-spun, and dyed by the workers. The tweeds were blends inspired by the surrounding countryside; embroidery on woven jackets, linens and pictures portrayed such motifs as the country dance, boys skating on a pond and local landscapes. By 1921 $1200 was being paid to workers. Products were exhibited at the British Empire Exhibit at Wembley 1925. In 1932 about fifty women were employed and in 1937 approximately $8000 was being paid to workers.[23] The work was being sold through the shop particularly to Americans and country-wide, in part through the CHG network.

During the 1920s Mowat brought in two experienced potters, Bernard Kane and son Bernard, from England to set up a pottery. Initially local clays were used but when they needed a white body clay was bought from Sovereign Pottery, Hamilton. Work was fired in a hard wood fired kiln. Two local apprentices were employed, one of whom learned to throw. Mowat apparently taught school children to decorate, Frances Wren and Helen Hallet of St. Andrew's also decorated pots. Frances Wren also painted picture maps "showing by place and person the homely history of these honest folk."[24] There is conflicting information about when the Kanes left,[25] however

---

[21] Cunningham p.40d

[22] type written sheet from Charlotte County Cottage Craft n/d [pre-early 1940s] USK.A J.E.Murray collection

[23] Bovey 1938 p.14 "A shop representing part of a New Brunswick county"

[24] Cunningham p.8 Frances Wren was later an instructor at Macdonald College PQ with Crowell

[25] NGC AC H.G.Mowat file: Kanes left before 1930 and operations stopped; however Tweedie says the English potters left in 1947. M.Dorothea Cox 'amateur' threw on the wheel c1941, Ed Murphy independently used the pottery 1950-51 when it burnt down.

there was still a small pottery in 1940.[26]

In 1933 products included woven market bags, sewing-bags, baby blankets, and tweeds, and embroidered samplers and pictures, picture maps, and pottery. At the end of WWII, there were more than 40 looms in operation, average production of tweed and homespun was about 6000 yards a year,[27] and Mowat retired handing over the operation of the business to Kent and William Ross, sons of a former pupil.[28] In 1954, work was still being done by "farm folks in their country homes" and the yarns used were still dyed and spun locally. Products included "tweed and yarn in boxed sets; embroidered hand bags; small knee rugs; suiting and coating materials yardage; large and small throws in plain, tartan, stripes; yarns by skein; hand knit Argyle socks, gauntlets, mitts; hooked and braided rugs."[29]

Romanchych AB 1928-c.1940
In Alberta, Hanka Romanchych,[30] an extension worker through the Alberta government's Women's Bureau, was responsible for helping immigrant women adapt to Canadian life. Working with 326 groups in the north east of the province, many of which were Ukrainian, she was aware of a scarcity of money. She agreed, in 1928, to find markets for the work of a loose network of Ukrainian weavers, in 1930 there were ten, by 1936 over thirty. She did not receive commission, nor was there government intervention although she combined this with her regular work for the government. The project continued for roughly twelve years, long after Romanchych had left that job.

Working out of their homes, weavers were responsible for materials and equipment, which were largely home grown and home built, and designs. Romanchych did supply items which were difficult to get such as white cotton warp and white wool weft, the latter was supplied from the Ukraine. "Patterns and colours were largely the artist's choice, but since traditional compositions

---

[26] Aida McAnn 'Busy Hands in New Brunswick' *CGJ* 1940 p.132

[27] Aida McAnn p.132

[28] Tweedie p.265

[29] *Blue book New Brunswick* 1954

[30] Romanchych 1907-1984 was also a collector, see chapter 6 UWAC:UMC, Saskatoon.

were familiar to the artisans and popular among clients, they were preferred by the weavers."[31] They made shopping bags, small blankets, bench covers, and kylyms, which were used as wall hangings and furniture coverings but not as mats.

Romanchych had wide contacts through her job and her affiliations with national organizations such as UWAC. She organized exhibitions and sales through the Hudson's Bay Company, Edmonton; the Junior League; the CPR Palliser Hotel, Calgary; the ethnic crafts section of Canadian National Exhibition (CNE), Toronto; Banff Springs Hotel; and Woodward's Department Stores. A special wedding kylym was commissioned for a member of the T. Eaton family being married in Winnipeg. Through a contact in the Ukrainian community who had moved from Winnipeg to work at Macy's Store in New York a standing order for kylyms from particular weavers, and pysanky, extended over a number of years.[32] There were orders from Boston but Boston women preferred predominantly blue tones and the weavers were not prepared to alter traditional designs to that extent.

Murray Tweeds BC 1932
Enid Murray's inspiration for Murray Tweeds (or Island Weavers),[33] Esquimalt, Vancouver Island came from watching the development of a Kashmiri community weaving project. Her husband's retirement from India to British Columbia revived the idea. A Scot, Murray returned as a mature student to learn handloom weaving at the Technical College at Galashiels, Scotland. In Esquimalt in 1932, she took over the old High School, setting up nine 54" treadle looms brought from Scotland. The project at the end of five years employed 10 people and had trained three or four. It had also tripled its output. They wove high quality lightweight tweeds for men and women's suitings using Scottish spun and dyed wool, cashmere and angora. Murray experimented with Canadian wools but found yarns spun in eastern Canada were too coarse, the threads were not smoothly spun[34] and they could not get the required quantities.

Despite being reduced to one man and several women weavers during the war, by 1943 Murray employed up to twelve weavers, many women trained after leaving high school. Difficulties with importing Scottish yarns during the war predicated a change to Australian wool. The tweed was sold through a branch in Seattle, and shops in Chicago, New York and San Francisco, and in

---

[31] Lazarowich p.71

[32] *Herstory* 1997 p.66 suggests that Romanchych marketed a wider range of products from a range of ethnic groups, at Macy's and Gimbels, NY.

[33] W.Garland uses 4 names, I have used the two most commonly used; also Murray Tweed Industry, Esquimalt Tweed Industry

[34] Romanchych got white weft from the Ukraine because the twist was tighter than Canadian spun wool

Canada, in Vancouver, Calgary, Banff, Winnipeg, Toronto and Quebec.

Canada Homespun Reg'd PQ 1929-1960

Karen Bulow, a native of Denmark, studied craft textiles at a Copenhagen technical school. She came to Canada in 1929, bringing her loom, and opened a weaving studio/shop in Montreal producing Danish-style yardage and woven articles. For some years, c.1932-5, she taught at the CHG weaving school with Mrs Bang. By 1935 she employed three weavers in her studio, 'Canada Homespun Reg'd'. This had increased to about six 'design-apprentices' by 1939. During this period Bulow also started a home industry to replicate her designs. She ran two to ten week weaving courses in her studio to train Québécois women, who then returned home to produce work under Bulow's supervision. After the war, the provincial government funded a weaving school for veterans under her direction. The school also attracted growing numbers of affluent women responding to the rising interest in craft weaving. At the height of Canada Homespun's production, more than 20 weavers worked in the studio, mainly young women but including a veteran, and within a 70 mile radius of Montreal 70 women wove at home.

The cottage industry produced 'peasant' skirts with overshot border pattern, ski hats, women's suiting material, woolen scarves, table linens, bags, belts and aprons. Rugs in rya[35] technique were made on up-right looms. In the 1940s, ready made and custom designed woven ties were the mainstay of the company but it became widely known for wall hangings and interior fabrics frequently commissioned through architects and interior designers for corporations, offices and homes. Bulow's aesthetic fitted well with the fashion for imported Scandinavian furniture during the 1950s. Three of her fabrics won National Industrial Design Council awards. CHG exhibited and sold Bulow fabrics through their outlets in CPR, CSL and Canadian National Railway (CNR) hotels. Bulow also employed travelling sales representatives.[36]

Gaelic College Highland Home Crafts NS 1944

It seems that neither Murray or Bulow depended on a specifically regional connection or motif to market weaving nor largely did Burke with the Cheticamp rugs produced under her direction, however work marketed by Mowat and Romanchych had a distinct regional or ethnic connotation. McKay argues that "since the 1920s tourism has figured centrally in strategies to cope with regional de-industrialization...the state aggressively intervened in civil society to construct such a [tourism] plant by paving highways, developing hotels, inventing new ethnic...traditions."[37] The Gaelic College of Celtic Folk Arts and Highland Home Crafts was established at St. Anne's, Cape

---

[35] Rya is a pile rather than a flat weave technique.

[36] G.Lesser 'Karen Bulow: Masterweaver' *Canadian Society of Decorative Arts Bulletin* 1990 p.8

[37] McKay p.33

Breton in 1939 by A.W.R.Mackenzie, a Scottish born Celtic revivalist, and his wife. Mackenzie, perhaps by analogy with Appalachia as a bastion of Elizabethan English life, saw Cape Breton as "the cradle of Celtic culture in North America." Neither Mackley nor Burnham show evidence of tartans being produced historically. Using the slogan "a loom in operation in every rural home and more sheep on the Cape Breton hills," a school for tartan weaving was opened, taught by Mackley[38] under the directorship of Mrs Mackenzie. Mary Black, Supervisor of Handcrafts for the Nova Scotia government, who also taught at the school, in the summers of 1943, 1944 and 1945, did not think highly of Mackenzie's weaving skills.[39] Weaving instruction was free, both a permanent craft building built in 1947 and instruction being underwritten by the provincial government's Handcraft Division. Tartans were then produced as a home industry and marketed, largely to tourists and by commission, at St. Anne's.[40] Within a few years demand had outstripped supply and spawned a number of similar tartan cottage industries, culminating in Bessie Murray's Nova Scotia Tartan Limited, 1955, which employed about 45 people in manufacturing, supervising, selling and bookkeeping .

These examples document a few of the better known individual initiatives. There appear to have been numerous smaller initiatives such as those of an American designer, Eloise Steele who worked with Acadian women in the Pubnico area, NS in the 1920s and 1930s to produce crafts sold through CHG and latter through a shop owned by two makers. The work included hooked rugs using dyed silk stockings, appliqued and quilted bedspreads, embroidered and appliqued cushions and embroidered pictures of local landscapes.[41] Mrs M.T. Barber at Craft Cottage, Hope, BC (located on the trans-Canada highway) was active by 1941 and had "built up a centre where skilled workers wove woolen and linen fabrics on hand looms...Mrs Barber taught many different kinds of hand crafts, and created a good trade in genuine British Columbian crafts."[42]

---

[38] Florence MacDonald Mackley (Mrs S.T.Mackley) b.1905 weaver; 1943 - taught at Gaelic Foundation; c1952 visited Lou Tate, Louisville, Kentucky discussion and comparison of old weaving drafts lead to small privately printed book *Handweaving in Cape Breton* 1967; started a chain of gift shops to sell local crafts; established museum to preserve Cape Breton heritage opened 1972 at North East Margaree.

[39] McKay pp.207-8

[40] A.Leitch 'The Tartan Weavers of Cape Breton' *CGJ* 1958(c) p.176 By 1958 20,000 visitors were expected each summer and 75 weavers had been in production

[41] E.Steele 'Acadian Handicrafts' *The American Home* October 1933 p.250 Steele describes CHG as "a subsidized Middleman for handwork in the Provinces". A bedspread won a prize at a [CHG?] Montreal exhibition, and an embroidered balsam stuffed cushion was sent to King George.

[42] Green p.219 (possibly M.A. Barber)

Missionary organizations

For some organizations, craft was a secondary concern, craft cottage industries being seen as a way of raising money for the betterment of the community. I have called them missionary organizations because although economic considerations moved craft production out of the domestic economy into the marketplace in many projects (in line with the development of a cash economy) and although some organizations with an entirely craft focus murmured about "facilitating and spreading habits of home industry and thrift,"[43] for these missionary organizations improved medical care, living standards and the rehabilitating benefits of diligence were primary. The initiators of these organizations were private people, religious societies, or the non-elected government elite, particularly the wives of the King's representatives who saw their task as that of instituting or lending their name to the institution of community improvement. Given the status of the organizers it is not surprising that there was frequently some level of government funding, usually small and erratic, and that at a later stage provincial or federal government became directly involved.

Bissel Institute AB 1930s

The United Church of Canada and other church societies had various home missionary services in large urban centres[44] as well as rural locations. Nellie McClung, a campaigner for women's political and legal rights, described in the late 1930s a visit to the Bissel Institute at Edmonton where she saw,

> "fifty women at work, making quilts, hooking rugs, sewing...They receive a forty-cent credit for three hours' work. When a woman has worked seven afternoons, her credit of two dollars and eighty cents entitles her to a quilt, or to this amount on anything she wishes [garments made with sewing machines were also produced]...The motto of the Institute is 'We will not give what they can earn'."[45]

The purpose was to keep women off relief with a secondary purpose of racial harmony, Finns, Russians, Ukrainians, Poles, English and French "work and talk and grow to understand each other." Surplus work was probably sold to raise funds for running costs which included child care. The organized production of crafts such as this may have been considerable in cities, the concentration in the literature has been on rural examples in eastern Canada.

Grenfell Medical Mission NFD 1905

The Grenfell Medical Mission was set up in 1905 by Wilfred Grenfell, a British doctor, in

---

[43] CHG document of incorporation 1906

[44] e.g. Winnipeg's All People's Mission Superintendent, J.S.Woodsworth wrote several books including *Strangers within Our Gates* 1909

[45] Quoted J.M.Gibbon *Canadian Mosaic* (Toronto 1938) p.421. CHG headed its note paper c.1925 'Self help, not Charity'

Organized craft

response to "scandalous" conditions he found among the permanent and seasonal residents of the Labrador coast.[46] The Dominion of Newfoundland with Labrador was not part of Canada, its affiliations and connections were with Britain and New England. Grinding poverty resulted from lack of civil administration, high duties on imported goods and the exploitation by fishing companies of poor and illiterate people.[47] Believing self-respect was not engendered by 'charity', Grenfell accepted barter for medical services in labour or goods, indigenous crafts such as beaded and embroidered work, sea grass baskets, some knitting, sea mammal ivory carving and hooked mats. These exotic Northern objects as well as providing funding through resale also provided excellent publicity.

The Industrial Department, a cottage industry branch, was set up in the first year. In 1906 Jessie Luther, an American, a graduate of the Rhode Island School of Design and experienced in the American Settlement House movement, was brought in to develop the Industrial Department.[48] Grenfell and his wife took an active interest, in addition to frequently changing professional and volunteer staff. Based at St. Anthony on the northern tip of Newfoundland, Luther spent the next ten summers organizing craft production. Luther encouraged continued production of indigenous crafts with little change. She successfully introduced weaving although it found only a local market. The agricultural Codroy valley in the south east, settled by Irish, Scots and Acadians, was the only area in which weaving was traditionally practiced. She was unsuccessful in establishing pottery using clay found in the St. Anthony area, or stone polishing using local semi-precious minerals.

Deciding that the traditional hooked rugs were virtually indistinguishable from New England designs and therefore were not capturing an adequate market, Grenfell intervened to design

---

[46] For much of my information on crafts in Newfoundland and Labrador, on the Grenfell Mission and on NONIA, I am indebted to Colleen Lynch's research, primarily for the Craft Development Division, Department of Tourism and Culture, Newfoundland and Labrador, and to that department who sent me the unpublished ms. 'A Handle on the Past: A Compilation of Research on Craft Design in Newfoundland and Labrador' 1994

[47] In R.Romkey ed. *Labrador Odyssey* (Montreal 1996), Curwen writes "the colony lives by the codfish caught, but the colony in no wise recognises that the codfish catchers are human." p.164 "The Merchants seem determined not to allow the people to make money...they take their salmon, cod, herring & fur at a price they name & give in return what provision they like, always arranging prices so that there is nothing on the credit side." p.170 "Food and clothing is very expensive here, & that's how the money is made; swanswool flannel 2/6 a ys., scotch yarn 6/- a lb. or 8 knots, linsey 15 cents." p.37
Along the coast the 1893 medical mission from the Mission to Deep Sea Fishermen constantly records large families in one room shacks, wearing rags and living through the winter on starvation diets of flour, hard bread, tea and molasses. It is probable there was little improvement by the 1920s.

[48] It is possible that it was through Luther that a Kentucky basketmaker was brought in to teach basketry despite an indigenous tradition (it did not succeed) and that Minnie Pike, who became the Mission's principal weaver in the 1920s was sent by the Mission to Kentucky to learn traditional American mountain crafts.

realistic 'Northern' motifs offering an 'exotic' appeal to a southern market. Pictorial designs continued to come into the repertoire from Mission workers and local craftspeople. Rugs continued to be made with rag. For personal use traditional motifs and techniques continued, remaining separate and largely unaffected by work produced for the Mission. Mission clothing items reflected current southern fashions and types (with occasionally modified northern wear) decorated with northern motifs.

The Industrial Department, based at Red Bay, Labrador and St. Anthony offered full-time employment to men and women. Weaving was done in the Loom Rooms at St. Anthony, also some sewing and carving; mat materials and embroidery projects were prepared and parcelled for shipment to makers and finished work returned there. Sewing, knitting, mat hooking and carving of bone and ivory were done at home. Grasswork and beaded skinwork were bought directly from settlers and Native people. Luther worked for the Mission for ten years, in the winters she was a pioneering occupational therapist at Rhode Island and sold Mission work through private sales, lectures and fund-raising events.

In 1920 demand necessitated a full-time director. The logistics were daunting, travel and communication between homeworkers, production centres and markets were sporadic and unreliable, there were supply shortages and cash flow was erratic. In 1958, the Grenfell Industrial Department at Harrington[49] on the Quebec coast, which supplied communities north to the Strait of Belle Isle, had mats picked up by boat twice a year and taken to St. Anthony for shipment by coastal steamer to St. John's and thence to depots across Canada.[50]

In 1906, Grenfell met with CHG to discuss the sale of Mission products. Two hundred pounds of wool for weaving and rags for mats were sent to the Mission from CHG, against this advance CHG hoped to receive pottery, fine leather coats and embroideries. In 1909 CHG became a distributing centre for the Mission. In the 1930s a Sales Director was added to the staff of the International Grenfell Association in the U.S.A.

To be accepted for sale under the Mission label work had to reach an acceptable standard. However as a charitable medical mission, sub-standard work from the destitute or less competent was accepted as was work produced as occupational therapy by hospital patients.

NONIA NFD 1920
The Newfoundland Outport Nursing and Industrial Association (NONIA) was established to

---

[49] A.Leitch 'Pictures on Brin - The Grenfell Hooked Mats' *CGJ* 1958(a) p.76

[50] SKAB SACS J.Murray Gibbon 1943, notes the first specimen of Grenfell Mission work he saw in Canada was in the house of Mrs Rose Dragan, Saskatoon, president UWAC, member SACS

Organized craft

provide nursing services in the scattered fishing outports which were facing much the same problems as Labrador. Through a cottage industry program, money could be raised to pay a nurse's salary. A nursing service was started in 1920 under the direction of the wife of the Governor of Newfoundland and a Board of prominent St. John's citizens but was reorganized to include the cottage industry component in 1924. Communities who wanted work had to provide a secretary and at least ten workers. All materials and patterns were supplied. The secretary was responsible for receiving materials from and returning produce to the St. John's depot, distributing, supervising and collecting work from her area, and paying the workers. Workers were paid by the piece with allowance for skill and experience but rates were low. By 1930 NONIA had 44 outport committees and 750 workers.

The market was to be St. John's more affluent classes who were not interested in traditional Newfoundland rustic crafts. The products used native knitting, furniture making and rug hooking skills but looked to Britain's Scottish Highlands Industry for inspiration. Shetland wool and Fair Isle products and patterns were sent to outports in 1922 to be used as examples. Paton's knitting yarns were imported from Britain. In 1927 more British samples were received, but students at the Nova Scotia School of Art were also designing patterns for NONIA.[51] In 1937 an American sweater pattern was introduced. The use of fine spun wools, multi-coloured patterns and garment design contrasted with traditional Newfoundland knitting of strictly functional garments in homespun wool mainly in shades of grey or white. A chair made at Scottish Highlands Industry was sent to furniture makers in Pools Cove in 1927 to be copied for production.

NONIA introduced weaving into the southeast of the province in 1922. Minnie Pike, a native of Red Bay, Labrador Straits, the chief weaver for the Grenfell Mission came to teach a two month course for NONIA in the Fortune Bay area. In 1923 and 1926, an Ontario weaver[52] taught dyeing and spinning in the Loom Room at Pools Cove. In 1927 a British weaver taught advanced pattern weaving on a 60" loom. Initially producing homespun for clothing, NONIA moved to four-harness pattern weaving for marketable household items, which had no distinctive local characteristics.

By 1933 Newfoundland was bankrupt, the fishing industry was decimated, the Depression was in full swing, and, as a result of the Amulree Report, the British Government set up an interim government by committee. One of the few submissions made to the Amulree Commission by

---

[51] Lynch 1994 p.135 refers to the "Halifax School of Art", The designing of patterns for the NONIA knitting industry by students at the Nova Scotia School of Art c.1925 is referred to in Soucy p.88

[52] Hepzibah Stansfield, wife of H.H.Stansfield Head of the Metalwork Department, OCA. NGC Canadian Artists files 'H.H.Stansfield' *The Romance of Weaving in Newfoundland* radio talk 23 January 1937

women came from Mrs Harold Mitchell, who with W.P.Hutcheson, described NONIA's activities.[53] Amulree noted with regard to NONIA that, "The places to which nurses have been appointed have not taken to home industries; those which have taken to home industries have not desired the appointment of a nurse...We hope that the industrial side of the Association will be kept in being. There exists a very real need for the promotion of home industries..."[54] The government took over health care and NONIA's production became strictly commercial.

Star of the Sea Handicrafts NS 1938

In Nova Scotia, the Antigonish movement of Catholic social activism based at the Extension Department of St. Francis Xavier University, which sparked the Cheticamp rug worker's revolt, amongst other activities saw craft production as a way of relieving economic distress among fishing communities in that province. Star of the Sea Handicrafts was started at Terence Bay in 1938 by the Sisters of Charity, Mount St. Vincent. Both supervisors of the weaving shop learnt designing and weaving at the CHG weaving school in Montreal run by the Scandinavian weavers, Mrs Bang and Karen Bulow. Sr. Gertrude Marie brought back two Norwegian looms from which the Terence Bay wood craft workers reproduced twelve more, but in soft wood. Producing woolens, linens and homespuns, the weaving shop ran from 1938 to the late 1960s. Some work was marketed through Simpson's and Eaton's department stores. The woodworking workshop seems to have got little attention, possibly the project was not successful, fishing revived during the war which also offered other alternatives for men, or perhaps this was because publications have focussed on the weaving revival.[55]

Summary

In all of these examples of cottage industries, women played the major part in initiation, direction and production. The examples chart distinctive organizational strategies, a variation in the degree of intervention by the directors and in the creative freedom of the maker. In all there was a demand for a high level of technical skill, which may have involved learning new techniques, and in most a radical change for the makers in design sources and products. The directors and teachers were largely American or British by birth, only four were (probably) Canadian born and of these perhaps one trained in Canada.[56] The imported craft influences were American, Scottish

---

[53] L.K.Cullum 'Under Construction: Women, The Jubilee Guilds and the Commission Government in Newfoundland and Labrador, 1935-1941' (Toronto 1993) p.51

[54] *Newfoundland Royal Commission 1933* (Amulree Report 1933) pp.213, 214 In 1933 Amulree reported only 4 nursing centres.

[55] Green p.49; Joyce Chown personal communication July 1996; McKay p.161

[56] Bell, Fairchild, Burke, Luther and Steele were American born; Murray, MacKenzie and Grenfell were British born; Romanchych (who was not a craftswoman as far as I can ascertain), Mowat and Pike were Canadian, the latter two trained in the United States. Sr. Gertrude Marie was almost certainly Canadian and trained with Bulow, Danish,

and Scandinavian, however these, with Ukrainian, were also inherent parts of the historical and contemporary Canadian cultural mosaic. The products were determined in large part by a perception of what the predominantly urban, distant, affluent market wanted, the market was almost never that of the maker's immediate community. Products may have sold within the province of manufacture either through tourists visiting the maker's region or through products shipped from rural to major population centres but they were as frequently sold widely throughout Canada and the United States. These cottage industries made articles which ranged from ethnic, regional and high fashion to folk fashion. The predominance of weaving in these cottage industries, particularly towards the end of the 1930s is related to government and other initiatives discussed below.

Craft organizations

Increasing access to tertiary education combined with obstructions to continuing a career after marriage[57] and an active philosophy of social responsibility, drove many women to find outlets for their skills, knowledge and energy in voluntary organizations. McLeod argues that men had established control of the prestigious fine arts organizations, galleries and markets, and that women moved in to establish their own niche through rediscovering, promoting, exhibiting and marketing crafts. Certainly many of the best Arts and Crafts exponents were women. The first decades of the twentieth century saw a network of women's organizations established across the country. The major craft organization was the Canadian Handicrafts Guild incorporated in 1906. It was involved in an extraordinary range of national activity. Before giving a brief survey of its history and endeavours, I would like to look at the marketing activity of a smaller, regional organization situated in western Canada. The Saskatoon Arts and Crafts Society files give a detailed and coherent glimpse of the activities of a philanthropic marketing organization, and offer insights into similar groups and comparisons with groups previously discussed.

Saskatoon Arts and Crafts Society, SK 1924-1956
The Saskatoon Arts and Crafts Society
> "had its nucleus in a small group in the Local Council of Women[58] which had felt for a long time that a useful and interesting piece of work might be done by studying and encouraging the handicrafts within the province of Saskatchewan...The impetus came directly from the variety of beautiful hand-work

---

and Bang in Montreal. Birthplace and training of Barber is unknown.

[57] S.Burt, L.Code, L.Dorney *Changing Patterns: Women in Canada* Toronto 1988 p.109 In 1931 the percentage of single women in paid employment was 43.8%, married women 3.5%; despite a rise during WWII, by 1951 the percentages were single women 58.3% married 11.2%

[58] Local branch of the Canadian Council of Women (LCW) aka National Council of Women (NCW)

of many peoples collected for a folk-museum in the University of Saskatchewan."[59]

The LCW set up an Arts and Crafts Committee in 1922. By 1924 the work of the committee had grown so extensive that it was decided to set up a separate organization, thus paralleling the emergence of the CHG from a committee of the WAAC:Montreal, twenty years earlier. Funds and property from the LCW committee were transferred to the new Saskatoon Arts and Crafts Society. The experience from those first "[t]wo years of extra-ordinarily successful experimenting in interesting the workers themselves in the artistic and commercial value of their crafts",[60] which included an unexpectedly large amount of volunteer labour and some misunderstandings with the makers, enabled SACS to set up an organization which operated successfully until WWII brought radical changes to the prairies.

The 1923 annual report of the LWC committee listed three aims: to encourage handicraft, marketing, and the development of resources in the province. Retention of handcraft skills was a concern and was directly linked with marketing, "A definite case was cited of two Ukrainians who, five years ago, were making rugs...and had stopped doing so because of their inability to find a market for their work."[61] Both retention of skills amongst pre-industrial communities[62] and the development of local resources were contemporary national issues. The raw materials for certain crafts were considered quite plentiful in Saskatchewan, for example clay, and Siberian willow for basketry and furniture; the promotion of flax and wool production, as elsewhere, met with varying degrees of success. In 1957, at the demise of SACS, Vivian Morton, a co-founder, summarized the aims of the society as,

> "Home Industries' - To encourage and retain unique and characteristic crafts within our province, and as far as possible find a market for the same, with a minimum of overhead and no profit. Educational - By having loan exhibitions from time to time of old or discontinued crafts within our province, and demonstrations or lectures at the regular meetings of the society."

She added,

> "besides the practical aspect of providing a market for work, a common interest in crafts often proved to be the first meeting place towards understanding and the

---

[59] Holmes 1928 p.4

[60] Holmes 1928 p.4

[61] SKAB SACS B88-B Minute book 1, Arts and Crafts Committee annual report 1923

[62] SACS was also very interested in First Peoples and promoted, exhibited and marketed local work, paralleling their work with New Canadians. In SACS financial accounts it is impossible to screen out the proportion paid to Native makers.

Organized craft

realization that many and varied gifts were being pooled in our Canadian life."[63]

"The first effort of the committee [was, in 1923]...to gather information as to what is being produced or can be produced in the province."[64] A number of the all-women membership were associated with the University through their husbands. Mrs.W.C.Murray, the first president was the wife of the President of the University and hosted the first LCW committee exhibition in their official residence. Vivian B. Morton, one of the founders of the enterprise and a driving force until its demise 35 years later, was the wife of A.S.Morton, first professor of history at the university and the initiator of the "folk-museum". This connection probably provided some initial contacts with community leaders and craftspeople, and led to makers being referred to SACS and work being marketed through people in the university network. Morton recalls a Ukrainian man who had drawn for her a map of Europe, traced Ukrainian settlements and told her what patterns were typical of various parts. "Then he enumerated to her the various Ukrainian settlements in Saskatchewan and told her where to look for workers in these same patterns."[65] Normal School students preparing to teach in country areas were also contacted as potential collaborators. Lydia E. Gruchy of Veregin taught at Kamsack and distributed linen and organized Doukhobor workers in that area for the committee.

> "The method of finding out what was the nationally characteristic handicraft of the settlers was to find out what they had brought to Canada with them from the Old Country. In the case of the Doukhobors it was drawn-thread work. This particular type of work, older than lace making, was unique among the Doukhobors. *It was replete with opportunities for self-expression.* The next problem was to adapt this work to articles which could be marketed in Canada." [my emphasis][66]

The first workers were primarily Doukhobor women producing linen and drawn-thread embroidery, and Ukrainian women producing cross-stitch embroidery although in 1924 there was more difficulty finding Ukrainian workers because, "The women-folk are probably earning more by digging seneca-root than by needle-work at the present time."[67] These two groups continued to be primary suppliers of work to SACS.

The organization of production was done by a 'work committee' in Saskatoon who would "receive

---

[63] SKAB SACS B88-D Dissolution of Society letter 31 May 1957

[64] SKAB SACS B88-B Committee Reports 1922-42 annual report 1923

[65] SKAB SACS B88 Minute book 2 newspaper clipping 15 April 1940

[66] SKAB SACS B88 Minute book 2 newspaper clipping 15 April 1940

[67] SKAB SACS B88-E Correspondence 1922-24 W.J.Mather to A.S.Morton 20 June 1924

and discuss work, price and mark pieces for the sales, keep inventories, and carry on the correspondence with the workers."[68] With no base the work was probably kept in committee members' homes, certainly in the 1940s the stock (and SACS collection) was kept at Morton's house. Early on there were also women in the countryside involved with organizing the work such as Gruchy and Jessie McKay, also in the Veregin area.

Problems quickly arose. McKay wrote complaining that the administrative work took considerably more time than she had expected and in December 1924 made a second plea for money to pay the workers,

> "The Doukhobor linen workers are becoming very impatient for their money for the work sent in [May 31]."[69]

Gruchy had earlier written to Morton,

> "I was afraid there would be dissatisfaction at this end when the women did not get cash for their work, and poor Mrs McKay has been besieged by them."[70]

In January 1925 Morton replied to McKay,

> "I am sorry you have been bothered so much by some of the women and that things at this end seemed to have moved so slowly when as a matter of fact Mrs MacDonald, Mrs Moffat and I have spent hours trying to straighten up after what almost seemed a deluge to us at times."

This deluge was caused not only by the ongoing work of the committee but by a major reorganization and review of accounts and inventories as the committee became a Society.[71] Morton goes on to say that she met with Mr Tarasoff of Langham and explained to him "very fully" about work which the committee felt was not of a high enough standard, pieces unsaleable because the size or design did not appeal to consumers, and that the committee did not work as a store and was unable to pay for pieces as they came in. Mr Tarasoff was also writing to various members of the Doukhobor community to clear up a misunderstanding over handloomed linen.

The teething problems of the 'work committee' centred on pricing work and payment of workers, 'standards', the desire to use home-produced linen, determining what was acceptable to the consumer, and volunteer time. Solutions to these problems were partial. That they did not overwhelm the Society was due to the dedication of the volunteers because the solutions tended to involve more rather than less time, and the need of the makers, which grew more desperate as the 1920s plummeted into the Dirty Thirties.

---

[68] SKAB SACS B88-B Committee Reports 1922-42 annual report 1923

[69] SKAB SACS B88-E Correspondence 1922-24 letter 31 December 1924

[70] SKAB SACS B88-E Correspondence 1922-24 Gruchy to Morton 24 July 1924

[71] Morton was also expecting her second child early in 1924

> "At the very beginning...it was decided to operate on a non-profit basis. They [the workers] were paid as nearly as possible on a yardage basis. The society added 10 per cent to the cost of material to pay for postage, insurance and loss."[72]

However it was not that simple as Margaret Lindsey pointed out in a 1938 report,

> "Sometimes it is not easy to be sure what is a reasonable amount to pay for some of the pieces; the amount of work is easy to estimate but, the difficulty of patterns, and perfection of needlework vary a great deal and should be paid for accordingly."[73]

Nor were the workers always satisfied. There were complaints at various times of how hard the work was on the eyes and in 1925 Haska Chutskoff wrote to Morton,

> "three dollars' is not enough for the work done on [the tablecloths]. It took one exactly three weeks to finish them, and I worked at them for at least nine hours each day. And another thing is that that material is too fine to work at. It wouldn't even pay to draw the threads for a dollar a day and it takes exactly a whole day to do it. I think the least amount that should be payed for these is ($9.00) 'nine dollars'."[74]

To which Morton replied,

> "if it took you as long to do the three cloths as you say it did, it would be bad business for you or for our society to go on together. We have workers who are quite satisfied to do the work at the rate I paid you. I fixed it by measuring the actual amount of work and comparing it with handkerchiefs done on the very same linen for which we pay the workers the amount they themselves asked in the first place...I am sorry you are not satisfied when so many others are."[75]

The price paid for fine needlework was certainly not good despite SACS's efforts to get the best price possible for their workers. Mrs Zaule was an exceptionally high earner making $250 in a winter for petit point pieces. As the Society got organized they were able to pay for "the work as soon as it comes in, if possible, and we handle as few articles as possible on the "Exchange" plan."[76]

---

[72] SKAB SACS B88 Minute book 2 newspaper clipping 15 April 1940

[73] SKAB SACS B88-B2 Financial report 31 September 1938

[74] SKAB SACS B88-E Correspondence 1925 Chutskoff to Morton 30 November 1925

[75] SKAB SACS B88-E Correspondence 1925 Morton to Chutskoff 14 December 1925

[76] SKAB SACS B88-F Articles and Speeches letter to a Mrs Macdonald n/d [probably c1934 after Violet McNaughton's visit to the 2nd Vancouver Folk Festival]

The standards which SACS applied to embroidery are inferred not articulated. New workers were tried "out on some small article such as a handkerchief or tray cloth first and we have them if possible send in some of their own articles for us to see."[77] If the work was not of an acceptable standard the reasons were explained. Young girls were given particular encouragement to continue, in line with the Society's desire to see traditional skills passed to the next generation. There were enough craftswomen producing satisfactory work that workers were dropped when they did not do "first class work."

The Society's desire to use local materials where possible, particularly linen, led initially to difficulties. A 1925 work committee report refers to "Native linen - much of it was unsatisfactory...some linen made on cotton warp, defective" and linen sent in as home made which "we were certain it was not."[78] The latter possibly reflects the committee's inexperience with highly skilled weavers. It was decided, "from now on all native linen will be bought by us as yardage and made according to our directions."[79] By 1928 it was reported that there was "some home made linen...but the rigours of this climate do not make it easy to persuade women to make linen if they can get some other work...one woman running her loom this winter."[80] As time went on there seems to have been an increasing use of imported Irish linen and by 1940, "Imported Irish linen had risen 125 per cent in price since the war...this created a problem which the society would soon have to face. The greater part of the work done by workers was done on this type of linen and local firms had cancelled their orders for it."[81]

From the beginning there seems to have been a conflict between the society's delight in the craftwork they were encountering and the demands of the market.
> "To our society this work is more of a study than a task. We are learning so much that otherwise we would never have known of the artistic background of these newcomers, who have so rich a heritage in the creation of beauty and handiwork."[82]

That "The articles suitable for sale and the articles the workers would make are often very

---

[77] SKAB SACS B88-F Articles and Speeches letter to Mrs Macdonald n/d

[78] SKAB SACS B88-B Work committee 2 March 1925

[79] SKAB SACS B88-B Work committee June 1926

[80] SKAB SACS B88-B Annual meeting 23 October 1928

[81] SKAB SACS B88 Minute book 2 Morton quoted in newspaper cutting 15 April 1940

[82] SKAB SACS B88 Morton quoted newspaper clipping [1928?]

Organized craft

different"[83] meant an accommodation had to be made between cultures. "It [Ukrainian cross-stitch in bright colours] had been a problem because of the difficulty of adapting it to our needs and tastes but this year we have had some articles - breakfast cloths, towels etc - decorated in an entirely acceptable way to us and yet adhering to the characteristic colors and designs of the workers."[84]

Workers were "encouraged to work out individual designs..."[85] The balance between conserving old designs, continuing to use them in new circumstances and adapting them to new uses, and the changing interests of the craftswomen encountering new influences and materials engaged both the originating communities and the dominant anglo-Canadian culture. The UWAC in particular, some of whose leading members were also members of SACS, collected historic Ukrainian samples and organized a vigorous campaign to disseminate these techniques and patterns and promote their use in traditional and contemporary ways within their community. SACS also conserved and adapted old designs, as Morton demonstrated,

> "To illustrate how some of our work develops I have brought an old runner from Bukovina and articles which we have had made from its designs. You can see it has been a veritable 'sampler'."[86]

SACS also noted the way in which craftswomen modified their work,

> "Mrs Morton pointed to the transition in Ukrainian patterns by showing samples done by a worker. A bedspread, shirtwaist and sampler show conventional patterns...typical of the section of the Ukraine from which the worker came",

however a blouse made a short time ago for a daughter was a radical departure with no black and the pattern floral. The woman had explained that since she came to this country she did not want to use black.

> "There are many people who will look at this and say it is not typical Ukrainian work,' Mrs Morton said. 'It may not be Ukrainian in the sense that it is what she would have done over there, but it is what she wants to do here. She also wants to experiment. Formerly she was confined by lack of dyes for many colours. Better this than to repeat the same thing over and over again.'"[87]

In part the problems of standardization and acceptability to a Canadian market were solved by

---

[83] SKAB SACS B88 Minute book 2 Morton quoted in newspaper cutting 15 April 1940

[84] SKAB SACS B88-B Committee Reports 1922-1942 1923 work committee

[85] SKAB SACS B88-B Committee Reports 1922-1942 January 1927

[86] SKAB SACS B88-B2 Report on workers 1939/40

[87] SKAB SACS Minute book 2 newspaper clipping 15 April 1940

labour-intensive strategies on the part of the committee. "In so far as possible we find it best to deal directly with the individual workers. To linen workers we supply the linen and threads. We then have control of the quality of the materials, also the sizes and types of articles."[88] In the 1926/7 year there were 21 active members and 19 associated members running a rapidly increasing marketing operation as well as the educational and exhibiting activities of the Society. The depression increased the workload as the Society sought to respond to the demands for work. In 1930 SACS had 93 craftworkers, in the following year, "the number of requests for work has been larger than ever before" and in the 1932/33 year six work convenors received work from over 100 women who were predominantly Doukhobor, Polish, Ukrainian and Swedish.[89]

> "There is no doubt that during the years of depression the small articles [needlebooks, pin cushions] have greatly helped us in earning on. While they have been a boon they have greatly increased the work. We are hoping to arrange for more members to help with the drawing of the linen."[90]

The work handled was primarily textiles and included Doukhobor drawn thread work, homemade linens and woven rugs (described as tapestry) and "Ghileem" (kylym) of Doukhobor and Ukrainian origin, Ukrainian cross-stitch and other embroidery, loomed, hooked, and braided rag rugs, hooked wool rugs, needle weaving, petit point, Hungarian and Polish embroidery, smocking, beadwork (Austrian), Hebdebo, Filet lace and Swedish drawn work. Basketry and pottery were also exhibited and sold in limited amounts, and possibly wooden articles particularly after an inquiry in 1940 from the "Czech and Sudetan settlement in the north of the province."[91] Knitting, crochet and tatting were seen as unmarketable as they were done by most women. In 1926 the Society found it necessary to say there was, "sometimes misunderstanding in regard to the class of people that the Society desires to help. Some people thought it was only the foreigners...The Society is just as anxious to help and encourage British-born people, but in every case the work must be typical and saleable."[92]

Marketing quickly expanded from local sales. Within five years work was being sold through craft shops and exhibitions in Regina, Montreal, Edmonton, Yorkton, Vancouver and Jasper. The Applied Arts Department of the Home Economics School, University of Wisconsin requested an

---

[88] SKAB SACS B88-F Articles and Speeches letter to Mrs Macdonald n/d

[89] SKAB SACS B88-A Minute book 1 AGM 20 October 1930, Work committee report 1930-31 Minute book 2 program 1932-1933

[90] SKAB SACS Minute book 2 Annual Report 1937-38

[91] SKAB SACS B88-B2 Report on workers 1939-40

[92] SKAB SACS B88 Minute book 1 21 June 1926

Organized craft

exhibit. In 1924 CHG had written requesting a Saskatchewan exhibit at their next National Exhibition[93] which gave SACS access to the CHG nationwide marketing network. By the mid-1930s they were selling in major centres from Nova Scotia to Vancouver, including Toronto and Montreal. In 1939/40, parcels went to individual women in eleven places, "who each showed the parcel to friends," and to nine shops and organizations.

> "You will realize from this list that our contacts are becoming wide spread and we are learning much about marketing. There is no doubt that personal contacts are the most valuable means. In these cases the goods are shown for what they are, - 'handicrafts' with peculiar geographic or national or artistic interest of their own."[94]

In 1939, Mrs Morton was responsible for 'private sales' worth $843.89.[95]

In 1926, total sales for the year were $907.16, disbursements totalled $842.89 of which $637.36 was paid out for work.[96] A 1937 report shows where $194 was paid to 23 craftswomen for 83 parcels of work, expenses amounted to $63.14 spent mainly on embroidery threads and on postage for 86 parcels, 89 letters and money orders.[97] It appears from these figures that overheads, materials and postage, formed a third of disbursements. Surprisingly sales climbed steadily through the Dirty Thirties, for 1933/34 receipts are $1,264.81, for 1935/36, $1,862.64.[98] In the year ending October 1939, sales reached $2,107.54 and disbursements $2,113.75. As the figures for 1939 show, local support brought in over half the Society's income: Christmas sales raised $795.02, May sales $107.90 and the Bessborough Hotel case $203.13, totalling $1106.05.[99] The war brought new customers, in 1941 "more than $2,500 passed through books during the year and sales had been unusually good"[100] and in 1943 the Bessborough Hotel permanent showcase had increased sales because, "The men in the forces are buying it and sending it all

---

[93] SKAB SACS B88 Minute book 1 28 October 1924

[94] SKAB SACS B88-B2 Private sale report October 1940

[95] SKAB SACS B88-B2 Treasurer's Report 13 October 1939 It appears from the Treasurer's report that these may be sales through shops and organizations other than SACS organized sales.

[96] SKAB SACS B88 Minute book 1 21 June 1926

[97] SKAB SACS B88-B2 Report 18 October 1937

[98] SKAB SACS B88-A Minute book 2

[99] SKAB SACS B88-B2 Report 13 October 1939

[100] SKAB SACS B88 Minute book 2 annual meeting 29 October 1941

over the world."[101]

For the craftswomen, the financial rewards may look slim. Edith Fraser for 1935/36, reports she sent 51 parcels to Doukhobor workers, chiefly eight former workers but with eight new workers doing embroidery, and 49 parcels were returned completed. In addition, from other workers she received 11 rag runners, 3 wool rugs and 23 yards of native linen. The total payment for this work was $176.06.[102] However the Society had many more requests for work than they could fulfil.

> "I am now working hard and can't get a cent from nowheres. I got your address from my neighbors place and surely think that you will help me out of my big trouble. I would kindly ask you to send me out some work to do for I am poor now as our home burned."[103]

The correspondence, particularly between 1933 and 1937, is a heart-rending litany of the economic stresses of pioneering, the drought and the depression - poor crops, new babies, ill health, breaking new ground, living on relief. Sewing was interrupted to put in gardens, drive tractors, feed threshing teams, make hay and through sickness. The small sums made by embroidery appear frequently to have made the difference between surviving and not. "In the Summer the daughter of one of our first workers (whose picture was on our folders)", a young married women from a "drought stricken farm where she said she had not even weeds she could pull...came saying she wanted something to be busy with and she knew her mother had received help and encouragement and friendship from us."[104] The work also filled the long winter days, when outside work was finished, for the isolated farm women.

Despite good sales for the Society, WWII brought many changes. Imported materials used in embroideries became unobtainable. The organizers and many of the makers turned their energy to the war effort working through the Red Cross and associated organizations. As men enlisted and the farm community geared up to war production, farm women became an essential part of that production taking over the work of absent men. Climatic conditions on the Prairies changed and the desperate economic need of the Thirties receded. The war brought more money into the Prairie economy and more choice of work into the province. As a result of this combination of circumstances the Society became inactive in February 1945 although the executive continued to meet at infrequent intervals.

---

[101] SKAB SACS B88 Minute book 2 18 January 1943 (p.243)

[102] SKAB SACS B88-B2 Report Edith P. Fraser 1935/36

[103] SKAB SACS B88-E Correspondence 1933-37 to Mrs Moffat from Mrs Milse Hedale, Parkerview 20/3/1933

[104] SKAB SACS B88-B2 Report Vivian Morton

Organized craft

In 1950 the society reconvened. Although "some of the old workers...were inquiring about work...It is not felt that this is the time to try and revive the handicraft end of the society."[105]

"Economic and social conditions had changed since the society had been organized in 1922, she [Vivian Morton] pointed out, and a second generation had grown up since the new Canadians of that era had done handiwork for sale through the organization. However she was convinced that in many cases the children were keeping up their national handicraft work, but economic conditions were such that they did not have to do it for pay. The new settlers now coming to Canada were in many cases being looked after by their own national organizations."[106]

It was decided to dissolve the Society. The last minutes of the Society are dated 1956. A list of members shows that a number of the original members were still active. The intervening five years had been spent trying to wisely dispose of the Society's assets which included their collection and a substantial sum of money.[107]

The paths of the Society and CHG crossed. In March 1925, CHG wrote requesting a Saskatchewan exhibit[108] for their next national exhibition. In September CHG wrote requesting more Saskatchewan linen, it seems that they were already buying work through SACS, and asked the Society to affiliate. The pressure to affiliate was renewed in 1928 when Mrs Harry Bottomley travelled through Canada to organize provincial branches of the Guild and the handcraft section, in conjunction with the CPR, of the New Canadian Folk Song and Handicraft Festival at Winnipeg. Bottomley argued that the affiliation of all handicraft societies under one head, CHG, would develop a national consciousness, "Canadian Craft formerly meant Indian and Habitant - the time has now come to develop a real Canadian Craft"[109] and that Saskatchewan was the only province with no affiliation.[110] The Society hesitated largely because it feared losing its identity in joining. SACS sent an exhibit to the Winnipeg Festival under its own name. In 1929 the Western Festival was held in Regina, again under the auspices of the CPR and CHG. The Society asked for adequate space "to set up and take complete charge of its own exhibit, selling if it were possible to so without a percentage going to the Handicrafts Guild and, in any case, taking

---

[105] SPL LHR SACS file Minute book February 1950 p.57

[106] SPL LHR SACS file p.5 newspaper clipping attached minutes 16 January 1950

[107] see chapter 6 for further discussion of the collection and assets

[108] The exhibit won a prize of $5

[109] This is a rather odd remark considering that by 1909 CHG already marketed work from BC to PEI and NFD.

[110] SKAB SACS B88 Minute book 23 January 1928

orders."[111] It was settled, after some contention, to the Society's satisfaction. The Society continued to sell through CHG affiliated outlets.

Canadian Handicrafts Guild 1906-1974
The Canadian Handicrafts Guild[112] was the outcome of a WAAC:Montreal committee interested in the conservation of "the minor arts", including those of Aboriginal peoples, New Canadians and rural Québécois. By 1905 the committee had organized two successful major craft exhibitions in Montreal which had given them some working capital. Committee members had spent several summers searching out craftspeople, mainly in rural areas along the lower St. Lawrence, organizing exhibitions and sales at summer resorts such as Malbaie (Murray Bay) and Metis, and establishing a number of independent village industries for *catalognes* and weaving, this included sending a woman to "revive" vegetable dyeing.[113] They had also opened a permanent sales outlet in Montreal, 'Our Handicraft Shop'. Using their connections with the major women's organizations and with the industrial and government elite with whom they socialized, they had addressed the NCW in Toronto and (later) Winnipeg on the "handicrafts movement", the Royal Society of Canada had requested information,[114] as had the Royal Commission on Industrial Training for Women and the Royal Technical Society, Ottawa. In 1904, at the government's request, an exhibit was sent to the St. Louis World's Fair, USA, accompanied by a woman[115] who promoted Canadian craft over a six month period. By 1905, it was obvious that the WAAC charter "was not elastic enough for the enterprises on which the Montreal Branch had embarked, and it was decided that a separate charter should be applied for."

The Canadian Handicrafts Guild[116] was incorporated in 1906. The preamble to the incorporation of the Guild describes it as a
> "benevolent association for the purposes of encouraging, retaining, reviving and

---

[111] Interestingly CHG in that year was involved in a similar situation when they were invited by NCW to participate in a national women's display at CNE. They accepted with reservations, "the Canadian Handicrafts Guild, Headquarters, does not wish to lose its identity in this Exhibition...if we exhibit, it will be understood that our exhibit will be attractively displayed in a space of its own, and distinctively as an exhibition sent from Dominion Headquarters of this Guild." McLeod p.93

[112] I am indebted to Ellen McLeod's research on the founders of CHG and the organization's early years.

[113] Peck 1934 p.204

[114] This was incorporated into a 1905 report, discussed at the meeting in Winnipeg of the Royal Society of Canada and British Association for the Advancement of Science, where it was noted that handicraft underlies the "creation of national schools of design." L.Nowry *Marius Barbeau* (Toronto 1995) p.87

[115] Peck 1929 p.5 Miss Robertson, a member of the WAAC:Montreal Committee

[116] CHG is also referred to as the Dominion Handicrafts Guild, and at a later date as Canadian Guild of Crafts

Organized craft

developing Canadian handicrafts and home and art industries, providing markets for the same, facilitating and spreading habits of home industry and thrift, holding and taking part in exhibitions, providing any kind of instructions connected with the objects aforesaid, and carrying on all sorts of business operations necessary for the said operations, but without personal profit to the members of the Guild."

It is apparent that CHG not only called itself a national organization but intended to be one. Certainly in 1906,

"The Atlantic and the Pacific seemed a far cry from each other, but it was the aim of these enthusiasts to reach from sea to sea...by 1909 this aim was no longer a dream, for by that date craftsmen and women from Prince Edward Island to British Columbia were sending in their hand-work for exhibition and sale."[117]

The first decade was spent in consolidating the Guild as the national organization. This was done through exhibits, within Canada and abroad, and by the executive travelling across the Dominion to identify craftspeople and set up marketing arrangements, to promote crafts and the Guild, and to set up a network of Guild branches and selling outlets.

In 1906, exhibitions were sent to sixteen centres in eastern and central Canada, in 1907 to five. In 1910, May Phillips, a co-founder, travelled through western Canada visiting fourteen centres which included Victoria, Vancouver, Calgary, Edmonton, Winnipeg,[118] Kenora and North Bay. As early as 1904 the Guild's precursor was accessing Doukhobor,[119] Galician (Ukrainian), Welsh and Swedish work from Western Canada. Personal contacts with the NCW and their network of regional women's organizations, and with such people as Sydney Fisher, Federal Minister of Agriculture and Donald Smith[120] of the CPR, both concerned with immigration, probably pinpointed settlements likely to be producing crafts and their community leaders. Fisher certainly provided letters of introduction to the Premier and Lieutenant-Governor of Saskatchewan and to

---

[117] Peck 1934 p.202

[118] 1904 Peck had represented WAAC:Montreal at the NCWC meeting in Winnipeg, giving a report and taking a craft exhibit. McLeod p.170; at the first annual CHG exhibition 1905 Sir Daniel MacMillan, Lieutenant Governor of Manitoba gave a prize for leather work. McLeod p.90

[119] Through the NCW Phillips had contact with Mary Fitzgibbon (Lally Bernard) who went out to the Doukhobor settlements in 1899. In 1902 some monies collected by NCW to help the Doukhobors establish themselves was passed to the WAAC: Montreal. Personal communication McLeod 16 December 1996
The NCW had sent 50 spinning wheels and 12 handlooms to the community c1899 when they first arrived. D.K.Burnham *Unlike the Lilies: Doukhobor Textile Traditions in Canada* (Toronto 1986) p.15

[120] Smith, Lord Strathcona, a major stakeholder in the Hudson's Bay Co. and the CPR syndicate opened the WAAC craft exhibition 1900 and the Lady Strathcona Capital Fund 1902 with publicly raised money gave Our Handicrafts Shop the capital to advance purchase stock. He was also the first named corporator for CHG.

Thomas Sharp at the Experimental Farm, Agassiz, BC. Phillips visited promising communities to see and encourage craft making, to identify intermediaries and to buy work. She also, through women's organizations, gave talks in urban centres to stimulate interest and support and to gain new members for the Guild. A map pinpointing marketing craftspeople c1910,[121] shows a scattering of dots across western Canada indicating 57 locations, the major concentration is along the St. Lawrence River valley but (surprisingly) the Niagara Peninsula and southern Nova Scotia have moderate concentrations too.

The next year, 1911, Madeleine (Mrs Harry) Bottomley took an exhibit to the Winnipeg Industrial Fair, Québécois crafts were admired and purchased. She also made a four day visit to Doukhobor settlements around Veregin, SK. This was facilitated by Bruce Walker, the Immigration Commissioner in Winnipeg. She met with Peter Veregin, the Doukhobour leader and Mr. Cazakoff, manager of the Doukhobour Trading Society and placed orders for furniture, spoons and vessels for the Montreal shop.[122] Katherine Campbell went east to Prince Edward Island, Picton and Halifax, NS, and Moncton and Saint John, NB, with lantern slide lectures. In 1912 Christine Steen, CHG shop manager, took an exhibit to the Third Vancouver Annual Fair[123] and talked to the Women's Canadian Club which resulted in 55 members joining CHG, and to Victoria. En route she visited the Ruthenian (Ukrainian) settlement at Mundare, AB, where contact was through the Ukrainian Catholic Church. Based on SACS's practice, it is probable that many of these meetings also dealt with how to make traditional ethnic products acceptable to a wider market. To have 'revived' vegetable dyeing among Quebec weavers so early on suggests a conception of how products looked historically and a need to accommodate contemporary tastes, expectations and usage.

By 1916, five branches were operating in Edmonton 1911, Summerside PEI 1911, Vancouver 1912[124], Winnipeg 1913[125] and Charlottetown PEI 1916. Numerous sales outlets in the USA, Britain and Canada existed besides the Montreal shop. Externally, CHG continued to be responsible for Canadian craft exhibits at the government's request and despite inadequate

---

[121] Peck 1934 p.206

[122] McLeod p.149

[123] later the Pacific National Exhibition (PNE)

[124] C.Wilks 'PNE Arts and Crafts Program: historical overview' (Vancouver 1994) quotes the Daily Province, Vancouver 1910 "the exhibit of the handicrafts guild which has been arranged under the auspices of the Local Council of Women."

[125] From 1910 to 1915, Winnipeg had either visits from CHG:HQ personnel or exhibits.

government funding, and sent work to major exhibitions in Eire and Australia 1907[126], and in Britain 1908, 1909 and 1911. By 1914, 143 exhibits had been generated through the Montreal shop and by 1917, an estimated $106,654 had been paid out to craftspeople.[127] The war curtailed some of the Guild's activity as organizers' energy and materials were diverted to the war effort, however,

> "during the War the sales of our craftsmen and women were enormous. In one year payments were made to them of $113,000."[128]

The second decade from 1917 to 1927 seems one of retrenchment and recovery. War production,[129] social disruption and racial tension engendered by Anglo-Canadian patriotism, and a major post-war influx of immigrants combined with the demands of a fast-growing centralized national marketing endeavour done by volunteers took their toll. The first generation of organizers were ageing. It was decided it would be more efficient to establish autonomous Provincial Branches, which appear to have been envisaged as encouraging and identifying regional craftspeople in order to funnel work through to CHG:HQ. Most of the original branches seem to have become inactive. Lack of personnel and lack of means in a volunteer organization limited contact between the branches and CHG headquarters, even in 1949 the president of the Alberta Branch would say, "Westerners don't, of course, get down there [Montreal, to the annual general meeting] very often."[130]

Activity was concentrated at CHG:HQ. The Guild continued its annual national exhibition and the assembly of a collection based at MMFA. From 1922 to 1936 CHG:HQ ran needlework classes for Montreal children of Jewish, Russian, Greek, Syrian, Italian, Hungarian, Roumanian, Armenian and English origin as part of their program to retain and encourage heritage crafts. The Guild collected and disseminated information on techniques, designs and materials preparation. In 1926 and 1927, the Guild co-sponsored with McGill University a series of public lectures by consulate officials speaking on their country's crafts. In 1926 CHG:HQ also arranged for information about the Guild to be available on CPR immigrant ships. Travelling exhibition cases, possibly to demonstrate the kinds of craft the Guild was interested in, were also in circulation.

---

[126] Peck 1929 p.9
"[A letter] came from Australia saying that the Exhibit sent to that Colony had aroused so much interest that a sister organization had been started in that Country."

[127] Statistics Canada estimates $100 c.1917 approximately equivalent to $1470 in 1996; therefore $106,654 is equivalent $1,567,818 currently; McLeod personal communication

[128] Peck 1929 p.10

[129] see chapter 3, 'community projects'

[130] NAC Massey Files C2005 8:13:124

Our Handicrafts Shop, which changed its shop front name to 'The Canadian Handicrafts Guild' in 1926, was the centre of operations. In 1904 it was staffed by a paid woman shop manager and by volunteers; by 1927 CHG:HQ employed a stenographer, a book-keeper and sales women, in addition to volunteers. Craftspeople were requested to send priced samples of their work to be presented to a judging committee. There was an emphasis on maintaining a high standard of work and the use of native materials. CHG encouraged "craftsmen to develop individuality of design, and to specialize in crafts that will be representative and distinctive of their background and locality."[131] Work of an acceptable standard was held for sale for a year, then it was reduced in price or returned freight paid. The Guild added its percentage and work was sold and exhibited with a CHG label. Sales percentage and member's fees covered overhead expenses including the shop, exhibition production, expenses relating to marketing such as the cleaning and shrinking of homespun, and helping out craftspeople "when necessity arises." By 1934, "the Guild has paid out to craftsmen and women, many of whom are not in a position to sell for themselves, over one million dollars."[132] Their account books were scrupulously accurate. In contemporary terms this is a rough equivalent of 15 million dollars over thirty years and indicates the volume of business both of individual craft production and of a volunteer organization.

A 1932 account lists CHG's major craft interests as reflected in the shop: basketry; beadwork; weaving and embroidery on canvas foundations; woven blankets; chairs with rush, thong, elm bark or 'babiche'[133] seats; linen; hand knitting; homespuns "of all weaves, light and heavy, making excellent men's clothing; lace; needlecraft; pottery; quilts; rugs; batik; woodwork and woodcarvings.[134]

As Peck points out in her 1934 article, there were enormous differences between similar societies in Britain or Europe, "settled countries" dealing with "one language, one religion, with established standards, ideals, conditions, and over an area of hundreds of miles", and CHG which dealt with
> "peoples of many tongues, many religions, differing standards, conditions that change constantly, and over an area that covers thousands of miles; miles that during the winter are deep in snow...the notice board lately bore information in nine foreign languages, besides English and French."

However,
> "Everyone who serves in any capacity, from the President to the packer of parcels...becomes willing to give long hours of overtime to advance the work,

---

[131] NAC Massey Files C2005 8:13:126 1949

[132] Peck 1934 p.209

[133] rawhide thongs or lacings, used in snowshoes

[134] 'The Handicrafts of New France' *The Seigneur* January 1932 p.19

because they believe that not only individuals are benefitted but that an art-foundation is being laid for Canada."[135]

The third decade, 1927-1937, of CHG saw a renewed high national profile through the series of Folk Festivals organised in conjunction with the CPR. The first Canadian Folk Song and Handicraft Festivals took place in Quebec City in May 1927 and 1928. They resulted from the CPR's need to boost tourist traffic, the interest of their Publicity Director, John Murray Gibbon,[136] in music particularly but also in handcrafts, and the Québécois folk culture activities of Marius Barbeau of NMC. In a letter to the Director of NMC, tourism was not mentioned, the festival's object was of "increasing the interest in the folk songs and handicrafts of Quebec, [of helping] along the market for some of the handicrafts of the Province...[and] exhibiting some of the beautiful textiles which are in the possession of your Museum."[137] The Museum felt it was "well justified in lending assistance [through Barbeau's services] to an undertaking of such prospective artistic and ethnological interest."[138] The CPR's close association with CHG has already been mentioned, many of their hotels had gift shops selling CHG work[139] and in 1927 the Federal Department of Colonisation, CNR and CPR jointly provided transport for another western trip by Madeleine Bottomley on behalf of CHG. Barbeau was only interested in the promotion of Québécois culture and took no future part in the CPR festivals after 1928.

For the Western festivals, Gibbon delegated full responsibility for the handcraft exhibitions to CHG. Branches were revived or reconstituted at each location. The 'New Canadian Folk Song and Handicraft Festival' took place in Winnipeg, June 1928, in Regina in 1929, the 'Great West Folk-dance, Folk-song, Handicrafts Festival' in Calgary March 1930,[140] the First Annual Folk Song and Dance Festival in Vancouver 1933 was followed by another a year later and appears to have become an annual event. CHG:Alberta, Edmonton, had already held a 'First Exhibit' in 1928 in the Palm Room of the Macdonald Hotel, opened by the Lieutenant-Governor of Alberta.

---

[135] Peck 1934 pp.211-2

[136] Gibbon became CHG President c1942

[137] CMC.A Gibbon to W.H.Collins 20 January 1927

[138] CMC.A Collins to Murray 26 January 1927

[139] Mrs Kate Stovel Mather was a buyer for CPR gift shops in Banff, Victoria and the East c.1924, she had trained in Applied Arts at the Pratt Institute, New York, travelled in Europe, stayed 3 winters in one of Emily Carr's apartments, worked for many years doing occupational therapy in a Winnipeg mental hospital, and corresponded with Barbeau.

[140] The CPR were more interested in Calgary than Edmonton because of its proximity to Banff, where they were to institute 'Indian Days' as a tourist attraction.

Over four hundred articles,
> "done by the clever fingers of women who have brought this greatest of gifts to the new world with them...[gave] not only a revelation of beauty and color, but a new appreciation of the good fortune to which Alberta has fallen heir, in her years of new settlement."[141]

The Handicraft Association of Canada, ON also ran 'The Canadian Craft Festival', a mix of song, dance and crafts in 1931, 1932 and 1942 based at Eaton's College Street store in Toronto.

In the case of the Winnipeg festival, three members of CHG:HQ went to Winnipeg to talk with local women's groups, however it appears that the Manitoba branch had "already done considerable spade work, both through the securing of the present exhibition and in surveying the 'crop'."[142] With the co-operation of the provincial government, the Women's Institute and the United Farm Women, a Manitoba branch was formed initially for the purpose of organizing the festival. CHG:MB continued to work closely with the WI and the Manitoba government's Agricultural Extension Service[143] in the following years.

The festival itself seems to have followed the pattern of those in Quebec. Located in a major hotel, each of the 13 ethnic groups represented[144] had a booth, usually representing a typical room in which, dressed in national costume, craftspeople demonstrated their skills, "long discarded in Canada".[145] All exhibited work was competitively entered and prizes were given.[146] The prize list shows about forty categories, the recipients coming mainly from Manitoba but some from Saskatchewan and a handful from Alberta and British Columbia. Work was for sale. At all the festivals, CHG:HQ had a separate exhibit. Other festivals showed historical as well as

---

[141] USK.A J.E.Murray File IV 1925-33 Edmonton Bulletin clipping n/d

[142] USK.A J.E.Murray file newspaper 'The Future For Handicrafts' n/d c1928

[143] Esther Thompson who was the second Head of Women's Work, an enthusiastic arts and crafts supporter, was also one of the first committee members of CHG:MB.

[144] n/a *The Manitoba School Journal* April 1957 says 20 'national' groups were involved of which 14 joined CHG:MB.

[145] USK.A J.E.Murray file newspaper clipping 'Picturesque Scene Marks First Western Canadian Handicrafts Exhibition 20 June 1928. This article is the least sympathetic, teetering on the verge of hostility: the hotel rotunda "presents a motley scene...transformed into a typical European market street where the traveller delves for curios", "Garbed in seemingly grotesque clothes of many bright hues the European mingles with the conservatively-clad westerner. The new Canadian seems perfectly at home in this setting...the westerner is bewildered." In the same column is a political agenda, including amongst "Other important stands...an immigration policy which will insure the permanency of British institutions and ideals..."

[146] PAM CGMB archives, Winnipeg Tribune, 19 June 1928 says over 1800 pieces of handcraft were submitted.

Organized craft 137

contemporary ethnic and studio craft.

CHG:MB, with an eye on the success of SACS, hoped that the exhibition would prove the spring-board to a provincial handcraft industry. Festival entries gave CHG:MB a list of expert craftspeople, Manitoba was seen to have "a far more varied field to draw on than there is in Quebec and at least as good workmanship."[147] Emphasis was to be on the preservation of distinctive ethnic designs and colours but transferred to articles, garments and accessories which were acceptable to the wider community and the "vagaries of the market." The worker set the price for work, CHG:MB added twenty percent for expenses. The worker had to be a member of CHG:MB, the dollar fee being subtracted from the first sale. At the annual meeting profits in excess of a working fund, used to finance Guild operations including educational work, were redistributed among the workers on a co-operative basis.

For CHG:HQ, the Festivals were seen as being "of great value",[148] branches in seven of the nine provinces were now active, 'agencies' established in 1909 were reopened, new ones were established so that by 1930 there were 38 Summer agencies and about twenty working year round. In 1933 the Montreal shop moved to permanent quarters. The building also contained the CHG:HQ office and board room, the library and a weaving school, the first stage it was hoped in the development of a Handicraft School, for "[Montreal} should have its crafts school if it is to take its place as a fully equipped centre of cultural development."[149] The Depression, in contrast to SACS, weakened CHG sales and in 1935 the President of CHG, Lt.Col. Wilfrid Bovey, appeared convinced that national headquarters should not be so involved in commerce.[150] Given the Guild's marketing efforts this would mark a major reorientation.

Over thirty years both internal and external conditions had changed. The founders were elderly, Phillips died in 1937, Peck, aged 88, in 1943. The governing committee had, since WWI, been composed of both men and women, and remained an elite of wealthy patrons, academics and administrators rather than craftspeople. Externally, the level of government and other agencies' involvement in craft had risen, following in part where the pioneering Guild had led although with different agendas. The activity of the Quebec government in establishing a handcraft school at Quebec, 1930, and taking over craft training in francophone rural areas, the Guild's earliest and most sustained area of interest, appears to have precipitated a crisis c1936 for the Montreal-based Guild.

---

[147] USK.A J.E.Murray File newspaper clipping Winnipeg [?] Press 23 June [1928?]

[148] Peck 1934 p.213 repeated twice

[149] Peck 1934 p.216

[150] Despite this the shop expanded into the neighbouring building in 1936, and acquired the third in the row in 1949.

"[T]he Guild felt that the work in that field [Quebec] had been largely accomplished and it was following that that the Quebec branch [formerly CHG:HQ] was established as a branch."[151]

However "the premises and the possessions and the endowments which had been built up during the years"[152] remained with the new branch, CHG:PQ, which undertook to continue for the next five years as a national headquarters providing secretarial and other services as before. In addition they received 10 cents per member per year from all branches. Nearly 15 years later in 1949 CHG:PQ was still acting as national headquarters[153] and CHG was the only national craft organization.

As one of CHG's autonomous branches, CHG:MB was situated in the most populous and, at that time, powerful city in the West, Winnipeg, a city of sharp economic and ethnic contrasts. At first, craft groups were organized in national groups under "Guild supervision" and met in churches, community halls and homes.[154] By 1939, groups were reorganized according to craft media or technique rather than national origin "with good results."[155] By 1945 eleven different nationalities were affiliated with CHG:MB and five had representatives on the executive,

"It means that the exchange of ideas on a mutually helpful basis can do much to breakdown the barriers of seeming difference between those who are native Canadians and those who are New Canadians. It is a potentially powerful weapon in the hands of women, who, using the loom, the needle and the thread, can help to bring about a state where we are all simply Canadians."[156]

The CHG Annual Report 1948 for Manitoba said that Mrs Zoltan Istvanffy "a member of our Hungarian group" (and one of the award winners at the 'New Canadian Folk Song and Handicraft Festival' in 1928) had organized a class in Hungarian embroidery by request.

"It is interesting to note that this group was not only comprised of mothers and daughters, but was made up of many national origins - Belgian, Ukrainian, Hungarian, Austrian, English and French - all equally interested in learning how to do Hungarian embroidery."

---

[151] NAC Massey files C2005 8:13:126 CHG National Committee

[152] NAC Massey files C2005 8:13:126 CHG National Committee

[153] NAC Massey files C2005 8:13:126 CHG National Committee

[154] n/a *The Manitoba School Journal* p.14

[155] NAC Massey File C2005 8:13:126 'Notes on Canadian Handicrafts Guild 1901-1948'

[156] NAC Massey File C2005 8:13:126 CHG 1944 Report, Mrs Bruce Chown, CHG:MB president and a member of CHG executive committee, quoted in *Family Herald and Weekly Star* 11 April 1945

Organized craft

The same report notes members of the Ukrainian Handicraft Guild, Winnipeg[157] giving classes arranged by CHG:MB, with a member on the CHG:MB executive, and Norwegians teaching CHG:MB members.[158] Over a twenty year period, this suggests an interesting picture of both retention and dispersal of particular ethnic craft skills and traditions, and of the retention and accommodation of ethnic allegiances.

Unlike SACS, CHG:MB had established a headquarters and "a shop, with an instructress in daily attendance"[159] by 1935, when through the social connections of CHG:MB's president and the generosity of the Winnipeg Power Company, CHG:MB acquired space in the Power Building. When the Power Building was sequestered for the war effort in c.1941,[160] the Guild moved its shop to a room in the Paris Building, where although short of space sales boomed. Their classes and equipment, library and permanent collection went to two attic rooms at the Winnipeg Art School. Post-war expansion in the Art School c.1947 forced the Guild into a series of moves ending in 1949[161] with no base, the Guild's equipment and other assets were stored in member's homes. In 1951, a purpose-built building to house their collection, archives, classes and shop was opened in downtown Winnipeg.[162]

Like CHG:HQ, CHG:MB used its social and organizational connections to situate itself and its activities. The Guild remained closely connected with the Women's Institute (WI) and the Agricultural Extension Department, and thence with the University of Manitoba where the Agricultural College also housed Home Economics. In 1945 the University's Evening Institute

---

[157] I don't know whether this is the same society, given constant changes and/or incorrect reporting of names, as the Ukrainian Arts and Crafts Society founded in 1931 in association with the Ukrainian National Home, part of whose museum collection was purchased by UWAC:MB. N.Kohuska *A Half-Century of Service to the Community: An outline of the Ukrainian Womens' Association of Canada 1926-1976* (Winnipeg 1986)

[158] NAC Massey File C2005 8:13:126 CHG Annual Report 1948 pp.7,8

[159] n/a *The Manitoba School Journal* p.14

[160] 'Crafts Guild of Manitoba Inc: A Brief History' ms written by CGMB Archives Committee 1997 says the Paris Building was home from 1944-1950, but Gibbon in his account of his western trip in 1943 notes that Mrs Eric Bergman was already running a shop in the Paris Building. Dot From 'The Crafts Guild of Manitoba Celebrates Sixty-Five Years' *Manitoba History* 25 1993 p.30 dates the Power Building occupancy from 1935-1941.

[161] NAC Massey File C2005 8:13:126 CHG:Montreal Annual Report 1946 p.16 CHG:MB moves from Art School after 5 years, looms and books are at the Public Library, permanent collection is at a member's house. As detailed in the previous footnote there is conflicting chronology of Guild moves and locations of various activities.

[162] In 1968 CHG:MB became the Crafts Guild of Manitoba (CGMB). The 1990s saw a decline in membership, volunteers and shop sales. In May 1997 the Guild was dissolved and the Kennedy Street building sold. The permanent collection, antique spinning wheels, and the library became the Manitoba Crafts Museum and Library, sharing a space with the Manitoba Craft Council. The Guild archives went to the Provincial Archives of Manitoba.

held a series of 12 lectures on "Handicrafts for Leisure", and again in 1947 Guild members lectured on craft,[163] 12 week practical courses attracting more than 40 students a session were also organized.[164] Early association with the Junior League and the Red Cross, and no doubt through doctor husbands, involved the Guild in occupational therapy, particularly in the 1940s with child polio patients and with war veterans. The Winnipeg Art Gallery gave space for meetings and exhibited work, an exhibition in 1946 attracted more than 7000 visitors, a "far larger number than it has been usual to record for any other exhibition in the gallery,"[165] and "[i]n spite of bad weather the attendance was outstanding"[166] at an exhibition and demonstration in February 1947. Earlier in 1944, CHG:MB had been responsible for organizing and assembling a national needlework exhibition, 'The Travelling Canadian Needlework Exhibition' with work from all CHG branches, which included a Victory Banner competition and samplers representing each province. The exhibition travelled from CHG:HQ to Halifax, under the auspices of the Nova Scotia Department of Industry and Publicity, through four western cities "through the courtesy of the Hudson's Bay Company", to the Banff School of Fine Arts, and the Regina Arts and Crafts Society where it was exhibited at the Saskatchewan Hotel.[167] The exhibition at the Bay in Winnipeg was augmented by demonstrations by Guild members and attracted 30,000 people over ten days. Four years later the Guild produced the exhibition 'Embroidery Old and New in Manitoba'.[168] The Winnipeg Art School[169] and the Winnipeg Public Library lent space for classes. Despite the disruptions caused by lack of a permanent home during this decade CHG:MB continued with a varied and energetic program.

Government intervention

Governments and rural women, and related ventures
Federal Department of Agriculture and CHG

As CHG's experience showed, from the beginning various government organizations were interested in aspects of craft production, particularly as a function of the rural home economy and

---

[163] NAC Massey File C2005 8:13:126 'Notes on Canadian Handicrafts Guild 1901-1948'

[164] n/a *The Manitoba School Journal* p.15, From p.31

[165] NAC Massey File C2005 8:13:126 CHG Annual Report 1946 p.6

[166] n/a *The Manitoba School Journal* p.15

[167] PAM CGMB.A One of two sheets with pictures marked CHG 1946, the other shows examples from a Canada-wide weaving exhibition 1946

[168] NAC Massey File C2005 8:13:126 CHG Annual Report 1948

[169] The association of CHG:MB and the Winnipeg Art School is discussed in chapter 5.

as a women's industry. The Guild received funding through Sydney Fisher, the Federal Minister of Agriculture. The Guild had started campaigning for government funding in 1906. They not only needed the financial support but considered such a grant recognition of their merit and national standing, and it was on the grounds of being a national organization[170] that in 1910, they received a grant of $1000. The grant continued for several years but an attempt to have it doubled in 1912 was unsuccessful. During the war the grant ceased but was reinstated after, increased to $2000 and then discontinued. In 1927, their 21st anniversary, CHG campaigned unsuccessfully for $10,000 to extend their education and outreach programs.[171] The Guild probably came under the rubric of the Department of Agriculture because some of their constituency consisted of rural and immigrant populations.[172] However the agenda of the Guild and other craft organizations was to encourage and promote the whole range of craft production, "Handicrafts and Art Industries",[173] as an integral, valued part of the cultural life of the nation. Collecting, exhibiting and marketing paralleled fine art activity although lacking the financial investment, prestige and patronage of the fine arts. Creativity, individuality, skill, innovation, beauty were part of their vocabulary of craft as of the arts, although the hierarchy was frequently acknowledged[174] and the discourse often confused. Their agenda was substantially different from government departments and other rural women's organizations such as the Women's Institutes and United Farm Women's Association despite the fact that in the regions there was often a long history of association.

Provincial Departments of Agriculture and the Women's Institutes

The aim of the Women's Institutes, operating as the women's branch of the Farmer's Institute and started in Ontario in 1897 by Adelaide Hoodless, a social reformer, was to raise the standard of homemaking and health and to improve the intellectual and cultural life of rural women. Thus the focus initially was only incidentally on craft, as part of the domestic economy or as a leisure activity, and the constituency was restricted. However craft seems to have become an increasingly important part of WI programs, the level of craft activity being such that by 1961, it was the Federated Women's Institutes of Canada (FWIC) who celebrated Canada's Centennial by producing *A Heritage of Canadian Handicrafts* (1967) and the Provincial and National handcraft competitions became an integral part of national WI craft programming.

---

[170] McLeod p.113

[171] McLeod says there is no record or activities to indicate such a large sum came to CHG. personal communication 23 January 1997

[172] In addition the Department also handled international exhibitions, as noted earlier an area of major activity for the Guild.

[173] Constitution and By-laws of the Canadian Handicrafts Guild, Objects 1906

[174] "The folk arts of a country are the roots from which the fine arts grow" provides an interesting reversal of the accepted genesis of folk art. NAC Massey files C2005 8:13:126 CHG National Committee letter 30 August 1949

Provincial governments, for reasons which differed according to region but mainly centred on preventing the drift of rural populations to towns, were also involved in improving rural life. The farm vote had an electoral strength increasingly out of proportion to its numbers, was well organized, and presented a nostalgic vision of a morally and materially wholesome agrarian Canada to policy-makers, the media and others. During the first decades of the century the WI, which by 1915 had 892 branches scattered through every province and a membership of 29,045,[175] became closely involved with provincial agricultural departments and while some craft programs were wide-spread and followed similar patterns of delivery, provincial populations, agendas and circumstances affected focus and effort.

The Alberta government ran a Women's Extension Service Program through home economics demonstrations at agricultural fairs as early as 1906. Over the next ten years WI branches were organised and supervised by the Department of Agriculture and the Alberta Women's Institutes Act was passed in 1916. Crafts were taught through the Home Economics Departments of the six Provincial Schools of Agriculture and Home Economics. A 1920 Department of Agriculture Annual Report said,

> "Many of our people have come from countries where arts and crafts are a well organised and paying industry. Through time we should discover those skilled and using the law of demand and supply as a basis bring people wanting goods into contact with those who have the training to carry out the specialized work here...It is an important factor in our development as a province that we get to know the possibilities that are within our own territory."[176]

Although Romanchych, of the Women's Program, had on her own initiative in 1928 facilitated the successful cottage industry amongst Ukrainian women described earlier, in common with all of the West official concentration was on primary products rather than diversification. The Alberta Department of Agriculture never seems to have been actively involved with marketing, did not cultivate a craft industry infrastructure and, by 1940, the domestic production of equipment and raw fibres had virtually ceased and Alberta had no small industries producing craft materials, equipment or products.

The University of Alberta also pioneered extension education through a department established in 1912. On an early lecture tour through the remoter areas of Alberta, the University President, Dr.H.M.Tory, "was impressed with the great desire of the people for good books, music, painting

---

[175] L.K.Cullum 'Under Construction: Women and the Jubilee Guild and the Commission of Government in Newfoundland and Labrador 1935-1941' (Toronto 1993) p.97
In Saskatchewan the equivalent of the WI was the Homemaker's Clubs, run through the University of Saskatchewan Extension Services, Department of Women's Work.

[176] Green p.191

Organized craft

and craftsmanship."[177] The department developed a strong cultural outreach program which included crafts, particularly under Dr.E.A.Corbett in the 1930s. References to a WI:AB biennial convention in 1921 which included a Handicraft Exhibition with "many beautiful articles made by New Canadians" and a joint WI:AB/CHG:AB sponsored handcraft exhibition in 1933, both held at the University suggest an ongoing association between the three groups. Corbett worked closely with CHG.[178] He accessed Carnegie Foundation funding to put together a craft collection[179] and in 1934-35

> "organized in the southern part of the province handicrafts exhibitions in co-operation with the Alberta Handicrafts Guild and the technical schools. These were accompanied by lectures and were displayed in 26 locations with attendance exceeding 20,000. Several district handicrafts guilds were organized as a consequence."[180]

CHG:AB and the Extension department, in collaboration with other groups, were involved with craft education, such as the "handicraft institutes" held in Lethbridge, Calgary and Edmonton in 1937.[181] In the late 1930s the department and CHG:AB used the University radio station CKUA to broadcast programs giving instruction on craft techniques.

Home economics societies started in Manitoba communities c.1910 and eventually came under the aegis of the Manitoba Agricultural College. WWI brought federal government money into the provinces, including Manitoba, to increase rural education. As a result one week courses taught by craft specialists were set up in rural centres. With the passage of the Manitoba Women's Institute Act c1920, responsibility moved to the provincial Department of Agriculture with services delivered through its Extension Service. The first Head of Women's Work for the Extension Department was Helen MacDougal, a home economics graduate from Nova Scotia, followed by Esther Thompson in 1924, a Norwegian by birth, who "brought her enthusiasm for

---

[177] Green p.192

[178] Corbett was CHG President 1936-1939

[179] This collection is discussed in chapter 6.

[180] R.J.Clark 'A History of the Department of Extension at the University of Alberta 1912-1956' (Alberta 1985) p.180
The tour ran from 28 January 1935 to 27 March 1935, two places were inaccessible because of impassable roads. The collection included samples of weaving in wool and rag, and the preparation of wool, cotton and silk; lace, embroidery, tie-dye, batik, petit point, crochet, earthenware from local clay, china painting, pierced and hammered brass and copper, tooled leather, forging, woodwork, reed and raffia, wood carvings etc. from various sources including CHG:AB at Edmonton, Calgary and Macleod. UAB.A Extension Annual Report 1935 p.25-7

[181] UAB.A Extension Annual Report 1936-7 p.33

arts and crafts to her new position."[182] The Western Canadian Folk Song and Handicraft Festival, Winnipeg, was to take place through a collaboration between the provincial government, the WI, the United Farm Women and the newly revived CHG:MB. The aims and objectives of CHG:MB influenced WI:MB's crafts programs, not surprisingly as the Guild and WI:MB "were inextricably linked during the early years. People used to belong to, and volunteer at, both organizations."[183] The Extension Department "felt it was easier to maintain good standards by adopting Guild standards which were already recognized as being of high quality."[184] At the start of the Depression, Extension Department programs were curtailed and CHG:MB filled the gap. By the early 1930s WI:MB local branches were mounting craft exhibitions and the FWIC convention, Winnipeg 1933, featured a major craft exhibition and demonstrations paralleling the earlier Festival. As in Alberta and Saskatchewan, government involvement was aimed at raising rural living standards and Canadianizing non-anglophone immigrants. Voluntary organizations or private individuals developed any limited marketing activity.

In the Maritimes, the New Brunswick Department of Agriculture was giving instruction in household crafts in conjunction with the WI:NB by 1911. The WI in Nova Scotia was affiliated with the Nova Scotia College of Agriculture and the Nova Scotia Department of Agriculture in 1913. The first Superintendent of WI:NS was Jessie Fraser, a home economics graduate of MacDonald College, the agriculture college of McGill University. At that point WI:NS had fourteen branches and a rapidly growing membership. In 1928 'Handicraft Exchanges' were set up at strategic locations to sell handcrafts to the public, particularly tourists. "Considered a success in its first couple of years of operation, this endeavour led the Department of Agriculture to create the Home Industries Division, a more ambitious marketing project, which promoted provincially-made products both at home and further afield."[185] It was probably this department which sold Nova Scotia crafts on Cunard boats calling at Halifax.

In Quebec, a francophone organization modelled on the WI,[186] the Cercles des Fermières (CdF), was established by two agricultural experts in 1909 under the provincial department of agriculture

---

[182] Green p.147

[183] Margaret Gaunt CGMB letter 28 May 1995

[184] Green p.149

[185] Robson p.23

[186] The WI seems to have been an anglophone organization in PQ.

Organized craft

and incorporated in 1915.[187] These groups of women "were again to be taught the old crafts."[188] The attraction of booming industrialized Montreal for the rural population gave official concern. Catholic values (Catholics formed 85% of the population) affected women's lives. Church control of education largely restricted secondary education to males destined for the professions and priesthood until the 1950s,[189] women did not get the vote until 1944 in contrast to the Western provinces and Ontario,[190] and in the early 1950s there were still almost 60,000 women in 140 religious communities who provided a basic social service, which saved both the government and anglo-Quebec business money. These combined with the regionalism common to all provincial politics and reinforced by an active Québécois nationalism fed into an officially promoted 'Back to the Land' movement and the 'revival' of rural crafts delivered through CdF.

The emphasis was on weaving, which was seen as a traditional Québécois craft reflecting the total self-sufficiency of farm folk. In 1924 the Quebec Department of Agriculture organized a competition for a new type of loom to replace the large traditional models. The winning design would be endorsed by the Department. The competition was won by Nilus Leclerc of l'Islet who designed a four harness counter-balance loom. His company started production of the loom, which was shown at the Quebec Exposition 1926. The department of agriculture used it in their teaching programs and also aided its purchase by CdF members.[191] The looms were sold through mail order catalogues, initially the Leclerc company employed no dealers. In 1925 CHG sent a hundred copies of the French version of "Receipts for Dyeing" to M. Desilets, Chief of Home Economics at the Department of Agriculture.

In 1928 Henri Turcot of the Department of Trade and Commerce in Ottawa wrote that "French-Canadian homespuns are sought and valued by connoisseurs the world over",[192] that one hundred and nine CdF, with a membership of 7000, were producing homespun articles valued at $616000,

---

[187] J.S.Crosby 'A History of the Evolution of the Teaching of Textiles and Weaving in Quebec since 1905' (Montreal 1987) p.27

[188] Beriau 1943 p.22 This was at least 10 years after CHG had started their revival, promotion and marketing of Quebec crafts. A co-founder of CdF, Georges Bouchard became President CHG 1940-41

[189] As early as 1905 lay-women were involved in the founding of schools such l'École Normale Classico-Ménagère (later Institute Chanoine Beaudet) at Saint-Paul de Kamouraska which educated women to become teachers or homemakers. They came under the department of agriculture. Crosby pp.10,11

[190] MB 1916; AB,SK,BC,ON 1917; NS and Federal 1918; NB 1919, PEI 1922

[191] In 1915 members paid 25c membership fee a year. Crosby p.28 By 1943 it was a dollar a year which was matched by a government fund for the purchase of looms, spinning wheels etc. J.M.Gibbon 1943(a) pp.140-1

[192] Turcot p.5

and that the growth of the industry was steady. The weavers sold to specialty shops which in turn sold the bulk of the produce to American tourists visiting the province.[193] The industry, he points out, was concentrated in Charlevoix, Pont Neuf, Gaspé and Bonaventure counties and in some parts of the lower St. Lawrence but "[i]n the environs of Montreal very few have taken to the native woollen industry even for domestic purposes."[194]

Despite, or perhaps because of, this evidence of production stimulated by the department of agriculture, in 1929 the provincial government investigated rural home industries. The conclusions were that old techniques had been lost in almost all parts of the province, looms still in operation were unfit for new conditions of weaving, there was a noticeable lack of artistic taste in work being produced, women were eager to learn about these "neglected crafts" but the facilities for training were lacking. It was decided to create an organization for the revival of Quebec handicrafts and rural industries. A study was done of handcraft practice, in particular weaving and spinning, in the United States and Europe and a collection, which eventually numbered 2500 pieces, was made of rural art from various countries and exhibited at the Provincial Exhibition of Domestic and Foreign Handicrafts 1930.[195] The government founded and the department of agriculture funded l'École des Arts Domestiques de Quebec (EdAD), Quebec City, which opened in 1930 under the direction of Oscar A. Beriau, Director-General of Handicrafts for Quebec, to train leaders "who are now working in the field, teaching the arts of spinning, weaving, dyeing, rug making from various fibres, especially those produced on the farm."[196] The first group of 59 students, many of whom were nuns,[197] came from Écoles Ménagères Regionales. "The initial staff was composed of a few teachers from the very best educational centres of Europe and America and...two or three of our old Canadian weavers."[198] In the next three years twelve Canadian women qualified as teachers, "bringing the actual staff to twelve in the Department."[199] Two graduates of the School of Fine Arts helped students with the preparation of drawings, "Canadian

---

[193] Turcot p.17

[194] Turcot p.17

[195] Beriau 1933(b) p.143

[196] Beriau 1943 p.22

[197] photos of classes 1930, 1933 from O.Beriau *Tissage Domestique/ Home Weaving* (Quebec 1933); "during the summer months nuns from the convents in all parts of the province receive lessons and practical demonstrations." MacKay p.29

[198] Beriau 1933(b) p.147 September

[199] This seems to suggest that the foreign teachers were temporary.

artists were employed to prepare suitable Canadian motifs."[200] A manual was published on natural dyeing containing "hundreds of recipes"; Beriau himself wrote a weaving manual published in English and French.

For 1933-34 the CdF reported 8877 members,[201] in 1940 according to government promotional material there were 60,000 looms, 1000 CdF and 35,000 members, in 1943 Beriau reported 800 CdF and 91 branches of the WI in Quebec, with 32 leaders travelling throughout the province teaching, "tens of thousands of looms and spinning wheels are in use in rural Quebec."[202] In 1938, Bovey suggested that, "The economic implications of the [Canadian handweaving] movement are somewhat difficult to ascertain owing to the lack of complete statistics." In 1933-34, CdF members made over $14,000 worth of linen selling about 10%, and out of about 138,000 lbs of home-produced wool used almost 134,000 lbs. Farm women from the South Shore of the Lower St. Lawrence, who were producing almost half the provincial total, in 1937 produced approximately 1,200,000 lbs of wool, 70% of weavers used their own wool, the average production per weaver per year was 25 yards. Bovey costs production and comes to the conclusion that the return on sold woven homespun was about twenty cents an hour. He postulated that the real importance was in the production of textiles for home use, by far the bulk of the production, on which he put a value of $750,000 a year. Turcot, ten years earlier had conceded that "prices are rather low in comparison with the quality of the goods produced, but this industry is remunerative in this sense that the work is performed in the long winter season...[when] nothing else could readily be done, the utilization of spare time meaning...double saving."[203]

La société d'enseignement postscolaire du Manitoba MB
The Catholic church through its adult education organization, la Société d'enseignement postscolaire (SEP), promoted weaving in other francophone communities. In Manitoba, teaching of weaving, sponsored jointly by the Manitoba Department of Education and SEP:MB began in 1941 with instructors drawn from the Order of the Holy Names of Jesus and Mary, Quebec. Students were selected by their parish priest, did not pay tuition and room and board were provided, however they were required to pass on the skills acquired to other interested people in their community. Courses were based at St. Joseph's College, St. Boniface where each student had a loom. A comprehensive study of four harness woven structures and techniques was taught

---

[200] MacKay p.28

[201] Divided into 5,379 spinners, 4,939 weavers. Bovey 1938 p.14 Crosby indicates numbers have continued to grow pp.29, 14: 1959 741 groups 41,175 members; 1969 membership doubled; 1975 70,000+ 795 groups

[202] Beriau 1943 p.22

[203] Turcot p.11

using fine yarns, primarily cotton with some wool and occasionally linen, and dense weave. Yarns were brought from Quebec. Courses were also taught in rural Manitoba and Winnipeg. Between the Fall of 1941 and Summer 1942, Sr. Donalda taught in five parishes, spending at least five weeks in each, boarding in local nunneries. Classes were held in parish halls, looms were dismantled and taken from community to community, attendance was often high and included people of all ages, lay and religious. By November 1943 about 400 Manitobans had been taught to weave and SEP:MB had about 30 looms. SEP:MB kept stocks of materials for courses but war shortages caused problems. In 1944 SEP:MB ran fourteen courses for 182 students and sold 47 looms,[204] in 1945 courses were taught to 80 students and 50 looms were sold. The demise of formal courses in 1948 coincided with the end of grants from the department of education.

Searle Grain Company weaving program MB, SK, AB
The Searle Grain Company weaving program in Manitoba,[205] Saskatchewan and Alberta also started in 1941. Major Strange, a director of the company, was inspired by the success of Quebec's handweaving revival. His first purpose was to improve individual surroundings rather than to start a cottage industry; later, to provide activity for post-war unemployment amongst women and demobbed service men. Strange contacted Beriau, whose daughter Renée came to Manitoba in 1942. She recruited four local farm girls who spoke English and another language, two French, one Swedish, one Ukrainian and Russian, suggesting that, although there was no discrimination, courses were aimed at communities which were perceived to have an active hand weaving tradition. After four months intensive training, each went to a community in their language area.[206] Some courses were taught in Manitoba, but because of SEP:MB's activity, most were taught in Saskatchewan and Alberta.

Courses were taught in towns or villages with a Searle elevator so that looms could be shipped by rail and the local agent could assist with unloading and setting up looms. Each instructor had five looms for class use and her personal loom. Classes, held in church basements or town halls, started with twenty pupils but when this was found to be unmanageable, they were reduced to twelve. Wives of Company customers had first choice, farm women had preference over town women, there was no religious or ethnic affiliation. Classes lasted for six weeks, five days a

---

[204] It is highly likely that these were Leclerc looms; under the Searle Grain Co. weaving program, 246 45" Leclerc looms were in use in Saskatchewan and Alberta within three years.

[205] Manitoba Pool Elevators, a grain handling co-operative decided in 1942 to develop a Rural Art and Handicraft Exhibition to stimulate interest and raise standards. The exhibition would be non-competitive although appraised by qualified judges. The first of many well-patronized exhibitions took place in 1948. Green p.158

[206] Hoskins p.64 Helen Boiley, Germaine Chaput - francophone, went to Legal and St. Paule, AB; Laura Muirhead (McHugh) - swedish, to Melford, SK; Ann Yakimischak - ukrainian and russian, to Blaine Lake, SK.

week. Students were asked to form a weaving circle for which there were explicit rules and regulations to provide a mechanism for the continuation of the weaving program after formal instruction ended. There was no charge for instruction and a nominal fee of 50 cents a year for weaving circle members. As well as looms, materials were provided for classes but students paid the wholesale cost of yarn for any work they kept. The Company sustained the entire costs of the program, thus having received instruction free, weaving circles in turn were to provide free instruction. By July 1944, 62 classes had been held for 794 students, 260 looms had been purchased[207] and an estimated 10,000 yards of 45" fabric had been woven for clothing and home furnishings. In that year the program was brought to a halt by gas [petrol] rationing which prevented students driving in to classes. Searle weaving groups also created interest in communities where classes had not been held and informal classes continued until the 1950s when materials became more expensive and local weavers had to compete with low-priced, imports of small household linens from China and Taiwan.[208]

At least as important as the weaving program was the Searle Farm Weaving Service opened at the Company's head office in Winnipeg to act as a retail outlet for equipment and materials in 1941. It became the first dealership for Leclerc looms, and also imported from the US 'Hand Skill' looms by Elphege Nadeau. Looms and weaving accessories were sold without profit. A large variety of yarns were stocked including linen from Ireland and France and tweed yarns and fine wools from Britain, although it should be noted that the Company encouraged farms to keep some sheep for wool and had experimented with fibre flax growing. A large proportion of sales were to Winnipeg weavers but mail order sales went beyond isolated prairie farm women, and the Service eventually shipped yarns and equipment world wide. The Service also employed a consultant, Dorothy Brownell Rankine, and each month with the invoices a bulletin, *Searle Suggestions*, was sent out. The Weaving Service shut in 1965 with the amalgamation of Searle and Federal Grain, which lead to Searle shedding all peripheral operations. The reason given for closing was the change to group purchasing by weavers to obtain yarn at lower cost.

A 1947 article said "Hundreds of weavers in Canada weave entirely for their own pleasure, defraying the cost of the materials by small-scale selling."[209] Enjoyment aside, the enormous increase in handweaving amongst rural women can only be explained by the amount of government promotion and subsidy, a cash-poor economy which necessitated home production rather than purchase, the continued systematic exclusion of women from the workforce ensuring that their "primary economic functions [remained] curiously frozen in the unpaid work of the

---

[207] CMC.A n/f 'Will Profitable Hearthside Industry Develop From Revival of Handloom Weaving in West?' Kathleen Strange reprint from *Saturday Night* magazine c.1944

[208] P.Perry *Traditional-Functional Weaving in Saskatchewan* Regina 1976

[209] NAC Massey files C2005 8:13:126 p.9 'Craft of Handweaving Canada 1947' by E.M.Henderson and Mary Sandin

family"[210] and, latterly, war shortages of manufactured textiles. Tweeds had become very fashionable[211] and variations on the rustic look continued to be a staple of interior design but these were probably marginal considerations for weavers who were not selling.

Jubilee Guilds NFD

In Newfoundland and Labrador, an equivalent of the WI[212] was not started until 1935, when the Jubilee Guilds were formed in response to increasing economic distress in the outports and the belief amongst the governing classes that self-help was better than charity. Lady Anderson, wife of the Governor of Newfoundland, had started the British Empire Service League (1933-1935) to collect and distribute clothing to the needy, primarily of St. John's. In 1934 she "independently hired a young female weaving instructor [possibly Maggie George of Heart's Content, Trinity Bay], purchased a loom and sent her on a teaching tour of St. Mary's Bay and Placenta Bay."[213] Homespun for clothing and domestic linen production was a major incentive behind the Guild's weaving program. The Jubilee Guilds were established to further "home improvement and community betterment...To develop home and local industries, and to cooperate with all Departments of the Commission of Government...To encourage the sale of Newfoundland-made goods..."[214] Three of the six Departments of the Commission of Government had representatives on the Guilds' Board of Trustees - Natural Resources, charged with the economic regeneration of Newfoundland (and its subdivision, the Department of Rural Reconstruction which included Cooperatives, Land Settlement and Agriculture), Public Health and Welfare, and Education.

Like NONIA, the Jubilee Guilds were governed by a male Board of Trustees in St. John's and

---

[210] Finkel p.204

[211] eg. *Canadian Home Journal* October 1932 p.78 "Fashion has gone British...the rough and tweedy swagger coat"

[212] The Jubilee Guilds were largely a women's organization because the organization's focus of interest represented a middle and upper class gendered view of homemaking skills (which did not necessarily correlate with outport women's experience.) Men were involved in constructing looms and in 1936, Cullum p.168 reports a dozen men were actively involved with the formation of Guilds and the *teaching of weaving.* [my emphasis]

[213] Cullum p.89 As President of NONIA, Lady Anderson must have known of NONIA's weaving program in the Fortune Bay area a decade earlier which continued to be co-ordinated by Rev. Hugh MacDermott and his wife. Also the Department of Public Health and Welfare started, when it took over NONIA's nursing responsibilities, "employing supervisors and trained instructors of weaving on the South West Coast and particularly along the route served by the 'Lady Anderson' [hospital ship]" in answer to requests for training. This trespassing on established territory caused conflict with the Department of Health and Welfare and ended with an agreement that the Department would be responsible for weaving programs along the south coast from Port-aux-Basque to Fortune Bay.

[214] Cullum p.100

Organized craft

run by a committee of socially prominent women, headed by the Governor's wife,[215] who employed an Organizing Secretary and from 1937 a number of Field Workers, all young single women. Also like NONIA,[216] communities had to petition the St. John's headquarters, showing that at least ten women representing the whole community (ie. all religious groups) were interested, and there was a rigorous approval system. Seventeen branches were formed in the first year and by 1947 over 3000 women were involved in 116 branches. As with similar organizations the emphasis was on crafts and domestic skills, taught through Field Workers going to the outports, staying several weeks at each place before travelling on to the next, and through short courses in St. John's. These included, in 1937, instruction in carding wool, weaving, knitting, quilt making, glove making and making of vegetable dyes. Field Workers took materials and supplies with them, including demonstration looms. Local men copied the Canadian and Norwegian looms for use in their communities. During the winter the Field Workers attended courses in a variety of craft and other subjects at the Guilds' school, known as the Weaving School, in St. John's.[217] The head office provided patterns for projects free but sold materials and equipment on the "nothing for nothing" principle. Lynch's conclusion is that training concentrated on technique rather than encouraging design or personal creativity, each course's contents were designed at head office and the Guild provided all the materials as a course package.[218]

By 1937, the Grenfell Mission, NONIA, the Department of Health and Welfare, and the Jubilee Guilds were all running weaving programs, with some territorial jostling, as well as promoting rugmaking, knitting and other textile handcrafts. At this time the Co-operative Division also became involved with weaving and other craft projects with outport women, running Summer schools in St. John's and Corner Brook in 1937, 1938 and 1939 and outport classes in collaboration with the Guilds. The Co-operative Division workers were trained at and came from the Coady Co-operative Movement at Antigonish, NS and encouraged women to improve domestic incomes through earnings from the production and marketing of handcrafts. The Guilds, despite their statement of intent to develop and encourage home industries, strongly opposed the Co-operative Division's proposal to introduce cottage industries and their provision of tools and materials in communities too poor to make start-up purchases. The Guilds saw their survival threatened by proposed government programs, including competition from the Co-operative

---

[215] Lady Eileen Walwyn, second President 1936-1946, purchased a loom and learned to weave and "personally supplied raw wool for weaving and knitting to outport communities, provided a loom to a needy group or turned over the basement of Government House for experimental dyeing of yarns and cottons for weaving." Cullum p.123

[216] NONIA and the Jubilee Guilds collaborated and overlapped, mainly to their mutual benefit.In the Summer of 1938 they joint funded and shared the teaching services of Elsie Bell of the London School of Weaving.

[217] In 1939 Oscar Beriau "former Director of the Provincial School of Handicraft", Quebec taught there. Cullum p.216

[218] Lynch 1994 p.146

Women's Guilds, and desperately needed funding to continue. Apart from its own fundraising efforts, the Guilds received in its first two years a grant from the Carnegie Corporation, New York, amounting to $4000. The Department saw the Guilds as an established network delivering education to a population not otherwise reached. Negotiation and compromise resulted in the Department of Rural Reconstruction starting annual funding of $9000 to the Guilds in 1938. The craftswomen themselves forced the issue of marketing through the Guilds by their need for cash income. After some years of private sales and sales through the Co-operative Division, in 1946 the Guilds' head office opened a store to retail member's work.

The Department of Rural Reconstruction was responsible for an effort to improve small-scale wool production by importing high-grade breeding stock, the introduction of drum carders, mechanical spinners and knitting machines into the outports in the 1930s, and sponsorship of rural exhibitions, the responsibility for the Women's Section of the latter soon became the Guilds' responsibility. The sheep breeding program had limited success, the Guild imported New Zealand fleeces for weaving until WWII. Lynch suggests that the knitting machines had only limited acceptance unlike the drum carders which some women's groups purchased for communal use.

By 1945, there were 106 local Jubilee Guilds, and a provincial exhibition showed the range of woven articles being produced. At this time, the government decided to rationalize handcraft education and set up a National Handicrafts Centre (which duplicated the Guild's office and school.) Again some of the Guilds' staff were seconded to the government's Women's Programme. A year later the government asked the Guilds to amalgamate with the Women's Programme. This was not well received by the Guilds. The dispute was resolved when, in 1949, Newfoundland and Labrador voted for union with Canada. The new provincial government, strongly in favour of an expansion of the handicrafts program as an integral part of a development plan for the province,[219] withdrew the proposed amalgamation of programs, asking the Guilds to continue running their programs for rural women with funding from the Department of Education.

Governments and rural men
It is noticeable that little government support through agricultural departments was given to other media. Woodworking was included as part of agricultural college courses but agricultural extension dealt with farming, there occurs no equivalent profiling of woodwork and blacksmithing to women's textile production. Quebec was unusual when in 1932 the department of agriculture "included in its division of handicrafts a well organized and clearly enunciated ceramic program."[220] A later project, the 'peasant potters of Beauce', was launched in 1941. Under this project a group of farmer's sons were established on small holdings of about nine acres. They

---

[219] Green p.17

[220] R.Home 'Pottery' 1944 p.72

were given training in carpentry, drawing, modelling and pottery. They were required to build their own houses and furniture, farm during the summer and make pottery in the winter. They appear to have produced a variety of work as a group rather than working in individual potteries. It was hoped that this experiment might produce a solution to the financial problems of subsistence farmers, fishermen and other seasonal workers. In 1961, one could still buy Beauce pottery, "highly glazed a royal blue, with simple designs."[221] Funding also went to a training shop in wood carving, directed by Médard Bourgault at St. Jean-Port-Joli.[222]

Governments, reconstruction and marketing

During the Depression and WWII there was increasing government intervention, particularly in the national organization of industry and the institution of social programs. Concern at levels of unemployment and poverty with their potential for social upheaval and political unrest, war-time shortages and preparation for the return to peace-time conditions coupled with the profitable activity of individual craft ventures and organizations attracted government interest and are reflected in the departments involved.

Federal government: initiatives

At a national level, the Dominion-Provincial Youth Training Program was instituted in 1937, a late response to the Depression's economic crisis. In New Brunswick, for example, the Department of Education joined the program in order "to train rural young people in long forgotten crafts."[223] Courses included weaving, sewing, crocheting, needlepoint, quilting and rug making. Month long courses were held in 62 communities and about 1500 unemployed young women received training, of which 604 specialized in weaving. Boys learnt to design and make furniture from New Brunswick birch and maple, and one group learnt how to build and repair looms. The programs seem to have been delivered through vocational schools and youth organizations. The focus echoed earlier women's rural programs but appears more controlled and sophisticated. At various schools, including those in Woodstock, Saint John, Fredericton and Moncton, women graduates of the project held fashion shows in which they modelled their handwoven tailored clothing, knitwear and accessories. The Youth Training Program lapsed at the start of the war.

---

[221] Green p.123

[222] see chapter 3

[223] Green p.82
In Saskatchewan it was administered through the University of Saskatchewan Extension Services, and for girls was under the Women's Program and closely associated with Homemaker's Clubs' activities.

Federal government: reports
In the early part of the war a 'Composite Report to the Minister of Agriculture'[224] was published, which considered the development of a "typically Canadian national handcraft programme." Representatives from the Departments of Agriculture,[225] Trade and Commerce, and Fisheries, and the Foreign Exchange Control Board and Committee on Rehabilitation each presented briefs which looked at the economic, cultural, social and educational values of craft. In addition there were representatives from the Departments of Transport, Labour (Youth Training Branch), Mines and Resources (Indian Affairs and the Archaeological Division), and from the Ethnology Branch, NMC (Marius Barbeau), the National Research Council (Textile Division) and the RCMP,[226] making a committee of thirteen in all. The committee looked at American government activity during the Depression through the Division of Self-Help Co-operatives, Federal Emergency Relief Administration,[227] and at handcraft programs in the Southern Highlands. They suggested other federal departments which might be involved with a national craft program and listed agencies dealing with "the welfare of handcraftsmen in Canada, and the successful marketing of their products."

The published report is unsophisticated in its analysis. A page headed 'Comment' states,
> "The privilege of being able to work at a craft...make quite unnecessary and, indeed, undesired, countless services and possessions which others feel so all-important in order to secure and keep a place in society...while a mere wage earner seems always to desire more money...Thus, many a present-day craftsman is getting along comfortably and happily, according to his more simple standard of living."

The report omits to mention that many 'craftsmen' were, in fact, 'craftswomen' which perhaps accounts for the casualness with which adequate financial recompense for skilled work was treated. "Encourage marketing agencies to look to interests of craftsmen", identified as one of five "Pressing Programme Problems", hints that, economically, all was not well. The report concludes that "desirable programmes" would: assist rural people to supplement their cash earnings, increase

---

[224] Russell 1941

[225] The Agriculture Department representative was Georges Bouchard, co-founder of CdF and by 1941 Assistant Deputy Minister of Agriculture and President of CHG:HQ. His booklet *The Renaissance of Rustic Arts* was one of the briefs.

[226] Royal Canadian Mounted Police, the federal police force, as opposed to provincial and municipal forces.

[227] There was no Canadian equivalent to this program. Also products under this program had to be non-competitive with industrial products.

Organized craft

the inflow of US dollars,[228] and provide occupations for demobilized service men.

This committee seems to have spawned the Provisional Interdepartmental Committee on Canadian Hand Arts and Crafts which sat from 1942 to 1944. With the exception of the RCMP and Transport, representatives (often the same people) from all the departments and organizations sitting on the first committee sat on the second. They were augmented by three staff from NGC including the Director, H.O.McCurry, three staff from the Art and Printing Branch of what later became the Wartime Information Branch, Dr.E.A.Corbett, formerly of the University of Alberta Extension Division now involved with CHG:ON, Dr.G.W.Simpson of the University of Saskatchewan Extension Division and John Grierson of the National Film Board, a committee of twenty.[229]

During 1942, the Committee's Secretary visited the Antigonish Conference, NS,[230] the Director of WI:NS, a Canadian Arts and Crafts exhibition sponsored by CHG:ON at Eaton's Store, Toronto, and Montreal[231] where he had "27 direct contacts with institutions encouraging handcraft programmes, guilds, professional and amateur craftsmen."[232] He also went to the Women's International Exposition of Arts and Industries, Madison Square Garden, New York, which provided an opportunity for meetings with government officials of other countries running craft education and marketing programs and with various American officials, including a visit to America House, the headquarters of the American Craftsmen's Co-operative Council, "a national organization offering educational and marketing services to American craftsmen." The Secretary was also 'visited' by 23 officials from craft and associated institutions. They came mainly from Toronto (6) and Montreal (8), and included four past, present or future presidents of CHG (two past presidents sat on the Committee) and four officials, including their president, of CHG:ON. The remaining Canadian visitors came from Western Canada.

Information about their country's craft programs came from six foreign legations in Ottawa, and reports and correspondence were received on government sponsored programs in Norway, Sweden

---

[228] Canada had an ongoing trade deficit with the US; this was exacerbated during the early part of the war when UK exchange controls on converting sterling to dollars and wartime purchases in Canada escalated Canada's huge sterling surplus and created a crippling deficit of US dollars. With the UK/US Lease-Lend agreement, extensive US war effort purchases in Canada reversed the trend. However tourists' US dollars for Canadian craft purchases were always a government consideration.

[229] All were seconded to war work, 5 returned to civilian occupations during the course of the committee.

[230] The conference is discussed below.

[231] It is noticeable that despite the level of activity no visits were made further west than Toronto.

[232] Russell 1944 p.19

and the United States, the latter from eight State or Federal bodies. The Deputy Ministers of all provincial government departments of agriculture were surveyed about current organized "efforts to encourage useful rural art and craft activities." Helen Mowat of Charlotte County Cottage Crafts, NB, Bertha Oxner of the Extension Service, University of Saskatchewan, CHG:HQ, CHG:MB, CHG:ON and CHG:AB were other major correspondents.

The first of the "major findings" was "that Canada appears to be alone, among the larger nations of the world, in not having so far established a national service to encourage useful characteristic hand art and craft activities." The remaining six findings identify a national need to improve household economic and cultural living standards, the former with particular reference to low income groups through self-sufficiency and marketing; the need for a central service offering sources for educational and technical information, suppliers of materials and equipment, marketing opportunities etc. to makers or potential makers; the improvement of industrial products through input from craft designers and "specialists"; and the potential of craft, "a subject of such a common-denominator and non-contentious nature",[233] to provide a common meeting ground in a multi-cultural society and a national domestic culture, recognised as such within the country and abroad. The Committee commented that their survey showed that craft enjoyed "an unusual national-scale interest."

The Committee dealt with the first issue by identifying a major role for NGC, with the co-operation of the Department of Agriculture and rural organizations, in establishing a national service for the encouragement of Canadian craft through an extension of NGC's outreach program, a national survey and a major national exhibition. At that point, this was an untenable proposition on financial, political and philosophical grounds.[234]

Of the other four issues, two are not discussed. Employment, referred to constantly in relation to low-income earners and seasonal workers, did not produce any coherent plan or new ideas, despite the Committee's wide-ranging examination of Canadian and foreign practice. Craft as an aspect of national culture was linked to women's work in a 'motherhood' statement. There was an effort to identify "economic interest fields", which included professional craftsmen, interior decorators and the tourist industry, and to forecast the economic value of craft activity broken down into producers and suppliers of raw and semi-processed materials, tools and equipment valued at $50,000,000 annually and products and services valued at $150,000,000 annually. The obverse to the predicted generation of wealth was that "federal governments of many countries have observed...in encouraging useful handcraft programmes, they have found themselves less

---

[233] Russell 1944 p.5

[234] The position of NGC is discussed in chapter 6.

Organized craft

obliged to consider problems of direct relief."[235] It was also noted that "some countries offer full-time employment to craftsmen working in more than 60 different fields, highly skilled craftsmen may find practically untouched fields in Canada" although there were limited suggestions as to what these were. Although not going as far as the earlier committee, this one also was unable to divorce "the purely economic benefits of handcraft practices from the many other benefits: cultural, social, educational, therapeutic and aesthetic."[236] These benefits were considered intrinsic to the activity of making, and to the national welfare and ethos.

The decade ended with the Royal Commission on Arts, Letters and Sciences (Massey Commission.) In contrast to the federal department committees above, the Commission was independent and the focus was on a wide range of issues affecting Canadian culture. Acknowledging that "some measure of official responsibility in this field [cultural affairs] is now accepted in all civilized countries,"[237] the Commission was sensitive to the problems of providing consistent aid within the federal structure without stifling individual and community initiative or intruding on provincial jurisdiction. The Commission of five members went to their constituency, travelling across the country to listen to briefs of which an unexpectedly large number as far as the Commission were concerned (44) came from craft organizations.[238]

The Commission questioned whether craftspeople, given the economic return for their work, could produce enough to make a living. The President of CHG:HQ, Mrs G.S.Currie replied that the Guild had a number of people "who try to do that...in exceptional cases it can be entirely an economic means of a livelihood...some of our branches would like to stress and develop that economic angle of it. The Guild is ready to support them."[239] CHG:ON proposed that "with proper direction and adequate incentive young men and women may make a living as full-time professional craftsmen...[and] that crafts can play such an immediate part in helping to solve the economic problems of Canada."[240] The Community Arts Council of Vancouver propounded "the importance of developing markets for the best of the work being done."[241] Ivan Crowell of the New Brunswick Government, Department of Industry and Reconstruction, Handicrafts Division

---

[235] Russell 1944 p.28 Canadians seem to have feared a return of the Depression.

[236] Russell 1944 p.27

[237] Massey Report p.5

[238] chapter 6, Massey and craft

[239] NAC Massey Commission C2005 8:13:126

[240] NAC Massey Commission C2005 8:13:128 CHG:ON presentation

[241] NAC Massey Commission C2006 9:16:161 p.20

(see below) discussed this project and presented a series of proposals. The Commission in its report[242] considered, apparently *de facto* as no reasons are given, that "the formal encouragement of handicrafts is a responsibility of the provinces and of the various voluntary organizations." They therefore made no formal recommendations in the belief "that handicrafts in Canada can be most effectively and suitably aided through the strengthening of the appropriate national voluntary organisation, the Canadian Handicrafts Guild." How CHG was to be 'strengthened' was not indicated although as early as the 1941 Composite Report CHG had been described as "weak" and in desperate need of a full-time business secretary and two women organizers with sufficient funds to travel.

Provincial government initiatives

In 1940, Jean Marie Gauvreau, director of l'École du Meuble, was funded by the provincial government to do an inventory of Quebec craftspeople.[243] This was publicized through articles and in *Artisans du Quebec* 1940. In 1945 the Quebec Ministry of Industry and Commerce, under pressure from the CdF to "co-ordinate the efforts of Quebec artisans", set up l'office de l'Artisant et de la Petite Industrie, Gauvreau was the first Director. The mandate was to gain information concerning the state of crafts in Quebec, to educate the public about crafts, and to "help artists and artisans progress in their work, and assist them in developing their livelihood."[244]

As the economic crisis had deepened in Atlantic Canada, social activism in sectors of the Catholic church had mobilized economically depressed communities through adult education leading to the establishment of co-operatives, credit unions[245] and community self-help projects including craft cottage industries. In Nova Scotia, much of this work centred on the Extension Department of St. Francis Xavier University at Antigonish, which had stimulated a number of small craft initiatives including Star of the Sea Handicrafts at Terence Bay, promoted craft development through short courses and exhibitions, and helped sell work through their publication 'Maritime Co-operator'.[246] In 1942, the Extension Department organized the 'Antigonish Conference' attended by 65 craftspeople and others involved with crafts in rural areas, including representatives from the Quebec Department of Handcraft, the Newfoundland Department of

---

[242] Massey Report p.237

[243] How complete an inventory it was is not clear from *Artisans du Quebec* which is largely based on craftspeople taking part in the first Île Ste. Helene fair, 1939.

[244] Crosby pp.17-18

[245] community owned, co-op banks

[246] Since 1917 Mount St. Bernard College had offered several craft courses, in 1943 the program was seen as "one of the most comprehensive in Canada". A 3 year course led to a diploma recognised by the Nova Scotia Department of Education as craft teaching certification.

Reconstruction and the federal Interdepartmental Committee. The Conference resolved to appoint a committee to present a proposal for craft development to the Nova Scotia government. It also requested a study of crafts "with a view to inaugurating a province-wide movement under government direction."[247] The Nova Scotia government responded with surprising promptness, this time by establishing a Handcrafts and Home Industries Division under the Department of Trade and Industry rather than under the Department of Agriculture as before the war. In February 1943, Mary E. Black was appointed Supervisor of Handcrafts, she became Director before she retired in 1955.

The Handcraft Divisions established in Nova Scotia and in New Brunswick, under the Department of Finance and Industry in 1946, intensified the commercial direction of initiatives in those provinces. Although Black wrote, "The Nova Scotia handcraft programme is largely concerned with the training of individuals to utilize their leisure time to produce handcrafts either for use in the home or for sale outside to augment family incomes,"[248] the focus was on developing craft as small business rather than on the improvement of rural standards of living or support for a much wider range of craft activity which might include making a livelihood and marketing. Harold Connolly, Minister of Trade and Industry stated in 1945, "Our first thoughts are to make the crafts commercially worthwhile to the people of the rural districts. If we succeed in improving their revenues we can then proceed to the cultural."[249] The spur was a worsening economic situation caused by de-industrialization and fluctuating incomes from primary resource occupations, and increasing economic dependence on tourism.

McKay argues that Black's appointment and the handcraft program smacked of tokenism. Harold Connolly, the minister, distanced himself from handcrafts and gave Black no terms of reference
> "nor any specific directions as to procedure...and altho [although] I outlined what I felt should be attempted little was said as to how to go about it or where to start. I had the distinct feeling that they could not care less whether or not N.S. had a Handcrafts program - and I found out later how right I was!"[250]

---

[247] Lotz pp.16-18

[248] M.Black 'Improving Design in Handcrafts' *CA* 1952 p.158

[249] quoted McKay p.182

[250] Black quoted McKay p.170 Black is unusual in that she left, to quote McKay an "illuminating series of 'diary notes', handwritten extracts from her personal journal that frankly describe the day-to-day decisions...Even in this presumably edited form, Black's candid comments on her contemporaries in the state and on the handcraft revival make revealing reading." p.165

Despite this perceived lack of support, Black, "an incredibly good crafts administrator",[251] started on an ambitious development program. This was outlined in 1944 in a ten point agenda which covered exhibitions, teaching and dissemination of information and ideas, and the establishment of standardized pricing and a juried level of design and technical competence which would permit work to be sold with the Division's stamp of approval.

Promotion and information started in January 1944 with a quarterly bulletin, *Handcrafts*, sent free of charge to Nova Scotia craftspeople and others. Initially going to 250 people, by 1952 it had a mailing list of 9000. This was followed in 1947 by *Where to Buy Crafts in Nova Scotia*, an annual booklet listing distributors, shops, Tourist Bureaus and marketing craftspeople. Forty outlets included in the first had increased to 136 by 1956. The first of the annual "Craftsmen-at-Work" exhibitions opened at Simpson's department store in Halifax in 1945. With a large number of service people in the city, attendance was even higher than expected. From 1947 to 1955, the exhibition moved around the province, to Sydney, Amherst, Yarmouth, Truro, Lunenburg, Halifax, Antigonish and *HMCS Cornwallis* giving handcrafts maximum exposure. Also in 1945 a film on Nova Scotia crafts, produced with the co-operation of the Department, was premiered. Black travelled constantly, encouraging the setting up of craft groups (guilds), particularly for weaving, searching out established craftspeople and "especially talented individuals interested in adding to income through the sale of their products,"[252] and, with other field workers, conducting classes.

In 1946 the Division had seven employees and by 1950, ten, including an assistant director, a librarian,[253] a secretary, an instructor in silver jewellery, woodworking and leather tooling, a pottery instructor, a general instructor, two weaving instructors and a tapestry weaving instructor. The emphasis on weaving fitted with the general pattern of activity across the country and with Black's own expertise. Black had trained as an Occupational Therapist at the Royal Victoria Hospital, Montreal and worked from 1922 to 1939 at various hospitals in America. In 1937 she spent some time at the Saterglanten Weaving School, Sweden and by the mid-1940s was an Accredited Master Weaver of both the Boston Society of Fine Arts and the Canadian Guild of Weavers, which she helped found. She had also written *Key to Weaving* (now reprinted 19 times). Her first weaving instructors came from the Acadian area in the extreme south west of the

---

[251] Joyce Chown letter 27 March 1995 Chown studied and taught weaving in Nova Scotia, at Mount Allison University and NSCAD, and for 3 years published with Black *Shuttlecraft Guild Bulletin*

[252] M.Black 'Weaving in Nova Scotia - Yesterday and Today' *Handweaver and Craftsman* 1951 p.7

[253] The Division's office and then the Handcraft Centre had a library of international craft books, bulletins from other craft organizations and designs. In 1952, 495 books and 294 designs were loaned to craftspeople. McKay pp.172-3

Organized craft

province and were probably[254] taught their skills by nuns in Quebec, later weaving instructors were trained at Mount Allison University. However by 1951 many of the students had reached the level of the "junior instructors." As in other rural programs, they travelled through the province with looms, materials and literature teaching groups of six. The first set of lessons dealt with basic weaving, the second with theory and application of theory to projects for home use, and the third covered projects designed for sale through gift shops.[255] The courses were also designed to cover the basic and intermediate requirements of the Guild of Canadian Weavers. The Division set up a Handcrafts Centre in Halifax in 1948 which, amongst other services, ran two week, live-in courses for "weavers interested in production for sale." These students were chosen on merit and returned to pass their skills on to their group. In 1947 there were more than 33 weaving groups receiving teaching and about 20 established groups with approximately 400 members, many in communities devastated by the decline of coal mining. By 1951 there were "probably between six and seven hundred weavers in Nova Scotia, most of whom have received their training through the Provincial Handcrafts program."[256]

Black saw two serious difficulties challenging the success of this commercial handcraft program, the lack both of "good design", particularly that which would "attract the attention of both the discriminating purchaser and the souvenir hunter,"[257] and a smooth and consistent flow of goods from artisan to retailer. Black had a low opinion of both traditional and contemporary Nova Scotian crafts production, McKay suggests that she viewed "local weaving as uninteresting because it simply reproduced standard patterns and did not evoke the creativity of the individual craft worker."[258] As with other cottage craft enterprises, the director's training and perception of market taste influenced products. Like Mowat, Black wanted to create a distinctive regional iconography, particularly related to natural objects, but also to Nova Scotia's history, costumes, legends and industries, "The problem is how to teach people to see these things and how to incorporate them into their handcrafts."[259] However "[w]e cannot afford to alienate our craftsmen by forcing them to use designs which they do not understand and therefore do not like."[260] There

---

[254] Chown letter 27 March 1995 "I am told..." Possibly they attended l'École des Arts Domestiques de Quebec or one of the École Ménagères Regionale.

[255] Black 1951 p.8

[256] Black 1951 p.8

[257] Black 1952 p.159

[258] McKay pp.166-68

[259] Black 1952 p.162

[260] Black 1952 p.160

is a Modernist insistence on simplification and on the articulation of an aesthetic vocabulary, "efforts are constantly being made to awaken producing craftsmen to the innate beauty of his material, with a stress on form and finish, design and mass rather than on ornamentation."[261] Black also separates "technicians" from designers although the program appears to have encouraged potential designer/makers. Solutions to the problem were sought in the creation of 'good' designs sent out as examples or in kits to makers; in the up-grading of instructors through advanced training; through visiting instructors with specialized craft training; and through the employment of European-trained craftspeople living in Canada as designers, teachers and mentors. "Fine crafts"[262] and "artist-craftsman"[263] occur, for the first time in this context, as part of this vocabulary. The Division also started a collection of work presumably exemplifying the best in design from Nova Scotia which numbered 104 pieces[264] by the time Black retired in 1955.

The problem of marketing was two-fold, succinctly stated as "the establishing of better understanding between the producing craftsmen and the retail outlets."[265] Potential retail outlets were either new, small provincial businesses or major chain stores. Small outlets, Black noted, were operating with little or no capital and little knowledge of marketing, inferring that they were without the ability to buy work outright rather than on consignment or to select and promote work appropriately. Major stores, unless they incorporated a specialist craft shop like some branches of Eatons or Simpsons, expected handcrafts to compete with manufactured, and often imported, wares in consistency, quantity and price. The craftsperson was working within small financial margins and was caught between the repetitive production of large quantities of successfully selling articles and the desire or need to spend time developing new designs. Black said that she was "continually hearing criticism of our Nova Scotia, as well as of all Canadian, craftsmen for not producing attractive handcrafted souvenirs, on a mass production level, at a price that the tourist was willing to pay." Her response was that to ask an "artist-craftsman, regardless of his media, to personally mass produce his creation is, to me, a gross fallacy and impossibility."[266]

---

[261] Black 1952 p.162

[262] Black 1952 p.160

[263] McKay p.195

[264] Excluding dolls and toys. The collection continued to be added to until 1982; since then there have been a limited number of acquisitions.

[265] Black quoted McKay p.182

[266] Black quoted McKay p.195

During the pre-war Youth Training Program, the New Brunswick government had employed Aida McAnn, a Masters graduate of Columbia University, New York, to make a thorough study of the development of a handicraft industry in the province and to promote activity through writing articles and representing the province at handcraft exhibitions in Boston and New York. They also opened a school of handcrafts to train Program leaders.[267] This was reinstated in 1946 when New Brunswick set up a Handicrafts Branch under the Department of Finance and Industry. Dr. Ivan H. (Bill) Crowell was appointed Director.

Crowell, a Nova Scotian, graduated from Teacher's College and taught manual training for some years in Nova Scotia. He earned a science doctorate and taught at various colleges. At MacDonald Agricultural College, McGill University, he started "an experiment" in students making for sale handcrafts to pay for their schooling.[268] "This personal project...attracted far wider attention than anticipated. In a few years the project grew into a full Division of McGill University"[269] of which Crowell became first Director in 1943. He was also Administrator for the Canadian Legion Educational Service Handicrafts Project and in the same year the Canadian Red Cross hospital handicrafts course began at the College. This ten week course to prepare women for teaching forces convalescents included the construction of simple equipment and techniques in weaving, leatherwork and rug hooking. In conjunction with these activities Crowell started a Handicrafts Store, "a co-operating organization" of CHG, where various supplies and tools could be purchased (or mail ordered) in kit form and produced a series of inexpensive instruction booklets on various crafts. Initially the *McDonald College Handicrafts Series*, they were reissued as the *Craftsmen's Library*. Edited by Crowell, a projected fifty or so titles, many written by established craftspeople, covered leather, metal, textiles, wood and "sundry" crafts.

The New Brunswick Handicrafts Division operated through the Provincial Handicrafts School in Fredericton which was fully equipped to teach weaving, wood-turning, leatherwork, rug hooking, cutting and polishing of gem stones, fish fly tying and "several sundry projects"[270] and offered a one year advanced courses for program leaders. The school also tried to develop distinctive

---

[267] Beriau 1933(a) p.10

[268] This was hardly a new idea, Mount Allison [University] Handicrafts Guild 1932-c.1944 was established to help students in the weaving school and other craft courses to market their produce thus helping them financially, see chapter 5.

[269] I.Crowell 'Teaching Handicrafts in Canada' CGJ 1943 p.vii Crowell implies that the experiment started when he was already teaching handcrafts. How he moved from plant pathology to handcrafts is not explained, although MacDonald College had had a Home Economics Department at least as early as 1910 and these departments commonly taught crafts.

[270] NAC Massey C2013 16:26:299 Handicrafts Division, New Brunswick Department of Industry and Reconstruction Crowell presentation

saleable articles, presumably as exemplars. As in Nova Scotia and other rural areas, instructors also went to country areas to teach where a minimum of six people requested a course. No course fees were charged and materials and tools were sold at wholesale prices for the first two weeks of a course. For weaving, New Brunswick-made looms were sent ahead to students houses, the rent could be put towards buying the loom. The objective was to promote handcrafts in the province with "most projects slanted to economic ends." The Division co-operated closely with the Guild of New Brunswick Craftsmen, set up in 1947, which set product standards, juried work and awarded a seal of approval valid for one year to work meeting its "standard of excellence." Crowell c.1949 said that more work was bought by the local market than by tourists.[271]

Summary

The craftspeople involved in the activities described in this chapter were predominantly women, producing or embellishing textiles, rural, cash poor and working at home where they frequently provided their own materials and equipment. Choice of product, product design, skills upgrading or teaching, and marketing organization were largely done by 'outsiders'. Where these, as was usually the case, were academically trained craftswomen, design and product were mainly dictated by their perception of outside market demand and tended not to be typical of articles made in the maker's community. Despite the pressure of economic circumstances, makers chose whether to discard or modify traditional products and designs, by not working through marketing organizations or by choosing sympathetic markets, by continuing to make traditional articles as well as producing non-traditional commercial products, or by upgrading skills[272] or learning new techniques and designs which might also become a part of the community's repertoire. Although many commercial products demanded of the maker little more than a basic knowledge of technique, the required level of manual dexterity and an ability to follow instructions, others required creativity, initiative and knowledge. Some makers functioned as technicians, some as designer/makers, others moved between the two or developed from the former to the latter. Craftspeople also moved to being marketers and there were many individual and smaller scale marketing initiatives by craftspeople within a community and by local or outsider entrepreneurs, these appear to have increased with the development of tourism.

Where craftspeople worked in a centre, it was perceived as full time work however home-based work was disparaged as a spare time activity, "The loom is permanently set up and sometimes, while waiting for dinner to cook or the men to come home, another inch or two is added."[273] The

---

[271] NAC Massey C2013 16:26:299 Crowell, discussion

[272] I am not inferring a low level of skill in traditional work however standards acceptable in a domestic setting were not necessarily so in the market.

[273] A.Leitch 'The Tartan Weavers of Cape Breton' *CGJ* 56:5:197 1958(b)

amount of time home-based makers spent on their craft was probably dictated by financial need and the demands of household, farm or other duties. Haska Chutskoff, Saskatchewan worked at "least nine hours each day" for three weeks on one project[274] and there are other examples of long working days. Work also may have been intermittent or seasonal. The financial rewards for labour-intensive, skilled work were, for the makers, poor. Entrepreneurial middlemen (or women) appear to have fared well. The market value of craft work probably varied depending on the point of sale or commission.

The voluntary organizations involved in conserving, reviving and/or marketing craft, and in promoting it through exhibitions and education were conceived and run by women. National organizations such as the WI and similar rural women's organizations, and ethnic, provincial or local organizations such as SACS focused entirely on craft or included craft as an important part of their program. They provided a community which supported and recognised makers, upheld standards and through their craft education programs provided work for trained women instructors. Given its time-frame, vision, national and international scope, and achievements, CHG was the national craft organization and appears an organization unique to Canada during this period.

Government departments' initial involvement with crafts was aimed at rural women through programs to improve living standards and, in western Canada, to Canadianize non-anglophone immigrant groups. There was little vision of craft beyond the making of functional domestic furnishings and clothing aiming at self-sufficiency for cash-poor settlers. Craft was seen as a moral good and productive of contentment. As a result of successful private initiatives in cottage industries and the private and corporate use of distinctive regional crafts as tourist attractions, governments, particularly in eastern Canada, began to consider craft as an income generator to supplement seasonal or part-time employment in depressed or unstable economies and as an adjunct to an increased dependence on tourism in areas of de-industrialization. Most government action was politically driven and reactive, and therefore unstable and short term. Federal government reports indicate that, unlike the elite fine arts, crafts were so genuinely embedded in community life that bureaucrats had problems in separating the component parts, and in dealing with the scale of production which was that of small, independent units producing small quantities of relatively low-priced goods.

Positioned against the historiography, this account both diverges from and reinforces aspects of it. In particular, this account details and underlines the contribution of New Canadians, noticeably lacking in the historiography.

This account also touches on two activities of relevance to museums. The first concerns the

---

[274] SKAB SACS B88-E Correspondence 1925 Chutskoff to Morton 30 November 1925

intervention of mainly academically trained craftspeople as organizers from outside the makers' community, and the concurrent demands of a non-traditional market. Recent and deliberate outsider intervention would, in the view of an ethnologist such as Barbeau, disrupt the clear line of transmission in makers presumed isolated and inviolate. Barbeau in a 1948 article 'Are the Real Folk Arts and Crafts Dying Out?' answered in the affirmative,

> "In the last two decades, a well-meant but misleading educational effort has heavily contributed to demoralize handicrafts...talent among weavers has been snuffed out; ancient patterns...have fallen into discredit; invention and self-reliance...have been branded as futile...A centralized control, through the agency of rural clubs, has proved efficient but deadly..."[275]

However it is clear from WAAC/CHG accounts at the turn of the century that the organization was 'reviving traditions', that is encouraging the use of older motifs and vegetable dyeing. It is open to question how divergent WAAC/CHG's researches and 'revivals' were from Barbeau's conceptualization of traditional Québécois textiles, and given WAAC/CHG's thirty years or longer of activity in the province before Barbeau started collecting, how many 'revivals' became part of Barbeau's collections. The second activity is that of craft collecting throughout the period by craft organizations.

---

[275] M.Barbeau 'Are the Real Folk Arts and Crafts Dying Out?' *CA* 1948 p.133

CHAPTER 5
STUDIO CRAFT:
"NOT ONLY A CRAFT BUT A *MAJOR* ART"[1]

Positioned against the craftspeople defined by the activity of many but not all of the organizations discussed in the previous chapter, the historiography refers to another group - "professionals", "craft designers", "artists", "Studio Crafts" - and infers a hierarchy. Barbeau presumed a hierarchy of media and maker. Makers are contrasted professional/ folk, formally trained (which does not necessarily mean academic training)/ informally trained and urban/ rural. Ringland echoes this. Thus the literature defines the studio craftsperson by class, income generation and formal education which are components of 'professional', and media which is allied with formal education, and self-concept. The literature also shows 'craft' positioned with 'art'. 'Studio' therefore also links craft to the elite fine arts and suggests a stronger emphasis on an articulated aesthetic, and on 'decoration' rather than 'function'. This chapter will survey academic craft education and the activities of studio craftspeople.

Academic craft education

Academic craft education is defined as that taught through a recognised tertiary level education institute,[2] whether public or independent, in which a standard program leading to a paper qualification is taught to groups of students.

Lack of published data affects all aspects of this area. The Canadian Almanac[3] lists no art schools in the first decades of the twentieth century although between 1900 and 1919 I know of seven.[4] The Almanac does list craft media and applied art courses[5] in women's colleges, however even

---

[1] Wood 1944 p.191

[2] Tertiary is used with the proviso that the period saw changing standards, requirements and achievements, and the growing and uncertain hierarchy of universities, colleges, institutes etc.

[3] *The Canadian Almanac* (Toronto 1889, 1901, 1913, 1915, 1916, 1920, 1925, 1926)

[4] These are probably only a fraction of those that existed.

[5] Including 'manual training' and 'shop work', the first often taught by women. F.Simon *History of the Alberta Provincial Institute of Technology and Art* M.Ed. thesis (Calgary 1962) p.23 suggests that 'manual training' consisted mainly of woodwork.

these listings disappear by the late 1920s. The few art schools that have a published history tend to priorize fine arts.

Tertiary level craft education in Canada became available through a variety of institutions which in the first decades of the twentieth century included art schools, independent or attached to museums, colleges or universities, with public funding or privately run; and technical, vocational, education (Normal) or domestic science schools/colleges. I have chosen to look at eight institutions which offered a range of craft courses but vary in locale, institutional situation, focus, history and influence. By 1900, three of these institutions were active. They were the Owens School of Art at Sackville, NB, the Ontario School of Art, Toronto and the Victoria School of Art and Design, Halifax, NS. The second decade of the twentieth century saw the establishment of a linked gallery and art school in Winnipeg, MB; an art school linked with a technical school, the Provincial Institute of Technology and Art, Calgary, AB; and two important craft departments within technical schools, the pottery department of the Toronto Central Technical School and the cabinetry department of l'École Technique, Montreal which became an independent craft school in 1935. The Vancouver School of Decorative and Applied Arts opened in the mid-1920s

The Dominion government took an early interest in 'vocational', as opposed to 'professional', education and made a number of funding initiatives which affected the economic viability of many 'art schools' or student's ability to access craft education. The first of these was the Royal Commission on Technical Education 1910-1913. Resulting from this Commission, funding was designated to support the implementation of vocational education under the 1913 Agricultural Assistance Act. However WWI delayed implementation until 1919 when a new act was passed. This act, made in agreement with the provinces, provided $1,000,000 to be spent over a ten year period with the provinces matching the Dominion contribution.[6] The 1937 Dominion-Provincial Youth Training Program[7] was another federal/provincial matching funding program. The federal annual appropriation of $1,000,000 was under the Agricultural and Employment Relief Act. Both World Wars brought Dominion government assistance for the rehabilitation of disabled and returned soldiers which affected craft education directly through increased enrollment, of veterans and of students interested in occupational therapy and teaching.

---

[6] Simon pp.109,110

[7] referred to in chapter 4, Governments, reconstruction and marketing: Federal government initiatives and reports

Owens Art Museum[8] and Owens School of Art, Saint John, 1884-1893/ Mount Allison Ladies' College, Sackville, 1854-1937/ Mount Allison University, Department of Applied Art, Sackville, 1937-1961, NB[9]

In 1854, a "Female Branch"[10] was added to the Wesleyan Academy, later to become Mount Allison University, in the small town of Sackville. The art teachers were women until 1869 when John W.Grey became first Professor of Art and Head of the Department. In 1893,[11] the Owens Art Institution was attached to the Ladies' College. The Institution had been set up in 1884 in the largest city in the province, Saint John, as the result of a bequest. By 1893, it included a school directed by John Hammond R.C.A. (1843-1939), a collection of paintings, prints and sculptures, and financial problems. The negotiations with Mount Allison provided that the collection and school would be housed in a specially erected building. John Hammond remained head of the Art School.

When Hammond retired in 1916, Elizabeth McLeod R.C.A,[12] who had joined the teaching staff while still a student in 1896, ran the department (she was not officially recognised as Head of Department until 1930.) The staff, with one brief exception, were all women until the advent of Stanley Royle as Head of the Fine Art Department just prior to the closing of the Ladies College in 1937. Most were graduates of the College and had post-graduate training which qualified them to teach both fine and applied art. Amongst the earliest were Christian Harris McKiel,[13] later to

---

[8] The school continued to be referred to as the Owens Art Museum after it moved to Sackville.

[9] all abbreviated to UMA

[10] Women's education, as in many Ladies Colleges, was taken seriously. In 1872 a motion was passed:"Ladies having regularly matriculated and completed the course of study prescribed by this board shall be entitled to receive the degrees in the arts and the faculties upon the same terms and conditions as are now or may hereafter be imposed on male students of the college." Three years later the first woman in the British Empire to be awarded a degree (B.Sc) graduated from Mount Allison, followed seven years later by the first woman to be awarded a B.A in Canada.

[11] Dates given frequently vary, usually only by a year. If possible I have chosen the date most frequently mentioned, if not the earlier.

[12] Elizabeth McLeod RCA (1875-1963)Educated: Mount Allison Ladies' College; "advanced study" 1902-1906 at the Student's Art League, New York, Columbia University, and "under such outstanding teachers as Maud Mason, Robert Henri and Charles Hawthorne. She also spent a year abroad studying in the museums of Europe." *Mount Allison Record* Winter 1964 47:1:25 obituary

[13] Christian Harris McKiel (1889-1978) Educated: Mount Allison Ladies' College to 1911, then New York. Taught at Mount Allison 1913-1917, 1922-1950, becoming Head of the newly formed Department of Applied Arts in 1938.

become Head of the Applied Arts Department, and Sarah Stewart Hart[14] who taught from 1908 until the Department closed in 1961. Cliff Eyland, Fredette Frame[15] and Ruth Stanton comment on the commitment to teaching and to being practicing artists characteristic of the staff and particularly of McLeod.

Crowell says that "certificates of proficiency in handicrafts" were awarded from 1904,[16] and according to Ryder in 1910 the school began offering a three year course in applied arts.[17] "In 1908 applied art courses in leatherwork, woodcarving and copper etching were introduced, followed by metalworking in the newly completed basement of the Owens Gallery."[18] Frame adds china painting and basketry in 1908.[19] The 1910/11 Prospectus offers courses in Design, including "the study of historic ornament and the application of its principles, also the development of original ideas in the decoration of book covers, wall paper, textiles, etc"; Leather Work, "tooling, modelling, incising, staining, stencilling, etc."; Wood Carving; Metal Work, "hammered and chased brass, copper and silver utensils, such as bowls, trays, candlesticks, etc., and jewelry; also the setting of semi-precious stones"; and China Painting as well as other arts courses. Accompanying pictures of students' work in wood carving, metal working, jewel setting and china painting show a range of contemporary Arts and Crafts style motifs.[20] Frame comments, "the finished pieces were of a highly developed nature."[21]

Ruth Stanton recalls that as a student in 1920 she was required to complete a year of basic qualifying courses equivalent to a final year of high school before embarking on the three year

---

[14] Sarah Stewart Hart (1880-1981) Educated: Ontario Provincial Art School, certificate in wood carving 1899; Womens' Art School and Cooper Union School, New York c.1900 to 1906. Mount Allison University Archives biography file (pre 1981) Also taught weaving, leather work and silver smithing.

[15] F.Frame *Mount Allison Ladies' College 1854-1937* catalogue (Sackville 1994) n/p McLeod was particularly well thought of. Ruth Stanton, one of her students, says "she was a wonderful, strict, v[ery] talented teacher." letter 28 June 1997

[16] Crowell p.87 These may have been a teaching qualification.

[17] Tweedie p.264

[18] C.Eyland et al *Atque Ars: Art from Mount Allison University 1854-1989* catalogue (New Brunswick 1989)

[19] Frame n/p

[20] UMA.A Mount Allison Ladies' College prospectus 1910-1911 p.71, [73, 75]

[21] Frame n/p

diploma course in applied arts.²² At that time McLeod taught drawing, painting and china painting, McKiel taught drawing, painting and design. Florence Huestis taught wood carving, silver working and jewellery, and Miss Hutter taught basket weaving. Textile painting, copper work, batik, history of art and English were also taught but leatherwork was not. There already seems to have been a division into a fine arts and an applied arts department. The former, painting, drawing and wood carving, was "upstairs", the applied arts studios which consisted of large, well-lit workrooms were "downstairs." Katherine Hammond Krug, a 1927 graduate recalled, "Fine Arts students were required to do courses in design and crafts as well, including printmaking, leatherwork, metalwork, weaving²³ and batik."²⁴ Winifred McGill Fox, a 1930 graduate, said that when McLeod heard of her experience looking at cross-sections through a microscope, she sent her entire design course to the University's biology laboratory to study microscope slides as an inspiration for design.²⁵

Despite the application of the students and the high standard of work, for women students, "Expectations of a job - we did not have any beyond getting married",²⁶ however a proportion did find employment and Ryder says,

> "The resulting well-trained corps of graduates slowly spread through the province, teaching and instructing other schools and groups in the fundamentals of good workmanship, the use of colour, and the importance of design."²⁷

In 1930 McLeod officially became Department Head. In 1935 Stanley Royle, trained at Sheffield

---

[22] Ruth Stanton (b.1905 Yarmouth NS) graduated in May 1924 aged 19. "My graduation thesis was on Cezanne - That was v[ery] daring and considered a most unusual choice." Ruth Stanton letter 28 June 1997.

[23] Stanton is quite definite that weaving was not taught while she was at the Ladies College. In 1932 there is correspondence between CHG:HQ and University President, G.T.Trueman about sources of looms for a prospective weaving school (Ellen McLeod personal communication) and in Massey C2005 CHG 'Notes on CHG 1901-1948' Mount Allison is noted as starting weaving courses in 1932.

[24] Eyland p.17

[25] Interview with Winifred Fox 1 November 1997

[26] In fact, on graduating Mrs Stanton went to Boston where her first job was painting cards for Rustcraft. She then applied to Bloomingdale ['Mental'] Hospital to take a six month occupational therapist course "a new course at the time" and on graduation worked as an occupational therapist. In the 1930s, after a number of misfortunes, she trained as a nurse - reluctantly, "it was far from my beloved arts and crafts" - graduated with Honours and a scholarship to University of Toronto where she took Public Health Nursing. In the 1940s she went to Yellowknife, NWT with her doctor husband, where in 1946 she started the CHG:Yellowknife Branch. On her husband's retirement she moved to Saltspring Island where she started a weavers guild. Ruth Stanton letter 28 June 1997

[27] Tweedie p.264

School of Art, moved from the Nova Scotia School of Art and Design to become Head of the Fine Art Department, displacing McLeod.[28] In 1937 the Ladies' College was closed and the University of Mount Allison absorbed the fine and applied arts programs. At this time Mount Allison started a four year degree program with specialization in the last two years in fine arts or public school art teaching. This appears to have been the only university degree of this sort at the time. "The two year diploma course in applied art also continued."[29]

With integration into the University, McKiel became Head of the newly designated Applied Arts Department.[30] A fellow faculty member was Ellis Roulston, also a Mount Allison graduate who gained an Applied Arts Certificate in 1937, and a B.A. in 1941. Ellis Roulston was to become the last Head of the Applied Art Department in 1951[31] teaching, with his brother Maxwell Roulston and Sarah Hart, until the department closed in 1961.

The School was affected by the Depression and by the War. Under the direction of McLeod the Mount Allison Handicrafts Guild was set up in 1932 to form an outlet for the work of art students, in order to help fund schooling. In line with production outside the University, the Guild turned its energy to the weaving of tweeds "using exclusively wools from the Maritime provinces." A range of suitings, drapes, runners and upholstery material was produced, some to customer's specifications. The quality must have been high and the tweeds were renowned for their "beautiful pastel shades." By 1939, up to 1200 yards of material a year was being produced and sold through the Guild office, the CHG:ON shop at Eaton's, Toronto and other outlets in the Maritimes, and was exhibited at the Sportmen's Show in Boston and New York, and at the 1938 British Empire Exhibition in Glasgow, Scotland, and the New York World's Fair.

---

[28] McLeod taught until her retirement in 1947. Royle left in 1945.

[29] J.G.Reid *Mount Allison University: A History to 1963* (Toronto 1984) p.126 However Reid later says, referring to the early 1950s, in applied arts, a new 2 year diploma course in handicrafts, designed for those who wished to acquire craft skills for their own use, was added to the existing 3 year applied arts certificate course, taken primarily by teachers. p.258

[30] Eyland p.15

[31] Ellis Roulston d.1973 learned silversmithing from Jean Dixon, a Ladies' College graduate, who was taught by Jean Smith educated at the Pratt Institute, Brooklyn, New York one of the first schools offering courses in art metal and jewellery. Jean Dixon had a silver necklace and a bracelet of silver, ivory, coral and green enamel c.1930 in the exhibition curated by Frame 1994. Dixon only taught metalsmithing for one year at Mount Allison, her salary for the year was $35. Roulston also studied with Eric Fleming at the Konstfackskolan, Stockholm 1950-51. Both Roulston and his brother Maxwell who joined the faculty in 1948 were described in Tweedie p.269 as exceptionally skilled and gifted silversmiths, pictures show hollow-ware and cutlery. While he was in Sweden, Ellis Roulston did a weaving course at the Handarbetets Vanner, Stockholm. He is described (by Chown) as a traditional weaver. From 1961 until his death in 1973, he was Chief of Handcrafts Instruction, Continuing Education Division, Department of Education, NS.

Studio Craft

The 1939-40 year saw only 12 full-time students, 20 University students taking one course, 30 "not otherwise registered in the University, taking one course[,] 6 taking two or more courses."[32] That year the 'Arts and Crafts Department' offered programs in "Commercial Posters and Advertising, Costume Design, Lettering and Manuscript Work, Weaving, Wood Carving, Jewelry and Beaten Metal, Leather Tooling, Leather Carving, Basketry, Pottery, Lino-Blocking, Batiks."[33] Pictures of work c.1943 show wheel-thrown pottery and some imaginative leatherwork motifs. This program must have continued through the next decade as Royle's successor as director, Lawren Harris, stressed in the early 1950s that,

> "Mount Allison School did not cater only for those who wished to become professional painters, but also provided training for careers in commercial and advertising art, industrial design, and teaching of the fine and applied arts."[34]

During this half century, other tertiary institutions providing a craft education opened in the province. In 1926 the Saint John Vocational School opened on Douglas Avenue near the Museum. The Department of Fine and Applied Art was headed by Violet A.Gillett A.R.C.A.,[35] who came from teaching at the Central Technical School (CTS), Toronto (see below). In 1928 she took educational leave to study design at the Royal College of Art, London and toured Europe on a scholarship. Gillett was assisted by Julia Crawford, who had gained an Honours in Design from the Pratt Institute, New York one of the earliest American schools to teach art metal, jewellery and ceramics. Details of their craft programs are not available,

> "There was very little published during the time that Violet Gillett and Julia Crawford were at the Vocational School."[36]

Given the vicinity of the Museum, it is to be assumed that Gillett was aware of the collection of "Industrial Art" and contemporary New Brunswick pottery and weaving put together by Alice Webster, particularly as Webster was an enthusiastic educator and had chosen works for their educational value and in the hope of encouraging production in home industries.[37] In 1949/50 the Vocational School calendar for the Department of Fine and Applied Art says,

> "The school is fortunate in being situated near the New Brunswick Museum,

---

[32] UMA.A Report of the President 1939-40

[33] UMA.A Report of the President 1939-40

[34] Reid p.258

[35] Gillett (1898 -?) educated at the Normal School, Fredericton to 1915; 1920-1925 Ontario College of Art

[36] Peter Larocque Curator NBM personal communication 23 September 1997

[37] see chapter 6 Eastern Canada: New Brunswick Museum

where a splendid art library, exhibitions of art of the past and present...are available for study."

In 1946 Gillett also became Consultant to the Handicraft Division of the Department of Industry and Reconstruction,[38] which in 1946 restarted the New Brunswick Handicraft Training Centre under Ivan Crowell.[39] At this time the Centre provided one year technical courses primarily for adult education craft instructors.[40] Gillett was also involved with the Guild of New Brunswick Craftsmen.

Victoria School (College) of Art and Design 1887/Nova Scotia College of Art 1925/Nova Scotia College of Art and Design, Halifax 1963[41]
Thirtytwo years after the Mount Allison Ladies College and three years after the Owens Art Museum and Art School were established in the neighbouring province of New Brunswick, the Victoria School of Art and Design was started in 1887 in the provincial capital of Nova Scotia, Halifax, as the result of energetic activity by a group of women led by Anna Leonowens.[42] The Constitution of the School was:

> "a) to provide technical instruction and art culture to persons employed in the various trades, manufacturers, &c., requiring artistic skill;
> b) to open up new and remunerative employment for women;
> c) to prepare the teachers of the Province for the teaching of industrial drawing in the Public Schools;
> d) to educate public taste by establishing exhibitions and classes in the fine arts as far as practicable."[43]

---

[38] In 1948 Gillett resigned both positions to start her own studio at Andover, NB, with her sister and some local women, producing a range of crafts but becoming famous for Gillett's hand stencilled fabrics. Gillett produced and/or designed for clay sculpture, stencilled fabrics, enamels, book binding, hooked rugs and quilts.

[39] Crowell had formerly been Director of a handcraft department at MacDonald [Agricultural] College, McGill University primarily concerned with adult education and leisure crafts.

[40] In the mid 1940s courses included woodturning, weaving, stonework, leatherwork and pottery. In 1952 55% students came from New Brunswick, 30% from the USA, 15% from other provinces. In 1969, the renamed New Brunswick Handicraft School offered a 2 year course and direct community instruction had largely ended, the concentration on technical training did not end until 1978.
New Brunswick College of Craft and Design 1995-6 prospectus pp.3-4

[41] all abbreviated to NSCA

[42] formerly tutor to the children of the King of Siam

[43] D.Soucy, H.Pearse *The First Hundred Years: A History of the Nova Scotia College of Art and Design* (Halifax 1993) pp.14-15

Studio Craft 175

Survival as an independent institution meant ongoing effort for its predominantly female supporters and Board to ensure the support of the Halifax public. For its mainly female staff it meant uncertain prospects, poor pay, and a wide range of clients and facilities. In 1900 Alice Egan Hagen taught china painting at Halifax Ladies' College under the aegis of NSCA,[44] Marion Graham taught 'elementary'[45] classes from 1892 to 1913 and "served with little pay for 21 years", and in the 1920s and early 1930s Margaret Brodie, and later Nellie Adams, taught a class at Dalhousie University dental school in metal work, carving for teeth and colouring for teeth.[46]

In the first two decades of the twentieth century, there are barely more than hints that the School taught crafts.[47] In 1904, a year after the School moved into the top floor of the old National School Building,[48] an exhibition of hand and loom work by Doukhobor women coincided with the annual School exhibition, "Large crowds attended, paying a small fee and sipping tea as they viewed the crafts and art."[49] A. McKay, the School Secretary, wanted to increase the School's emphasis on applied design, by teaching design applied to book covers, advertisements, furniture, interiors and other objects associated with the home or with small industry.[50] Around 1910-11, Lewis Smith, the Principal, "increased the number of courses available by including work in crafts", in 1912 these included "Repousse Metal, Wood Carving, etc."[51] There is no indication of who taught craft courses. From 1913 to 1916 there was only one member of staff.

Arthur Lismer[52] came to the School as Principal in 1916. At that time it was still struggling for existence, it had 12 students. In 1917, referring to Halifax, he wrote,
"In the field of industrial design and in the endeavour to instruct sound principles
of order and beauty and the need of good workmanship to make a useful thing

---

[44] Soucy p.47

[45] Soucy p.26 The elementary or C class was for specialist art teachers who would teach in private schools or academies, and for others interested in a fine arts career.

[46] Soucy p.103

[47] It is not clear whether this reflects Soucy and Pearce's focus on fine arts, or a dearth of records from this period. According to Soucy it is by a fluke that the records still exist.

[48] The bottom floor was rented out to provide the school with income.

[49] Soucy p.51

[50] Soucy p.53

[51] Soucy p.60 The latter is quoted from a Victoria School of Art and Design 1912 flyer.

[52] Lismer 1885-1969 Educated: Sheffield School of Art, Academie des Beaux Arts, Belgium

also a thing of beauty, there is wide scope for the foundation of a good technical school of art."[53]

A pamphlet for the School said,

"The Victoria School of Art aims to supply facilities for thorough and practical study of Fine and Applied Art, and offers interesting and valuable courses of instruction to students, craftspeople, teachers and public school scholars"

which included,

"The Principles of Design and their application to Decoration and the making of simple and useful articles."[54]

However it is not made clear whether craft courses *per se* as well as Principles of Design were taught under Lismer.

Under Lismer's nominee and successor in 1919, Elizabeth Styring Nutt,[55] who was also educated at Sheffield School of Art, the fortunes of the school improved and stabilized. Nutt promoted the importance of commercial art and crafts, claiming that the College was training much needed art workers. In 1919 classes in embroidery, modelling, metal work and basketry were taught, "enrollment and spirits were high." Margaret Brodie was hired to teach two craft courses and was soon promoted to full-time head of crafts. In 1920 jewellery and leatherwork courses were added. By 1921 the School curriculum was in seven sections, one being Crafts. "Students were encouraged to engage in crafts, applied design, commercial art and other forms of art for practical ends."[56] By 1924 Nutt required students to take at least one course in the craft department because, "Crafts alone can make a design a real thing."[57]

By 1925, Nutt had persuaded the province and the city to match the annual funding for vocational education provided by the Dominion government since 1919.[58] In addition, through a Provincial act the Victoria School of Art and Design became the Nova Scotia College of Art. Its college status allowed it to affiliate with a university and confer degrees. Nutt proposed an

---

[53] Soucy p.71

[54] Soucy p.74

[55] Nutt 1870-1946 Educated Sheffield Art School; post-graduate studies with Stanhope Forbes; a year's study on a scholarship at the Sorbonne, Paris; two years with Professor Sim in Florence; an Art Masters Diploma from the University of Sheffield.

[56] Soucy pp.87-8

[57] Victoria School of Art and Design Annual Report 1924 quoted Soucy p.196

[58] NSCA continued to receive federal, provincial and city funding until 1936 when the federal funding ceased, however provincial and city funding continued.

affiliation with Dalhousie University in 1938 to offer a BFA degree but the College did not take advantage of its status until 1962.[59]

From 1925 to 1931 when Margaret Brodie retired, 'Design, Decorative Art and Crafts' formed one of six curriculum areas. Serious students usually received diplomas from more than one area. Fine arts students were required to study applied design and to produce craft objects. The College offered at least basic instruction in batik, weaving, basketry, raffia work, leather work, stencilling, toy making, jewellery, rug making, wood carving and the production of lamp shades. Brodie had been joined by Marjorie Robertson, teaching evening craft classes, Nellie Drysdale as student assistant, and S.L.Shannon teaching wood carving. All were graduates of the School. Between 1919 and 1943, when Nutt retired, teaching was also done by student teachers and by volunteers. I have come across no pictures of work so it is impossible to tell what range and standard of work was being produced.[60]

Facilities at the College continued to be poor. Local women's groups, including LCW:Halifax, IODE and the Catholic Women's League, continued to support the College and had long campaigned for a new building which would house both the College and a provincial gallery. This campaign had included, in 1928, asking every woman in the province to contribute a dollar towards the College building fund. Lack of space and facilities meant that when Brodie retired in 1931, her successor as head of the craft department, Ellen Adams, could only teach a basic program of leatherwork, clay, lampshade making and weaving "on the College's small loom." Adams, another NSCA graduate (1930) "who had earned five scholarship years," had previously taught at the Nova Scotia Tuberculosis Hospital, the Young Women's Christian Association and private classes in her own home. In 1935-6 the craft department took over the *ground* floor of the college building and was "now able to have suitable rooms for clay modelling and work in other media."[61] But from 1939 to 1945 "Nellie Adams continued to teach craft classes in the *basement* which housed the kiln...Teaching a wide range of crafts to a broad spectrum of students under such cramped, drafty, and fume-filled conditions took its toll on Adam's health and she resigned in 1945." (my italics)[62] Despite these conditions, pottery, weaving, "exquisite

---

[59] Soucy p.125

[60] Frame said of 'Mount Allison Ladies' College 1854-1937' "Much of the artwork for this exhibition came from private collections, particularly those of family members, passed on through generations, or from old friends. Sadly there is little trace of these women artists in public collections."

[61] Soucy p.127

[62] Soucy p.132

needlework...and embroidery of great beauty" was taught.[63]

As with other art schools, enrollment during WWII dropped to a "handful of full-time students", "dozens of school children" and, not surprisingly in an Atlantic port city, a "steady flow of service men and women" who wanted to study art, hone previously acquired skills or relax.[64] For a small fee materials were supplied, no prescribed program was followed.

The post-war period saw the largest enrollment in the College's history as discharged service personnel looked for career training.[65] The College claimed almost 500 students, although full-time, "professional" students comprised only ten per cent.[66] Between 1945-1950, the craft department was particularly active.

> "A hundred or more study pottery and weaving, work in leather, metal and jewellery...Wood carving and other crafts in newly equipped work rooms have attracted many spare time craftsmen and women and their work shown in recent handicraft exhibits has been very well received."[67]

Even if newly equipped, the department was still desperately short of space, the "cramped, drafty and fume-filled" conditions had not improved. An oil-fired kiln was used which had to be constantly monitored during firing, Homer Lord[68] expected to spend two or three nights a week at the College. Lead glazes were sprayed, and scraped up for recycling, leaving "a sweet taste in the mouth."[69] Materials were expensive and in short supply. Experiments were made in using

---

[63] E.Florence Blackwood, Acting Administrative Head 1943 quoted Soucy p.131

[64] Soucy p.131

[65] Discharged servicemen were offered housing or education.

[66] Mrs Betty Lord, wife of Homer Lord, interview Halifax July 1995. "When you finished there were no openings, no jobs. Some of the men went into television props and graphics...It was harder for girls...I can't remember anyone making a living." Betty Lord graduated in 1950. Work with the Handicraft Division was unobtainable because the government would not employ married women. Lord taught classes in occupational therapy part-time, leather work, weaving and pottery with Homer Lord, she also taught at the tuberculosis hospital part-time, at the Y[WCA?] and the School for the Deaf. Most of this may have been volunteer.

[67] *Chronicle* January 1946 quoted Soucy p.136

[68] Homer Lord Educated: NSCA, a student of Church, who was herself a student of Hagen; taught NSCA 1948-1988 becoming Head of Crafts to 1969. Homer Lord also worked with Hagen for a period, firing kilns for her. Betty Lord also went to Hagen as student although she says that Hagen's pottery was poor.

[69] Interview Mrs Betty Lord, July 1995. Homer Lord suffered emphysema directly attributable to working conditions.

Studio Craft

local materials such as clay for pottery, and amethyst, agate and other semi-precious stones for jewellery. Employment conditions for staff had not improved, Homer Lord taught for nine years before becoming full-time, pay was poor and there were no perks.[70]

Staffed, at various times, by Mary Chute Powers, John Bradford,[71] Emelie 'Nim' Church (Roulston),[72] Mary Armitage, Maxwell Roulston, Adele Hunter, Joan Frazer, Phyllis LeBlanc, Bessie Murray[73] and Homer Lord, classes were taught in silversmithing, jewellery, weaving, needlework, embroidery, wood carving, leather work and pottery. Donald C. MacKay,[74] who became principal in 1945, was particularly interested in the work of early Nova Scotia silversmiths,[75] and organized and promoted classes in silversmithing. In 1949 silversmithing had an enrollment of 50 students which gave rise to the Nova Scotia branch of the Metal Arts Guild in 1951. Whatever the facilities, by 1950 NSCA had a well-established crafts course and a second Principal with an interest in craft.

Mount St. Bernard College, Antigonish, from 1917 had offered training in crafts and by 1943 the program had expanded to be, according to Crowell,[76] one of the most comprehensive in Canada. The three year course leading to a diploma was recognised by the Nova Scotia Department of Education as a license to teach crafts in the province. Regrettably Crowell does not detail the

---

[70] Staff had to wait until the advent of G.N.Kennedy as President (Principal) in 1967 for a rise in salaries and pensions. Betty Lord, interview July 1995

[71] John Bradford self-taught, founder-president Atlantic Wood-Carvers Guild, 1st president Nova Scotia Craftsmens Guild, 1942-44 correspondent with Interdepartmental Committee on Canadian Handicrafts, exhibited widely.

[72] Emelie (or Emily) 'Nim' Church married Max Roulston. A student of Alice Hagen and a "talented potter." 1946-1950 taught at Acadia University with Helen Beals

[73] Mrs Elizabeth Rosemary Murray b.1912 England, Lancashire College of Art with City and Guilds Embroidery, to Canada 1938, taught NSCA 1940-49 embroidery; Halifax Ladies College 1950s art; NS Handcraft Centre consultant designer 1950-60; co-author with Mary Black *You Can Weave* 1974

[74] MacKay (1906-)Principal 1945-1967 grad NSCA 1928, post-graduate studies, Chelsea School of Art London, Academie Colorossi, Paris, University of Toronto with Lismer; taught Northern Vocational School, Toronto, education staff Art Gallery Toronto 1933-34, instructor NSCA 1934, vice-principal 1936, lecturer art history Dalhousie University 1938, war service.

[75] MacKay became foremost connoisseur and collector of silver in Nova Scotia, published books, and advised Henry Birks on the Birks Collection of crafted silver pieces.

[76] Crowell *CGJ* p.87

program although pottery was one craft taught by 1947.[77]

Mary Black, Head of the Nova Scotia Department of Trade and Industry, Handcraft Division (1943), offers a critique of college courses. She "was deeply convinced that handicrafts could and should be a profession; weaving, for example, should be governed by accreditation procedures."[78] McKay argues this and her unsuccessful search for handcraft teachers she considered competent, led Black to have "little confidence in the existing centres of craft training" in Nova Scotia. In 1946, "[a]fter a 'thorough investigation' of Mount Allison's program, Black decided to give the students a 'stiff orientation course' herself."[79] In 1943, of a handcraft class at Mount St. Bernard "she wrote tersely: 'no originality, designs poor.'"[80] She wrote that the setting up of a training centre would encounter,

> "many problems - one of the most acute being the securing of properly trained personnel to direct its activities. In all likelihood these teachers will have to be brought in from outside the Province."

In the late 1940s Black complained that she could not find anyone to teach "advanced craft techniques."[81] McKay argues that Black was convinced that only Europeans would be able to teach crafts at an advanced level and introduce more sophisticated concepts of design, and that she actively recruited craftspeople such as Konrad and Krystyna Sadowski,[82] Mrs Valborg Pedersen[83] and Bessie Murray. It is hard to discern what interaction and cross-influences there were between NSCA and the Handcraft Division's Handcraft Centre and marketing and exhibition programs, both in terms of the organizations and in terms of their craft communities.

---

[77] *Where to Buy Crafts in Nova Scotia* Handcraft Division, Nova Scotia Department of Trade and Industry 1947 "Mount Saint Bernard School of Pottery"

[78] McKay p.191

[79] McKay p.191

[80] McKay p.167

[81] Contrary to what he has implied earlier about the program at Mount Allison, MaKay then says "Although veterans from the Mount Allison program and the Newfoundland Handcrafts Centre in St. John's could fill this gap to some extent." p.191

[82] McKay describes the Sadowskis as Polish emigres who "represented Black's ideal of European handicraft culture." p.193 The Sadowskis had been invited to come to Canada from Brazil. Krystyna Sadowska's training at the Academy of Fine Art, Warsaw included weaving, she became renowned for her tapestries. Konrad Sadowski studied painting in Paris briefly. Konrad and Krystyna studied ceramics with Dora Billington at the Central School of Arts and Crafts, London after the war. From 1953 to his death in 1960, Sadowski was Head of Ceramics at OCA, and Sadowska taught tapestry there.

[83] Pedersen was a weaver, a graduate of Kage Technical School, Denmark who operated her own studio in Copenhagen before WWII.

Studio Craft

Ontario School of Art, Toronto 1876/ Central Ontario School of Art and [Industrial][84] Design 1890[85]/ Ontario College of Art 1912[86]

The Ontario School of Art situated in Toronto, the centre of what was fast becoming the most highly urbanized and industrialized area of Canada, was started in October 1876 by the Ontario Society of Artists with the aid of an Ontario government grant. Although the Ontario Minister of Education sat on the governing Council from the School's inception, the School was not integrated into the provincial education system until 1882. At that time the emphasis was on industrial art and teacher training. By the turn of the century, instruction, given in three terms of 30 lessons each, concentrated on art and industrial design.

George Reid (1860-1947), principal from 1909 to 1929, saw the stabilization and development of the school. A follower of William Morris, he promoted the integration of the various arts and reform in design.[87] In his 1911 report Dr. John Seath, Superintendent of Education for Ontario, advised that suitable accommodation, a greater range of courses, and an increase in staff and equipment were necessary if the School was to train both artists and skilled workers. The following year with the incorporation of the College, it was given an annual grant of $3,000 and free premises on the third floor of the Normal School on Gould Street. The act of incorporation stated the aims of the College were, "the training of students in the fine arts...and in all branches of the applied arts in the more artistic trades and professions...the training of teachers in the fine and applied arts."[88] Training now was based on that of the Royal College of Art, London, rather than on the Kensington School system as it had been earlier, and a "Diploma of Associate of the Ontario College of Art" was awarded.[89] A member of the College faculty c.1913 wrote,

"all teaching...must make it its aim to keep the students' individual feeling pure

---

[84] 'Industrial' was inserted in the 1905/6 to 1909/10 prospectuses. *100 Years: Evolution of the Ontario College of Art* catalogue (Toronto 1977) p.14

[85] There appear to have been a number of Acts of Incorporation and there is conflicting information in the literature. Marie Fleming and John Taylor say an application for Incorporation of the Central Ontario School of Art was filed in 1890 and the School opened in 1981. An "Act incorporating the Ontario College of Art" received royal assent in April 1912. *100 Years* pp.14, 15. However Wright says the Central Ontario School of Art continued "during the First World War" and the Act of Incorporation of the "newly reorganized school" was 1919. Wright p.104 "[T]he archives of the Ontario College of Art is almost hopeless. Almost nothing has been saved except for the calendars listing courses of study and faculty; many of them are missing or were not printed at all (esp during WWII years) and at times, faculty are not listed at all." Gail Crawford personal communication 2 September 1997

[86] all abbreviated to OCA

[87] Katharine Lochnan et al *The Earthly Paradise* catalogue (Toronto 1993)

[88] Wright p.104, *100 Years* p.15

[89] *100 Years* p.15

and unspoiled, to cultivate it, and bring it to perfection."[90]

In 1921 the College moved into its own building, on a Grange Park site provided by the Art Gallery of Toronto and financed by the Provincial and Federal governments.[91] The College appears to have been comparatively well financed,[92] receiving c.1926 $25,000 in annual appropriations from the Provincial and Federal Governments.[93]

In 1927 the College was arranged in five departments[94], which included Applied Design.[95] Second year students did practical work in stained glass, woodwork, metalwork and pottery. In the third and fourth year students could specialize in jewellery and enamelling, stained glass or pottery and ceramics.[96] Herbert H. Stansfield, a metal worker, taught from 1922 and was head of the department from 1926 until 1933.[97] In 1930 interior design was added which included furniture design. The college prospectus said that the course would be thorough and practical, work would be as professional as possible and the new courses in combination with crafts and design studies

---

[90] C.M.Manley in *100 Years* p.20

[91] Fleming and Taylor suggest it was the first building in Canada erected solely for the purpose of art education. *100 Years* p.16

[92] In 1925 NSCA received $3,440 in city, provincial and federal funding. Soucy p.104

[93] Lars Haukaness to W.G.Carpenter, Head of the Institute of Technology and Art quoted V.Greenfield *Founders of the Alberta College of Art* catalogue (Alberta 1986) p.7

[94] The other four were Elementary Art and Teacher Training; Drawing and Painting; Graphic and Commercial Art; Modelling.

[95] Departments tended to change names, in 1930 it was the Department of Industrial Design and Applied Art. *100 Years* p.19. Wright also notes that these studio activities were variously referred to in the 1929 prospectus: design, industrial design, applied art, applied design, craft. Virginia Wright 'Craft Education in Canada: A History of Confusion' in Hickey ed. *Making and Metaphor* (Ottawa/Hull 1994) pp.80-81

[96] Fleming and Taylor, referring to "weaving, pottery *and such*" [my italics] say "there had been visiting instructors in some of these subjects in the 1920s." p.21

[97] Herbert Henry Stansfield (1878-1937) b. Sheffield; educated Sheffield and Manchester Schools of Art as scholarship student, Royal College of Art winning King's and National scholarships, studios Julian and Colorosie, Paris, also Antwerp and Berlin. 1910-c1914 by invitation chief goldsmith at Kaiser Wilhelm's studio, Germany. Ran Guild of Handicraft at Cromer, UK, for 9 years, taught at Ipswich and Norwich Art Schools, also author and journalist. Invited to take post at OCA, 1936 taught at Northern Vocational School. With wife Hepzibah, a weaver, set up a studio at Limberlost c1933-36, set up studio/shop in 'The Village' Toronto 1936. NGC DCA file

Studio Craft

would prove of great value to the serious student.[98]

F.S.Haines was Principal from 1933 to 1951. The College grew from one to four buildings, the number of staff increased from 15 to 60, and the student body increased from 130 to more than 500. Haines insisted that instructors be exhibiting artists or practicing designers. Fleming and Taylor say that in 1945, courses in "weaving, pottery and such" were introduced with the opening of the Design School. However pottery in "dreadful facilities" was already offered as a major by 1939 under Cameron Paulin.[99] Luke Lindoe who studied at OCA c.1940 says,

> "It was unbelievably primitive. It was no more than the level that a good high school ceramic course does now. But it was very advanced then because Toronto, at least, was trying to escape china painting...
>
> Both industry and the school were oriented to something else; a populist thing. There were lots of little plaques and things done by people who had art training but it was acanthus leaf work with no thought of using the medium creatively...I just felt that there should be a use for clay rather than just a method to reproduce something...
>
> There were lots of black panthers, mallard ducks, little funny primitive portraits of people standing under trees and native worms with scratches and green, green glaze put on. Everyone was delighted if the thing didn't blow up in the kiln or the glazes were fired and came out looking like anything. Nearly always the form was entirely covered with glaze and the firing temperature was 010."[100]

Over the next decade Gladys Montgomery, an OCA graduate and student of Paulin's, John B. McLellan from Glascow School of Art,[101] and Grant Wylie in succession taught the pottery courses which included drawing, theory of colour, design and function, history of pottery, preparation of clay, technical research, and stacking and firing a kiln. As part of the first year course, pottery was allotted 3 hours a week; in addition there was a special class requiring 6 hours a week.[102] Ruth Home,[103] who came to OCA to teach Museum Research Studies in 1946,

---

[98] Wright p.35

[99] Crawford fax 2 September 1997 Cameron Paulin, Canadian, studied in New York [at Alfred University ?], exhibited CNE 1937

[100] *Studio Ceramics in Alberta 1947-1952* catalogue (Alberta c.1981) Interview with Luke Lindoe p.8 Some allowance should be made for exaggeration, particularly in the light of later work; pictures accompanying Home's 1944 article also show competent thrown functional ware, most undecorated.

[101] McLellan taught the first Modelling and Pottery program at the Banff Summer School of the Arts, Division of Applied Arts and Handicrafts 1941. He enlisted in 1942.

[102] Home *CGJ* p.72

said in 1944 that OCA (and CTS below) produced,
> "objects with a high standard of design and of ceramic excellence. They have broken entirely with the curse of 'arty-crafte' vases and sculpture."[104]

Around the time of the setting up of the 'Design School' in 1945, Principal Haines described the aims of the College's craft program as "the developing of designers for the various crafts and industries; second, the training of craft teachers; and, third, encouraging adults to take up handicrafts as hobbies."[105] As part of the Design School program, Harold Stacey[106] directed a full-time jewellery and metalwork program for discharged servicemen.[107] Furniture and cabinet making was taught by Frank Carrington[108] and Gordon Yearsley. Bookbinding was taught by Amy Despard and leather work by Frances Neil. Wanda Nelles founded the textile department, which "languished" between her departure[109] and the arrival of Helen Frances Gregor R.C.A[110] in 1951/2 to teach textile design. Presumably the 12 handmade looms built by the College and stored unused in an attic came from this interim period. Gregor says that in the late 1940s College Board members visited a number of Scandinavian art centres and as a result decided to stress the development of 'fine crafts'. The General Course, a new department opened in 1949.

---

[103] Ruth Home went to ROM in c1928 as the third in a succession of women museum educators. She lectured in ROM of Archaeology (ROM was still 5 separate museums), gave general tours and expanded the children's programs, a "brilliant" educator, she "effected dramatic changes."
Lovat Dickson *The Museum Makers: The Story of the Royal Ontario Museum* (Toronto 1986) pp.61-2
In 1948 Home was Executive Secretary of CHG:ON.

[104] Home *CGJ* p.72

[105] Wright p.104

[106] Harold Stacey 1911-1979 silversmith, educated at Central and Northern Technical Schools, Toronto, pupil of Renzius; taught at Central and Northern Technical Schools 1935-38; OCA 1945-51; opened first studio 1931; involved with organizing Ridpath Gallery exhibition 1931, Metal Arts Guild 1946.

[107] He was disappointed in the lack of interest in craftsmanship and lack of creativity. n/a *Mayfair* p.56

[108] Carrington, British born, furniture maker, worked first with Guild of All Crafts, Scarborough; set up business in Toronto; taught at OCA. Wright 1997 p.106 remarks on the "anti-production conservatism" of the Furniture and Cabinet Making course in the late 1940s in contrast to Ryerson Institute of Technology which offered two year diploma courses in Furniture Design or Furniture Crafts, emphasizing the technical nature of the courses in modern well equipped studio shops and laboratories.

[109] NGC.A DCA H.F.Gregor file OCA *Aluminus* Spring 1990 np.

[110] H.F.Gregor *The Fabric of My Life* (Toronto 1987) p.43
Gregor was trained at the Central School of Arts and Design, London; Newark Technical College; Birmingham College of Art and taught at Newark Technical College.

Studio Craft

It gave special attention to a knowledge of materials.

In Toronto there were "two centres of work between which the potters shuttle back and forth."[111] One was OCA, the other the Central Technical School. Its pottery department, was initiated in 1915 by Alfred Howells who employed a part-time instructor. Under Bobs Haworth,[112] who arrived in 1923 and was Head of Ceramics from c.1942 to 1957, it became a centre for a number of high-profile Ontario potters who formed the Canadian Guild of Potters in 1936. Both institutions and the Guild benefitted from the encouragement and technical expertise of R.J.Montgomery, professor of ceramics at the University of Toronto and of the Canadian ceramic industry.

In 1944, the pottery course had 20 to 25 day students and about 28 evening students. Pottery was taken in the third and fourth years of a four year course, and varied from 5 hours to a day a week depending on the degree of specialization. Evelyn Charles, a potter and early member of the CGP, rated instruction as "high quality."[113] Bailey Leslie's[114] remarks in 1957 indicate that Haworth moved with the times,

> "This group of potters had been doing many traditional things...and it was Mrs. Peter Haworth, ceramics teacher at Central Technical School who felt that new techniques would give us more freedom of expression. She suggested the ancient coil built and slab methods - a combination of the potter's wheel and a lot of free-hand work.'...The clay body is a mixture of several clays, plus large quantities of grog...The pieces fit the emphasis on texture which is such a strong part of the decorating trend. 'We think these particular examples have sculptural value even with nothing in them...although most of them are functional in design.'"[115]

---

[111] Home p.71

[112] Zemma 'Bobs' Coghill Haworth (1900-1988), born: South Africa, educated: Royal College of Art 1919-1923 under Eric Gill, Edward Johnston, and Dora Billington (Design and Pottery). Also taught in the Fine Art Department, University of Toronto 1928 to 1962.

[113] E.Charles 'A History of the Guild' *Tactile* August 1976 p.3

[114] Bailey Lesley b.Poland 1904 Educated: University of Toronto MA 1928; CTS with Haworth as a special student "for many years"; 1945 Alfred University, NY summer school, stoneware and porcelain; exhibited internationally; founding member CGP; one of Five Potters group.

[115] M.Jukes 'New Pottery Designed to Suit Modern House' *Globe and Mail* (Toronto 1957)

I have found no good illustrations of Haworth's pottery.[116]

Haworth came to CTS with her husband Peter Haworth,[117] who became Director of Art there from 1928 to 1956. Through his mentor at the Royal College of Art, Robert Anning Bell, Peter Haworth was linked to William Morris and Burne Jones which is reflected in his early work. He completed more than 60 stained glass commissions for churches, synagogues, schools and other buildings in Metro-Toronto, southern Ontario, Calgary, Montreal and Halifax. The School also ran an Art Metal course, taught between 1935 and 1938/9 by a graduate, Harold Stacey, who concurrently taught at the Northern Vocational School, Toronto from 1935 to 1938, as did his teacher, Rudy Renzius from 1932 to 1936.

Although it may be assumed that the many technical and normal schools throughout urban southern Ontario ran craft courses during this period, they are rarely mentioned in the craft literature. Crawford refers to Vera McIntyre Cryderman, a jeweller, who for 35 years was a pioneer in art education in London, Ontario, creating a vocational art department at H.B.Beal Technical School in 1927, which included jewellery making.[118]

Winnipeg School of Art 1913/University of Manitoba School of Art 1950[119]
Like the established centres of Eastern Canada, the small but fast growing city of Winnipeg at the end of the nineteenth century[120] also had a series of art schools and teachers, amongst them: "Miss T.C.Young (late of Buffalo art school) is now prepared to give lessons in embroidery, point lace, Paris tinting, and all the latest decorative arts", the Winnipeg School of Art and Design 1894, the art school of the Manitoba Society of Arts and Crafts c.1907-1914, and The

---

[116] NGC.A DCA Bobs Coghill Haworth file lists her work as paintings, murals, illuminated MS, illustration. The file concentrates on her paintings; there is a small indecipherable picture of a table setting. The only other picture, also small, of her pottery I have found is another table setting with decorated soup bowls by Haworth, 1942. Home *CGJ* p.70

[117] Peter Haworth R.C.A. (1889-1986) born UK; educated: Accrington School of Art; Manchester School of Art 1911-13; Royal College of Art 1914/15 [war service, Distinguished Flying Cross] 1918-1921 studied with Robert Anning Bell, graduated Associate of RCA with University of London Fellowship degree. The translation of his designs into windows was done by Pringle and London, Toronto; Haworth closely supervised the work, often going abroad to select glass.

[118] Crawford ms 'Movers and Shakers'. Cryderman (1896-1969) trained at London Normal School, WSA, OCA, and "special training" in Detroit, USA. She designed jewellery for Tiffany's, New York and was described as a fine craftsperson.

[119] all abbreviated to WSA

[120] Winnipeg's population was 241 residents 1871; 7985 in 1881; 25,639 in 1891; 42,340 in 1901

Studio Craft

[A.S.] Keszthelyi School of Fine Arts 1908-1912.[121] Also like a number of Eastern art schools, the Winnipeg School of Art was closely linked to an art gallery. In 1912 the Civic Art Gallery and Museum opened in the Exposition Building of the Industrial Bureau and a year later the Winnipeg School of Art opened in the same building, mainly through the support of the Winnipeg Industrial Bureau who saw a need for industrial designers in the city. The School was also funded initially by the Industrial Bureau, as well as by student fees, donations and the city, but financial support was unstable and decreasing.

The first joint Principal and Curator was Alexander Musgrove, a graduate of the Glascow School of Art and of the Scottish Department of Education art instructors training. Musgrove's qualifications included, "pottery, the design and execution of the article, and Ceramic Decoration; Design and Execution in Metal-Work."[122] The 1915/16 prospectus offered three professional programs: Drawing and Painting; Modelling and Sculpture; and Designs and Crafts. Each program required three years full-time attendance and study in four groups of topics of which group one were core courses for the first year and common to all three programs. There is no mention of what crafts were offered.[123]

In 1921 Musgrove resigned to start the Western Art Academy, and was replaced from 1921-23 by Frank (Franz) Johnston, Toronto born and educated, a painter and commercial artist. In 1923 the Winnipeg Art Gallery and School were incorporated by a special act of the Manitoba legislature and made independent of the Board of Trade.[124] The following year C.K.Gebhardt, an American educated at the Chicago Art Institute took over as head of the Gallery and School, and the city cut funding from $3500 to $2500. In 1925 there was no city funding, the gallery was in stasis and the small collection was at the School. During the early 1920s Baker suggests an emphasis on fine and commercial art, however in 1927/28 courses offered included Design,

> "A study of the manipulation of form, colour and subject matter in decorative applications; a training of the inventive faculty basic to all manner of creative work in painting, illustration and the decorative arts; an introduction to the principles of ornament and in a measure an application of these to simple handicrafts."

---

[121] *150 years of Art in Manitoba* catalogue (Winnipeg 1970) pp.12, 78 (under Ewart, Mary Clay), 86

[122] M.Baker *The Winnipeg School of Art: The Early Years* (Winnipeg 1984) p.29 The first curator of the Winnipeg Art Gallery was also a graduate of Glasgow School of Art, Donald McQuarrie.

[123] Baker's history concentrates on fine arts. In addition much space is devoted to Brigden's, a graphic design firm who employed many graduates of the School, sent their workers to the school, were on the Boards of the School and Gallery and collected works later donated to the Gallery. The impression is that Design and Crafts became primarily graphic design.

[124] *150 Years of Art in Manitoba* p.16

Lionel LeMoine Fitzgerald who taught at the school from 1924, becoming principal from 1929-1949, "also embossed in copper and other material."[125]

In 1933, the gallery separated physically from the School, going to "provisional and...inadequate quarters in the Civic Auditorium."[126] The School itself moved in 1935, and again in 1938 to the old Law Buildings on Kennedy Street. Around 1942[127] CHG:MB moved into two attic rooms at the School, where apart from housing their collection and their library, "a fairly full program was carried on...The school of weaving was particularly active - over 100 persons received instruction."[128] In 1945/6 the "weaving school" was "under the capable direction" of Mrs Inga Roos, a Swedish born weaver, and theory of weaving was taught by Mrs Ethel Henderson,[129] who was also head of the weaving program at the Banff Summer School of Fine Arts 1942-63.[130] Banks does not say whether craft courses were being taught by the Art School at this period nor is there any indication of intercourse between the CHG:MB weaving school and the Art School. By 1950/51 when the School came under the aegis of the University of Manitoba, 'Household Crafts' and 'Modern Handicrafts' were "related courses by other departments of the University", namely the Department of Home Economics, although pottery was taught at the University School of Art from 1952.[131]

---

[125] *150 Years of Art in Manitoba* p.78 Fitzgerald studied in Winnipeg and at the Art Students League, New York.

[126] *50 Years of Art in Manitoba* p.16 The gallery was also renamed the Winnipeg Art Gallery Association. Alvin C.Eastman was appointed Director in 1950, Dr. F.Eckhardt in 1953. In 1963 the gallery was incorporated as The Winnipeg Art Gallery and in 1969 its present building on the Mall was constructed.

[127] NAC Massey File C-2005 8:13:126 CHG Notes 1901-1948 say that in 1942 CHG:MB "opens weaving classes." The Annual Report for 1946/7 p.16 says that CHG:MB moves from the Art School after 5 years. However Hoskins says that the first 4 week weaving course was run in 1943. Jo-Anne Tabachek 'Our Weaving History' 1997 p.2 says that CHG:MB extended their courses to include weaving in 1934 and that in the mid to late 1930s weaving was taught throughout Winnipeg in private homes and the Guild shop by Gladys Chown, Kitty Churchill and Miss Hunt among others.

[128] n/a *Manitoba School Journal* p.14

[129] Mrs Ethel M. Henderson d.1965 Education: V.Runstrom and T.Hewson studios, Los Angeles, USA; graduate Shuttlecraft Guild of America/M.M.Atwater. 1941 Atwater's assistant first Banff weaving and design course, 1942 Head weaving program with assistant Mary Sandin, both from 1944 published *Loom Music* monthly instructional weaving bulletin. Founding member Guild of Canadian Weavers and GCW:MB.

[130] NAC Massey File C-2005 8:13:126 CHG Annual Report 1945/6 p.19

[131] Taught by Cecil Richards.

Studio Craft

Alberta Provincial Institute of Technology and Art, Calgary 1916/ Alberta College of Art 1960[132]
To the far west of the Prairies in Calgary, the Institute of Technology and Art, founded in 1916, was to comprise four schools of which one was a school of fine and applied arts.[133] Leo E. Pearson was hired as art instructor, teaching evening and Saturday classes.[134] In the following year,

> "Thought was given to the expansion of the art department also. Announcing that an art exhibit was planned for the coming autumn, Dr Miller [Principal] expressed the expectation that the Institute would become in time "the home of fine and applied art," and he intimated that arrangements would be made in the new permanent home of the institution for an art gallery."[135]

However during that year the Institute was taken over by the Military Hospitals Commission[136] and did not return to civilian hands until 1920.

Although art courses for teachers and commercial artists were offered from 1921 and taught from 1926, it was not until the advent of Alfred C. Leighton[137] as Head of the Art Department in 1929 that the department had a full-time teacher. Four courses were offered, 'elementary' which was a course required before proceeding to 'fine art', 'commercial' or 'applied arts and crafts'. Units of instruction were grouped to form "certificate subjects", a diploma was given on successful completion of the required number of "certificate subjects" which included day or evening classes. For example, the requirements for a diploma in Applied Art in 1930 were lettering; modelling; theory - science; commercial design - drawing for reproduction; industrial design - craft design and application; craft work (special).[138] Students were required to be at least 16 years

---

[132] all abbreviated to PITA
Simon p.291 "When the Institute in December, 1960 was renamed the Southern Alberta Institute of Technology, the art department...was given individual identity as the Alberta College of Art."
Greenfield catalogue p.7 "In 1985, after a highly publicized struggle for autonomy, the Alberta College of Art gained the status of being a wholly independent art school."

[133] Simon p.44

[134] Pearson, an American, was educated in California, Minnesota, Chicago, and New York and had taught day art classes at Canmore Normal School, AB from 1913-1916.

[135] Simon p.91 There were also plans for a natural history museum as part of the Institute.

[136] The Military Hospitals Commission provided programs to rehabilitate disabled soldiers and veterans.

[137] Leighton b.1901 in Britain, first studied architecture then art; taught at Dartford Art School, England in 1920; worked as a toy designer and model maker, and in Canada as a commercial artist for the CPR. In 1929 he became a full member of the Royal Society of British Artists. Greenfield catalogue p.13

[138] Simon p.194,95

and a full high school education was desired.[139] The diploma course took approximately four years, of which a minimum of two years residence was required. This made the Art Department courses considerably longer than any of the Institute's other courses. Simon's figures show that although relatively large numbers of students took classes, a very small proportion got diplomas, over a 16 year period from 1929/30 to 1944/45, 33 diplomas were awarded of which 10 were 'elementary', 16 'fine art' and 3 'applied art and craft'.[140]

Instruction was aimed at producing art teachers, design specialists, commercial artists and illustrators, fashion and costume designers,[141] interior decorators, and "craft workers." To cover such a range, instruction was largely individual. Crafts taught were metalsmithing, leather work, stencil, batik,[142] woodcarving, china painting and pottery.[143] In 1929 Marion Mackay Nicoll[144] also arrived at the Art Department as a student, having transferred after two years at OCA. In 1931 Nicoll became student instructor and, with only two breaks in 1937/38 and 1940-46,[145] taught exclusively design and crafts at the Art Department/College until her retirement in January 1966.[146] Although "Nicoll clearly felt that painting was the highest calling to which one could aspire",[147] she was a committed craft teacher with a thorough knowledge of design and jewellery,

---

[139] Simon p.191

[140] Simon pp.177, 184, 214, 228, 229, 243
Enrollments 1-4 year course

	1929/30	31	32	33	34	35	36	37	38	39	40	41	42	43	44	45
day	20	40	44	44	47	62	57	43	50	44	33	31	52	32	42	61
eve	57	90	68	33	29	28	38	36	57	45	20	30	21	46	72	91
craft eve																13
diplomas	-	1	-	5	5	1	5	2	5	1	-	-	3	1	-	3

[141] Greenfield catalogue p.16 "magazine illustration for costume and fashion design"

[142] Greenfield catalogue p.16, obviously quoting from the same sources as Simon, says "stencil batik"

[143] Simon p.192-3

[144] Marion Mackay Nicoll 1909-1985 b.Calgary; educated OCA 1927-29, AB:PITA 1929-32, Banff Summer School 1932,33,34; 6 honour certificates in teaching from Royal Drawing Society, London, UK; 1937-38 Central School of Arts and Crafts, London, UK with Duncan Grant (Greenfield catalogue p.21 calls it the London County Council School of Arts and Crafts.)

[145] There is no mention of who taught craft during this period.

[146] Greenfield catalogue p.21 Nicoll concurrently taught at the Banff Summer School; Baker Sanitorium, Calgary; and UAB Extension courses in Black Diamond and Medicine Hat.

[147] Greenfield catalogue p.21 quoting Eileen Taylor, a student of Nicoll's

Studio Craft

leather, weaving, ceramics and batik techniques. Her students were expected to be equally committed and hardworking.

During the Depression there was a downward trend in the number of students attending the Institute, however art classes increased in size. The evening art class declined but it was the only evening class during the depression. The mid-1930s seem to have been an lively time for the Art Department. In 1934/5, the Art Department took part in a china painting contest organized by the Paragon China Company, Staffordshire, England in conjunction with the Hudson's Bay Company, Calgary. Rather than award one prize, the 42 contestants were each given a cup and saucer decorated with one of designs submitted (at a cost to the china company of 5 pounds sterling.)[148] The exhibition of "handcraft done in Alberta...to which technical schools in Calgary and Edmonton contributed generously",[149] organized in co-operation with the Extension Department of UAB and CHG:AB, toured the southern part of the province at the beginning of the year. Noting an increasing interest in handcrafts, Dr Carpenter, Provincial Director of Technical Education and Principal of PITA, recommended that the work of the art department be directed along the lines of applied art. The provision for increased facilities and instruction in this branch of the department was planned for 1936.[150]

In 1935,
> "H.G.Glyde[151] and I [Luke Lindoe][152] appeared on the scene on the same day. I was green right out of the bush and he was green right out of Jolly Old...we were in the old original building, the west end of it and the normal school was on the

---

[148] Simon p.193
Calgary is relatively near the major Canadian clay deposits and clay products industries on the southern Saskatchewan/Alberta border. However Lindoe says that even though his course was titled 'Industrial Design', there was no emphasis on a commercial product, "it was necessary to pay lip service to the words." *Studio Ceramics in Alberta* p.10

[149] Simon p.193 This exhibition is discussed in detail in chapters 4 and 6.

[150] Simon p.196

[151] H.G.Glyde b.UK c1906, educated RCA, London; taught at Croydon School of Arts and Crafts 1929-31, Boraegh PolyTechnic 1929-35, High Wycombe SA 1931-35, all in UK. Glyde was known to Leighton in England and was brought in to teach drawing in the Art Department on contract, he became Head in 1935. Greenfield catalogue p.16

[152] Luke Lindoe was to become a major Canadian potter. b.1913 Bashaw, AB; educated: PITA 1935-37/38, OCA 1940-41; taught PITA 1947-57. 1941, 1957-64 worked in ceramic industry. 1953 started Lindoe Studio, 1964 started Plainsman Clays, a major supplier of clays to studio potters, schools etc.

east end."[153]

On the ailing Leighton's recommendation, Glyde took over the Art Department. A year later Lindoe recalls,

> "Doris Le Coque [sic][154] came onto the staff...fresh from art school in England. Her major was sculpture. Le Coque employed models, molds, and slip casting to reproduce small sculptural objects in low temperature ceramics. I was in her classes in my second year. This was my introduction to the contemporary ceramics process...Le Coque stayed at the school for most of two years."[155]

Le Cocq had studied and worked as a studio assistant with Professor Richard Garbe at the Royal College of Art. Garbe was a "highly regarded modeller who favoured Art Deco forms, particularly cubism. From 1933 to 1939 he became a modeller for the Doulton Potteries." In 1937/8 Marion Nicoll went to London to study at the Central School of Arts and Crafts under Duncan Grant and was undoubtedly introduced to the very different style of the Bloomsbury Group in ceramics and other materials.[156]

Between c.1940 and 1946 the Art Department moved from the Institute campus to Coste House. In 1946, it moved back to campus, Glyde went to UAB to "start an art division within the Department of Fine Arts",[157] and J.W.G.Macdonald who had taught at VSA since 1927[158] became Head of the Art Department. In 1947 Macdonald left for OCA and Dr. Illingworth Kerr, on Macdonald's recommendation became Head.

In 1947 the Art Department "consisted of a few rooms spread over the main building of the

---

[153] *Studio Ceramics in Alberta* p.6

[154] NGC.A DCA file Usually spelt Le Cocq, also Lecocq. Doris Le Cocq b. Lethbridge AB; educated: private school, England; Central School of Art, London; Royal College of Art, London (3 years)and after became assistant to Professor Richard Garbe in his private studio. Taught sculpture in London County Council Schools 1934-5; instructor ceramics PITA 1935-38; 1940-[1948] instructor pottery and modelling VSA. Le Cocq appears to have left PITA on her marriage

[155] Greenfield catalogue p.7

[156] Elsewhere Lindoe says, perhaps implying a difference between Le Cocq's program and wheel thrown work, "Nicoll initiated the ceramic program. The classes hadn't started. This was something she had taken in her studies in England and was something that she knew was going to come...As soon as I showed up on the scene, she said, 'YOU can have the ceramics department'...She wanted it there and she really hadn't wanted to run it." *Studio Ceramics in Alberta* p.10

[157] Greenfield catalogue p.18

[158] Macdonald, Diploma in Art, Edinburgh had taught Design and Crafts at Vancouver School of Art

Studio Craft

Institute and had 60 students."[159] Up to that time all staff, apart from the Head of the department, had been part time.

> "Unlike his predecessors, Kerr was allowed a full-time staff because war veterans had swollen the ranks enormously...he sacked everybody who had been teaching in the department. Kerr's four new staff members had all studied at the Institute: 'All were Westerners sharing my regional patriotism and were perhaps best fitted to understand prairie students.'"[160]

Nicoll and Lindoe were hired as full-time instructors, Nicoll to continue teaching design and crafts, Lindoe to teach sculpture and ceramics (and painting). In 1948 a fifth diploma course was added to the existing four: Applied Art and General Crafts; Commercial Art; Advanced General Art; Fine Art, Advanced. This was a three year course in pottery, ceramics and industrial design taught by Lindoe.[161]

Lindoe recalls that in 1947:

> "The ceramics section...was in a corner of the tractor shop and so they quickly whipped up some thin plaster board, just to do about a 30' x 30' corner in the tractor shop...after the first year or two, we put in a mezzanine floor that added to the area by about 50 percent. It was enough to accommodate as many people as wanted to go in that direction anyway, which was only about eight or ten at a time...
> One wheel, one gas kiln, some tables and chairs and sink and some shelves."[162]

Basic clay came from Medalta Potteries, Medicine Hat but other Alberta clays were used on an experimental basis. Stoneware was primarily produced. Glazes were made in the department, also often using local clays. The basic text was Norton's book on ceramic glazes, first edition. Work was handbuilt, slab and modelling,

> "Very little wheel work. I didn't even permit people to go to the wheel until their second year in the shop. They had to have a basic understanding of clay before they got that far."[163]

Cast work and mould making was also taught.

---

[159] Greenfield catalogue p.28

[160] Greenfield catalogue p.27

[161] Simon p.297 Simon's figures appear to show 'craft' as a distinct subject in day classes in the two years 1946/7, 1947/8. In evening classes 'craftwork' continues, with no figures for 1948/9, from 1945/46 to 1954/55. In 1949/50 'ceramics' and 'weaving' are added and continue to date.

[162] *Studio Ceramics in Alberta* p.11

[163] *Studio Ceramics in Alberta* p.13

The Art Department continued the provincial tradition of circulating exhibits. In 1948, for example, there was the annual Spring exhibition; an exhibition touring through the Western Art Circuit which included Winnipeg, Regina, Saskatoon, Edmonton, Victoria and Calgary; an exhibition of work at the Calgary Exhibition and Stampede which attracted an estimated 40,000 visitors; a small exhibition touring Saskatchewan towns organized by a student; an exhibition going to Vernon, Kelowna, and the Okanagan, BC organized by Lindoe; an exhibition at PNE; and a small display of commercial art and craftwork at the Legislative Building, Edmonton.[164]

Vancouver School of Decorative and Applied Arts 1925/Vancouver School of Art 1933/Emily Carr College of Art 1978/ Emily Carr Institute of Art and Design, BC, 1995[165]

On the Pacific coast, separated from the rest of Canada by mountain ranges, Vancouver established its art school in 1925. It had been preceded in 1904 by the Vancouver Studio Club and School of Art, S.P.Judge the first instructor was later to teach at VSA. Judge and John Howard Kyle A.R.C.A. (London) were founders in 1906 of the British Columbia Society of Fine Arts, an exhibiting group. Kyle[166] also started evening art classes in Vancouver and as Director of Technical Education for the province "talked art education to every School Board in British Columbia."[167] In 1920, The Art League was formed with the aim of getting a provincial art school and a gallery. The League, which included Charles Scott,[168] swung into action to raise public support across the province and in 1925,

> "following several meetings between the Vancouver School Board and the B.C. Art League, the Board agreed to the opening of a Vancouver School of Art as an integral part of the school system."[169]

The VSA Advisory Board, at least until 1928, consisted of five members of the League and a representative from the Trades and Labor Council, the Architectural Institute of BC, the Manufacturers' Association and the Board of Trade. These groups, with the Vancouver Exhibition Association and a number of private and commercial patrons, also supported students through scholarships and prizes.

---

[164] Simon p.290

[165] all abbreviated to VSA. ECIAD.A denotes the school's archives. ECIAD is a degree granting institute.

[166] In 1913 Kyle was associated with the Provincial Normal School, Vancouver and McGill University College of British Columbia. He was responsible for getting a pottery instructor from Ottawa for a summer school for teachers in Victoria c1927. He retired as Director of Technical Education, British Columbia, in 1938.

[167] C.Scott 'A Short Art History of British Columbia' *Behind the Palette* VSA student annual publication 1947/48 n/p

[168] H.Dickson 'The Vancouver School of Decorative and Applied Art' *Canadian Forum* 1931 p.102

[169] C.Scott *100 Years of B.C. Art* catalogue (Vancouver 1958) n/p

Studio Craft

The School opened in September 1925. Initially G.Thornton Sharp, a city architect, was Director of the School and Charles H. Scott,[170] the former superintendent of Art in the public schools, was Principal but at the end of first session Sharp resigned and Scott was appointed Director. Scott, Mrs Kate Smith Hoole and Miss Railton taught drawing and painting, Charles Marega, a sculptor, taught modelling, Mr. Semeyn taught Design and Mrs Sharland taught Costume Design.[171] The School was located on the top floor of School Board Office building, where the "several rooms are well lit and contain all the necessary equipment."[172] The School also had "the nucleus of an art library" which included "current art periodicals".[173]

The 'Objects of the School' were:
> "To give a through practical knowledge of industrial design, drawing, modelling, and decorative painting; and to furnish a sound training to those following, or intending to follow, the various trades, manufactures, or professions requiring such knowledge.
> To keep in close touch with established industries and professions in the city and province, which are dependent on art for their success."[174]

Scott later said,
> "The aim of the School was to steer a course in Art which would enable students to land either on the shores of industry or the less secure footing of the fine arts."[175]

In that first year seven classes were offered: Drawing; Design - composition, lettering, patterns, conventional studies, history of ornament and styles; Poster work and Commercial Illustration; Colour; Modelling - plaster work and pottery forms, china painting, study and history of ornament and style, practical work; Interior and Exterior Decoration - painting and use of colour, furniture and woodwork, stained glass, tiles, electric fixtures, stencilling and wall treatment; Costume Design and Embroidery. All students took drawing. Examinations and work produced determined promotion, pass lists and awards were later published in the Prospectus and there was

---

[170] Charles H. Scott 1886-1964 b.Scotland; educated Glascow School of Art, also Belgium, Holland and Germany. Came to Canada 1912, first to Calgary.

[171] ECIAD.A *The Paint Box* 1:1:np 1926 VSA Art Student's Club annual publication

[172] ECIAD.A 1926/7 Prospectus p.3

[173] ECIAD.A Prospectus 1926/7

[174] ECIAD.A Prospectus 1925/6 n/p

[175] *Behind the Palette* n/p

a year end exhibition. Day, evening and Saturday classes were offered.

The School seems to have got off to a strong start, in 1927/28 it had a 100 students.[176] The staff increased and so did the subjects offered, by 1928/29 there were four full-time staff: Scott, F.H.Varley A.R.C.A., J.W.G.MacDonald D.A. (Edinburgh) teaching Design and Crafts, Grace Melvin D.A. (Glasgow)[177] teaching Lettering and Illumination, Embroidery and Pottery; and nine part-time staff including Marega, Hoole, and R.P.S. Twizell A.R.I.B.A. teaching Perspective and Architecture; S.P.Judge, Teachers Classes and Miss J. Allen, China Painting.

The School was offering a course it considered "of university standard." Students attending the day school had to be at least 17 years and give evidence of high school training or equivalent. They appear to have been overwhelmingly female, of first year students in 1927/8 37 were women, 3 men. Not surprisingly women also scooped awards and scholarships, 13:1.[178] The "Professional Training" of Art Teachers required Junior Matriculation, the Diploma Course of VSA and a teacher training course of thirty weeks which it was hoped would be offered by the University of British Columbia (UBC) at the end of which "successful candidates would be recommended to the Provincial Department of Education for the Art Teachers' Certificate."[179]

All students were required to take a first year "general art training carefully organized" comprising Drawing, Composition, Design, Commercial Art and Modelling. The second year course was an extension of first, with the addition of a choice between Modelling and Architecture. Certificates were given for completion of units. The third and fourth years constituted the Diploma course. In 1927/28 the following were recognized as Diploma Crafts: Needlework and embroidery, leatherwork; Lettering and Illumination; Ceramics; Rug-weaving; Costume design (this was dropped the following year); Posters and Advertisements. Candidates were required to work in two of these areas in their third year. The third year course consisted of: Application of Design; Constructive Patterns; Woven and printed fabrics, carpets, rugs, tapestries; Drawing from Plant, Bird and Animal Form; Colour Study; Figure Drawing from life;

---

[176] ECIAD.A newspaper article in *The Paint Box* 1928

[177] Grace Melvin 1890-1977 b.Scotland educated Glasgow School of Art, by Maurice Grieffen Gagen and Robert Bell c1910-1915; student work exhibited 1912 includes art needlework and embroidery based on Ann McBeth and Margaret Swainson's teaching program *Educational Needlecraft* (1911), jewellery and lettering in Jude Burke *Glasgow Girls* (Edinburgh 1990) p.154; taught needlework various primary schools 1912-1913; GSA Travelling Bursary 1914 study in London and Paris; taught GSA 1920-27 lettering and illumination, also Scribe to Corporation of Glasgow. Came to Vancouver, Canada 1927 taught at VSA 1928-c1953, becoming Head of Department of Design; also Provincial Examiner, Home Economics Applied Art, BC. Sister-in-law to Charles Scott.

[178] ECIAD.A Prospectus 1927/8 pp.17-18

[179] ECIAD.A Prospectus 1928/9 p.15

Studio Craft

Museum Studies;[180] Styles of Architecture; Interior Perspective. In the fourth year, there was specialization in one craft, with advanced design for all forms of textiles including embroidery, drawing, museum studies, and the production of a special piece of diploma work in the chosen craft.[181]

In 1927/28 a pottery kiln and looms for the making of hand-woven rugs were acquired. Pottery, which was taught both as part of the day courses and as an evening course, included designing, cutting of templates, production of works by various processes including moulding, pressing, casting in slip etc., and decoration with underglaze, overglaze, majolica, and slip-painting etc., the making of tiles and pottery panels in bas-relief, colouring and firing.[182] In 1941 Doris Le Cocq arrived to teach ceramics and modelling on a part-time basis. The school in 1943 had three kilns.[183] In 1931, "the clay is dug a short distance from Vancouver at Haney and Pitt Meadows."[184] By 1940, clay was mostly from Medalta Potteries.[185] 'China-painting' covered the "suitability of design to the article. Nature of paints and materials. Application of lustres, enamels, golds, satsuma, tinting, etc."[186]

'Hand-weaving' taught silk and wool weaving "on frame" of personal and household articles. Embroidery covered design and execution on a variety of domestic articles, using silks and fine wools on fine materials and wools and cottons on rough materials, also applique, needleweaving and stitchery. A reviewer commented,
> "The needle work and illumination are exquisite. Indian legends and legendary figures are often developed in designs for stitchery."[187]

---

[180] It would be interesting to know what 'museum studies' consisted of. Vancouver City Museum and Art Gallery est.1894, "principal exhibits: Ethnographical material of the Northwest coast Indians; Siamese Collection; Nigerian Collection, ECIAD.A *Who's Who in Northwest Art* (Seattle 1941) p.79

[181] ECIAD.A Prospectus 1927/8 p.8

[182] The School did not teach wheel-throwing until 1952/3 when Reg Dixon and David Lambert started teaching.

[183] SKAB SACS J.M.Gibbon 1943.
These seem to have been electric according to Elsa Shamis 'The Development of Pottery through the VSA Growth Years' *Vancouver School of Art, The Growth Years, 1939-1965* catalogue (Vancouver 1983) n/p.

[184] Dickson p.102 An article in *The Sun,* Vancouver 6 September 1940 also says, "some very attractive jars had been made of clay from potteries right on our own doorstep, in Haney."

[185] VAG.A 'Fine Showing of Pottery and Textile Designs at Gallery' *The Sun,* Vancouver 6 September 1940

[186] ECIAD.A Prospectus 1928/9 p.13

[187] Dickson p.103

Leatherwork included the making of bags, purses, gloves, cushions etc with suitable decorations; from the illustrations of work these included the full range of leather techniques. In total,
> "the student body of the school has produced more talent in design and commercial art than in the fine arts. There were many fine pieces of designing to be seen, and not a few excellent bits of illuminating, pottery and lettering."[188]

Although the School appears to have continued teaching decorative techniques for furniture,
> "As a practical application of study to industry, the set for a Swedish cafe, with the Scandinavian motif directing it, a screen, stool, and chair, deserve commendation"[189]

furniture making skills - woodworking, carpentry and joinery, machine construction and drawing, cabinet making, bench work, heat treatment, etc. - were taught through the Vancouver night schools according to the VSA Prospectus.[190]

In 1931, The Art League's second objective of a provincial art gallery was achieved through the generosity of private donors. The School promptly took advantage of the Vancouver Art Gallery (VAG) to hold its annual exhibitions there. However the splendour of the new Gallery building contrasted with the deteriorating conditions at the school. In 1928, a reviewer of the students' annual publication *The Paint Box* said,
> "It is nothing less than remarkable that the school is able to produce such work as is seen in the book under the conditions which now obtain. Vancouver needs an art school, just as any city of importance needs one. It has the faculty and the students. One hopes that suitable accommodation will soon be provided."[191]

In 1931, despite
> "student personnel...keen as mustard and brimming with talent...The strongly modernistic trend of the design may not appeal to all critics, but no one can fail to admire the thoroughness of the craftsmanship. The sloven and the dilettante have no place...
> It is a matter for deep regret that the people of Vancouver have not yet risen to the heights of housing their art school in decent quarters. They are at present occupying rooms in an old school and in the School Board building, which are

---

[188] ECIAD.A newspaper clipping in *The Paint Box* 1928

[189] VAG.A *Herald* newspaper Vancouver 30 May 1934

[190] ECIAD.A Prospectus 1927/8

[191] ECIAD.A newspaper clipping in *The Paint Box* 1928

Studio Craft

wholly inadequate in every way."[192]

The Depression was in full force when Melvin wrote to Marius Barbeau[193] in March 1933, "Vancouver tottering financially, all education grants etc. are lowered. They nearly wiped our department off the slate! - but thanks to Mr. Scott's influence and ingenuity, we are still going strong, but have to be a self supporting body - it will mean more work, and much less money, but so long as we can hold and develop the school - that is our main concern."[194]

But later that year,[195] Melvin says she is,

"superintending the reconditioning and colour schemes for our BEAUTIFUL NEW SCHOOL...it is an old building but has been entirely overhauled and modernised to suit us."

Despite all difficulties, the second annual exhibition at VAG was a

"marvellous exhibition - the best by a long way the school has ever had - authorities - Public - and papers are all unanimous on that point - and the whole town is ringing with its praises - which is very satisfactory...."[196]

"The exhibit of the VSA at the AG is thronged with visitors...As a practical application of study to industry, the set for a Swedish cafe, with the Scandinavian motif directing it, a screen, stool, and chair, deserve commendation...The pottery and similar work is excellent, the students in some cases having made every necessity for a summer camp."[197]

Reviews of exhibitions give some idea of production, focus and new developments. In 1940,

"About 20 different kinds of crafts are taught at the school...The value of good training in design and in the general basic laws of art is fully exemplified in this exhibit...The textile section comprises many fine examples of the arts of wood

---

[192] Dickson p.103 December 1931

[193] Melvin and Barbeau had a long and friendly relationship, mainly through correspondence. Barbeau's research brought him to the West Coast frequently, he lectured at UBC, and in 1926 was involved with preparations for 'Canadian West Coast Art, Native and Modern' at NGC. It is not surprising he met Scott and Melvin. Melvin later illustrated some of his books.

[194] CMC.A Barbeau files Melvin to Barbeau 13 March 1933

[195] CMC.A Barbeau File, Melvin to Barbeau The letter is undated but other parts of the letter suggest that it belongs to 1933

[196] CMC.A Barbeau File, Melvin to Barbeau 6 June 1934

[197] VAG.A *Herald* (Vancouver) May 30 1934

block and silk screen printing. The latter is a new method and has been handled here with excellent results. Many local motifs have been used including natural forms, heraldic designs and native Indian art."[198]

At the 19th annual exhibition in 1943,

"The pottery section as usual shows many beautiful examples of this fascinating work. While plenty of clay is still available from Canadian deposits, the lovely glazes that used to be imported from England are now almost a thing of the past - another war casualty...[S]ome very good work in silk screen textile designs applied to curtains...Original designs adapted as decoration for furniture translates several small coffee tables into works of art...Design and color are outstanding features in the needlework section where wide use has been made of felt and wool."[199]

At the end of 1936 Melvin wrote,

"school grows apace...our influence is growing rapidly - the Department of Education wishes us to introduce new classes - and in fact is trying to insist that we hold an advanced summer school."[200]

In 1939, when Barbeau lectured at the school, Melvin mentions an important summer school in July, and in July 1940 a "big Summer school". Melvin was also working for the Provincial Department of Education, in September 1940 "My first 'Students Manual' in applied art at press this week".[201] As Provincial Examiner of Applied Arts, Home Economics she toured the province regularly. In July 1941,

"tour [3 weeks] - all over mountainous country of BC - visiting all the High Schools for the Department of Education - to see and examine the art work is a wonderful experience - but as I lecture on an average of twice a day - it is strenuous."[202]

In 1945 the post-war surge of veterans hit the school, increasing the teaching load. In January 1945 Melvin wrote, "very large school and exceedingly heavy classes,"[203] in May, "the largest

---

[198] VAG.A 'Fine Showing of Pottery and Textile Designs at Gallery' *Sun* (Vancouver) 6 September 1940

[199] VAG.A 'Art School Students Stage Exhibition' *Sun* 9 September 1943

[200] CMC.A Barbeau file Melvin to Barbeau 10 December 1936

[201] CMC.A Barbeau file Melvin to Barbeau 9 September 1940

[202] CMC.A Barbeau file Melvin to Barbeau 27 July 1941

[203] CMC.A Barbeau file Melvin to Barbeau 24 January 1945

Studio Craft

enrolment on record...900 day and evening students",[204] and in September, "over 80 first year students - 30 rehabilitation soldiers - and oudles of others - and it is almost impossible to house them all comfortably...We now have 4 final year groups instead of the normal one."[205] In January 1946, she wrote,

> "[S]everal new groups of 'rehabilitation boys - and girls' - and I had to start four new classes in 'basic design and colour' on top of all my existing classes which means that from Monday A.M. to Friday P.M. I am lecturing and teaching five and six hours each day and on several days I have two large groups working - in different rooms - at the same time - so - from now until May, most of my creative energy will be given to teaching."[206]

One of Melvin's last remarks about the school in her correspondence is in 1951,

> "I had a magnificent show of student work in May...and one of my best students - a Chinese boy - has done particularly well - winning third prize in a big New York International Fabric design competition - and this same lad is handling some very important commissions that I cannot accept [a Book of Remembrance] and is producing them under my direction."[207]

A year later she wrote, "a wonderful new school opened by Charles last Friday."[208] The new school was opened and handed over to Fred Amess, one of the first students at VSA, who became the second Director.[209]

Melvin refers to "The Opposition" running an exhibition, at the same time as VSA's "marvellous exhibition" in 1934, but they got "only one quarter column Press notice."[210] The opposition was the H.Faulkner Smith School of Applied and Fine Art/Academy of Art which appears to have

---

[204] CMC.A Barbeau file Melvin to Barbeau 2 May 1945 [?]

[205] CMC.A Barbeau file Melvin to Barbeau 14 September 1945

[206] CMC.A Barbeau file Melvin to Barbeau 14 January 1941

[207] CMC.A Barbeau file Melvin to Barbeau 14 August 1951

[208] CMC.A Barbeau file Melvin to Barbeau 7 April 1952

[209] In the early 1950s, the School merged with the larger Vancouver Vocational Institute, possibly the "wonderful new school." The School regained its independence in 1978. ECIAD 1995/6 Calendar

[210] CMC.A Barbeau file Melvin to Barbeau 6 June 1934

lasted until 1937/8.[211] Crowell in 1943 refers to crafts being taught through the Extension Department, UBC, Vancouver.[212]

In Victoria, the province's capital on Vancouver Island, the Island Arts and Crafts Society opened a School of Handicraft and Design in 1913. Amongst the staff were Karel Bergrelt trained at the Amsterdam School of Art, Miss Lang, Miss L.M.Mills trained in Paris,[213] and L.L.Mold trained at the Birmingham School of Art, UK. Victoria appears to have had an early pottery school, or possibly two. Prior to c.1920, according to a 1927 MacLean's Magazine article, there were experiments with clay but firings were unsuccessful, however

> "[pottery] has grown to surprisingly large proportions during the last half a dozen years...through the efforts of Mr. [John] Howard Kyle, the organizer of technical education in the province, an instructor was sent out from Ottawa to the summer school for teachers. From three or four earnest workers, the class grew to large proportions. Today, at the summer school, one may see a score or more of women...manipulating the plastic clay, on potter's wheel or table..."[214]

In 1923 Margaret Grute[215] attended the pottery summer school.[216] MacLean's refers to the school

> "of which Mrs Margaret Grute is the head...She has a large following here, and teaches in the summer school as well. She uses the potter's wheel and her work is always glazed...By the use of the wheel, more delicate shapes can be evolved, even tea sets and gracefully moulded vases."[217]

Grute was, according to a fellow member of the Pottery Club, Elizabeth Burchett,

> "One of the real Pottery Pioneers, getting clay from the beaches, fitting the glazes and doing a great deal of experimental work...She works three or four days a week

---

[211] VAG:A VAG Annual Reports refer to exhibitions annually 1934-1937 The applied arts seem to have been largely graphic design.

[212] R.Boux *CA* p.113 1954 "about five winters ago [1949] the University Chapter of the I.O.D.E. made a grant for the establishment of a crafts workshop...The extension department assumed the administration of this workshop..."

[213] Lang trained with Sangorski and Sutcliffe, location not known; Mills with Callot and Delaborde.

[214] De Bertrand Lugrin *MacLean's Magazine* p.78

[215] Margaret Grute b.Queenstown Eire Educated: Cork School of Art; Goldsmiths College, London UK, qualified as an art teacher, worked as a designer for Liberty's, London; Victoria Summer School 1923 pottery. SKAB SACS Gibbon 1943 p.5-A

[216] SKAB SACS Gibbon 1943 p.5-A

[217] De Bertrand Lugrin *MacLean's Magazine* p.79

Studio Craft 203

at the Pottery Club. Has taught the Night School ever since it started."[218]
A 1939 article locates the Pottery Club at the Kingston Street School.[219]

The MacLean's article makes no mention of Ina Uhthoff,[220] another graduate of the Glascow School of Art, who from c.1926 ran a private art school from her studio, apart from teaching at the Department of Education summer school for teachers and at the Night School. Her studio school developed into the Victoria School of Art, also referred to as the Kingston Street School, supported by the Department of Education from 1935 to 1940 (or 1942). The program, taught almost entirely by Uhthoff, included textile design, including lino block printing; clay modelling including bas-reliefs, and pottery, and students finishing the first year could transfer to the second year at Vancouver School of Art.

> "Protesting that she was not a potter, she had nonetheless given in to the urgent request of provincial authorities that she take over the Kingston Street Pottery School as well. The school had brought in a technician from one of the British commercial potteries who was sound on technique but innocent of any inkling of ceramics as an art form. "The next thing...was to eliminate scratched logs and other horrors...Realism was rampant, and it was hard to convince students that pure form was something to be desired." Glazes had pretty well been restricted to the 'Brown Betty' type, and so she set herself, with complete success, to experiment with glaze formulae to bring in a wide range of new colours."[221]

Uhthoff was instrumental in the establishment of the Art Gallery of Greater Victoria 1951.

L'École Technique, Montreal 1911/ l'École du Meuble, PQ, 1935-1958[222]

Quebec, in response to growing industrialization, had by 1880 13 trade schools approved by the

---

[218] SKAB SACS Gibbon 1943 p.5-A

[219] J.E.M.Bruce 'Adult Education' *The Daily Colonist* (Victoria 1939) Third section p.1 Caption "The kiln, Presented by the City to the Pottery Society. This Kiln is Used for Firing Various Articles Made by the Pottery Class.

[220] Ina Campbell Uhthoff 1889-1971 F.R.S.A. UK b. Scotland Educated: Glasgow School of Art, Dip (Painting) 1912, with C.R.Mackintosh, Maurice Grieffenhagen R.A [Uhthoff doesn't mention the former in her NGC DCA file], also Metalwork, Silversmith, Enamels, Leather, Woodwork. Taught Glasgow High School. Came to Kootenay Lake, B.C. 1913 taught; returned a war bride at the end of the war to Kootenay, "seeing little future for her at Crawford Bay" in 1926 she went to Victoria with her 2 small children. Uhthoff with Emily Carr organized master classes by American Mark Tobey in 1929 and 1930. Uhthoff was art critic for the *Daily Colonist* for many years.

[221] *Ina D.D.Uhthoff* catalogue (Victoria 1972)

[222] abbreviated to EdM.
By 1958 all courses, apprenticeships and diplomas previously offered by EdM were at Institute des Arts Appliques. J.Crosby *A History of the Evolution of the Teaching of Textiles and Weaving in Quebec since 1905* MA thesis (Montreal 1987) p.34

provincial government; Simon comments, "in some of these schools...more attention was given to the fine arts than to the manual arts."[223] A 1897 provincial act put grants for existing schools under the control of the Arts and Trades Council incorporated in 1872. L'École Technique, Montreal, opened in 1911, initially taught technical courses in carpentry, ironwork and smelting, etc. A course in cabinetry was added by 1920. In 1930, early in the Depression, under Jean-Marie Gauvreau,[224] Professor of Cabinetry 1930-32 and Director of Cabinetry 1932-35, the cabinetry course became a department and started a two year apprenticeship program. In 1935 the department became a separate school, l'École du Meuble (EdM), set up under the Quebec Ministry of Youth, with Gauvreau as Director. The School taught interior design, cabinet making, woodcarving, upholstery, wood finishing, ceramics, weaving and other applied arts including bookbinding. L'École Technique through the 1930s and 1940s continued to supply custom designed wrought and hammered iron accessories for EdM furniture.

Both Gloria Lesser and Virginia Wright argue that, under the direction of Louis Athanese David, the Provincial Secretary,[225] and Gauvreau, EdM had a very focused provincial and economic agenda,

> "[T]he school adhered to French craft traditions, emphasizing woodworking skills. This was seen to be a positive nationalist strategy to provide skilled employment and regionally distinctive furniture for Montreal's rapidly growing population. The example of fine craftsmen using Québécois woods was also intended to promote lumber sales to local and foreign furniture manufacturers, architects, and interior decorators."[226]

Gauvreau trained at École Boulle in Paris and used that school as a model for the interior design and applied art program at EdM. In furniture Gauvreau rejected mass-production design and many of its materials and techniques in favour of hand-crafted, solid wood construction in a variation of Art Deco.

The furniture program offered a two year Apprenticeship program leading to a Certificate of Furniture Carpenter and a four year Artisanship program leading to the Diploma of Cabinet-Maker. Lesser describes the first as essentially a practical cabinetry trade program, with the

---

[223] Simon p.9

[224] J-M Gauvreau 1903-1970 b.Rimouski, PQ Educated: l'Ecole Technique 1920-22, Diploma in Cabinetry; University of Montreal 1924, Literature; l'Ecole Boulle, Paris, Interior Decoration. 1924-5 Assistant supervisor, J.W.Kilgour furniture manufacturer, Beauharnois; 1930-35 professor l'Ecole Technique; 1935-58 Director l'Ecole du Meuble; 1945 Director, Office de l'Artisanat et de la Petite Industrie, Quebec Ministry of Industry and Commerce.

[225] Lesser catalogue 1989 p.93 footnote 7. Under David "it was possible for a student to live and study in Europe with a yearly stipend of $1.200."

[226] Wright p.36

second year project being production of a simple piece of furniture such as an occasional table with marquetry designed by the student. The Artisanship included the apprenticeship program leading in the final two years to specialization, advanced studies in furniture design and carving applied to cabinetry. Gauvreau taught Technology of Wood Construction and History of Furniture and Alphonse Saint-Jacques[227] was Technical Director of the carpentry and cabinetry workshops aided by "experienced cabinet makers" Alberic Gagnon and Léo Fontaine. Wood carving was taught by Bernard Dagenais[228] with Elzéar Soucy.[229] In 1937 Soucy took over from Dagenais and was joined by Louis Parent[230] who succeeded Soucy in 1950.

In 1948, art critic Pearl McCarthy of the Toronto *Globe and Mail* in an article called, 'Ecole du Meuble Joins Carpentry and Culture', described these courses as startling and "worth heeding in other parts of Canada." "[H]idden behind the apparently conservative curriculum" of EdM, she suggested that a reappraisal of the status of craftspeople and their education was in process.

"As some of the students of cabinet-making are college graduates, one visitor expostulated to Jean-Marie Gauvreau, the director: 'You want to make carpenters out of bachelors of arts?' To which Mr. Gauvreau replied: 'Exactly, but in the manner of an earlier age, highly cultivated artisans capable of being real masters."

McCarthy goes on to say,

"The Ecole du Meuble is not trying to turn out graduates in large numbers: rather, to turn out masters equipped either to direct industrial work or set up their own shops, with the hope of having more good, native design in mass production and less pedantic 'artiness' in private craft work. Special attention has been given to

---

[227] Alphonse Saint-Jacques b.1911 Educated: École Technique, did a specialized additional year, 1934; trained by Gauvreau for the position of Technical Director, taught full time 1934-46, part-time 1946-61.

[228] Dagenais ?-1973 b.France educated: École Boulle, Paris; taught: EdM 1930-1937

[229] Soucy 1876-1970 b.Kamouraska PQ Educated: École des Arts et Manufactures 1891-2; apprentice Alfred Lefrancois sculptor and Phillipe Laperle studio 1892-95. Worked with G.W.Hill 1898-1912, war memorials, interiors, reproduction period furniture; 1912 owner Hill's workshop; 1912 working for Bromsgrove Guild on MMFA; 1950-1960 own workshop, interiors, carved furniture, church furnishings, sculpture etc. Taught: 1913/4-1928 École Provinciale des Arts et Metiers and École des Arts et Manufactures; 1928-50 EdM. Secretary Society of Modellers and Woodcarvers of America 1906-8, President 1909/10
Lesser 1989 p.45

[230] Parent 1908-1982 Educated: École Saint-Louis science degree; École des Beaux-Arts, Montreal, architecture, fine arts 1932; Pennsylvania Museum School of Industrial Arts including ceramics 1935; 1939-43 Haute Études Commerciales, intensive study science of ceramics; 1939-43 summer school New York State School of Ceramics, Alfred University B.A.; 1941-2 McGill U engineering;1942 McGill U fine arts. Taught EdBA professor Modelling; 1931-43 drawing Montreal Catholic School Board; summer school Alfred U.; 1937-74 EdM. 1939 La Maîtrise d'Arts workshop commercial contracts for craft shops, Henry Morgan, Birks stores decorative ceramics. Lesser catalogue 1989 p.49-57

use of Quebec wood. The modern designs from the school rouse controversy, but design is a very proper subject for debate. Only bad workmanship is a question on which there cannot be two opinions."[231]

Another course, introduced in 1935, which extended the Apprenticeship program was Interior Decoration. Lesser notes that in the 1930s and 1940s the term referred to "a multi-skilled craftsman in an age which required generalists."[232] In the first and second years, students also studied history of art, drawing, mechanical design, colour theory, and water colour and gouache techniques. In the additional two years, students studied planning and presentation drawing for interior designs and made larger pieces of furniture or suites, working in pairs. Work was sold at the end of the year to defray the cost of wood. Work was commissioned by Gauvreau, his clients, friends, or commercial interior decorators and designed and made by students or made to Gauvreau's designs. The Head of the Interior Design department, from 1936 to 1945, Marcel Parizeau[233] taught furniture making and architecture. Lesser suggests that Parizeau's furniture reflected both Art Deco and Quebec country furniture. Henri Beaulac[234] also taught interior design from 1942, becoming Head of the Department on the sudden death of Parizeau in 1945. In addition Beaulac taught theory of machine printing and silk screen fabric design, handprinted fabrics were produced at EdM under Professors Beaulac and Maurice Felix.[235] In 1940 Marie-Alain Couturier, a French priest, painter, art critic and co-director of the magazine *l'Art Sacré*, taught 'art sacré' canons at EdM, introducing church crafts and furnishings.

In 1940, fire destroyed sections of the buildings and the school museum craft collection[236] and the school had to move to new premises. A year later Parizeau designed an extension to accommodate increasing numbers of students. The main building and its extension contained lecture rooms, studios, workshops, a museum and an auditorium seating 400. In 1946, there were

---

[231] P.McCarthy 'Ecole du Meuble Joins Carpentry and Culture' *Globe and Mail* 3 July 1948 p.8 I am grateful to Beth Greenhorn for drawing my attention to this article.

[232] Lesser catalogue 1989 p.93 footnote 6

[233] Parizeau 1898-1945 b.PQ Educated: École d'Architecture 1921. Architect, artist, interior decorator

[234] Beaulac b.1914 PQ Education: École des Beaux-Arts de Quebec 1938-41; 1937-39 worked with Les Frères Lebrunn, Ferronnerie d'Art, Trois Rivières working with wrought and cast iron; Pratt Institute, New York 1940-42. 1946 on private practice interior design

[235] Lesser catalogue 1989 p.35.

[236] see chapter 6

Studio Craft

551 registered students,[237] which no doubt already shows a response to veteran enrollment; in 1949 there were 200 regular day and 375 evening students.[238] About this time the School had 45 full time and 3 part time staff.[239] Tuition was $50 a year with materials supplied.[240]

Pierre-Aimé Normandeau,[241] a graduate of l'École des Beaux-Arts de Montreal, studied at Sèvres and returned to open a four year ceramics program at EdBA in 1935. In 1945 the program was transferred to EdM, with four Beaux-Art graduates who wished to specialize in ceramics. The accommodation was better but difficulty with funding meant that only two kilns were installed. The ceramics program covered copper enamelling (mandatory in the first year), handbuilding, throwing, production of plaster moulds, design and manufacture of serial-made articles including tea and coffee services, and clay modelling which included bas-relief and maquettes for monumental sculpture.[242] Graduate students were engaged by ceramic companies, opened workshops or taught. Apart from veterans, it seems that about this time EdM found itself faced by a growing influx of women students who wished to study ceramics and in 1947, when that department was started, textiles.

Basic weaving became a required course for students in interior design, unlike ceramics, as it was hoped that interior design graduates with experience of weaving would integrate textiles into their designs or would make their own textiles and train others, emulating a number of successful weaving studios in the Montreal area. Jacques Plasse Le Caisne,[243] a Parisian master weaver and tapestry artist, became Head of the Textile Department from 1947 to 1949 when he returned to France. He was succeeded by his student Jeanne Dansereau[244] who taught there until her

---

[237] Crosby p.18

[238] Lesser catalogue 1989 p.15

[239] Crosby p.32

[240] McCarthy *Globe and Mail* p.8

[241] Normandeau 1906-1965 Education: worked for an Italian sculptor; EdBA Montreal; apprentice École Nationale de Ceramique de Sérvès, Paris c1932-34; Beaux-Arts de Paris, Colorossi Academy, Paris; `École Royale de Ceramique de Faenza, Italy. Visited ceramic factories France, Holland. Married Gilberte Gambier, graduate chemist l'Institut Français de Ceramique and specialist in glazes. 1935 returned to Canada, toured Quebec with Barbeau. Taught: EdBA 1935/6-1945; EdM 1945-c1955. Gilberte Normandeau taught at EdM. Lesser catalogue 1989 p.59

[242] Lesser catalogue 1989 p.61

[243] Le Caisne 1901- b.France

[244] Jeanne Dansereau 1909-1983

retirement in 1973.[245] The weaving course took three years. For entrance a secondary school diploma or family institute certificate was required. It included multiple harness loom techniques, weaves and rules of construction, instruction in design, composition and decoration, as well as research and practical work in a well-equipped studio.[246]

Through Maurice Gagnon, Professor of Art History and librarian, students were exposed to books and journals containing the work of contemporary designers and artists in America, Germany and France.
> "In the 1940s, École du Meuble became the meeting ground for artists of multi-vocational orientation, while the École des Beaux-Arts was considered too staid and retardataire an environment for the learning and practice of art."[247]

Quebec had a number of tertiary level schools teaching crafts. L'École des Arts Domestiques de Quebec (EdAD), discussed earlier,[248] founded in 1930, developed a textile program which went beyond the needs of CdF members, as shown by pictures of woven drapery and a hooked rug (c.1941) in contemporary designs. Students had provided upholstery cloth for EdM furniture before the EdM textile department opened.[249] A 1943 article by Oscar Beriau, Director of EdAD, is accompanied by pictures of weavers at vertical warp tapestry (Gobelin) looms at the "Quebec Provincial School of Handicrafts."[250]

Summary

Throughout the period, principals and heads of craft departments were well educated, the majority having extensive post-graduate training. In the early part of the century Maritime graduates, maintaining traditional links with the New England states, tended to go there for post-graduate education, particularly to the New York schools. In British Canada there was a strong tradition of employing senior staff trained at major British art schools including Sheffield and Glascow, in addition a number of influential teachers graduated at Canadian art schools and went to Britain, particularly to the major London schools such as the Royal College of Art and the

---

[245] Yvonne Rouleau was also teaching there in 1950.

[246] Crosby p.33

[247] Lesser catalogue 1989 p.43

[248] Chapter 4 under Provincial Departments of Agriculture and the Women's Institutes.

[249] Lesser catalogue 1989 pictures of drapery p.64, rug p.65; p.67

[250] Beriau *CGJ* pp.21,22 This appears to be an anglicization of EdDA which Beriau refers to as "a school of handicrafts", a later picture similarly captioned shows teachers from Écoles Ménagères at the school.

Studio Craft

Central School, for post-graduate study. European travel and study was a less frequent component of post-graduate training. When Ellis Roulston went to study in Sweden in 1950, it marked belated recognition of the influence of Scandinavian craft, which had been largely disseminated through teaching outside the formal system. In French Canada staff post-graduate education took place in France and to an almost equal extent in New England, and there was a tradition of bringing in relatively short term teachers from France to establish new directions. The schools and their influences were an intrinsic part of the dominant culture.

Apart from OCA and EdM, craft teaching was the province of women.

Staff were expected to be, and were, practicing artists, although not necessarily in craft.[251] Male staff in particular disciplines - furniture, stained glass, art metal - designed and/or executed regular commissions. Staff hired for their technical expertise and with manufacturing or commercial experience are occasionally referred to, perhaps less frequently as the century progressed. Equally infrequently referred to is contact with related local industries or specialist workshops, these occur most commonly in pottery and furniture.

Despite the varied initiators of arts and crafts schools, their aims were similar. Craft programs were to cover "technical" instruction in various media and "art knowledge" to produce practitioners and, particularly, designers for the "artistic trades and manufactures", teachers at all levels in formal and informal education and occupational therapy, and makers who were presumed to be learning a craft as a leisure activity. Simon's PITA figures for numbers taking courses in proportion to the very small number gaining qualifications, taken in conjunction with the apparently high numbers of women students, who through much of the period had poor employment prospects and domestic commitments, would indicate that many students did not expect to or intend to use the skills gained as a career. The media taught reflect the demands of this clientele, the school's budget and facilities, available teaching expertise, local markets and changing fashion. The twentytwo crafts identified can be grouped, with some overlap, into techniques and products associated with architectural and interior design, classroom teaching, occupational therapy, and with independent craft production. Certain crafts such as stained glass, furniture making, weaving, textile silk screen printing and pottery require considerably more in the way of dedicated space for machinery, tools and materials storage and processing. Staff expertise may be reflected in embroidery being taught at only two schools, VSA and NSCA, although in the beginning at NSCA it may have been seen as a marketable skill for women. Stained glass teaching at OCA was probably supported by a number of stained glass companies in the vicinity. The teaching of craft was carried out against a background of changing interior

---

[251] A number of craftspeople considered themselves primarily painters, and published records reflect this. How much this is due to a lack of critical interest in crafts and its low position in the fine arts hierarchy can only be speculation.

and personal fashions which favoured different skills, this is reflected in the implementation of weaving programs from the mid-twenties on in almost every school and in the introduction of textile silk screen printing in the 1940s.

Of the eight major schools discussed only one, EdM, was set up specifically to teach crafts, producing skilled designer/makers in three areas - furniture, ceramics and textiles. Two other craft schools were EdAD and the New Brunswick Handicraft Training Centre, both primarily trained craftspeople for adult education in rural areas. In the other schools craft was part of a program associated with fine arts (6) and/or with technical education (2).

Within the educational system, craft found itself located at the wrong end of three sets of oppositions: art/craft, art/science, and textbased/skills-based knowledge. The association with fine arts made craft vulnerable to an established hierarchy which strengthened through the period, reflected in the few histories of art schools[252] where craft programs and practitioners are neglected in favour of fine arts. When two art schools were integrated into universities, at Mount Allison 1961 and Winnipeg 1950, craft programs were dropped.

At Mount Allison, the hierarchies were stated from the beginning. Mary Electa Adams, chief preceptress of the Ladies College in 1855, said,
> "The ornamental branches without being depreciated or displaced will always be pursued in subserviency to the solid studies...the introduction of the abstruser sciences into a course of study for females is of the highest utility."[253]

In the late 1950s, a review of the Home Economics, Music, and Fine and Applied Arts departments taken over from the Ladies' College raised the question of the extent to which practical instruction could be part of an academic discipline. It should be noted that these questions are not raised about the male-dominated bastions of medicine and dentistry, which contained practical and skills instruction. In 1959 a University Special Committee recommended that the BFA be retained with more academic content, namely the text-based body of historical, critical and theoretical discourse which had developed in relation to the fine arts but not the lowly applied arts. The Certificate in Fine Arts and all work in applied arts was abolished. Ellis Roulston's arguments in favour of applied arts, which are not quoted, were denied by the committee, "such courses were below University level."[254] A 1944 government booklet indicated that art schools as "specialized teaching centres for arts and crafts" were almost singular in not being part of or a preparatory for the university system. "[T]here are few professional or higher

---

[252] These were written after 1950

[253] 'Grace Annie Lockhard' *Mount Allison Record* (NB 1994) p.37

[254] Reid p.304-5

technical schools in Canada which are...not...part of the university systems."[255] In addition, art schools were described, contrary to many published art school calendars, as "not requiring any fixed academic standing for admission [because they] concern themselves more exclusively with the technical development of the artist."[256] Despite their anomalous position, craft programs in art and technical schools were flourishing in the post-war boom at mid-century.

These eight major schools seem to have had discrete histories and characteristics. The impression received from the limited material is of schools working in isolation from each other. Although there was some movement of staff and graduate students between schools, senior staff tended to have long careers in one institution and students often graduated to teach or returned to teach in their alma mater. This isolation may have been exacerbated by the scale of the country and the regionalism that engendered, which included jealously guarded provincial control over education.

From 1900 to 1950, paralleling the growth in universal schooling, tertiary craft programs provided a particular kind of education in particular crafts. The graduates of these courses holding a 'professional' qualification became the next generation of teachers and practitioners disseminating a particular philosophy of craft and divorcing craft further from artisan knowledge and practice, frequently having to reinvent technical knowledge. Many of these graduates became studio craftspeople.

Studio Craftspeople

Database

As noted in the historiography chapter, there appears to be little published biographical or critical writing within the period about individual craftspeople. Craftspeople at all levels are frequently anonymous,[257] yet an inherent component of the concept 'artist' is that he (or she) is named. From the beginning of my research I have recorded all names of craftspeople on file cards, information and references have been added as they occurred. Many have remained names. In addition a search was made of the Artists in Canada database,[258] initially through CHIN to identify media

---

[255] *Handbook of Canadian Universities, Colleges and Private Schools for Use in Other Countries* (Ottawa 1944) p.83

[256] *Handbook of Canadian Universities, Colleges and Private Schools for Use in Other Countries* pp.53-4

[257] In *Canadian Art* XI:3:112 two decorated pots are featured with no named attribution, which is consistently done with crafts in this magazine but no work in fine art media is unattributed.

[258] I know of only 2 other directories of names being compiled, both regional:
of Manitoba women artists and craftswomen by Marilyn Baker and Claudine Majzels, not currently published; and artists and craftspeople of the Atlantic provinces computer document described in J.Murchie 'Here and There, Now and Agin, Regions End Where Countries Begin' *Art Libraries Journal* pp.16-23 1997

categories and makers likely to be active during the period, then through a physical search of artist files, which contained mostly newspaper articles, at NGC archives.

Fifteen craft media categories[259] gave a total of 5114 names[260] of which 406 (>8%) could have been active between 1900 and 1950. I identified these by birth dates from c1850 to 1926. Experience showed that 1926 was a late date for three reasons: makers born in 1926 were just graduating in 1950, WWII disrupted to varying degrees the time at which makers became a student or started their career, and rearing families frequently meant that women had a gap in their career or did not start until child-rearing was finished. A very large number of makers only had 'address dates', the year in which information was acquired or published, with no other indication of the period of activity; as most of these dates were outside the period the file was not opened unless the maker's name was familiar. In addition a maker may turn up in more than one category and a few names on the list do not have files at NGC. As a result only half (193) of the identified makers were found to be active and a quarter of the files (100) had more than minimal information.

[259] Identified areas	total	poss numbers	found active in period	info
Bookbinding	14	5	4	2
Calligraphy	40	4	1	1
Enamel and Enamelling	61	2	0	0
Furniture Design	67	5	4	1
Glass	150	3	2	0
Glass painting/staining	289	26	19	15
Jewellery making	364	21	9	5
Metalworking	174	38	19	15
Pottery	1573	119	37	30
Silversmithing	65	4	0	0
Tapestry*	110	4	0	0
Textiles	1540	169	92	30
Embroidery	43	6	6	1

Mosaic 51/26, woodcarving 573/50 were not pursued

| Totals | 5114 | 406 [8%] | 193 [48%] | 100 [52%/25%] |

*Tapestry was used as a synonym for wall hanging.

[260] This is a very small proportion of the total in the Directory.

Studio Craft

My card files, including AC makers,[261] totalled 642 names.[262] Almost half have minimal information (date, place, media, country of birth etc.), many of these are from exhibition lists or reviews. Approximately a third have brief anecdotal, academic or biographical details. A tenth may have significant information. Barely 2% have extensive information such as a scholarly article, interview, extensive biographical or archival material. Distributed by decades from 1900, numbers are 43, 40, 130, 210, 219; these hardly reflect population growth and relate only to what is a very fragmentary and random sample. There is a remarkable lack of information about individual craftspeople in this period.

The lack of information within the period combines with elapsing time and neglect to make difficult reconstruction of craftspeople's lives during the period. Carolyn Robinson says of ceramic sculptor Dora Wechsler[263] who received "so much acclaim during her lifetime" including having her work singled out by major critics as being "consistently brilliant and witty, *'the most outstanding in its field*'",

> "Finding her again has been a challenging odyssey for a number of reasons, the most difficult of which have been the passing of the majority of her closest friends and the lack of documentation."[264]

Lack of documentation includes personal sketchbooks and journals as well as published material. In addition, craftspeople themselves may obfuscate. Elsa Schamis says of David Lambert,[265]

> "Any attempt to describe in detail what he has been doing for the past forty years is hampered by the complexity and variety of his activities and by his playfully vague answers...This elusiveness protects his privacy and envelops him in a becoming mythical aura. Many anecdotes about him circulate within the potters circle, sometimes contradicting one another."[266]

In a hierarchical arts system, Kenneth Saltmarche could say of Peter Haworth,

> "His accomplishments as a painter are well-known: his influences as an

---

[261] Most of the 193 AC names were added to my card file but many duplicated names I already had. Some major names were missing from the AC list.

[262] BC 71; AB 30; SK 60; MB 68; ON 180; PQ 98; NB 41; NS 66; PEI 3; NFD 20; NWT 5; YT 0.
There are a small number of grouped makers under these names, eg unnamed employees or family members.

[263] Dora Harris Wechsler mrs (1897-1952) After a career in teaching and social work educated: 1934 Central Technical School, pottery with Bobs Haworth; 1937 London School of Arts and Crafts with Dora Billington.

[264] C.Robinson, K.Carpenter *Caricature and Conscience: The ceramic Sculpture of Dora Wechsler 1897-1952* catalogue (Toronto 1992) pp.8,9

[265] David Lambert (1919-1995) "master potter who came from England after the war"

[266] E.Shamis 'David Lambert, Vancouver's First Potter' ms 1984

educationist, as a director of art at the Toronto Central Technical School and as an instructor in design and drawing at the University of Toronto, has been felt by several generations of Canadian artists. His work as a designer of stained glass windows, beginning in 1923 and continuing up to 1968, remains virtually unknown."[267]

At the beginning of the chapter, craftspeople were defined by class, formal education, income generation, media and self-concept. In addition, 'studio' was seen as implying an artist-maker, working alone, with complete control over the work. My research shows that the reality was considerably more complex.

Class and education
Class (defined by education, lifestyle, income level and community mores) in the disrupted, fluid and multi-cultural milieu of Canada during the period becomes, outside the established Anglo-Canadian and French Canadian areas and elites, a chimera. However, the impression from the available information is that studio craftspeople came from and moved in a middle class or affluent milieu and had many of the attributes of that class.

Academic art education was not a critical factor in becoming recognised as a studio craftsperson although increasingly qualifications lent credibility or were required in craft-related jobs, such as teaching. However Home notes the length of practice necessary to become a competent craftsperson, "it takes seven years to make a wood carver."[268] Georges Delrue[269] "has the old-fashioned idea that years of study and work under a master are necessary before you can call yourself a serious craftsman."[270]

Paul Beau,[271] Montreal, "[i]n the first decades of the 20th century...perhaps the most prominent

---

[267] P.Duval *Glorious Visions* (Ontario 1985) p.3 Over 4 decades Haworth completed commissions for more than sixty churches and schools, some including more than 20 separate windows. His wife Zema Bobs Haworth was also an accomplished painter and educator, under Craft Education:CTS I have commented on the lack of any record of her pottery.

[268] NAC Massey C-2005 8:13:128 CHG:ON discussion

[269] Georges Delrue b.1920 Education:1936-47 apprentice with Gabriel Lucas, Montreal; 1940-45 evening courses EdBA, EdM. 1947 opened studio "in the one room where he lived with his wife"; by 1951 had a large new workshop and a couple of apprentices; 1960-82 proprietor Galerie Libre

[270] R.Ayre 'Creative Craftsmanship in Jewellery' *CA* 1951 p.104

[271] Paul Beau 1971-1949, born Montreal of French parents, restaurant owners; began his career as a clockmaker and antique dealer.

Studio Craft

Canadian craftsman working in brass, copper and wrought iron" claimed to be self-taught although Rosalind Pepall suggests that "he must have spent some time observing the techniques of the ironworker and coppersmith in Europe" on his frequent visits there.[272] By 1915, "Paul Beau & Co., Artistic Metal Workers",[273] located in a building which was Beau's residence and shop, was producing vases, jugs and desk sets "usually made of brass, often with repousse decoration and touches of copper in the design or as border trimming." Pepall reports that gifts of Beau's work were more highly regarded than gifts from Henry Birks and Sons, leading Canadian silversmiths.[274] He also sold work through CHG and exhibited there and at MMFA, the Royal Canadian Academy and various arts and crafts societies.

In addition, Beau worked for architects such as Edward and William Maxwell, for whom between 1902 and 1916 he executed numerous commissions designed by the Maxwells for interior ironwork in houses and churches. In 1918 Beau was selected to execute the interior wrought iron work for the rebuilt Houses of Parliament, some to designs by government architects and some to his own designs. Beau moved his workshop to the Ornamental Wrought Iron Shop on Parliament Hill and between 1919 and 1926 worked there with four blacksmiths and two finishers.[275]

Stan Clarke,[276] a Vancouver potter active from the mid-1940s, was also
"almost entirely self taught, learning by reading, experimenting and attending

---

[272] R.Pepall 'Montreal Metalsmith Paul Beau' *Canadian Collector* 1979 p.34

[273] Many craftspeople in fine and base metals, and other media, ran workshops employing highly skilled and largely anonymous craftspeople or artisans. Workshops appear rigidly hierarchical or co-operative. In some, as Sara Rossi suggests of the English metalsmith Omar Ramsden who exhibited at CNE, the principal was largely a 'facilitator'. Pepall (and others) infer that Beau not only designed but made works. Pieces could be signed "Paul Beau & Co./Montreal" or "Paul Beau" but Pepall does not indicate whether the latter were made solely by Beau.

[274] Henry Birks and Sons Ltd, founded as a retail jeweller and silversmith 1879, absorbed the earlier Hendery and Leslie production firms 1899; and established a national network becoming Canada's leading jewellery store. Employed highly skilled craftspeople such as Clifford Brown, Halifax, from 1920, appointed Jeweller to Queen Elizabeth, the Queen Mother, 1939, Warden of Metal Arts Guild:NS 1951; also designers such as Margaret Chivers, educated WSA, OCA, Industrial Arts Institute and ASL, NY, in the 1920s.

[275] Pepall says that by his death, Beau was a forgotten artist. He apparently left no written records of his work or activities, and friends and relatives met requests for information with "stony silence", possibly because Beau committed suicide.

[276] Stan Clarke b.1914, worked shift work for Air Canada for 34 years which "provided a good deal of spare time for 'artistic' activities." c1946 on had "a thriving pottery" producing mainly functional stoneware. 1953 opened Greenbarn Pottery Supply Ltd, 1955 Founder member Potters Guild of BC, c1959 started a ceramics department in the Education Faculty, University of British Columbia, teaching pottery design methods;. Wife Jean Reagh, a sculptor, studied ceramics at the Art Institute of Chicago 1945.

workshops. As I had an airline pass I was able to attend workshops all over Canada and in the UK...David Lambert had a working pottery and sold materials and equipment. I bought a kick wheel from Lambert and had my one and only lesson throwing pots."[277]

Clarke's 'workshops' mark a change through the period in the transference of craft knowledge. While Beau undoubtedly also read and experimented to inform himself about his craft, his technical expertise was acquired by observation of craftspeople and artisans (probably including consultation with his own skilled employees) in a production milieu as opposed to short term 'workshops' organized by studio craftspeople specifically to teach skills or concepts to a group.

Douglas Shenstone,[278] pewtersmith, took another common craft education route, that of working and studying in a craftsperson's studio for a period ranging from a few months to several years. In Shenstone's case, it was a traditional apprenticeship with Rudy Renzius[279] after taking some night classes from Renzius at Toronto's Northern Vocational School. At that time Renzius had a pewter studio on Gerrard Street, Toronto, in a polyglot area known as The Village where a number of craftspeople and artists had taken over small, rundown houses. The apprenticeship lasted for three years, Shenstone was Renzius' only apprentice. Mary Muff Hogg,[280] after war service, did a general crafts course at MacDonald College, McGill University and then apprenticed for 6 months at Karen Bulow's studio in Montreal and later wove at the Gaelic Foundation, Cape Breton. Ellen Simon[281] graduated from OCA, studied with the Art Students League, New York and c.1940 apprenticed, and became a partner, in the Toronto stained glass

---

[277] Letter from Stan Clarke 10 February 1996

[278] After completing his apprenticeship, Shenstone spent a brief period in California then returned to set up a shop in Hamilton, ON where he made his 'masterwork' a pewter wine decanter for presentation to Renzius. Shortly after war was declared and Shenstone enlisted. As pewter was not available after the war, he did not return to pewtersmithing for 30 years.
Douglas Shenstone *For Love of Pewter (Toronto 1990)*

[279] Hakon Rudolph Renzius 1899-1968 Born Malmo, Sweden. Educated Malmo Technical University (electrical engineering), Copenhagen (metal design), 1923 Chicago (art metalwork). Worked in father's wrought iron, copper and brasswork business. 1923 to USA, 1930 to Toronto. Taught 1932-36 Northern Vocational School, Toronto; 1936-61 Pickering College boys school.

[280] Mary Eileen 'Bunty' Hogg, Member of Order of Canada, 1949-1978 hired by Ontario Government, Education Department, Home Weaving Service as an instructor, later a consultant, organised 60 weaving guilds; helped found Ontario Handweavers and Spinners Guild 1955, Ontario Rug Hookers Guild 1960. Founding member Ontario Craft Foundation, Ontario Craft Council, Canadian Craft Council of which she was Director for 6 years and represented Canada on the World Craft Council.

[281] NGC CA Ellen Rosalie Simon 1916-? worked and lived in Toronto and New York until c.1985 when she moved permanently to New York. First commission for Holy Blossom Temple, Toronto 1941.

Studio Craft

studio of Yvonne Williams.[282] Crawford says that Williams hired students from OCA, "about three trainees at a time", who were exposed to all aspects of the work, "all functioned as both independents and collaborators in a radically egalitarian working environment."[283]

Income generation

The histories of these craftspeople also indicate that, like fine artists, craftspeople able to generate an adequate livelihood purely from studio production were relatively rare. Almost all serious craftspeople supplemented their income with activities directly or indirectly related to their craft, or moved back and fore between different modes of income generation as employee, employer or independent, working to commission or speculation. In some media such as stained glass, craftspeople worked almost exclusively to commission.

For these craftspeople, as for others discussed in earlier chapters, making a livelihood took place against a world economy of two major wars, an economic depression and changing fashions, a national economy responding to rapid changes in scales and loci of production, and major settlement expansion and immigration, and their local economy and patronage. The first quarter century saw the negative impact of settlement and a world war, the second quarter had perhaps eight years unaffected by Depression and war, thus the macro-economy played a major role during the whole period in what was a modest luxury trade. In addition craftspeople had to finance learning their craft and establishing a market.

The negative effects of the economy show up particularly in metalsmith's histories,
> "My father was a designer of jewellery and in Toronto in the Twenties we did fine. Our own house, we ate well, we belonged to a skating club. By 1932 we weren't doing so well at all; there were still plenty of his clients around and prosperous but they thinking of other things. A lot were buying houses, land, dirt cheap and not thinking of bracelets and such.
> Dad lost the business, of course. That came about early in '31. Then the house went...Then his savings. Broke. He wouldn't take relief...
> So Dad got a "Liberty Magazine" route. You've got to picture it. A man of 50, tall

---

[282] NGC CA Yvonne Williams RCA b.1905 Educated OCA 1922-25/6; apprentice stained glass Charles Connick studio, Boston 1927-30; self-directed study Chartres, France 1936. Set up studio Toronto c.1934. Spent 10 years working in studio and doing window dressing at Eaton's department store. Demonstrating stained glass at CNE attracted her first architectural commission. By 1954, 250 windows for 56 churches, chapels and schools in every province and NWT. In 1954 working with Williams were Ellen Simon, Gustav Weisman who also taught painting and glass painting, and George London, who apprenticed in a Toronto glass studio in 1907 and worked with Williams from the 1930s until at least 1962.

[283] Crawford ms

and slim, white-haired. From an old and proud Austrian family and peddling door-to-door..."[284]

Pepall says of Paul Beau,
> "by the 1930's his handcrafted pieces had become too expensive for clients who could buy similar machine-produced wares more cheaply."

and

> "By World War II, Beau was getting on in years and the times were difficult for metal workers, since metal was scarce. Brass and copper went into the production of cartridge cases and artillery shells instead of decorative vases and jugs."[285]

Carl Poul Petersen came from Denmark, where he had trained under silversmith Georg Jensen, to Montreal in 1929 at the beginning of the Depression. He got employment at Henry Birks and Sons Ltd. as their master goldsmith. In 1937 he opened a small studio but returned to Birks in 1939, and when silver became unavailable at the beginning of the war, became involved in specialized manufacture using his metalworking knowledge for the war effort. Thus it was not until 1944 that he set up an independent studio.[286]

For Shenstone,
> "Six years later [1945] I found myself back on civvy street and learned that tin, the principle ingredient of pewter, was still a strategic material not available to the artisan. Thus began a 25-year hiatus..."[287]

In these difficult economic circumstances, patronage and personal capital became important means to establishment. Carl Petersen, in opening an independent studio in 1944, was encouraged by the patronage of Saidye and Samuel Bronfman, of the Seagram whiskey distillery family. Their first orders were used to establish credit and were followed by commissions for family presents, corporate gifts and community service organization awards.[288]

---

[284] Broadfoot 1975 pp.81-82

[285] Pepall p.36

[286] Lesser 1996 pp.47-48

[287] Shenstone p.18

[288] Lesser 1996 p.48

Studio Craft

Kjeld and Erica Deichmann,[289] potters, came back to New Brunswick from studying in Denmark to set up their pottery[290] in Spring 1934. Their first firing, which was a failure, was in August 1935. By June 1936,

> "we were beginning to notice definite progress in our work...Slowly, we began to sell.
> Writers and photographers[291] had been coming, and we were given a great deal of publicity,[292] which helped us to become known quickly and brought many people to our door."[293]

In addition,

> "there used to be a wonderful person from St. Andrews who was a great patron of all the arts and crafts anywhere. And she would buy, oh, when $200 was an awful lot of money...
> Patrons help a great deal...Very early on Mrs. [Alice Lusk] Webster came to see us and we became very great friends and she bought quite a number of things for the N.B. Museum. All of the wedding presents the Websters ever gave, they gave Deichmann pottery. Their interest just helped us enormously...Dr. Webster was one of the most important people in the province."[294]

---

[289] Kjeld Deichmann 1900-1963 b.Copenhagen Educated: University of Copenhagen (Philosophy) 1919; painting, Paris 1920-21; wood sculpture Toulouse 1921-22, Vienna 1922-23; self-directed studies Florence and Ravenna 1924-25; 1933-34 Denmark, worked with potter Axel Bruel.
Erica Deichmann b.c1912 Educated: 1933-34 Denmark, weaving
The Deichmann Pottery 1935-1963, moved from Moss Glen, Kingston Peninsular to Sussex, NB 1956. Kjeld did all the throwing and some decorating, Erica decorated and made ceramic sculptures.

[290] Erica was weaving at this point, she exhibited weavings in the Paris Exposition 1937, however by 1936 she was increasingly involved in the pottery.

[291] Edith Marjorie (Madge) Smith 1898-1974 photographer also had a gallery/shop in Fredericton, NB, was a close friend of the Deichmanns and sold their pottery through the shop

[292] The Deichmanns were probably exceptional in the amount of publicity they garnered. Between 1938 and 1956, there were at least 19 articles about or referring to them; between 1952 and 1964 the National Film Board of Canada made 4 films, *The Story of Peter and the Potter* 1953 was one of NFB's most popular films.

[293] CMC.A Deichmann exhibition file Erica or Kjeld Deichmann 'A Study of Canadian Handicrafts with Particular Reference to New Brunswick' typescript of Submission to Massey Commission p.19

[294] Quoted from taped interviews with Erica Deichmann in Peter Thomas 'One Voice, Erica and Kjeld Deichmann' *ArtsAtlantic* 30 (Halifax 1988)
Dr and Mrs Webster may be the "doctor and his family" met about 1936 and recalled in 'Some Personal Experiences'. "Without their steadfast friendship throughout the years, we wonder what our lives would have been."

Despite "beginning to send our work farther away to exhibitions and to shops....we were not earning enough to live." On the death of Kjeld's parents c.1933 he had inherited "a fair amount of money...up until about 1940, we lived on Danish money..."[295] For the Deichmanns, even with generous patronage it took at least seven years to master their craft and establish a market sufficient to support a simple lifestyle.

Duncan Douglas[296] returned to Toronto from learning his craft in Paris, France, to set up as an art bookbinder in the Fall of 1928,

> "At first and for some time I imagine, my binding will only keep me in chocolate peppermints. Dividends etc provides me with a fairly certain background."[297]

For others the economic situation spelled defeat. Kristine Frederickson Smolleck[298] studied at WSA and the Art Students League, New York to 1925. After four years in New York, she returned to Winnipeg where she reluctantly worked as a fashion illustrator. During that period she took up ceramic sculpture and pottery. In the 1930s her story appears to end, "life closed in on her...she lost her job and had to go on relief."[299]

Mitzi Andersen Dahl[300] came to Winnipeg from Norway in 1926. A tapestry weaver working in the Norwegian tradition 'Billedvaev', who also dyed and spun her wool, she had eight years training in "the best handicraft schools of Norway" and her work had been exhibited to acclaim in Norway, Denmark and Germany. Within five days of her arrival she had secured a position as designer in the needlework department at Eaton's store, Winnipeg, where she worked for eighteen months. Her experiments with dyes from Canadian flora came to the attention of the CPR who,

> "being interested in preserving the arts and handicrafts of new settlers, invited her

---

[295] Thomas p.27

[296] Douglas Duncan 1902-1968 Educated: University of Toronto; Sorbonne, Paris 1925. In Paris the Canadian-born bookbinder Agnes St John d.1927 "whose bindings were, and are, prized in France, England, and the United States, though all but unknown in her own country" introduced Duncan to masterbinders Jean Domont and Henri Noulhac with whom he apprenticed 1926-1931, when both masters died. Studio in Paris 1928-mid 1930s, studio Toronto 1928 to c1942, after 1938 worked with Madeline Glenn who did much of the binding. Duncan bound his last book in 1949.
Alan Jarvis ed. *Douglas Duncan* (Toronto 1974)

[297] Jarvis p.20

[298] Kristine Frederickson Smolleck b.c1895 Yorkton SK Education: WSA 1915-19; ASL, NY 1923-1925

[299] Baker pp.110, 111

[300] also anglicized to Dale, Mitzi Andersen seems to have married c.1930

Studio Craft

to go to Ontario where she found many specimens to supplement those of Manitoba."[301]

Dahl was also invited to demonstrate her weaving[302] at the CPR sponsored New Canadian Folksong and Handicrafts Festivals in Winnipeg and Calgary.

In 1933, A.Y.Jackson wrote to Marius Barbeau,
> "Yesterday a very charming little lady came to the studio. Mrs Dale, or Dahl...She undertook to make a tapestry last Spring from one of my Arctic Drawings...She and her husband have been living in Winnipeg, and having a difficult time. The husband making skis, looms etc and she teaching weaving. This tapestry she has made is a beautiful piece of work about 48 by 50 inches, it took her over three months to do it. It is much richer than the sketch I made, technically I should say about perfect. She and her husband are trying to get something to do here, and failing that are going on home to Norway..."[303]

As Dahl's name does not reoccur, I assume that she did return to Norway.

Self-concept
The lack of autobiographical writing makes it a matter of speculation as to how craftspeople conceived of themselves. The lack of extensive information about craftspeople makes it difficult to categorize with accuracy. Thus activity becomes an indicator. These include the setting up of an independent studio, exhibiting and exhibit location, and media or maker associations.

Studios
There is evidence of studio craft activity from the beginning of the century. Alice Egan Hagen established a studio in the Roy Building, Halifax where she practiced and taught china painting for several years at the turn of the century.[304] Her marriage did not interfere with continued production, experimentation and teaching of china painting and later pottery through a long life.

---

[301] 'A Norwegian Woman Who Weaves Pictures' *The Western Producer* 27 February 1930. Dahl brought spinning wheel, table tapestry loom and examples of tapestries and other hand weaving to Saskatoon at the invitation of SACS, where she gave demonstrations and talked of the history of her craft. Dahl had a "charming personality and unfailing patience in answering many questions...in excellent English."

[302] Beriau *CGJ* 1943 p.28 shows a Dahl weaving after a lost painting by the Norwegian Gerhad Munthi, who was involved as a designer with the Norwegian tapestry revival.

[303] CMC:A Barbeau correspondence A.Y.Jackson to Barbeau 10 November 1933

[304] Alice Egan Hagen (Mrs J.C.Hagen) 1872-1972 Educated: NSCA; china painting with Mrs Bessie Brown, Halifax, Adelaide Alsop-Robineau Studio, New York, Osgood Art School, New York. Taught: NSCA: china painting Halifax 1889-1912, Jamaica, Halifax 1916-1930. Set up a pottery studio and kiln at her home in Mahone Bay c1930, experimented with clays and glazes, taught students and teachers.

Marie Hewson Guest also opened a studio/shop in Halifax, in 1905, in partnership with another woman, a china painter. Guest designed and made art metalwork in copper and silver, leatherwork and basketry. The studio seems to have lasted until 1913 when Guest returned to travel and study in Europe and America, and also taught crafts for WAAC:Ottawa and at UMA.[305]

In 1923 SACS records a "Canadian woman" selling homewoven articles including a skirt length, bags and scarfs in both wool and silk.[306] This is probably Maril Wells, a farmer's wife who wrote,
> "I have two more silk tunics and a skirt length that I could send...I can weave to a width of thirtyfour (34) inches on my loom...but the idea is this - to make a garment that cannot be bought in an ordinary store something different from the usual line of goods - I never make two alike in every respect...the designing and weaving is quite enough for me - I am absolutely lost when it comes to selling."[307]

Both the type of work and the maker's perspective suggest formal training and studio production. In same year in Saskatoon, Miss Kende exhibited embroideries and "exquisitely executed" illumination. Kende, who had received her craft instruction in her home city of Budapest, Hungary, was also "so proficient in the book-binding craft...that she is prepared to do book-binding by hand as a commercial industry. Her work occupies a table by itself and is a revelation of skill."[308] Whether Miss Kende and Mrs Wells were able to find a steady market for their work is unknown.

SACS continued to record through the 1930s craftspeople who may well have been studio craftspeople. These included weavers such as Mrs H.R.Clark, who in 1936 took second prize at CNE for a display of handloom weaving, and in 1938/9 took prizes at Victoria, BC, and attended

---

[305] Marie Olivia Hewson Guest (Mrs B. Guest) 1880-1966 Education: 1896-c1900 UMA, Eric Pape School of Art, Boston, Art Students' League, NY. Guest moved to Winnipeg after her marriage in 1919 and concentrated on painting and exhibiting, in 1931 doing a portrait of Mitzi Dahl, 'The Tapestry Weaver'. Guest also taught basketry and other crafts at evening classes.
Claudine Majzels 'Constructing the Woman Artist: Marie Hewson Guest in Winnipeg' *Manitoba History* 29 1995 pp.2-10

[306] SKAB SACS B88-B Committee reports Arts and Crafts Committee annual report 1923

[307] SKAB SACS B88-E(1) Correspondence 1922-1924 Maril (or Maret) Wells, Glenbush, to Mrs Marshall 20 September 1923 There is no further mention of Mrs Wells, although the first work sold for $45 and over $60 worth of orders were taken.

[308] SKAB SACS B88-4-H 'Throngs attend arts and crafts exhibition organized by L.C.W.' newspaper clipping

a class sponsored by the Weaver's Guild in Victoria.[309] Clark wove 'Harris tweed', "some very lovely curtains,...towels, shopping bags and purses in attractive designs." In 1939 Mrs L. Baumeister, who moved from Holland c1936 to the Prince Albert area,

> "showed some samples of her extremely fine weaving, colourful and extremely well made...articles woven in wool...other samples of intricate pattern...a particularly well made piece of suiting."[310]

SACS reports that Mrs Baumeister had taught weaving and bookbinding in Holland and was giving instruction at night classes in the [Saskatoon?] Technical School. She also opened a small shop in Saskatoon, and in June 1940 offered to display SACS work in the shop. The work would be sold on a percentage basis as a trial run through the Summer; by November 1940 SACS decided that sales justified the consignment arrangement.[311] Within the next year, Mrs Baumeister moved to join her soldier husband stationed at Kingston, ON, where she was involved with the Kingston Hand-Weavers and established a studio/shop, 'The Weefhuis'. In the interim the family also anglicized their name.[312] In 1948 Rie Donker Bannister[313] moved to Toronto with her family where she established another weaving studio, teaching both there and at Ryerson College.

Bannister's history is not untypical, many craftswomen accompanied their husbands in their search for work. People who had taken up land continuously left, particularly from drought-stricken or marginal farms, throughout the five decades. They tended to move to the larger urban centres, particularly the booming economy of Ontario. The second World War intensified this movement. Craftspeople also moved back and fore across the country in pursuit of commissions, teaching jobs and sustaining markets.

Theoretically, Toronto at the centre of Canada's major, most affluent conurbation with a number of colleges running craft courses and with major venues for exhibition (discussed below) should

---

[309] SKAB SACS B88-B2 Report 1939/9 and p.166
Victoria Spinners and Weavers Guild (Handweavers' Guild of Victoria) est.1934 in 1939 held "the first weaving institute" in BC with the influential American weaver Mary Meigs Atwater instructing. Beriau *CGJ* 1943 p.29

[310] SKAB SACS B88-B2 newspaper clipping p.171 16 October 1939

[311] SKAB SACS B88-B2 Entries 18 October 1939, 7 June 1940, 21 October 1940

[312] Personal conversation 2 April 1998 son William Bannister, who continued to run the South Landing Craft Centre, Queenston. Established in 1953 by Rie Bannister, it became "the province's best known and most influential resource centre for weavers" according to Crawford. William Bannister ran a mail-order supply business, his wife Carol taught using Rie Bannister's looms.

[313] Mrs Rie Donker Bannister (Mrs Louis Baumeister) 1902-1981 b. Rotterdam, met her husband a Canadian soldier in Holland. Came to Canada to be married bringing with her a large, traditional floor loom and wool wrapped around her china. Lived on a farm at Whitestar, moved to Prince Albert, then to Saskatoon.

have provided a substantial market for studio craftspeople. An initial survey may suggest this was so, however whether Toronto and environs did sustain a proportionately higher population of craftspeople or is simply better documented[314] remains open to question in the current state of Canadian research. Attention has primarily focussed on a group of fine metalsmiths and potters, mostly associated with CTS and involved with founding the Metal Arts Guild (MAG) and the Canadian Guild of Potters (CGP).

One of the earliest of this group of potters was Nunzia D'Angelo,[315] who studied with Bobs Haworth at CTS, graduated in 1926 and became Haworth's teaching assistant from 1927 to 1934. Home said in 1944,

> "[She] has been the most consistent worker, earning her living as a teacher and as a producer. Mrs Zavi has always been a crusader in the pottery cause and has furthered its welfare by much good propaganda. She was the moving spirit in the organization of the Canadian Guild of Potters in 1936 and in the Canadian exhibit at Syracuse."[316]

D'Angelo, uniquely, exhibited consistently at CNE Applied Arts exhibition from 1928 on. Making distinctive low fired majolica, "reflecting her Italian background" and an interest in folk pottery, Crawford says that in the 1930s she bisque fired in her parent's backyard and fired at Sovereign Pottery, Hamilton. However by the time D'Angelo and Jarko Zavi, her future husband, met in the late 1930s she had a kiln, apparently the only private one in Toronto at the time.[317] From 1941, D'Angelo and Zavi ran a joint pottery studio on Gerrard North in the Village area. Both were interested in experimenting with Ontario clay bodies and glazes.[318] In 1946 they moved to Coburg and D'Angelo, Crawford says at Zavi's behest, stopped making pottery. D'Angelo was one of the earliest of a group of Toronto women potters who flourished from the mid-1930s on. Home, in her 1944 survey, says,

> "Of the forty working potters, seven might be classed as professional handicraft

---

[314] Gail Crawford kindly allowed me to read various drafts of her comprehensive book on Ontario craft, due for publication in Fall 1998 *A Fine Line: Studio Crafts in Ontario from 1930 to the present* Dundurn Press.

[315] Nunzia D'Angelo Zavi 1906-1968 married Jarko Zavi c.1938 joint pottery studio 1941-1946. Zavi born in Czechoslovakia, graduate School of Fine Art, Prague, potter and later jeweller, d.1987

[316] Home *CGJ* p.72

[317] Zavi used to joke that he met D'Angelo through searching for someone with a kiln and married her for her kiln. Mrs Mary McMillan Prower personal communication 1 April 1998. If it is the kiln shown in Home's article it is small.

[318] Among the glazes they experimented with were uranium glazes accessed through government sources. Sarah Prower, CMC, has a ceramic horse originally given to her mother, which has a green uranium glaze. D'Angelo and one of her daughters died of cancer.

Studio Craft

potters, though the others all sell varying quantities of their output either privately or through the Canadian Handicrafts Guild's shop at Eaton's and the Women's Art Association."[319]

All accounts until late in this period indicate the restrictions imposed by lack of access to affordable or adequate kiln technology for studio potters producing relatively small runs. Home makes a point of saying of "a Mrs. Edwards"[320] in Manitoba c.1944 "owns her own electric kiln that fires to 2000F." She also notes that in British Columbia, "of the six kilns available in the province, five are owned by the schools" and Alberta had three kilns, one in private hands.[321] David Lambert, Vancouver, manufactured kilns in the late 1940s, "without David Lambert's small electric kilns many people would have waited a long time for the opportunity to do their own firing."[322]

Nancy Meek[323] was a co-founder of MAG and one of the group of jewellers and fine metal smiths working in Toronto which included Renzius, Fussell,[324] Stacey and Shenstone. Like D'Angelo, Meek and her classmate, Rosina White were consistent exhibitors in the CNE Applied Arts section from 1932. Meek studied at CTS and OCA with Harold Stansfield. After graduating in 1930, Meek spent a year in Paris studying with Paul Babelet and jewellery designer, Grebel. Like most craftspeople, Meek made commissioned and speculative work, taught[325] and on occasion, such as the copper convector grilles for the new British American Oil headquarters,

---

[319] Home *CGJ* p.71

[320] Mrs Edwards trained in England, "working before her marriage at the University of North Wales, Bangor." Under her "inspiration" a small group of women made lamp bases, book-ends, cups and saucers, jugs, teapots and cigarette boxes which they sell to local stores or gift shops. Home *CGJ* p.69
I assume from the tone of the article this is thrown pottery.

[321] Home *CGJ* 1944 p.69 These are not necessarily accurate figures, Home's article appears a solid overview but the account of the Deichmanns has major inaccuracies.

[322] BC Potters Guild [?] Georgina Huges 'Early Pottery Classes in British Columbia' ms

[323] Nancy Meek Pocock 1910-1998

[324] Andrew Fussell 1904-1983 Educated:1926-32 CTS nightcourse, brief course with Henrik Beenfeldt; NVS Rudy Renzius. Taught: own studio 1932-62; CTS 1963-72. Worked gold sterling, copper, bronze, brass, aluminum, stainless steel; hollowware and jewellery, particularly ecclesiastical pieces.

[325] Taught 1937 New York School of Handicrafts, NY city; University of Toronto Occupational Therapy Course; c1948 with Pocock at Madsen Folk School, Unionville; CTS night school etc.

worked to other's designs.[326] In 1942 she married John Pocock, taught him her craft and they worked in partnership in a studio on Gerrard Street.

Hepzibah Stansfield, Herbert Stansfield's wife, was a weaver "known as a fine craftsman." It is possible that she was a member of the Guild of Handicraft at Cromer, UK. After she came to Canada she continued to weave. She taught weaving and dyeing at Pools Harbour, NFD, for two summers, c.1923 and 1926, at the invitation of the Governor of Newfoundland and his wife. She, with others, initiated the Ridpath Gallery exhibition in 1931, and at some stage, possibly as late as 1933 when Stansfield finished teaching at OCA, she and her husband set up their own studio and workshop at Limberlost in the Muskoka.[327] It is possible that a combination of the effect of the Depression on affluent cottage owners and the remoteness effected their move back to Toronto in 1936 where Stansfield returned to teaching, at Northern Vocational School, and they set up a studio/shop in the studio Renzius had vacated on Gerrard.[328]

Outside the nascent media guilds, studio craftspeople are even less well documented. Painted and stencilled fabrics were taught and exhibited early in the century. Alice McCabe, a classmate of Nancy Meek at CTS, supplied batik and printed fabrics to the Guild of All Crafts in the late 1920s,[329] as did Constance Pole who exhibited batiks at CNE in 1933 and 1934.[330] In 1930 Mathilda McCulloch exhibited two batiks selling for $125 and $150.[331] Arthur Smith, a "member of the Canadian National Academy, Ottawa" in 1933 had just completed six large batik panels representing the great lovers of history "on muslin and silk and done after an old Japanese

---

[326] B-A Oil c1950 employed a number of craftspeople to make hangings, metalwork, carvings, woven and printed fabrics, and furniture for various corporate headquarters in Canada. The works used Canadian motifs, and often materials, many of which were designed by Thor(kild) Hansen, art director for the company.
Hansen 1903-1976 born in Denmark was involved in the folk art revival there. In 1930 he and his wife Dagmar Mortsen set up a handcraft shop in Regina, SK which despite going broke in two months had some impact. In 1938 he went to B-A Oil as staff artist but continued to be involved with the craft community, designing, teaching and speaking on their behalf.

[327] The Muskoka is a wilderness area of lakes and woods north of Toronto and a popular summer cottage area. Limberlost Lodge was a well-known resort.

[328] The shop lasted briefly as Stansfield died in early 1937, "The long hours of over-work taxed his never robust constitution. So quiet and self-effacing was this man that few realized his true greatness, and even those who knew him best knew little of his achievements." NCG CA H.H.Stansfield file Obituary *Globe and Mail, Toronto* 17 May 1937. Nothing further is known of Hepzibah.

[329] Crawford personal communication 2 April 1998

[330] CNE Fine Art, Graphic and Applied Art, Photography catalogue 1933, 1934

[331] CNE Fine Art, Graphic and Applied Art, Photography catalogue 1930

Studio Craft

method", had made batik theatre curtains and the "largest batik ever made" for Trinity Methodist Church, Springfield, Mass.[332] Marion Mackay Nicoll,[333] while a student at OCA c1937, became interested in batik through a friend who was making "tapestries" for hotels in New York. Nicoll returned to Alberta and,

> "in the depression years...was able to earn money by producing batik scarves and other items for a city merchant...her skilful fingers have turned out hundreds of pieces of Batik including, tapestries, wall hangings, scarves, curtains, portraits and runners."

In 1945, Angus Macdonald[334] and Elizabeth Wilkes Hoey[335] set up a hand-screen fabric studio, Wilcam Fabrics.[336] Wilkes had unsuccessfully tried to sell her fabric designs in New York, which was suffering war time restrictions. Macdonald was working as an Interior Designer for Simpson's Department Store, Toronto. The partnership was brief, Wilkes married and her husband became involved in the fabric printing. During a long career, they produced custom designed and hand printed fabrics including silkscreened fabrics for the B-A Oil project c1950.

Studio craftspeople in embroidery and associated needle techniques seem even less well documented. In the late 1920s and early 1930s embroideries by Margaret Middleton and by Hilda Benjamin Sexton, creator of two major works *The Hunt* and *The Seasons* selling at $2,000 respectively, were shown at CNE Applied Arts exhibition.

Exhibitions

Where more extensive evidence is lacking, I have assumed that a craftsperson who successfully entered work for juried exhibition both conceives of him or herself as a craftsperson and is acknowledged as such. While exhibitions held in art galleries clearly signal affiliation with fine arts, crafts exhibited at industrial/agricultural exhibitions are not so clearly signed but it would be unwise to underestimate the level of entrants as these adjudicated exhibitions offered an

---

[332] NGC CA Arthur Smith file Washington, DC *Star* 10 December 1933

[333] see Craft Education: PITA

[334] Angus A Macdonald OSA, ARCA 1909-1986 Education: mainly self-taught, brief college c1929; 1953 to Europe to study stained glass. Various jobs including Interior designer (fabric and furniture) 1938-45. Continued to design fabrics and stained glass windows until at least 1966.

[335] Elizabeth Wilkes b.1915-c.1997 m. William Hoey c1945 Education:OCA. Designed draperies for commercial and industrial operations; screen print design and printing; batik; also sheep breeder, spinner and weaver. Her career designing and printing fabrics seems to have covered at least 20 years and included commissions for Atlas Steel, Imperial Oil and the Canadian Government for whom she designed draperies for the Parliament buildings.

[336] Described in B.Button *I Married an Artist* (Toronto 1951) pp.214-226

important showcase, recognition and sales for craftspeople often not available elsewhere in the early decades. Exhibitors or prize lists give minimal information - place, date, maker's name, media and in some cases price, however my discussion of industrial/ agricultural exhibition lists[337] indicated that a proportion of entrants were working and/or exceptionally skilled craftspeople.

While some classes suggest a continuation of artisan traditions, many others would allow for design skills, significant innovation and reflect a formal education. Percy Inglis, Mahone Bay, NS, an exhibition judge "who, himself, hooks beautiful mats" was "one of those who is doing much to encourage the workers in mats and other handicrafts to a higher standard of taste and workmanship."[338] Rug hooking, in particular, attracted the attention of a number of artists such as Pegi Nicol MacLeod, who made and designed hooked rugs.[339]

The PEI:PE award lists indicated out-of-province entrants including Mrs A.G.Savage of Listowel, ON, who took eleven prizes in 1930. To my knowledge no-one has done a comparable Canadian study to that on two Australian women, Elsie Wright and Mary Dwyer, who through the 1930s to the 1950s competed aggressively and very successfully for embroidery prizes in agricultural shows throughout Australia.[340] Craftswomen at this level have to be acknowledged as experts in their fields, deeply committed in time and energy to their craft.

The award lists for the New Canadian Folk Song and Handicrafts Festival, Winnipeg 1928, categorized by media and ethnic group (excluding British and French) suggests that these are examples of traditional skills, however many of these countries already had craft schools and a lively interest in the development of craft. Esther Thompson, the second Head of Women's Work, Manitoba Department of Agriculture, and involved with the Festival was a Norwegian-Canadian. Nor were participants necessarily 'peasants', award-winners Gustav Roos was one of the designer/makers mentioned by Nobbs and Mrs S.Istvanffy was running embroidery classes for CHG:MB twenty years later.

The major industrial/agricultural exhibitions such as PNE, Vancouver and Canadian National

---

[337] chapter 3, 'Sources of information'

[338] G.Pearson 'The Art of Rug Hooking' *MacLean's Magazine* 1927 p.59

[339] J.Murray *Daffodils in Winter* (Ontario 1984) p.45 One of MacLeod's rugs won an award at 'The Arts in Therapy' exhibition, Museum of Modern Art, NY, in 1943. Other exhibitors were Louise Nevelson and Louise Bourgeois. In 1943 the AGO showed an exhibition of rugs by American artists which originated at MOMA. MacLeod's designs were made by several New Brunswick women under the supervision of Madge Smith for sale in her Fredericton gallery.

[340] F.Kenneley 'A Tale of Two Champions' *Piecework* January 1998 pp.22-24
Dwyer's winnings in one year during the Depression kept her family farm from foreclosure.

Studio Craft

Exhibition (CNE),[341] Toronto had a number of venues for exhibiting craft, some linked with women and/or domestic arts[342] and some with fine arts. At PNE:1910 crafts under Fine Arts included woodcarving, basket making, bead work, furniture, pottery, china painting and glass blowing. At CNE:1915, WAAC showed 'Crafts and Home Industries' in the Applied Arts Building. At CNE:1922 the 'Three Arts Room' in the Women's Building[343] exhibited painting, music and crafts by Canadian women. The latter included jewellery, weaving and batiks again exhibited under WAAC's auspices.[344] Also at CNE:1922 the Fine Arts catalogue, for exhibitions in the Fine Arts Building, included for the first time an 'International Graphic and Applied Arts' section. This exhibition seems to have been a selling exhibition by established artists. For the next decade 'Applied Arts' included Canadian craftspeople although identification is difficult from 1922 to 1927 as the country of origin is not given.

Thus at CNE not only was there a variety of locations (the Applied Arts Building, the Women's Building and the Fine Arts Gallery) and allocations (Canadian women, women and children, non-gendered) but there was a further division into exhibitions, competitive exhibitions and selling exhibitions by accredited artists. The decision to exhibit under Applied Arts as opposed to (or including) other options indicates that these craftspeople conceived of themselves as studio

---

[341] CNE had its roots in the 1840s through organizations such as the Agricultural and Arts Association of Ontario which had expanded their exhibition to include manufactured goods, machinery, domestic products, arts and crafts circulating annually to different towns in southern Ontario. A coalition of organizations c.1880 established the first of the annual exhibitions on a permanent Toronto site. It was not called the Canadian National Exhibition until 1919. The first exhibition on the permanent site attracted over 100,000 paid admissions to see 8234 exhibits, including crafts.

[342] CNE: 1879-1938 "has general prize lists that include handicrafts"; 1919-28 and 1931-39 separate prize lists for work done by women and children; 1941 "simple Handicrafts" prize list; 1942-46 closed for WWII; 1947 Women's Prize list; 1948-50 separate prize lists for handicrafts, art work etc submitted by women and by school children. Fax Linda Cobon CNE:A 3 February 1998

[343] The Women's Building erected 1908 contained a wide range of displays and activities presented by all the national women's organizations, including public health and home nursing, literature, housing and town planning, occupational therapy, cookery, and applied art and crafts, the last as part of the activities of a range of organizations not necessarily craft organizations. Apart from displays of entries in craft competitions, the WAAC put together exhibitions on an annual basis but these seem to have varied in their content, some containing artisan crafts or a mix of studio and artisan crafts. In 1929 WAAC and CHG:HQ ran a Handicraft Fair "which consisted of ten practical demonstrations of needlework, jewelry-making, weaving, painting on fabrics, batik, rug-making and lace making...held daily." In 1932 the WAAC demonstrations included "pewter modelling, studio weaving on a modern loom, bookbinding, spinning, jewelry-making, leather work." In 1934, metal workers demonstrated with a display of work "collected from all parts of Canada by the Canadian Handcrafts Association [this was probably CHG:HQ not CHG:ON]" Finlayson says that the West Wing of the Women's Building during the 1930s was "a demonstration wing where active workers carry on..." CNE.A M.Finlayson 'Women's Activities at the Canadian National Exhibition During the Years 1928-1937' ms (Toronto 1976) pp.7,9,11

[344] McLeod p.93

craftspeople. This is supported by the type of work, by exhibiting with high calibre international makers and by related activities in the Toronto craft scene. This was also a major market, in 1925 Miss Marjory Hicken of Toronto, amongst the large number of unmarried women exhibiting jewellery up to 1926, displayed 48 items of jewellery and uniquely gives her full address.

The Applied Arts exhibition was dominated by British craftspeople, reflecting the British predilection of anglo-Ontario. This suddenly ceased in 1932, I assume as a result of the Depression. The last of the huge British Applied Art Sections[345] in 1931 had 43 exhibitors in pottery, stained glass, jewellery, art metal, hollowware and flatware, needlework, ceramic sculpture, leatherwork, painted wood, weaving, enamels and bookbinding. In 1928 and 1929 there was a 'Canadian Applied Art' section, the first such recognition. Seven (and 8) exhibitors showed pottery, batik panels, large embroideries, silverware and bookbinding. In 1930, countries of origin were given in the International section, 12 Canadians were included. The Canadian Applied Arts section remained comparatively small in numbers and restricted in media through the 1930s, with between 5 and 15 exhibitors each year. It was lead by Nancy Meek and Rosina White, who in 1936 had their own section 'Handmade Jewellery' showing 19 pieces, and Nuncia D'Angelo as one of a growing group of women potters. In 1935 and 1938 only potters exhibited. The 51 craftspeople exhibiting between 1928 and 1938, included 27 potters, 2 or 3 clay sculptors, 11 batik makers, 2 embroiderers, 6 silversmiths and a stained glass designer/maker.

Parallel to the 1939 Applied Art exhibit, a 'Craft Exhibition' in the West Wing of the Women's Building "assembled by the Arts and Crafts Club" of WAAC included craftspeople who customarily exhibited in the Applied Arts section. Crafts included weaving, hooked rugs, pottery, ceramic sculpture, metal work, jewellery, stained glass, woodcarving, bookbinding, "ceramic decoration", batik, lacquer work, knitting, and block printing from the Central Technical School.

Although *Canadian National* Exhibition and '*Canadian* Applied Art' suggests national involvement, only 3 of the 51 craftspeople exhibiting between 1928 and 1938, and 4 of 57 exhibitors in the 1939 Craft Exhibition came from outside the Toronto area.[346]

Throughout the period CHG:HQ was the pre-eminent organization involved in exhibiting

---

[345] This exhibition must have offered a reliable market for British exhibitors to attract such numbers including people of the stature of K.Pleydell Bouverie, Michael Cardew and Charles Vyse.

[346] These were 1928-38 Kjeld and Erica Deichmann, NB, and Grace Melvin, BC; 1938 Deichmanns, Emily Carr (pottery) BC, and Edith Matheson, weaver, MB. Five rug hookers were not included in the total.
Competitive exhibitions may have had a more national representation. The 1932 CNE Annual Report said, "The handcraft associations of Canada have also been very helpful in connection with our aims to make the annual exhibits in the Women's Building one of the most nationally representative of Canadian arts." "Showings of work from Vancouver to Halifax were on display in non-competitive groups in the east wing" Findlayson says that there were 9 "handcraft organizations of Canada." Findlayson p.9

Canadian craft at major international exhibition venues, through national travelling exhibitions and annually at MMFA.[347] However, as there appears to be no extant archival information,[348] it is difficult to know what proportion of the work was by studio craftspeople.

In 1923 the Province of Quebec Association of Architects, the Art Association of Montreal and CHG held a joint exhibition at MMFA, which covered the whole gamut of crafts from furniture and stained glass to basketry, batik and weaving,
>"to demonstrate the capabilities of Canadian craftsmen in meeting the needs of designers and owners in the matter of artistically executed workmanship."[349]

That "the names of designers, craftsmen and producing firms were all given equal prominence" suggests the complexity of production which existed during the period.

Twentyfive years later, the CHG annual exhibition was described as "unusually varied and original and the specimens exhibited are of an increasingly high standard. Exhibits by mastercraftsmen." Some craftspeople are named including W.G.Hodgson, AB and the Deichmanns, NB.[350] Their work was also included in the exhibition of 'Contemporary Canadian Arts and Crafts' at the Paris International Exhibition of Art and Crafts in Modern Life. This exhibit was assembled by CHG and curated by Marius Barbeau. The work was in fact a mixture of Native, historical and contemporary pieces, the latter included work from 8 jewellers and silversmiths including Meek, White, Stacey and Fussell; 10 Toronto potters and Emily Carr, BC,[351] the Deichmanns and [Ida] Kay MacKay, PEI; and 3 bookbinders, Duncan Douglas, and Louis Forest[352] and Marguerite Lemieux,[353] PQ. This exhibition went on to the Scottish Empire

---

[347] see chapters 4 and 6

[348] personal communication Ellen McLeod 23 March 1998.
Newspaper articles seem to focus on the 'exotic' - work by Native peoples, New Canadians and Québécois; accompanying pictures show walls of textiles and rugs with showcases, furniture and other objects too small to see.

[349] n/a 'The Arts and Crafts Exhibit, Montreal' *Construction* November 1923 p.391 The exhibition coincided with the 16th annual assembly of the Royal Architectural Institute of Canada and the opening of the École des Beaux Arts.

[350] Erica Deichmann also had 3 weavings in the Paris exhibit

[351] Barbeau had included Carr's pottery and hooked rugs with Native motifs in an exhibition of 'Canadian West Coast Art, Native and Modern' at NGC in 1927.

[352] Forest taught various crafts including bookbinding at Reformatory St. Vincent de Paul.

[353] Lemieux also had two hooked rugs in the exhibition, and in 1939 at Île Ste Helene showed metal work, pyrogravure and bookbinding.

Exhibition in Glasgow, and in 1938 to the Women's International Exposition of Arts and Industries, Madison Square Gardens, NY.

In 1939 and 1940, CHG was the principal organizer of the Île Ste Helene Craft Fairs, Montreal, which seem to mark a transition from the earlier 'folk festivals' to showcasing studio craftspeople, many of whom were teachers or graduates of Quebec craft schools.[354] The 1939 exhibition had 50,000 visitors in 15 days.

In 1943, CHG achieved, due to the "investigation and persistence" of their president Dr.J.M.Gibbon,[355] the inclusion of crafts for the first time in the annual Royal Canadian Academy exhibition, the 64th in R.C.A.'s history. The work was selected by a R.C.A committee and CHG's design committee. This did not become an annual event.

In Toronto, the other national organization involved with craft and precursor to CHG,[356] the Women's Art Association of Canada (WAAC), more closely allied to the Arts and Crafts movement and to craft school programs in its choice of crafts, offered exhibition venues through its involvement with CNE and from 1900 exhibited crafts annually through its Toronto headquarters. The first exhibition was part of the Annual Member's Exhibition, 24 of the 79 women participating exhibited pottery, embroidery, weaving, rug making, lace, silk painting, woodcarving, metal work, bookbinding and leatherwork. The catalogue accompanying the exhibition noted,
> "A revival of interest in handicrafts has been quite marked of late in England and on the Continent. In the last decade much enterprise has been shown and there have been many new developments in the United States. Canada alone seemed to be dormant. By dint of much searching, isolated and desultory efforts have been brought together in the present Exhibition which show that even in Canada a beginning has been made."[357]

Through the next four decades WAAC continued to exhibit art and craft jointly or separately, in group or solo exhibitions. These ranged from an exhibition of batiks by Mrs Deeble, 1919, to the

---

[354] Gauvreau's *Artisans du Quebec* deals with the Fair and many of the exhibitors.

[355] NAC C2005 8:13:126 CHG annual report 1945/46 p.12

[356] In the first decades there appears to have been a high level of rivalry between WAAC and CHG, and some overlap of interests in the craft field. Their foci are different: CHG was entirely concerned with crafts; WAAC was concerned primarily with support for serious women artists and craftswomen, although men also exhibited at their gallery.

[357] A.Thompson *A Worthy Place in the Art of Our Country: The Women's Art Association of Canada 1887-1987* M.A. thesis (Ottawa 1989) p.104

Studio Craft

work of Charlotte County Cottage Crafts, NB 1921/22, 'Cartoons of Stained Glass Windows and Pottery by Mr. and Mrs. Peter Haworth' and 'Ukrainian Crafts', 1923/4, 'Hooked Rugs from all the Provinces of Canada' 1927-28, 'Fabrics from Ontario and Quebec' 1932-33, 'Exhibit of Bookbindings, Illuminations and Book Plates' 1933-4, 'Display of Pottery and Wrought Iron' 1935, 'Dora Wechsler - Ceramic Satires' 1938 and 'Church embroideries and furnishings' 1943. 'Pottery by Canadian Guild of Potters' 1939-40, was followed by two joint exhibitions by CGP and the Spinners and Weavers of Ontario (S&W.ON)[358] 1941, 1942.[359] Perhaps because of activity through its own gallery and CNE, WAAC did not develop with the Art Museum of Toronto, incorporated 1900,[360] or the Royal Ontario Museum, founded in 1912,[361] the close relationship CHG:HQ developed with MMFA as a public gallery.

In so far as a pattern can be discerned in public gallery activity, they played a passive role with societies generating annual exhibitions. From 1910, for example, AGO showed "Society Annuals" which for craft included in 1911 the Canadian Society of Applied Art[362] and from 1918 the work of OCA students.[363] In the early decades fine arts and crafts were frequently exhibited together. In 1912, the 'Manitoba Society of Arts and Crafts' with the 'Western Art Association' held their First Exhibition at the Carnegie Library, Winnipeg.[364] Although most of the work was paintings and drawings, 14 craftspeople showed pottery; metal and enamel work; jewellery; wood carving, inlay and burnt relief work; modelled leather and leather craft; stencilled and painted fabrics; clay modelling; and tapestry. Crafts were also exhibited as applied arts associated with architecture and with interior design.

---

[358] S&W.ON was in fact a Toronto Guild established 1939, c1955 it became Toronto Spinners and Weavers

[359] Thompson pp.188-193

[360] In 1900 the Ontario Society of Artists headquarters was used for exhibits. The society with the Toronto Art Museum Society held meetings towards founding an art gallery. In 1909 both societies, with the Royal Canadian Academy and the Canadian Art Club shared a gallery in the new Toronto Public Library. In 1911 The Grange was gifted to the Toronto Art Museum Society. In 1966 the Art Gallery of Toronto became the Art Gallery of Ontario (AGO).

[361] ROM grew out of University of Toronto collections. In 1912 a building was completed designed to house the collections and serve both the University and the public.

[362] founded as the Arts and Craft Society of Canada in 1903 by Mabel Cawthra Adamson (Mrs Agar Adamson)

[363] K.McKenzie, L.Pfaff 'The Art gallery of Ontario Sixty Years of Exhibitions, 1906-1966' *RACAR* pp.62-80

[364] The Civic Art Gallery was opened in the Winnipeg Industrial Bureau in 1912, which also housed the Winnipeg School of Art in 1913 and a branch of the Carnegie Library which contained 200 volumes related to the visual arts. Baker pp.31, 36

Through the period the hierarchical arts split into more strongly demarcated, esoteric territories. Architecture moved towards industrial components and a Modernist lack of integral decoration. The emerging discipline of interior design alone remained related to crafts and allied with 'design' gave rise to some exhibitions such as the Vancouver Art Gallery's[365] 'Miriam Peck'[366] (textile designs) and 'Marian McCrea'[367] (ceramics and fabrics) 1948, 'Ceramics, Textiles and Furniture' 1951, and 'Second annual B.C. Ceramics, Textiles and Furniture' 1952.

The fine arts increased their exclusive grip at the top of the hierarchy. There were a few hard won exceptions such as the 1943 R.C.A exhibition and at AGO, "The crowning moment [of Society Annuals] came in 1950, the Gallery's jubilee year, with ten societies joining forces to present *Contemporary Canadian Arts*",[368] these societies included CHG, CGP, and S&W.ON. On the rare occasion where a public gallery actively moved to exhibit craft there was, in Blodwen Davies' account of an exhibition proposed by ROM in 1948, a "lack of comprehension of the dignity of handicrafts and the difference between a hobby and a handicraft."[369] Studio crafts did not gain recognition as a facet of national culture through exhibition at NGC, despite government committee recommendations to that effect.[370]

Associations
Gallery activity during the period, particularly in Toronto, also records a change in the kind of craft organization fighting to exhibit. In 1938 CGP had the first of the annual exhibitions which continued until 1954 at the AGO.[371] In 1945, S&W.ON exhibited. The ROM, whose list of

---

[365] VAG, established 1931, like many galleries was closely linked to the local art school. From its opening it showed VSA student and graduate exhibitions which included interior sets.

[366] Miriam L.Peek 1900-? Weaver Education: VSA (1 year); University of Washington, USA, B.A., M.A. (Art). Taught art: Vancouver schools; University of Manitoba, Home Economics and College of Education. 1949/50 in co-operation with Verney Mills, Montreal was developing original handweave patterns, rayon and cotton in irregular twill, for use in mass production and was experimenting with producing non-flammable fabrics using glass and metal; promoted an experimental approach to weaving.

[367] Marian McCrea McClain (Marion/Marianne/McRae) 1920-? Educated: 1937-42 VSA; 1944 California School Fine Art summer school; 1946-48 Wimbledon and Camberwell Schools of Art, UK. Exhibited Syracuse, member BCPG, CGP. c1950 on, annually sold 6-8 designs to fabric company F.W.Fewks, Montreal and Riverdale, NY, also custom designed silkscreened fabrics. Some of the fabrics and pottery in this exhibition were related designs.

[368] McKenzie p.63

[369] B.Davies 'Generosity Of Craftsmen Too Long Exploited' *Saturday Night* 20 1948 p.18

[370] Chapter 6

[371] There are no lists or catalogues until a list in 1943, and catalogues from 1945.

Studio Craft

exhibitions starts in 1934, showed work by CGP in 1938, S$W.ON in 1946, and CHG:ON in 1947.[372]

Craft organizations generated exhibits and found exhibiting facilities in a wide range of locales which could up to WWII include gallery space in department stores[373] and in major hotels which played a relatively high profile, community role in cultural patronage. Typical of this was the exhibition held at the Ridpath Gallery, part of Ridpath's Furniture Store, Toronto, early in 1931. The organizers of this exhibition were two British immigrant couples teaching at CTS and OCA, Peter and Bobs Haworth and Herbert and Hepzibah Stansfield, Joseph Banigan,[374] a leisure craftsman and activist who in 1951 became director of the Ontario Government, Department of Education, Home Weaving Service, and Frederick Robson.[375] Ringland wrote,

> "Recently Ontario has wakened up to the fact that she is behind the other provinces, Quebec, the Maritimes and the West as well, ...This spring a comprehensive exhibition was held in a Toronto Gallery. It was attended by some 3,000 people interested in all the handicrafts, weaving, rug hooking, batik design, leather tooling, wood carving, jewelry making, metal work. Such enthusiasm was aroused that a new organization was formed, the Handcrafts Association of Canada. Its objects are threefold - 1. To promote greater interest in Canadian craft work. 2. To secure permanent displays in various towns and cities. 3. To collect literature, samples and records from all over the world on the development of craft work."[376]

In the following year, the Handcrafts Association of Canada[377] was involved with the Canadian Craft Festival in the new Eaton's department store on College Street, Toronto. The success of the

---

[372] ROM.A Record Group 107 'Exhibitions held at the Royal Ontario Museum, 1934 to 1979'

[373] Eaton's College Street, Toronto advertised in 1950 "In The Fine Art Galleries/...paintings from the past and present...And, from time to time, there are exhibits featuring Photography and Ceramics...ever-changing displays keyed to the interest of Connoisseur, Collector, Artist and Home-maker." *CA* 7:4:180 Summer 1950

[374] Joseph Banigan 1889-? Architectural engineer, art metal work leisure craft; 1930s vice-president De Havilland Aircraft; 1931 won essay competition in conjunction Ridpath Galleries exhibition, founding member Handcrafts Association of Canada, later President CHG:ON; 1949 presentation to Massey Commission; succeeded Beriau, first craft consultant, c.1946. Daughter Betty Banigan one of first 6 home Weaving Service instructors.
J.A.Norris *The Book of Giving* (Toronto c1980) p.2 refers to him as James Bannigan

[375] Crawford ms

[376] M.C.Ringland 'The Work of Canadian Hands' *The Canadian Magazine* 1931 p.37

[377] Handcrafts Association of Canada 1931, 1937 Canadian Handicrafts Guild of Toronto, c1938 joined CHG becoming CHG:ON, Canadian Crafts Council (Ontario), 1974 Ontario Crafts Council.

Festival lead to the opening, a few month's later, of a small permanent craft shop in the store, and to a second Festival the following year. In the process, as had happened over the years at CHG:HQ, control moved out of craftspeople's hands as the board accumulated 'big names' and "architects, artists, business men, teachers, museum authorities".[378] In 1949 CHG:ON, with 97 craftsmen members, had a 24 member board. Fifteen board members were chosen for special professional qualifications, three of these were craftsmen; the remaining nine board members were the presidents of nine affiliated guilds.[379]

In the early 1930s, single media associations of craftspeople begin to appear. The earliest seem to have been weaving guilds such as the North Lanark Weavers Guild, ON and the Victoria Spinners' and Weavers' Guild, BC[380] established 1934, and The B.C. Weavers' Guild 1935. The latter had eight founding members, including Honey Hooser[381] and Adelaide Ellis.[382] "To be eligible for membership, a person had to own a loom and pay a $1.00 annual fee."[383] The impetus for establishing this guild and the aims are unknown as "[d]ue to an accident our early records were lost", however membership requirements and the calibre of known members indicate a group of established weavers.[384] By the Guild's first exhibition at VAG in 1944, it had 56 members, and its work had been shown with CHG at the 64th annual R.C.A. exhibition.

Many local weaving groups and guilds during the 1940s started as a result of weaving programs supported by government departments such as Ontario's Home Weaving Service or the Searle

---

[378] A.Lighthall 'The Handicrafts Guild Program Encourages and Instructs' *Saturday Night* 1948 p.30

[379] L.D.Millar 'Guild-Community Programs For Richer Recreation' *Saturday Night* 1949 p.16

[380] also referred to as the Handweavers' Guild of Victoria

[381] Honey Hooser (Mrs) 1894-1984 started weaving in 1930s, weaving education England, affiliated with Royal School of Embroidery. "Throughout her life, Mrs. Hooser taught others to weave. People came from across North America and Britain to learn from her." Obituary *The Surrey Leader* 21 November 1984
SKAB SACS B88-4 H newspaper clipping 17 December 1937 "weavings - bags, shawls, scarfs, length suiting, some articles of her own dyeing with nettles and madder, walnuts and onions."

[382] The Guild history says "She learned her craft by taking a correspondence course with Mary Atwater" but Gibbon (SKAB SACS Gibbon 1943) says her mother was a weaver.

[383] *Weaving Our Way Through 50 Years: Greater Vancouver Weavers' and Spinners' Guild* booklet GVWSG c1985 n/p

[384] An early member was Ernest Beaver, "who had learned the weaving trade as a boy and had followed it all of his life, had retired from the firm of Gordon Campbell. He had a great fund of information regarding looms and commercial weaving." *Weaving Our Way Through 50 Years* n/p

Grain Company.[385] They provided the social support of mutual interest, and improvement and exchange of skills. The Halifax Weavers' Guild, NS, started in 1944, aimed,

> "to stimulate interest in the technical development of hand weaving, to encourage weavers in general to set the highest possible standards for their work, with emphasis on careful selection and suitability of materials, combination of colours and design, superiority of workmanship."[386]

As these guilds developed they arranged formal workshops, set up media libraries, acquired equipment and sometimes facilities, set guild standards, exhibited and in many cases found markets. They could also bulk-buy supplies. While many members did not have formal education, numerous workshops and personal dedication moved them from basic to high level skills, and beyond a leisure interest.

Nunzia D'Angelo, teaching at CTS,

> "observed the many keenly interested Students of Pottery, whom when they left school had no way of carrying it out...My idea formed into the thought of gathering together these students, in order to organize a group that would work together with the same objective..."[387]

As a result the Canadian Guild of Potters held its first meeting in March 1936, "30 of us in number." The Guild had Professor R.J. Montgomery as Chairman and six executive officers, "all active in some phrase of the Handicraft Pottery...the Technical and Artistic side." The Guild's aims were to "further the interest of Handicraft Pottery in a broad way, as well as obtaining suitable clays, glazes and facilities for firing," also "Pottery was to be Canadianized as work done in Canada with Canadian materials and Canadian influence." As with other guilds, CGP members met regularly to hear papers and discuss issues relating to their media, exhibitions were arranged, work was sold through CHG:ON. Although "an interest in Handicraft Pottery" was the only requirement for membership, the base membership was a group of practicing potters. Despite its title CGP was essentially a Toronto based group, with contacts in other parts of Canada. In 1944, Home said of CGP,

> "Of the forty working potters, seven might be classed as professional handicraft potters, though the others all sell varying quantities of their output either privately or through the Canadian Handicrafts Guild's shop at Eaton's and the Women's Art Association."[388]

By 1949, the situation seemed less flourishing,

---

[385] chapter 4

[386] Lotz p.21 Halifax Weavers Guild established 1944 ended 1954

[387] CMC Deichmann exhibition file, typescript Nunzia D'Angelo 'Canadian Guild of Potters' c1938

[388] Home p.71

"in Ontario at the moment...there are 4 struggling craft potteries and about 12 potters who produce occasional pieces for sale."[389]

The same report to the Massey commission said,
"there are 8 full time professional workers in metal and about as many who make considerable additions to their income;...most of the weaving is done by workers on a semi-professional basis."[390]

The Metal Arts Guild of Ontario (MAG), started in 1946 by Stacey, Fussell, Meek and Pocock, was intended to be a Canadian version of the English Worshipful Company of Goldsmiths. Its aims were "to promote and encourage the cultural and commercial development of metal arts and crafts both non-ferrous and ferrous." Its "objectives were to provide and arrange for instruction in metal arts, prepare and conduct tests and examinations of skill and proficiency, establish standards and give diplomas directly or indirectly."[391] Douglas Boyd[392] told the Massey Commission in 1949 that MAG had about 35 to 40 members in Ontario and two from Quebec, "professionals and amateurs," and that he hadn't "found anyone sufficiently interested [outside the two provinces], one possible artist on the west coast."[393]

"Our professional metal artists by and large are self-taught...No-one who is a member is not self-employed, no-one is working for a silversmith firm...The metal artist, as a rule, is a complete production unit in himself."[394]

All members worked in precious metals, no-one in iron. Like CGP, MAG was concerned with the development of a distinctively Canadian style, but above all, "we would like to be recognised as artists in metal."

---

[389] NAC C2005:8:13:128 Ontario Guild presentation

[390] NAC C2005:8:13:128 Ontario Guild presentation

[391] A.Barros 'Archives: The Metal Arts Guild of Ontario' *MAGazine* 1994 pp.13-14

[392] Douglas Boyd 1901-1972, like Stacey started silversmithing in the 1930s as a leisure craft, mainly self-taught, possibly a pupil of Renzius, "refresher" course with Eric Fleming in US; produced hollowware, ecclesiastical and domestic pieces, some jewellery, in silver, gold and platinum only.

[393] On the east coast, The Metal Arts Guild of Nova Scotia was founded in Halifax in 1951 by 12 people who had attended day and evening classes at NSCA but who were primarily silversmiths as a leisure activity; the exception, Clifford Brown, had worked for Birks for 31 years. The suggested aims were: standardization of work; standardization of prices; promotion of sales and care of exhibition work; wholesale prices for materials and Guild members; exchange of ideas and designs and tool-making; to make application for a sterling stamp (a Guild mark and the Canadian standards mark was granted by the Precious Metals Division Bureau of Standards, Ottawa in 1953.) M.Anderson *Metal Arts Guild of Nova Scotia, 25 Years, 1951-1976* ms (NS c1977)

[394] NAC Massey C-2010 13:22:276 Metal Arts Guild

Studio Craft

Another form of craftmaker-generated organization arose in 1947 in Nova Scotia and New Brunswick. Both provinces had active government craft development departments[395] and craft education programs, as a result there was a nexus of practising craftspeople and teachers, and a growing population of people with basic craft training looking to sell. In New Brunswick, Ivan Crowell, Director of the Handcrafts Division is credited with calling the meeting of craftspeople which resulted in the Guild of New Brunswick Craftsmen. Mrs Webster and Avery Shaw, Art Curator, of NBM were actively involved and the quarterly meetings of the executive were held at NBM, where,

> "among other business, they scrutinize examples of craft work submitted by various workers for approval. Seals of approval are given to craftsmen whose pieces have been accepted and letters, containing constructive criticism, are written by [Shaw]...to the others.[396]

In Nova Scotia, the Handcrafts Division under the active direction of Mary Black had become a member of CHG in 1944, which gave it access to "all current trends and developments on Canadian handcrafts."[397] As in other areas, craftspeople were also organizing themselves voluntarily or under slight coercion.[398] McKay says there were more than 20 weaving groups with about 400 members by the mid-1940s.[399] The Atlantic Woodcarvers' Group, credited with a membership of 50, formed in 1945, as did the Nova Scotia Craftsmen's Guild which served to bring these varied groups under one umbrella. "Working craftspeople, hobbyists, gift shop managers, and any other interested parties were eligible for membership" which led McKay to suggest that marketing considerations took precedence.

Canadian craft

In a country open to settlement, Canada saw amongst its many immigrants craftspeople trained in other than British, French or American schools. Although private schools teaching craft often seemed to have been run by Canadians of European extraction, on balance the public art schools through the period looked for senior staff from the dominant cultures and to their own graduates. Thus the institutional milieu, which extended to art galleries, was predominantly British. However

---

[395] chapter 4 'Provincial government intervention'

[396] CMC Deichmann exhibition file Deichmann 'A study on Canadian handicrafts with particular reference to New Brunswick' p.8

[397] McKay p.173

[398] The terms of many classes, under government departments or private organizations, required participants to form groups both to receive lessons and material aid, and to commit to continuing as a group to develop and disseminate skills.

[399] McKay p.174

craftspeople came into the country with formal training in schools and traditions throughout Northern, Central and Eastern Europe.

The historiography indicates that the issue of a distinctive Canadian style was under discussion throughout the period. To the establishment traditional crafts, techniques and motifs firmly tagged with their ethnic origin, the 'peasant' crafts, seem to have offered less problems than, as Carless said in 1926,

> "many crafts being practised in Canada...which, owing either to their late introduction or other causes, follow along the lines typical of modern work and show no characteristics which attach them to the place of their manufacture."[400]

Although divergent and fast evolving modern styles were international to some extent, their place of origin and national variations were discernable to the interested and educated eye.[401]

Canadianization of materials and design were part of CGP's agenda in 1936. A decade later, it was a concern of the newly formed MAG, which made the point that all its members were "native born". Boyd speaking on behalf of MAG to the Massey commission said they,

> "Would like to see a basic design developing so it could be spoken of as Canadian...Because of the population we have here the tendency seems to go to Nordic design...We find our great inspiration in the work from Sweden...favour Swedish over Danish...There aren't very many English designers...The English design doesn't seem to belong to us here."[402]

While Scandinavian influences and craftspeople found widespread acceptance, not only in handcraft but in the post-war domination of interior design, other studio traditions were less digestible. Robert Ayre says of Valentin Shabaeff,

> "Essentially a Russian, schooled in an ancient and narrow tradition, he brings to us an art that scarcely fits into the context of this country but that charms by its exoticism."[403]

Some of Shabaeff's work used iconic imagery and references (familiar to a large minority of the Canadian public if not that of the establishment) but his reliefs for the Montreal Central railway

---

[400] Carless p.5

[401] There are constant comments on and examples of the conservatism of Canadian audiences and patrons in the literature I assembled and in the fine arts literature. Isolation from major European or American centres of activity was a partial factor; Emily Carr's accounts of responses to her work in Victoria and Vancouver and CNE's large sector of British exhibitors suggest other factors.

[402] NAC Massey C-2010 13:22:276 Metal Arts Guild presentation

[403] R.Ayre 'Introducing Valentin Shabaeff' *CA* 1947-48 pp.80-83

Studio Craft

station were in a modern figurative mode. His ceramic reliefs made with moulds and crackled, gilded glazes were certainly out of step with the growing influence of British potters such as Bernard Leach. The following sentence possibly explains the first,

"Trained in Europe, he has a low opinion of Canadian standards and when he looks at our ceramics it is lower still."[404]

The information suggests that there was selective integration of influences and styles.

Within the country Luke Lindoe talking of the mid-1940s emphasises isolation from tradition and from other groups,

"Sibyl Laubental brought [European] folk pottery into Alberta [in 1952] and it is the only folk pottery I have seen done...
[W]e were able to be isolated and independent. Consequently ceramics in Alberta grew as a thing separate...There was very, very little exchange. I watched what was illustrated in Canadian Guild of Potters early shows...There was never any feeling that they were showing us how to do it or that we were showing them how to do it."[405]

Delrue, situated in Montreal, looked to young Quebec painters and sculptors such as Alfred Pellan and Louis Archambault, to European magazines and catalogues for the contemporary jewellery designs of Jean Puiforcat and Gerard Sandoz, and to the work of Arp, Miro and Lipchitz. Ayre in the same article could say

"Montreal, long used to peasant handicrafts, has learned to accept the sophisticated artist-craftsman, people like Louis Archambault, the sculptor and ceramist, and Mme. Desrochers-Drolet, of Quebec City, who does fascinating things with enamel on copper."[406]

Summary

Throughout this period, there appears to be a considerable level of activity in the area defined as studio craft. It is an area that has problems with definition through lack of indepth evidence and research, in positioning against current myths and practice, and because the definition resists anonymity. The 1940s saw a strong drive towards 'professionalism' conceived in terms of

---

[404] Jarko Zavi's opinion of Canadian work was similarly low. Moreover *Bulletin of the Canadian National Committee on Refugees* 1 January 1945 acknowledging a 1943/44 article in *Saturday Night* 'Jarko Zavi, Ceramic Pioneer' said "Jarko is not introducing a foreign art into Canada. He is not using foreign patterns of design. He is working out a style of design which is particularly suitable for Canadian homes, and for which Canadians have a particular use and liking."

[405] *Studio Ceramics in Alberta* pp.15,13

[406] Ayre 1951 p.103

standards of work and in manner of practice, that of the full-time independent artist-craftsman. Much of this emanated from the Toronto-based CHG:ON,

> "we in Ontario go our own way. We have our own ideas as to how this movement should be developed."[407]

Lillian Millar elucidates,

> "While the Canadian Handicraft Guild recognizes the recreational value of the crafts; its chief purpose is to stimulate as many people as possible to work in crafts with a professional approach to their work and with professional standards."[408]

This could make for a rather small and exclusive coterie of craftspeople,

> "there are perhaps not more than two dozen such full-time free lance craftsmen in Ontario."[409]

Standards of work, including skill, technique, artistry and innovation, had been an issue from the beginning of the century in all organizations marketing, exhibiting and/or promoting craft. Production situations during the period were diverse and the assessment (or knowledge) of the makers' independence within those situations is open to question. Moreover the requirement of finding a sustaining and sustainable market for craft in shifting, volatile social and economic circumstances led to a diversity of production situations within a maker's career.

I use 'artist-crafts*man*' in my definition above advisedly.[410] My research this far suggests that studio-craftsmen into the fourth decade were employees, employers or designers, working in production groups rather than singly. Undoubtedly this involved economies of scale, and lessening of risk and capital investment at one end and maximizing profit and the benefits of proprietorship at the other. During the same period it would seem that, because of social and legal restrictions, there were in fact more free lance craftswomen. Evidence from art school craft programs shows that women formed a majority of graduates and while a number went into craft related jobs such as teaching and occupational therapy, or a few as designers in firms such as Birks, some pursued their craft on a production basis. Women's lower expectations of employment and income counterbalanced the risks of self-employment. Even so to afford the long schooling, materials and set-up costs would have required private income or subsidy through scholarships, patronage or family support. Clearly there were enough highly talented and

---

[407] NAC Massey C-2005 8:13:128 Ruth Home presenting for CHG:ON

[408] Millar p.16

[409] Millar p.16

[410] The early organizations and the media guilds had non-gendered names; the provincial guilds established in the 1940s had gendered names. Craftspeople were referred to as 'craftsmen' throughout the period.

Studio Craft

committed craftswomen to challenge inherent difficulties.

Not only did women have a high profile in making, they maintained that high profile through teaching and organizing, not least through the national organizations CHG and WAAC. Women were also involved in the genesis of the early media guilds.

In educational level, class and social milieu, studio craftspeople (more than any other group of craftspeople discussed) were closest to both the writers on craft activity and museum curators. This made them not open to direct patronage or anthropological interest and, given the closed focus of the fine arts, deprived them of critical attention and at its most basic level scholarship and cultural recognition.

CHAPTER 6
MUSEUMS AND CRAFT COLLECTING:
"A COURAGEOUS BUT PRECARIOUS EXISTENCE"[1]

This chapter looks at the second of the two communities under discussion. As an institution, museums offer a smaller, more circumscribed field particularly in relation to the crafts community. In addition museums' interest in craft would be only a facet of their activity. It is in terms of the museum's role in assigning cultural value and acting as the nation's memory that the relationship between the two communities becomes significant.

The chapter surveys Canadian museum practice, giving particular attention to the findings of the Miers-Markham Report 1932 and the Massey Report 1949-51. It surveys craft collections, their initiators, focus, range, and philosophic underpinnings, through four museum collections and collections such as those of the Canadian Handicraft Guild (national and regional branches), the Saskatoon Arts and Crafts Society and others. It discusses in detail the activities of Marius Barbeau of the National Museum of Canada as the first identifiable museum professional to take an interest in handcraft.

Introduction

The problems of identifying craft collections encountered in my British research[2] are multiplied enormously for the early years of the developing Dominion of Canada. The Miers-Markham report 1932 appears the first serious published attempt at a national survey and identifies only four decorative arts collections. The paucity of published museum histories, and the huge scale of the country combine to make searches of primary materials both necessary and difficult. I therefore decided to note all collections that came to my attention but to look closely at four museums identified as being involved with 'craft collections'. The four museums, the Montreal Museum of Fine Arts (MMFA), the National Museum of Canada (NMC), the New Brunswick Museum (NBM) and the Museum of the Ukrainian Women's Association of Canada (UWAC:UM), are located in various regions of Canada and, with craft collections, are grouped for discussion by region.

---

[1] Massey p.92

[2] Flood pp.7-9

An overview of museum organization shows unstable coalitions of learned societies, individuals, wealthy patrons, and educational institutes, aided by occasional or unpredictable amounts of municipal, provincial or federal funds, each party pursuing its own agenda until well into the second half of the century. This situation did not go unnoted. Nobbs wrote in 1908,

> "[W}ithout an offer of state aid, it is difficult to see how these various interests are to be stimulated to common action along useful lines. The need of a museum, both in Montreal and in Toronto, is immediate and imperative. In other cities, museums will be necessary ten, twenty, or fifty years hence."[3]

Canadian museums to 1932

Museums in Canada paralleled the nineteenth century museum movement in Europe but under the very different circumstances of a country in the process of settlement, a colonial administration, no indigenous, wealthy aristocracy, and a sparse, scattered and increasingly migrant population. The first collections were primarily scientific and educational. Catholic institutions in Quebec and in predominantly francophone communities in the Maritimes had accumulated natural history collections for use as teaching aids since the eighteenth century. The adult education movement of the early nineteenth century typified by the Mechanic's Institutes were the genesis of many eclectic collections in the Maritimes, some of which escaped the decline of their originating organizations, neglect or fire to become the basis of museums.

A survey published in a 1903 *Bulletin of the New York State Museum* refers to 21 Canadian museums.[4] Nearly thirty years later the Carnegie Corporation, New York commissioned two senior members of the British Museums Association, H.A.Miers and S.F.Markham to research and publish a *Directory of Museums and Art Galleries in Canada* which listed 135 museums, archives and art galleries.[5] (Newfoundland, not yet part of Canada, had one.) The concentration of museums in Ontario, 37, and Quebec, 54[6] reflects patterns of settlement chronology, wealth

---

[3] P.Nobbs 'State Aid to Art Education in Canada' *Construction* (1908)

[4] A.F.Key *Beyond Four Walls: The Origins and Development of Canadian Museums* (Toronto 1973) p.92
This was published concurrently with the first museum directory published in U.S. by NYSM in 1903 which was limited to Natural History Museums. The location of museums were Maritimes 6, Quebec City 1, Montreal 3, ON 9, MB 1, BC 1. Key p.162

[5] The information in these reports is not comprehensive or necessarily reliable, see below the section on A.S.Morton and SACS

[6] Montreal had 22 museums, 14 at the anglophone McGill University

and population density.[7]

Miers-Markham suggested that none of these museums, apart from those in Ottawa and Toronto, were "really worthy of their province or country" and were, in buildings and equipment, far below the average US museum. Given their funding this was not surprising. Only seven museums had an annual income of over $10,000 and the total income for all Canadian museums was estimated at $550,000 at a time when London, UK, museums alone spent well over $5,000,000 annually. A 1938 Dominion Bureau of Statistics survey[8] "revealed that the total estimated budgets of all museums, art galleries, historic parks, and archives in Canada "is considerably less than one million dollars annually." Key suggests that,

> "governments at all levels were reluctant to provide fiscal aid to institutions which they viewed as esoteric, failing to recognize their educational value, and, more important their economic importance as showcases...of a young colony rich with natural resources overdue for exploitation."[9]

In addition he blames the economic demands of WWI, the burning of the Parliament Buildings in 1916 which "resulted in the virtual closing down of the National Museums complex for five years during a critical period in Canada's cultural growth", and the Depression.

Miers-Markham recorded that by 1932 the federal government funded three 'museums' - the Dominion Archives, the National Gallery and NMC all in Ottawa, and six national parks sites. Provincial governments funded 23 museums including 6 archives. Municipalities directly funded 19 museums but more frequently provided facilities, as a separate unit or shared, primarily, with libraries. Almost half the museums, 63, still formed part of educational institutions, in Catholic schools and missions particularly in Quebec, and in universities in the country as a whole. Museums supported by learned societies and private and corporate patrons, including the CPR, the Canadian Steamship Lines, Dominion Atlantic Railway and the Hudson's Bay Company (37) formed 20% of the total.

The principal concentrations of interest in these museums were on natural history (58), focusing on the region in which the museum was located or on lesser known parts of Canada, which frequently included anthropology with a particular emphasis on Canada's Aboriginal Peoples (24); and regional history (51). Twentythree museums dealt primarily with the fine arts and four with "related objects." Of these latter, three were situated in Montreal and included the Chateau de

---

[7] BC 9; AB 6; SK 6; MB 3; ON 37; PQ 54; NB 7; NS 11; PEI 0; (NFD 1)

[8] Educational Bulletin No.4 1938 quoted Key p.166

[9] Key p.9

Ramezay, which contained a Handicraft Room;[10] the Art Association of Montreal Gallery, which was "founded in 1860 as a gallery of paintings and sculpture", built splendid new premises in 1912 and inaugurated in 1916 "a museum to consist of objects of artistic merit" including "furniture, china, pottery, glass, metalwork, textiles and objects illustrating other decorative arts"; and the Redpath Library Museum, McGill University, which contained "examples of fine bindings and productions of modern private presses."[11] The fourth was the University Museum, Saskatoon, Saskatchewan (USKFM) which included "objects illustrating the racial customs, handicrafts and costumes of early European settlers."[12]

It was the collection at the Chateau de Ramezay that had attracted the notice of the founders of CHG. Opened as a museum in 1895 under the auspices of the Antiquarian and Numismatic Society, at that time it broadened its collections to include Canadian historical and social material including Québécois traditional crafts. However it was with the Art Association of Montreal Gallery that the CHG was most closely associated.

Central Canada: Montreal Museum of Fine Arts and the CHG collection
Art Association of Montreal 1860/ Montreal Museum of Fine Art 1916[13]
The Art Association of Montreal joined with the older Montreal Society of Artists (founded 1847) to campaign for a civic gallery. In 1879 a bequest from Benaiah Gibb and the gift of a site from the city secured their first building and attracted further large bequests including the 1892 donation of a major decorative arts collection from William and Agnes Learmont. In 1906 Percy Nobbs called for a permanent exhibit in the AAM Gallery to link art with industry but it was not until 1916, after the move to a new building, that the Gallery decided to collect "good examples of iron work, objects of artistic merit, embroidery, textiles, glass, and in fact all objects tending to the education of the designer and the worker",[14] a changing focus reflected in a new name, the Montreal Museum of Fine Art.

From the turn of the century the Women's Art Association Montreal Branch (WAAC:Montreal) had been exhibiting craft in the AAM/MMFA galleries. The CHG continued this close association by holding their National Annual Exhibitions there from 1905 to 1935 when the financial

---

[10] Judith Berlyn, Librarian, Chateau Ramezay suggests that the Handicraft Room was short lived. letter 26 April 1996

[11] As this collection was restricted to one medium, possibly peripheral, I decided not to pursue the enquiry.

[12] H.A.Miers and S.F.Markham *Directory of Museums and Art Galleries* (London 1932) pp.34,33,40,63

[13] all abbreviated to MMFA

[14] McLeod p.117

stringencies of the Depression caused the CHG to cancel the exhibition.[15] H.B.Wallen wrote to Wilfrid Bovey, President of CHG in 1935 that the MMFA was "greatly interested in the welfare and progress of the Guild" whose exhibitions "had been of increasing interest to our members each year."[16] However the Guild seems to have varied the venues for its exhibitions after this date.[17]

In 1908 Alice Peck, cognisant that the CHG:HQ shop harboured irreplaceable examples of fine craft pieces, suggested that CHG start a permanent collection. As the national organization handling a wide range of craft CHG had an unrivalled, educated overview of and interest in contemporary and historic Canadian craft. By 1915 about 70 articles had been purchased from surplus funds and in 1914 works from the Permanent Collection had been exhibited at the same time as the CHG Annual Prize Competition.[18] From 1917 to 1924, F. Cleveland Morgan was president of CHG:HQ, a man, Key suggests,[19] "whose interest in the decorative arts was responsible for it [the MMFA] becoming the first Museum of Fine Arts in Canada."[20] Concurrently (1918 to 1927) with Morgan's presidency, CHG funded the purchase of artifacts for MMFA and donated works, and their permanent collection was also housed at the MMFA in the Industrial Gallery and the Arts and Crafts 'museum'.[21]

Confusion seems to have arisen between donated works and housed works and in 1928 the CHG collection was dispersed; 54 works, mainly Inuit, went to the McCord Museum in the Ethnology Department of McGill University and 47 pieces remained at the MMFA.[22] A 1996 MMFA list of gifts from CHG between 1918 and 1927 shows these were predominately early textiles

---

[15] 1935 was also the year in which CHG:HQ was involved in a major reorganization.

[16] McLeod p.164

[17] In 1939 the first [Montreal] Arts and Crafts Fair took place at Île St. Helene/St. Helen's Island.

[18] McLeod p.117

[19] Key p.117

[20] Cleveland Morgan had a long association with both MMFA and CHG, in 1957 he was still Chair of MMFA's Decorative Arts Committee, in 1946 on CHG's Permanent Collection Committee.

[21] McLeod p.120 "Peck wrote [19 December 1927] that the CHG's Permanent Collection was housed at the AAM and McCord 'as we cannot yet afford a suitable place for it'."

[22] Between 1908 and 1915 CHG collected 70 pieces, averaging 10 a year. If their collecting continued over the next 13 years at the same rate, the collection would have contained about 200 pieces, double the number divided between MMFA and McCord.

(Coptic, Persian and Indian), only 5 artifacts were Canadian and only one, an Assomption sash (ceinture fléchée), was twentieth century.[23] This indicates a difference between the Museum's fashionable archaeological interests and what CHG:HQ customarily exhibited in the Museum or purchased to form the nucleus of the new "permanent" collection in 1930, namely twelve French Canadian, New Canadian and Native pieces.[24] However, even this nucleus reflected only part of the work CHG:HQ handled through its shop, which included studio and rural industries crafts.

A 1996 MMFA list of Canadian 'decorative arts' made and collected between 1900 and 1950 shows 13 craft works made within the period,[25] including 8 Quebec *tapis* from F. Cleveland Morgan. All were donated. Thus despite annual exhibitions of craft over a considerable period and the proximity and activity of CHG:HQ as the national craft organization, the Museum made little or no attempt to collect twentieth century Canadian craft.

In 1949 the CHG reported to the Massey Commission[26] that it had "a permanent collection of exceptional pieces of craftwork"[27] and their work was facilitated by the co-operation of, amongst other organizations, the national, provincial and university museums. In their presentation, 'Purchases for permanent collections' was one of nine areas for which CHG:HQ suggested Grants-in-Aid.

Collections at l'École des Arts Domestiques and l'École du Meuble
Two other major craft collections were made during this period by Quebec institutions. The first, collected in 1930, was predominantly non-Canadian however it is the only Canadian reference to such a collection I have come across. It was put together during the Quebec government study to support the "renaissance of peasant art in Canada" and the establishment of the handcraft

---

[23] Eric Vanasse, Archivist MMFA, 23 February 1996 list of works acquired through CHG 1918 to 1927

[24] McLeod p.119 For example in 1925 CHG Permanent Collection purchases were contemporary: quilt with double-faced weaving, two hooked rugs from P.E.I., several Roumanian embroideries

[25] Vanasse MMFA 26 February 1996 list of Canadian decorative arts objects produced between 1900 and 1960. 211 works, which are not dated are excluded from this list, compared with the dated list this suggests little increase in identifiable pieces possible.

[26] NAC Massey Commission C-2005 8:13:126 CHG National letter 30 August 1949

[27] In May 1969 works from the Permanent Collection formed an exhibition, 'Industry in the Homes of the People', at La Maison Del Vecchio, Montreal. In 1974, CHG as a national organization ceased to exist, CHG:HQ/PQ became the Canadian Guild of Crafts, Quebec. They retained their shop, archives and a small permanent collection, predominantly of Innuit and Native work. The bulk of the CHG permanent collection was divided among the McCord Museum, Montreal, the University of Montreal, ROM, NMC and OCC, some works were sold. The OCC collection came to NMC/CMC c.1995.

school, l'École des Arts Domestiques.[28] The study looked at handcrafts, particularly weaving and spinning, from the United States and Europe.

> "A very complete collection of specimens of rural art was obtained from the various countries of the world. This collection now [1933] comprises more than 2500 pieces."[29]

The collection was exhibited at the first Provincial Exhibition of Domestic and Foreign Handicrafts in 1930, and then seems to have gone to l'EdAD.[30] The subsequent history of the collection is unknown.

The second collection is also connected with a craft school, École du Meuble. The first museum and collection were destroyed when the building burned down in 1940.[31] Lesser seems to be talking of the second collection when she says,

> "[W]ith the expertise of Paul Gouin and Jean Palardy, he [Gauvreau] installed a museum on the premises of Ecole du Meuble. The collection included artifacts from Gauvreau's private collection as well as those acquired as gifts and bequests. Quebec traditional crafts and furniture and reproduction furniture for teaching purposes were amassed along with contemporary works. Original Art Deco furniture and decorative art objects were prohibitively expensive...so such luxurious goods were bypassed."[32]

Lesser says that "Gauvreau considered this 'museum' as his personal collection."[33]

---

[28] See chapter 4, Government Intervention, Provincial Departments of Agriculture and the Women's Institutes

[29] Beriau *CGJ* 1933(b) p.143

[30] Beriau *CGJ* 1933(b) p.148 says of the School, "The pupils are warned against the copying of foreign designs; *these being exhibited solely as examples of technique and workmanship."* my italics

[31] Lesser catalogue 1989 p.89 picture shows an exhibition of crafts from EdM "photographed just prior to the fire of 1941 [sic]."

[32] Lesser catalogue 1989 p.89

[33] In its later life the collection was stored in various places. Some pieces went to the Chateau Dufresne/Montreal Museum of Decorative Arts c1978; when this Museum switched to an international focus, some pieces were donated to the Musee d'Art de Saint-Laurent. Parts of the original collection seem to have been discarded at various times. In 1982 there was a public auction of remnants of the La Centrale/The Handicraft Centre collection of l'Association professionnelle des artisans du Quebec. This included work labelled 'office provincial de l'artisanat', EdAD textiles, and possibly works from Gauvreau's EdM museum. Lesser says in this account these were "not public collections". Lesser letter 19 October 1997
In the sense that they were not museum collections that is so; in the sense that they belonged to publicly funded institutions, they were.

Central Canada: National Museum of Canada and Marius Barbeau
Geological Survey of Canada (1841) museum/ National Museum of Canada 1927[34][*National Museum of Man, National Museums of Canada 1968/Canadian Museum of Civilization 1986*]
The National Museum of Canada was an off-shoot of the Geological Survey of Canada founded in 1841 and based in Montreal. This affected its activities, administration and development. Collecting was propelled by the exploration and potential for exploitation of Canada's natural resources. The Survey's first geologist, W.E.Logan set up a private museum which extended beyond geology and mineralogy to natural history. Logan proposed to the United Canadas parliament in 1853 that they erect "an appropriate edifice especially planned as a National Museum."[35] When Ottawa became the national capital in 1880, the Survey, with its museum recognised by an Act of Parliament in 1868, moved there.

The scientific exploration of Canada included contact with native peoples. In 1910, Edward Sapir, a pupil of the American ethnologist Franz Boas, took charge of Anthropology, a new division within the Geological Survey for "the scientific study of the [native] cultures of Canada".[36] This, Tom McFeat[37] argues was, under Boas' reconstructive ethnography, an extension of natural history.[38] Anthropology (and Biology), according to the writer of the 1926 Annual Report, were "maintained solely for museum purposes",[39] not being a means to economic development as other departments of the Survey were. The four disciplines within Anthropology were physical anthropology, ethnology, linguistics and archaeology. Marius Barbeau[40] joined the museum in 1911 as Associate Ethnologist and worked there until 1948. In 1925 Barbeau turned his attention to Québécois material culture. A memorandum, "C.M.Barbeau's contemplated folklore investigations in Eastern Quebec, from June to December, 1925" proposed:

"an extensive study of the folk technology and colonial arts and crafts of the

---

[34] abbreviated to NMC. Canadian Museum of Civilization (CMC)

[35] Key p.124

[36] CMC.A Ethnography records Edward Sapir correspondence 1-A-236M, Folder 'R.G.McConnell (1914-1915) Box 427f.76 letter 2 October 1914

[37] Chief Ethnologists were D.Jenness 1910-1948, Marcel Rioux (Barbeau's son-in-law) 1949-1955, T.McFeat 1959-1963

[38] T.McFeat in M.M.Ames *History of Canadian Anthropology* (1976) p.151

[39] CMC.A *Bulletin 50, Annual Report for 1926, National Museum of Man* (Ottawa 1928) p.55

[40] F.C.J.Marius Barbeau 1883-1969 Educated: Oxford University (1st French Canadian Rhodes Scholar) and the Sorbonne, Anthropology, thesis *The Totemic System of the Northwestern Indian Tribes of North America*, an area which was to absorb him for much of his working life.

ancient French colony of Quebec [city] and surroundings...particularly in a well-preserved old-time settlement; that is, at the eastern end of Île d'Orleans...

To make records of old wood carvings, statuettes, church decorations, silver articles, churches, houses, costumes, etc...

$300 for the purchase of museum specimens [for] the study of pottery, of sculpture, painting, decorative panels, sashes and other technological or artistic processes."[41]

This research was to push the Museum further in new directions.

When Barbeau arrived at the Museum it had a national mandate. R.W.Brock, Director, said in his 1910 report,

"For the present it is the intention to restrict the Museum to Canadian material...in order to make it, first of all, the great Canadian Museum, whose collections in Canadian Material will surpass all others. When this has been accomplished in all divisions it may be advisable to enlarge its scope and make it a world museum..."[42]

Physically, the museum was housed in 1910 in the Victoria Memorial Museum Building, the first building built specifically to house the Survey's collections. The building was shared with the Survey and NGC. When the Parliament buildings were destroyed by fire in 1916, the Museum Building was taken over by the displaced legislature, museum exhibits and staff were scattered throughout the city bringing work almost to a halt. In 1920, the Survey and museum returned to the Museum Building with NGC taking over the whole east wing. With growing collections, the economic strigencies and dictates of the Depression and WWII and incursion by war-time agencies, space for the museum[43] and its activities was increasingly at a premium.[44]

Administratively, the Survey and its Museum had always been directly under the control of the government, by 1910 as a Branch of the Department of Mines. Thus Museum personnel were "government scientists", caught between the differing organizational strategies and goals of government bureaucracies and scientific enquiry. In 1920 the Museum separated, theoretically,

---

[41] Dated 11 May 1925, unsigned, quoted Nowry p.270

[42] CMC.A 'Canada/Department of Mines/National Museum of Canada/Annual Report for 1926 (Ottawa 1928) p.46

[43] In 1910 the Museum had 6 public exhibition halls, due to the expansion of the Survey and NGC by 1920 it had 4, during WWII there were no exhibitions. CMC.A 'A Museum for Canadians' 1960-61 NMC Annual Report (Ottawa 1961) p.9

[44] The Museum did not have the full use of the building designed for its use until 1960; the Survey moved to its own offices in 1959 and NGC in 1960.

from the Geological Survey becoming the Victoria Memorial Museum with William McInnes as the first director. However in 1925, W.H.Collins, Director of the Geological Survey of Canada also became Acting Director of the Museum retaining both positions until 1936. Designation as the 'National Museum of Canada' became official in 1927. The Survey and Museum jointly continued under the jurisdiction of various Department of Mines and Resources Bureau Directors with a Curator handling Museum administration until 1950, when NMC became a Division of the Parks Branch of the newly formed Department of Resources and Development. A 109 year association with the Geological Survey ended but, despite the Massey Commission recommendation in 1951 that NMC should have independent status, the Museum remained a government department until the establishment of the National Museums Corporation in 1968.[45]

When Barbeau arrived at NMC he initially worked on the language, myths and songs of various Amerindian groups but in 1913 Boas directed Barbeau's attention to the folklore of his birthplace,[46] 'folklore' being oral rather than material culture. Between 1914 and 1924 Barbeau made at least six major field trips in pursuit of Québécois oral culture. In the 1918 season he also brought back to NMC nine tiny samples (approximately 3x2")[47] of homespun fabrics from the La Malbaie/Murray Bay area. In 1919 with Dr.E.-Z.Massicotte, Archivist of the Montreal Court House, he initiated a series of concerts in Ottawa and Montreal to introduce the traditional music of rural Quebec to urban audiences. At the St-Sulpice Library performance the stage was decorated to look like a Québécois farmhouse and as part of the program Barbeau gave a talk entitled 'Canadian Folk Arts and Architecture' illustrated by 36 lantern slides. Although only six were craft related (and none were from outside Quebec), it was an indication that he was already taking note of aspects of Quebec material culture.[48]

At the end of 1925, Barbeau wrote to his Acting Director, "The new field I have investigated this year is of the greatest importance. It amounts to a new discovery."[49] For the NMC the 'scientific'

---

[45] L.Russell *The National Museum of Canada 1910 to 1960* (Ottawa 1961) pp.6-9

[46] It is surprising, given Barbeau's education at the Sorbonne, tours around France and admiration for things French, that his interest was not sparked by activity in France. Segalen notes French interest since the Revolution in indigenous 'primitive' people, the collection of material objects in the second half of the nineteenth century, the first congress of popular traditions in Paris in 1889 and the work of "the great folklorist" Paul Sebillot. Martine Segalen 'Here but Invisible: The Presentation of Women in French Ethnography Museums' *Gender and History* 6:3:334 (Oxford 1994)

[47] They look like the kind of samples attached to a trade card.

[48] Barbeau took over 10,000 photographic negatives which were integrated with others he acquired. From the Gaspé peninsular, 1922, he brought back 200 songs and 500 photographs, Nowry p.268

[49] 5 October 1925 quoted Nowry p.273

examination of the material culture of a Euro-Canadian people, Québécois, rather than that of Aboriginal peoples was a new field and "he [Acting Director, L.L. Bolton] considered your French Canadian work really lay outside the scope of our Division" replied Diamond Jenness, Head of Anthropology to Barbeau.[50]

In any other sense this was not a new discovery. Nowry remarks of the region selected, "This well-chosen, relatively accessible repository of old French rural architecture and handicrafts, also served...the tourist business",[51] as a 1928 *Toronto Star Weekly* article 'Rug Hunting in Habitant Quebec' demonstrates. Barbeau himself wrote,
> "Until the depression period curio dealers were accustomed to go around the country districts twice a year, gathering items and shipping them to the United States, to be palmed off on credulous customers as New England colonial antiques or as relics from old France."[52]

Of his first encounter with the wood sculptor Louis Jobin[53] he wrote,
> "I had heard of the old carver of saints of the Beaupre coast: strangers - writers and photographers - used to go and see him in his little shop and publish stories about him."[54]

Moreover, the WAAC and the CHG, of whom Barbeau was not unaware, had been seeking out, encouraging, exhibiting and marketing rural Québécois crafts, particularly textiles, for thirty years. The WAAC in 1902[55] and the CHG in 1907 had exhibited and demonstrated the making of Assomption sashes (*ceintures fléchées*) at the AAM Gallery. At the latter Mme. Venne, "considered the last representative of her type of weavers"[56] demonstrated her craft. Seventeen years later Massicotte, who had been at Mme. Venne's demonstration, published a short monograph on the sash and its history in *Proceedings and Transactions of the Royal Society*

---

[50] 8 October 1925 Nowry p.273

[51] Nowry p.271

[52] M.Barbeau 'Laurentian Wood Carvers' *CGJ* 1935 p.183

[53] Louis Jobin c1851-1928 Trained: Quebec City with master carver Berlinguet

[54] M.Barbeau *Quebec, Where Ancient France Lingers* (Toronto 1936) p.82

[55] "At the 1902 exhibition for the first time something was done to prevent the loss of the art of the ceinture flechee, the sash...worn by voyager or coureur-de-bois...The weaving of this sash, now so highly prized by collector and museum, was on the verge of becoming a lost art." Peck *CGJ* p.207

[56] M.Barbeau *Assomption Sash* NMC 93 (Ottawa 1939) p.5

1924. Barbeau himself did not make his major collection of sashes until 1930 and did not publish his analysis until 1939. Following the activity of the anglophone CHG, the CdF rural women's groups had been founded in 1915 to encourage the production of traditional crafts particularly weaving, and in 1929 the provincial government had conducted its own investigation of Quebec crafts concluding that old techniques had been lost in almost all parts of the province.[57]

As the locale and objects for study were not unknown, so also Barbeau's approach and methodology were not rigorously 'scientific'. Nowry suggests in a critique of Barbeau's interpretation of and writing about Northwest Pacific Coast culture that he was primarily a collector and was not interested in synthesis or methodology.[58] Barbeau described himself as "an inveterate collector, always grabbing, as it were, all my life."[59] His Quebec field notebooks frequently read more like an inventory with prices and possible buyers. He referred openly in publications and in correspondence to collecting for private patrons[60] and a large number of institutions besides NMC, for example pottery for l'Hôtel-Dieu de Québec, l'EdAD, Salle d'exposition provinciale, ROM, Fort Chambley and Maison Laurier. Other institutions receiving artifacts included the NGC and the AGO. He also had a personal collection. He was an enthusiast, a tireless promoter in his areas of interest, corresponding with many major figures in the craft scene and going to considerable trouble to facilitate the sale of work of friends such as artists A.Y.Jackson[61] and Emily Carr,[62] woodcarver Médard Bourgault and country weavers[63].

---

[57] Discussed in chapter 4, Governments and rural women, Provincial Departments of Agriculture and the Women's Institutes.

[58] Nowry pp.237-57
Helen Knibb M.A (Museo), Visiting Researcher CMC personal communication 12 June 1996 suggests that Barbeau was neither untypical nor the worst, Margery Halpin 'A Critique of the Boasian Paradigm for Northwest Coast Art' Culture 14:1 1994 argues that Barbeau's on-site knowledge was advantageous.

[59] Nowry p.182

[60] CMC.A Barbeau B70F5 Homespuns collected at Île aux Coudres October 1932 lists 48 pieces: 29 bedcovers, 4 hooked rugs, 2 napkins, 2 tablecloths, a catalogne, 6 lengths drouget, with sporadic details of maker and work, and prices with destination in pencil or ink. Destinations include Museum I 4 works, Museum II 8, National Gallery 11, *chez nous* 2, Reserved/taken 12, named people 9

[61] CMC.A Barbeau/Jackson correspondence file 22 May 1926;4 June 1926

[62] CMC.A Barbeau/CHG file 1928

[63] CMC.A Barbeau B70F15 Handcrafts Association of Canada Toronto accounts 27 June 1933 to 20 February 1937; Barbeau/ E.A.Corbett, Director of Extension University of Alberta correspondence 18 May 1933, 12 June 1933

The Barbeau collection at NMC eventually numbered about 640 objects, most of which were collected in the field. Barbeau's first year of collecting material culture for NMC saw the largest number of objects come into the collection, 217, including 80 objects from the church of St. Pierre, about 20 sculptures and fragments from Jobin's workshop, tools, pottery, samples of domestic handloom textiles including *catalogne* mats, *boutonné, à la planche*[64] and *catalogne* bedspreads and linen towels, and braided garters. These, with the addition of Assomption sashes, rural furniture and hooked rugs were typical of the range of objects he collected and wrote about. Numerous small undated note books document Barbeau's progress from house to house in rural Quebec cataloguing items which interested him. There is little in these brief field notes to elucidate decisions about what or why objects should be collected.[65] Nor are objects methodically described. Typical are the collected references to hooked rugs from the note books. Sixtytwo rugs are listed, 44 have some description of the design, 23 have indications of colours used, 12 have an indication of size, 15 have a fairly precise indication of age - *"nouveau"*, *"fait ya a peu pres 30 ans"*, *"ya 20 ans"*. Comments consist of *"jolis couleurs, bien fait"*; *"très bon"*; *"exceptionnellement bon"*. Maker (*fait par*) is noted for 24. There is no information about materials, their sources, or the maker's (as opposed to Barbeau's) design references, or the design, placement and use of these rugs in relation to other floor coverings not collected. Provenance, other than the household, and history are noted for few of the objects which caught Barbeau's eye. Many things are described as *vieux* or *très vieux* without even a conjectural date. 'Presumably' frequently modifies attributions in publications. There may be anecdotal information. He says of Mme. Vve. Gauthier,

> "She span two pounds of wool this week. Does the housework [*berda* which could include women's farmwork]. Five hundred pounds of spun wool in the house. Won first prize at Canadian Handicraft [CHG?] For 29 years worked for her [CHG?] Five people work, two weaving, three spinning. Weaves boutonne bedspreads...two work on a coverlet [sitting side by side]. Half finished in a day."[66]

It may be that additional information about some objects was recorded in photographs.

Barbeau's copious publications, academic and popular, both illuminate the subtext of this collecting and reflect "untidy scholarship."[67] The latter includes clumsy translations of francophone words, technical imprecision, unsupported connections and discounted evidence.

---

[64] A way of extending pattern possibilites on the two shaft loom in common use by the insertion of a thin board over and under groups of warp threads, which when turned vertically opens a pattern shed.

[65] Of necessity I have looked at a sample of "the 80 linear meters of documents in 26 filing cabinets...over 5600 separate files." Nowry p.12

[66] CMC.A Barbeau Notebook XXXVII p.47, transcript p.4, my translation

[67] Nowry p.256

Boutonné/boutonnue, a tabby weave with loops hand-picked along the main or a supplementary weft to form patterns, he translated as 'wool buttons', 'button-like knots' or 'twisted knots' when the effect is neither button-like nor a knot, descriptions which could easily be confused with other techniques such as 'candlewick' popular during roughly the same period. In a Royal Society paper he says of mats,
> "When woven on the regular loom they are called catalognes. Their pattern consists of lateral stripes in colour, occasionally embellished with hand-inserted loops while the weaving is being done, or with what is called "*fleches*" (arrows)."

Catalognes are distinguished by being a tabby weave with a weft of fine rag strips and were made in different weights suitable for bedcovers or mats. Frequently but not always the rag weft only was used to make a striped pattern. The embellishment described is *boutonné*. He omits to describe *fléchées*, made by using contrasting coloured weft strips twisted together and laid in pairs, one twisted S and one Z to make 'arrow heads'.

These examples and others call into doubt his technical knowledge and his respect for technicalities, an inherent craft criterium. This is combined with the constant use of 'humble' in conjunction with crafts and makers, and covert references to social and art hierarchies. He suggests both his lack of knowledge of craft and a focus on aesthetics in choosing to consult the artists A.Y. Jackson and Arthur Lismer (rather than the knowledgable CHG women),
> "I wanted their judgement on the value of the folk arts...It was in associating myself with them that I realized that there was truly a domain of important study there to be cultivated."[68]

His pursuit of the subtext contributed to omissions and unsustainable propositions. The subtext was, as he stated in his initial proposal to NMC, "the colonial arts and crafts of the ancient French colony of Quebec", in which he argued the direct lineage of crafts in contemporary rural Quebec through New France to Renaissance France. From this four themes emerge: the quintessential Frenchness of Quebec, tied to the centrality of the Catholic church in cultural patronage and cultural diffusion through the continent, isolationism, and the demise of French-Canadian culture.

For Barbeau, Quebec was French Canada,
> "It differs from that of Louisiana and Acadia where advanced craftsmanship and intellectual guidance were lacking. The country folk there, left unaided to their resources, experienced an independent evolution of their own, away from their racial origins."[69]

---

[68] NFB film *Marius Barbeau et le folklore* 1959 quoted in Nowry p.275

[69] Barbeau 1936a p.169

In saying this he discounts the traumatic history and straitened economic circumstances of the Acadian communities with their consequent effects on production. Moreover as Burnham showed[70] the common use of a two shaft loom to produce tabby weaves patterned with weft banding and 'barberpole' lines (or doubled, *fléchées*), *à la planche* and *boutonné* are distinctive of all the historical Canadian-French areas, including Manitoba, Quebec, New Brunswick, Nova Scotia and Prince Edward Island. Local variations occurred, as the brightly coloured *boutonné* of Quebec show.

Barbeau saw the defusion of motifs and techniques as being one way, from seventeenth century France through the agency of the Catholic church to the general population and Aboriginal Peoples. In defending this he resorted to a number of strategies. He strenuously argued the originality and primacy of Quebec production, for example, against the achievements of Aboriginal Peoples in finger weaving in *Assomption Sash* and the wider origins of hooked rugs in *The Hooked Rug - Its Origin* using selected and often contradictory evidence. He overrode his own accounts of the influx and influence of British and other nationals in various crafts and of studio books from abroad.[71] He appears unaware of the "assimilation of British socio-cultural symbols", noted by Hood and Ruddel[72] and Burnham[73] in the relationship between nineteenth century Quebec b*outonné* coverlets and the fashionable, imported cotton *boutonné* coverlets from Bolton, England. In his account of the genesis of *boutonné* he postulates a substitution of local wool for candlewick by Île aux Coudres women during a time of scarcity in the early nineteenth century, crediting the forerunners of two modern artisan families and linking them to possible eighteenth century ancestors who were taught tapestry making by Ursuline nuns at Québec.[74] He consistently claims but does not prove direct lineage for artisans from original artisan immigrants to New France.[75] In his study of rural potters[76] he cites historical records of potters from at least 1666 but shows during the nineteenth century a movement into the craft by choice and with a family involvement of three generations at most.

---

[70] Burnham 1981 p.54-74

[71] Barbeau 1936a pp.77,78

[72] Pocius 1991 p.77

[73] Burnham 1981 pp.74,45

[74] M.Barbeau *The Kingdom of Saguenay* (Toronto 1936) pp.103-5

[75] P.Moogk *Canadian Historical Review* pp.418-9, 435-437 on craftsmen's associations in early French Canada argues that such a lineage did not exist because of greater colonial social and occupational mobility.

[76] Barbeau 1942a pp.115-184

Museums and Craft Collections

Whatever the criticisms of Barbeau's work, he extended the Museum's ethnological investigations beyond Aboriginal Peoples to the activities of Euro-Canadians, in particular to their aesthetic material culture. Although McFeat says,

> "I really do not think that Barbeau regarded his work on Tsimshian Totem Poles or French Canadian songs as essentially different"[77]

Barbeau himself labelled this research "folklore", "folk technology" and "colonial arts and crafts"[78] making explicit a differentiation from Aboriginal ethnology. Preston cites[79] Barbeau as an example of

> "the causal processes of individual personalities in the development of institutional structures. In this particular case, the process of differentiation of folklore from ethnology begun by Barbeau within the National Museum later became institutionalised as the Canadian Centre for Folk Culture Studies[80] and the Canadian Ethnology Service, respectively."[81]

However the first craft collection came into NMC under the Anthropology department and reflected the anthropological thinking of the period, particularly the ideas of Franz Boas. Focussed on 'primitive societies', the picturesque Other, which in Barbeau's case was the conservative, relatively isolated, cash-poor, rural 'habitant' communities of the eastern St. Lawrence river valley, anthropologists mounted, as Pascale Galipeau describes Barbeau's collecting,[82] "a salvage operation...to rapidly build up the national collection", to save the last remnants of 'dying cultures'.

McFeat suggests that Boas also influenced the display of artifacts in two possibly conflicting

---

[77] Ames 1976 p.156
Pocius suggests that material culture studies within "folkloristics" in Europe and French Canada are still called ethnology. G. Pocius 'Material Culture Research: Authentic Things, Authentic Values' *Material History Review 45* (Ottawa 1997) p.6

[78] Nowry p.270

[79] Ames 1976 p.123

[80] This department currently holds the Contemporary Fine Craft Collections.

[81] This development was slow. Human History, comprising ethnology and archaeology, was created in 1956; History in 1964, "the unit began as a collection...transferred from the ethnology collection"; Folklore in 1966. In 1960/61 the planned permanent exhibition halls showed that the Museum's emphasis continued to be on natural history (4 halls) and "anthropological sciences" (3 halls), "the Museum's large collection illustrating the development of European culture in Canada" was to share temporary exhibition space on the third floor. *'A Museum for Canadians'*

[82] P.Galipeau *Les Paradis du monde: Quebec Folk Art* (Ottawa/Hull 1996) p.32

directions, the contextualized and the aesthetic. Although the theoretical underpinning to Barbeau's research was an examination of a distinct pre-industrial ethnic/cultural group, presumed uncontaminated by other cultural influences, and the origin and diffusion of their craft techniques and motifs, Barbeau's exhibition format did not directly reflect this even given gross lack of exhibition space and the undeveloped state of exhibition design. Like Boas, Barbeau used both contextual, "grouped to illustrate a way of life"[83] in the "French-Canadian room" at the ROM, the Laurier House, St. Lin,[84] and Port Royal,[85] and aesthetic displays in NMC displays[86] and the exhibition, 'The Arts of French Canada'.[87]

Unlike knowledgable private individuals and organizations such as CHG, Barbeau's interests were legitimized, funded and given permanency by his professional standing as a museum ethnologist. However reluctantly, the NMC underwrote his research, collecting, exhibiting and, to some extent, publications.

Western Canada: Saskatoon collections and the Ukrainian Museum of Canada
University (Folk) Museum, Saskatoon 1910/17-1941
In 1917 when MMFA was receiving the first donations from CHG in Montreal, Canada's major city, the fourth of the craft collections identified by Miers-Markham as the 'University Museum, Saskatoon' (USKFM), came into being under the auspices of a university history department in a central prairie town. Saskatoon in a decade of frenzied activity, which included the acquisition of connections to all three transcontinental railways and the provincial university, had grown from a hamlet to a prominent city, from a population of 12,000 in 1911 to 26,000 in 1921.[88] Despite its prominence, Saskatoon was and remained the smallest of the five major prairie cities. The population of Winnipeg, the gateway to the West, was in 1911 thirteen times greater and by 1951 was still nearly seven times greater.

Arthur S. Morton, first professor of history at the University of Saskatchewan founded the

---

[83] Ames 1992 p.52

[84] Nowry pp.308-9

[85] CMC.A Barbeau correspondence letter to W.D.Cromarty 13 September 1940

[86] CMC.A Barbeau Photos: Art et Folklore, Quebec These appear to have been temporary exhibitions in the rotunda or main hall, interspersed with totem poles and skeletons. L.Russell in a brief rundown of permanent and temporary exhibitions does not mention any relating to Barbeau's collection.

[87] CMC.A Barbeau Folder:Photos:[Art et Folklore, Quebec]

[88] Friesen p.513

Museums and Craft Collections 261

Saskatchewan Archives and the Historical Society of the University of Saskatchewan, which through its Museum Committee initiated the acquisition of artifacts "to preserve the memory of the customs and art of the people from non-English speaking lands who have made Canada their home."[89] The collection seems to have spawned two related collections. All three overlap but only one survived.

Miers-Markham actually made no mention of A.S.Morton in connection with the University Museum, Saskatoon, linking him with an archaeology museum at Battleford, "Prof. Morton...is President of the Arts and Crafts Association [sic], which administers the Museum." This is one indication of ongoing confusion between the activities of A.S.Morton and his wife, Vivian B. Morton, a founding member of the Saskatoon Arts and Crafts Society. Nothing in SACS files indicates any connection with the Battleford Museum[90] nor was Professor Morton president of SACS.

The University museum, from dated correspondence, functioned between 1917[91] and 1941. Existing accession books in poor condition[92] dating from March 1921 indicate an eclectic collection. In 1931 the 'Ukrainian section' had both embroideries and ceramics.[93] It appears that artifacts were checked against records in 1944[94] and at about that time textiles and related objects were transferred to the Household Science department where they were "stuffed into the back of a storage area."[95] Under Madge Guilford,[96] who taught History of Costume, these textiles emerged

---

[89] USK.A file 'University Museum' HAUS phamplet n/d

[90] SACS supported, exhibited and marketed the work from a number of reservations. During the dissolution of SACS in the mid 1950s it was proposed "That the Indian things [from SACS collection] be loaned to Mrs Warden wife of superintendent of Indian Affairs to be used as a travelling exhibit to interest Indian Agencies and afterwards to be permanently placed in Fort Battleford Historic Park" which had happened by 1963.

[91] J.L.Teather 'Museum-Making in Canada (to 1972)' *Muse* 1992 p.26 dates the museum to 1910

[92] USKA Patrick Hayes personal communication "There was a fire in May of 1924 in the Physics Building where the Museum was housed at one time. I could not find a reference in our collection to what was damaged."
Rose Marie Fedorak personal communication 7 June 1996 says textiles were stored in a basement, possibly of the Physics Annex, which was flooded and a lot were damaged and/or destroyed as a result; at this time the textiles went to the Household Science Department.
These sound like separate incidents as textiles went to Household Science c.1944.

[93] Kohuska p.726

[94] USK.A file 'University Museum'

[95] Rose Marie Fedorak personal communication 7 June 1996

[96] died 1977/78

from obscurity. They were used in classes, and the collection was expanded by new acquisitions and samples made by students. Recognised officially as the Guilford (Historic Costume Society) Collection in 1984, its mandate was to collect and catalogue articles relating to the study of costume on the Canadian prairies. Starting c1985 Rose Marie Fedorak, a member of the department, accessed government funding for three summers to employ students to catalogue the collection and upgrade storage. Professor Morton is named, in the Guilford accession documents, as collecting in the 1920s from women whose names also appear as producers for SACS and the Student's Historical Association purchased from SACS. In 1989 what had become the College of Home Economics closed, Fedorak went to the Ukrainian Museum of Canada (UWAC:UMC) as Curator, the Ukrainian artifacts from the Guilford Collection went to UWAC:UMC on permanent loan[97], some Doukhobor artifacts went to SK:WDM and the remainder of the Collection was transferred first to the Diefenbaker Centre, USK campus, then to USK.A and in 1995 to USK Drama Department "for research and display."[98]

Saskatoon Arts and Crafts Society Collection 1925-[?]
"The impetus [to set up the Handicrafts Committee within the Local Council of Women which was the precursor to SACS] came directly from the variety of beautiful hand-work of many peoples, which was already collected for a folk-museum in the University of Saskatchewan"[99] and the first SACS Minute book is inscribed "University Museum, Arts and Crafts Committee, Local Council of Women". SACS set up an Archives Committee within two years of founding the organization in 1923. Apart from preserving all the documents associated with the operations of the society, newspaper references to the society and to arts and crafts in general, and research papers given at meetings, the committee was to be responsible for collecting and preserving photographs illustrating the lives and industries of the New Canadians, and for the collecting and care of work resulting from the decision that "an effort should be made to collect typical specimens of the various kinds of work passing through our hands...of educational and historical value." An accession book recorded each article, its maker, donor, value, history or interesting features.[100] SACS Minute books contain tantalizing references to a "permanent collection of

---

[97] In 1929 the National Executive UWAC gave to "the Ukrainian section of the University Museum" handicraft items and local branches donated $100 between 1931-34 for the purchase of artifacts. Kohuska p.974

[98] Cheryl Avery, USK.A, personal communication December 1995. It should be noted that the University has a full and a part-time curator and two galleries for its collection of paintings and prints.

[99] Holmes *The Country Guide* 1928

[100] SKAB SACS files B88-B Committee Reports: Archives 3 February 1926

historical or museum pieces"[101] but the only details extant are of a gift of "a beautiful piece of linen of native production" and by purchase, a collar of Roman cutwork and a piece of flannel homespun.[102] In 1951 an article on "a very fine collection...now in the care of Mrs. A. S. Morton" is illustrated with pictures of Hungarian, Ukrainian and Danish embroideries.[103]

Later in 1951 during discussion on what to do with the collection on the dissolution of the Society a Minute records, "Miss Wilnot had been contacted with regard to [insertion] where the Handicrafts from University Museum are."[104] Not surprisingly as the University Museum textile collection was at that point "stuffed in the back of a storage area" in the Household Science department, integration of the SACS collection with the University museum collection was not a viable alternative. The 1953 Minutes comment,
> "At the present time their [sic] are no facilities for accepting museum pieces in the province. It is interesting to learn that pressure is being brought to bear on the government to provide a museum.
> If this should come about it would solve our problem and provide a permanent home for the Arts and Crafts Societies collection of handicrafts."[105]

A few artifacts went to SK:WDM and a collection of Ukrainian embroidery and weaving went to the UWAC:UMC in 1956.
> "Vivian Morton and Rose Dragan were instrumental in seeing that the Ukrainian artifacts would be housed in a safe place. Unfortunately, we do not have the original records or accession books, or any records other than that these artifacts were received from the Saskatoon Arts and Crafts Society. In 1987, the Museum received additional artifacts from Vivian Morton. Apparently, when the Society dissolved, Mrs. Morton retained a number of pieces."[106]

---

[101] SKAB SACS files B88-B2 Archives committee report 21 September 1933

[102] SKAB SACS files B88-A Minute book February 1926

[103] R.Ducie 'Old-time Crafts Still Live' *Western Producer* 1951

[104] Saskatoon Public Library, Main Branch Local History Room (SPLm LHR) LH8542 Minutes 1 June 1951 p.67 The part deleted is "...to taking our collection to store at the University along with the other Museum collections..."

[105] SPLm LHR LH8542 Minutes 6 April 53 p.83

[106] Rose Marie Fedorak, Curator, UWAC:UMC, Saskatoon letter 15 September 1995

The SACS accession register is not with the rest of the archival material at SKAB[107] and presumably no longer exists.

During the 1949/51 Massey Commission hearings, Dr. Hilda Neatby, a member of the Commission and a professor of history at the University of Saskatchewan, "made mention of collections made in Saskatchewan of the groups that have settled in that province, which have been dispersed...and it is very difficult to get them again."[108] The histories of the craft collections of the University of Saskatchewan and SACS contrast with the officially sanctioned and financed activities of Barbeau at NMC and with the museums of the University of Toronto. At the University of Toronto active influential and affluent patronage, largely external to the university, endowed and propelled to independence the Royal Ontario Museum (ROM). The ROM's history would indicate that universities' priorities were not to their museums, particularly where collections were not germane to current academic interests, nor were staff expertise, tasks and focus the same. At the University of Saskatchewan, the 'folk collection' was under the aegis of the history department through the department's student society and linked to a historian with an interest in Western Canadian history. Academically, craft textiles interested neither history nor fine art.[109]

The Museum of the Ukrainian Women's Association of Canada 1941
The initiators of the third Saskatoon collection, that of the Ukrainian Women's Association of Canada (UWAC), were involved with the other two, through donations of artifacts and money to the University museum or by membership. Rose Dragan[110] convenor of the Handicrafts/Arts

---

[107] A SACS file containing much of the 1950s material was also separated from the main archive. I am grateful to Joan Champ for pointing me in the direction of the Saskatoon Public Library.

[108] NAC Massey Commission C2013 16:25:296 p.32
Dr. Neatby was approached by SACS to write a history of their work. The failure to find a suitable graduate student to do that may well have influenced the Society to donate to the University over $5000 in 1956 to set up the Saskatoon Arts and Crafts Society Trust Fund. The money first surfaced in 1983 as the 'Arthur Silver Morton Awards of the Saskatoon Arts and Crafts Society', soon shortened to the 'A.S.Morton Memorial Travel Scholarship' with the citation, "When the Saskatoon Arts and Craft Society ceased its operation on the death of one of its most prominent members, Arthur Silver Morton, the funds of the Society were donated to the University..."
Presented with the results of my research in January 1996, the History Department changed the name and description of the scholarship to 'The Vivian Williams Morton and Arthur Silver Morton Memorial Travel Scholarship'. fax Bill Waiser, Head History Department USK 9 October 1996
The only mention of SACS is Vivian Morton's part as co-founder, thus the name of the Society and the histories and efforts of the people and craftspeople involved are dismissed as of no historical value.

[109] Academic research on textiles is currently done almost entirely through University Home Economics Departments

[110] Rose Dragan fl.1927- embroiderer, weaver

Museums and Craft Collections

and Museum Committee, UWAC was an active member of SACS. If the University Museum and SACS, as representatives of the dominant British culture, were interested in studying, promoting and preserving the work of New Canadians, the UWAC as part of one of the largest and politically and organizationally most active New Canadian groups was intent on creating an awareness of Ukrainian national arts; within its own community as a means of maintaining and developing a distinct Ukrainian identity, without to celebrate ethnic roots in relation to the hope of a liberated Ukraine.

Predominantly poor, illiterate peasants determined to better their lot, the first influx of 70,000 immigrants, most from the western Ukraine, arrived between 1891 and the beginning of WWI to settle along the parkland belt from Winnipeg, MB through to Edmonton, AB. A second major immigration occurred in the 1920s. Winnipeg remained the major metropolitan centre for Ukrainians, 7001 in 1921, 41,997 in 1951. Saskatchewan had the largest rural Ukrainian population, 25,290 in 1921, 62,319 in 1951 but Saskatoon's Ukrainian community was small, 332 in 1921 and 4,257 in 1951. Mainly initiated by young first-generation Ukrainian women students associated with the Petro Mohyla Institute, Saskatoon, and public school teachers, the UWAC was established at a 1926 convention in Saskatoon. The development of the UWAC and the museum collection took place against the rigours of pioneer settlement, the early feminist movement, the drought and economic disaster of the Dirty Thirties, WWII and the devastation of the Ukraine with a resulting post-war third influx of displaced Ukrainians, who favoured central Canada.

From the beginning "a crying need" was recognized "for an organized effort to revive an interest in Ukrainian arts and crafts" and "a directing and informative agency to help maintain the high standards and old traditions of craftsmanship in those crafts which had as yet not completely vanished under modern influences."[111] This necessitated acquiring and exhibiting selected examples of Ukrainian crafts. Through its national, provincial, and local branches and in cooperation with other organizations, the UWAC sponsored and mounted exhibitions, workshops and festivals. In the late 1920s exhibitions were mounted in Winnipeg, Saskatoon, Edmonton, in Toronto at CNE, and Regina. Local branches were encouraged to institute collections in Ukrainian National Homes (community halls), with the idea of eventually establishing a Museum of Ukrainian Arts.

In 1937 a resolution was passed at the national UWAC convention outlining a policy for the collection of artifacts for a future museum. At that time approximately 200 items collected by Hanka Romanchych,[112] who for two and a half years had co-ordinated a cottage industry project

---

[111] R.Dragan *Ukrainian Embroidery Designs and Stitches* (Saskatoon 1957) p.10

[112] See chapter 4, Craft cottage industries, individual initiatives, Romanchych.

while working for the Alberta government, were acquired by donation and purchase to form the basis of the permanent collection. It included early embroidery designs, shirts, household weavings, belts and other items garnered from rural Western Canada, principally Alberta. There was a heavy emphasis on textiles, particularly embroideries, and the collection quickly became a mix of historical and contemporary work, brought in with settlers or generated in Canada or bought in the Ukraine on return visits prior to WWII. In 1939-40, travelling exhibitions of this permanent collection were used to encourage further donations of suitable artifacts; an Arts and Crafts Committee responsible for the museum was struck; the range of the collection was broadened and archival materials were added; and the first registration of the collection was made and published on the Women's Page of the weekly *Ukrainian Voice*.

> "The early collection was quite modest and was stored in suitcases and trunks in the homes of the national UWAC presidents in Saskatoon. As the collection grew, however, the safe housing of the collection became a priority."[113]

The Mohyla Institute was approached and provided a gallery to display the collection. Thus 'The Museum of the Ukrainian Women's Association of Canada', the first Ukrainian museum in North America, opened in 1941. The collection at that time included approximately 500 embroidery designs and 180 artifacts including weavings, folk costume items, wood carvings, *pysanky* (wax resist decorated Easter eggs) and other typical crafts.

Mary Tkachuk, who has been involved with the museum since c1936 sees 1941 as the end of the development phase of the museum. In the second phase 1942-1969,

> "internal growth and development was stabilised. Attention was focused on establishing a base for program functions such as acquisitions, care and management of the collections, permanent exhibitions, projects and publications."[114]

The promotion and revival of Ukrainian crafts were inextricably entwined with the museum collection.

> "At first the National Executive looked after matters pertaining to the folk arts, organized exhibits, gave lessons in embroidery and easter egg decorating, stylized Ukrainian folk costumes, preserved the integrity of Ukrainian embroidery, and collected items for the museum. The same functions were performed by the Arts and Museum Committee [from 1941 on]."[115]

Projects in 1939 included the adaptation of folk designs and traditional stitchery to contemporary

---

[113] Kohuska p.979

[114] Kohuska p.974

[115] Kohuska p.719

Museums and Craft Collections

dress, the revival of traditional weaving and the promotion of Ukrainian embroidery stitches.
"Precise directives for teaching embroidery courses included a kit with fabrics, designs, thread and examples of finished methods."[116]
From 1942 pamphlets were published in English and Ukrainian on embroidery, *pysanka* (1946), weaving, embroidery (1950) and the work of the museum. Rose Dragan, Museum and Handicraft Chairperson, was responsible from 1949 on for the publication of embroidery designs in the Women's Page of the 'Ukrainian Voice', the committee "strove to collect designs which would teach lesser-known embroidery stitches"[117] and, at the request of the members, provide suitable church embroidery designs for vestments, icons, banners and so on. This lead to the publication in 1956 of *The Album of Embroidery Designs* and to the definitive reference work, *Ukrainian Embroidery and Stitches* 1958 in English.

The museum and its outreach work depended financially totally on the support of the UWAC membership and on volunteer labour, particularly that of talented, dedicated committees. The Mohyla Institute provided some practical support and in 1948 the museum moved into a larger gallery there.[118] Also in 1948, the Museum and Handicraft Committee chairperson had investigated the possibility of establishing representative collections in national museums with apparently no response.[119]

By 1944 "the museum function had grown to such an extent"[120] that, under the UWAC executive, two branch museums were inaugurated, the Ontario Branch at St. Vladimir Cathedral, Toronto and the Alberta Branch in Edmonton, where from 1948 the collection, valued at $700, was divided between St. John's Orthodox Church and the M. Hrushevsky Institute. In 1951, it was united at St. John's Institute. In 1950, the Manitoba Branch Museum was set up and located, from 1952 in Holy Trinity Cathedral, Winnipeg.

---

[116] Kohuska p.976

[117] Kohuska p.985

[118] In 1979 a specially designed museum building was opened on Spadina Crescent East, Saskatoon.

[119] Kohuska p.991 This was not pursued again until 1958, when the national art collection was moving to a new gallery and the renovation of the space it had occupied "precluded the inclusion of an ethnic section in the national museum at that time." Continued enquiries "learned that the department of national museums was undergoing a period of major re-organization. Further overtures were shelved."

[120] Kohuska p.1018

Western Canada: CHG Collections
Canadian Handicrafts Guild: Alberta Branch

At least two western branches of CHG established permanent collections. The Alberta branch, started in 1920, came under the wing of the University of Alberta Extension Department. The director, Dr.E.A.Corbett, president of CHG in 1938, corresponded with Marius Barbeau between 1925 and 1937, writing in 1933,

> The [Quebecois] rug arrived, and I am making it the basis of a collection which I think we will gradually acquire of Canadian handicrafts...as soon as I hear from the Carnegie Foundation as to their attitude on the question of building up a carefully selected and comprehensive exhibit, I will let you know."[121]

In 1934 and 1935 amounts of $300 were spent purchasing artifacts for a permanent collection totalling 320 works, Corbett's correspondence hints that the collection was national rather than regional.

> "In 1934-35 Extension organized in the southern part of the province handicraft exhibitions in co-operation with the Canadian Handicraft Guild and various local agencies. These were accompanied by lectures and were displayed in 26 locations with attendance exceeding 20,000."[122]

Simon says that the collection of work in these exhibitions was of

> "handcraft work done in Alberta...
>
> The collection, to which technical schools in Calgary and Edmonton contributed generously, was intended to stimulate interest in such work by showing the public what it is possible to achieve in these schools."[123]

Whether Corbett's purchased collection was part of that travelling exhibition is unknown.

By the time of the Massey Commission in 1949 a craft collection was packed away at the Department of Extension.[124] In 1996 an extensive search of appropriate sources, including Director's correspondence with CHG from 1945 to 1950 "found nothing relating to the content nor disposition of any handicraft collection."[125]

---

[121] CMC.A Barbeau Correspondence B183 B97 14 June 1933

[122] Mark Vajcner Assistant Archivist UAB.A fax 3 June 1996 This tour is discussed in chapter 4, under Government intervention, Governments and rural women, Provincial Departments of Agriculture and the Women's Institutes

[123] Simon pp.193,196 quoting AB Department of Education, Annual Report 1934 p.77

[124] NAC Massey Commission C-2005 8:13:124

[125] Vajcner UAB.A fax 26 June 1996 Sources included UAB Museums and Collections Service; Faculty of Extension-Fine Arts Dept: Presidents Papers, Banff School Papers; Dept.of Extension Director's Files c1930-1950; Banff Centre Archives

Museums and Craft Collections

Canadian Handicrafts Guild: Manitoba Branch collection 1932/Crafts Guild of Manitoba museum 1968-1997/ Manitoba Crafts Museum and Library 1997

The Manitoba branch of CHG started its collection in 1932 in anticipation of the founding of the provincial museum and it has been added to by purchase and donation. Both CHG:MB and WI:MB[126] were involved in reviving old crafts at that time. Described as being predominantly of handcrafted textiles, the collection includes clothing and decorated household articles using techniques which include weaving, embroidery, crochet, tatting, knitting, needlepoint, and bobbin and needle lace. The textiles are historical (not necessarily Canadian) and contemporary, including ethnic embroideries "representative of the people of many nations who migrated from Europe to settle along the Red River valley...Many of the women of these communities were craftswomen and early members and organizers of the [CHG Manitoba branch]."[127] There is also pottery, hooked rugs, quilts, weavings, wood carvings, dolls, and basketry.[128]

A collection initiated by Lady Tweedsmuir, wife of the Governor General, in 1937 with the suggestion that if handicrafts were to become more than a "passing fad" the quality must be improved,

"I think a loan collection of good things to be circulated in country districts might help and we might have the first one in Manitoba as an experiment."[129]

The WI:MB voted $100 to purchase items for the collection and appointed three members of CHG:MB to purchase items of good workmanship and design to include, "knitted articles, small quilts, small rugs, simple loom and some woven articles, embroideries characteristic of different countries, handmade gloves, and articles carved from wood."[130] It remained a small demonstration collection. In 1992 the Guild received the 'Lady Tweedsmuir Collection of Crafts'.

Like a number of other organization's collections, CHG:MB's collection was peripatetic. By 1942 the collection was located with the library and weaving school in two attic rooms of the

---

[126] "The two organizations were inextricably linked during the early years. People used to belong to, and volunteer at, both organizations." Margaret Gaunt, Curator, CGMB, letter 28 May 1995

[127] CGMB 'Crafts Museum' pamphlet July 1993

[128] 'Crafts Guild of Manitoba' Margaret Gaunt sheet nd. In 1995 the guild had "a numerical listing of artifacts and are in the process of designing a computer programme which will enable us to catalogue and properly record the artifacts."
Margaret Gaunt letter 28 May 1995. This process was interrupted by the dissolution of the Guild and the removal of the collection to a new location in 1997.

[129] Lady Tweedsmuir, letter 20 March 1937 quoted 'Lady Tweedsmuir Collection' CGMB exhibition pamphlet March 1994

[130] 'Lady Tweedsmuir Collection' CGMB exhibition pamphlet March 1994

Winnipeg Art School. In 1947, when the Art School expanded because of post-war enrolment, the collection was stored at Guild member's houses.[131] In 1952 "the present site on Kennedy Street [Winnipeg] was purchased and a permanent home for crafts in the province was built."[132]

Eastern Canada: New Brunswick Museum

The contemporary craft collection at the New Brunswick Museum (NBM), Saint John was started by Alice Lusk Webster, who with her husband Dr. J. Clarence Webster, was on the museum Board and who were both directly engaged in the museum's collecting, research and exhibition activities. The museum was started in 1842 by provincial geologist Abraham Gesner and was located at the Saint John Mechanics' Institute. Run by the Natural History Society of New Brunswick from 1862 to 1912, NBM was incorporated as the provincial museum in 1929 and by 1934 was housed in a new museum building.

Born in New York, Alice Webster had a cosmopolitan education, initially in New York, later in Germany and in France, where she studied art and went to the Sorbonne. When a girl, she visited the Orient with her family and later regularly travelled to Britain and Europe. She had helped her husband with casts and water colours when he set up the University of Chicago, Rush Medical College museum.

In 1934 "Alice Webster wanted to broaden the policy of the Museum to include items from other countries and cultures." The Board initially turned down the idea, although because Saint John is a sea port city the museum collections already contained foreign curios. In response to continued application, the Board agreed with the understanding that Webster "would receive absolutely no assistance from them."[133] By 1936,

> "a collection of Industrial Art assembled and arranged by Mrs. Clarence Webster [affording] an opportunity to study the arts and crafts of Egypt, Greece and Rome...European ceramics, textiles and furniture...The arts of China, Japan and the

---

[131] NAC Massey Files C2005 8:13:126 CHG:HQ Annual Report 1946 p.16

[132] In 1997 CGMB was dissolved and the Kennedy Street building sold. CGMB archival material went to Provincial Archives, Manitoba. The CGMB museum collection and library moved to shared space with the Manitoba Crafts Council as the Manitoba Crafts Museum and Library. "The museum and library, along with antique spinning wheels, were placed under the auspices of Manitoba Crafts Council...and will remain the responsibilities of those committees [presumably CGMB Museum and Library Committees]. Looms and Spinning wheels have been placed with the Human Ecology faculty at the University of Manitoba, and teachers of those crafts will be allowed to teach there...Proceeds of the sale of the building and other valuable items will be administered by the Winnipeg Foundation, keeping the criteria in place that has funded crafts projects over the years." 'Crafts Guild of Manitoba Inc.: A Brief History' typescript CGMB Archives Committee 21 July 1997

[133] V.Simpson 'Our Gracious Lady: A Short Biography of Alice Webster' *Journal of the New Brunswick Museum* 1978 p.12

> Near East...A case has been provided for the pottery of New Brunswick, and its characteristic "homespuns" are also exhibited."[134]

The 'assembling and arranging' of this collection came entirely from Webster's own collections,
> "I have transferred my most treasured possessions to the Museum, or exchanged them for more suitable material,"

and her financial and physical investment in preparing the gallery and mounting the exhibits,
> "I was prepared to pay for the cases but was somewhat disconcerted to find myself personally responsible for all the incidental expenses, including structural changes and the painting of the gallery. The Museum was in financial difficulties and it was useless to make an appeal locally, for our people are not "givers".."[135]

> "Each article was carefully selected for its educational value, artistic quality or possible use in connection with the local handicraft movement...A case was added for the handicrafts of New Brunswick in the hope of encouraging production and promoting interest in home industries. The present exhibit the work of a Danish potter [Kjeld Deichmann] who is experimenting with glazes and local clays is exceptionally good."[136]

A list, "Homespuns woven by Mount Allison Handicraft Guild 1937/ Cottage Craft Tweeds Helen Mowatt 1937/ Textiles Miss Dorothy May Fraser, Lewisville, Moncton 1937", may indicate examples of the 'characteristic homespuns'.

In 1940 Edith Hudson Bishop, who had studied at the Newark Museum of Art, New Jersey became Art Curator, to be succeeded in 1946 by Avery Shaw. Both worked closely with Webster, who was Honourary Curator. A small collection (34) of contemporary ceramics, all but two the work of New Brunswick potters, was made between 1937 and 1954. Webster and Shaw were closely involved with the Guild of New Brunswick Craftsmen formed in 1947, in 1948 Webster was vice-president. In his submission to the Massey Committee, Kjeld Deichmann wrote,
> "We would like to pay tribute to the work and leadership of the New Brunswick Museum. During the years, The Decorative Arts Section, through the generosity of Mrs. J. C. Webster, has played an important role in the development of the Provinces' crafts, both by encouraging the worker, by buying his work for the permanent collections of the Museum, and by showing a personal interest in his progress. The New Brunswick craftsmen too have access to study rare books on arts and crafts. Furthermore, every summer the New Brunswick Museum has had

---

[134] *New Brunswick Museum Administrative Series* (a)1 1936-37 p.3,5; my emphasis.

[135] NBM.A Art Department Alice Lusk Webster File F544

[136] NBM.A Art Dept. Records F545 October 1936

in its main hall a summer showing of the craftsmen's most recent work."[137]
Concurrently J.C.Webster was on the Board of the CHG. On his death in 1950 he left an endowment sufficient to operate the Departments of Canadian History and Art. In the mid-1950s a new Art Curator with no interest in craft coincided with NBM's desire not to duplicate the collecting activity of the government department of tourism initiated through Dr. Crowell, Director of the New Brunswick Handicraft Training Centre.

Webster's comment, "It is obvious that in these days of specialization, the amateur labours under a heavy handicap,"[138] signals a change reflected in the NBM brief to the Massey Commission 1949-1951. It is not clear who authored the brief, possibly the former Director/Curator, Dr. W. McIntosh who retired in 1940 after more than 36 years at the museum.

> "Owing to the rapid expansion of the section devoted to Canadian history and the unforeseen development of the art collections, the Museum had ceased to be a unit and the functions of Director could no longer be combined with those of a Curator. The Museum became a Provincial Institute in 1941[139] but subsidies were not increased and to employ a competent executive with assistants to do the work was out of the question. The Museum was therefore divided into three departments and three young teachers of Science, Canadian History and Art were appointed curators."

The brief goes on to say that there was no activity in the Art Department until Mr Avery Shaw was appointed.[140] This brief seems extraordinary in the light of the work accomplished by the Websters and the employment of a qualified, if female, Art Curator. It marks museums' move towards professionalization and dependable and adequate public funding. The report of The Royal Commission on Arts, Letters and Sciences 1949-1951 (Massey Report), which included the first investigation of museums since Miers-Markham 1932, gives an overview both of the state of museums in Canada at mid-century and of the views of craft organizations in relation to museums.

---

[137] CMC Deichmann exhibition file 'A Study of Canadian Handicrafts with Particular Reference to New Brunswick' p.9

[138] NBM.A Art Dept. Alice Lusk Webster File F544

[139] NBM *M/J88* NBM incorporated 1929 as a provincial museum

[140] NAC Massey Commission C2013 16:26:301

The Royal Commission on Arts, Letters and Sciences 1949-1951

Canadian Museums 1932-1951

In its report, the commission refers to Miers-Markham,

> "Those who compare the record of our own impressions with the findings of the Report will see that the present shows little if any sign of improvement. The annual per capita expenditure on museums in terms of real value has probably decreased."[141]

The newly organised Canadian Museums Association (CMA) submitted a 'Provisional List of Canadian Museums and Art Galleries'[142], under the headings: A. Natural History Museums Including Archaeology (47), B. Historical Museums Including Military and Industrial (68), and C. Art Museums and Art Galleries (28). Ontario has the greatest number, 66.[143] The CMA boasted a membership of 30 from a total of 125 museums,[144]

> "It includes all the main museums; the majority of the museums in Eastern Canada...as you go further west the proportion of the total number of museums which is in the Association gradually diminishes."[145]

The CMA's objective was the advancement of public museum and art gallery services in Canada through improving museums services, acting as a clearing house for museum information, establishing museum staff training, promoting the exchange of exhibitions and exhibits within Canada and abroad, and involvement with other museum associations. Probably because of "the important part played by National Museum officials,"[146] its proposals revolve around the expansion and creation of national institutions, which were situated in Ottawa and, as briefs to the Commission showed, played a relatively limited role nationally. However the Report concentrates first and in some detail on NMC.

---

[141] Massey pp.99,100

[142] Massey Appendix VII pp.485-490

[143] The regional distribution is:
A: BC 3; AB 3; SK 6; MB 2; ON 16; PQ 11; NB 2; NS 3; NFD 1; PEI 0
B: BC 1; AB 1; SK 4; MB 2; ON 40; PQ 13; NB 3; NS 4;
C: BC 2; AB 3; SK 2; MB 1; ON 10; PQ 4;   NB 2; NS 2;   PEI 2
     6   7   12   5   66   28   7   9   1   2

[144] This total differs from that in the appendix

[145] NAC Massey Commission C2005 8-14-136a CMA brief

[146] Massey p.96

NMC was at that time a part of the National Parks Service of the Department of Resources and Development. Being part of a government department was seen as causing some confusion as to its independence, mandate and role[147]. Its premises, the Victoria Memorial Building, were considered totally inadequate condemning two-thirds of exhibits to storage. In an arrangement made forty years earlier, the NGC occupied one wing of NMC's building, the Geological Survey also occupied a large space. Its budget was also inadequate,

> "The National Museum operates on a budget appropriate to the modesty of its quarters...the budget of the National Museum of Canada in 1949-50 was $177,500."

This was compared with, among others, the budget which the British treasury granted to "ten important museums" in 1949, sterling 1,176,639, and the annual disbursement of the Smithsonian Institute "in approximately those fields covered by our National Museum," $1,062,737. "We have noted with interest that the American Museum of Natural History employs more full-time scientists in its Insect and Spider Division alone than are employed in our National Museum as a whole."[148] Dr Alcock, geologist and newly appointed Director of NMC, said, "I don't really pretend to be a museums man."[149] Not surprisingly the functions of NMC were priorized as research and collecting, with exhibitions and education coming second.

If the situation of the national museum was grim, the report on local museums was a song of woe reiterating the dearth of museums, their lack of adequate funding and accommodation, the ongoing loss of materials, and the lack of professional expertise. As with much of the material presented there was little in the way of hard facts and figures, however in the words of the report:

> "In Canada, with very few notable exceptions, local museums maintain a courageous but precarious existence, giving to their communities such services as their unsuitable quarters, inadequate budgets and the volunteer help of a few enthusiasts can maintain. It is probably true that most Canadian citizens remain throughout their lives quite unaware of the pleasure and enlightenment which an adequately planned and equipped museum could give them. The sorry plight of museums in Canada is appropriately matched by a widespread public indifference to their inadequacy...This indifference makes it the more difficult to secure exact information. In a western city we stumbled, as it were by accident, on a most interesting collection hidden in a basement. The curator gladly showed his exhibits and explained his problems, but modesty had restrained him from presenting a

---

[147] NAC was at this time under the Department of Agriculture

[148] Massey pp.88-9

[149] NAC Massey Commission C2013 16:26:297

Museums and Craft Collections 275

brief for our information."[150]

"There is general agreement...in the briefs...that Canadian museums, in relation to Canada's population and resources, are lamentably few and poor. Except in Toronto and Ottawa very little public money is granted to them. The combined annual revenue of all museums in Canada, public or private, would not pay the cost of one of the aircraft used in our transcontinental service."[151]

"The poverty and inadequacy of Canadian museums is regretted not only because of the present need for good museum services but because every year irreplaceable museum material is being lost. From all parts of the country we had reports on the loss or destruction of museum material."[152]

"Very few Canadian museums possess adequate buildings which are fireproof. Most are housed in improvised and temporary quarters. Not only do they lack money for new acquisitions; they have not the space to receive those that may be offered as gifts."[153]

"Any discussion of problems of accommodation and display leads inevitably to a consideration of the curator, and of his duties. The difficulty of finding a curator (and, we must add, the even greater difficulty of finding a curator's salary) was mentioned on several occasions."[154]

Craft and Museums

The Massey Commission had evidently not anticipated

"the spirited and good-humoured assaults made upon us by societies and individuals concerned with the fostering and growth of Canadian handicrafts...Some forty-four societies or individuals gave evidence before us on handicrafts in Canada...judging from the enthusiasm this subject has aroused, we are quite prepared to accept the statement made to us that handicraft workers in

---

[150] Massey p.92

[151] Massey p.93

[152] Massey p.93

[153] Massey p.94

[154] Massey p.95

Canada number well on to 300,000."[155]

Litt notes that the special study on handicrafts (written by the Deichmanns) was one of the last to be commissioned and came as an afterthought.[156]

The Commission seemed unaware of the findings and recommendations of the second of two committees, initially under the aegis of the Department of Agriculture, which looked at craft in the early 1940s. The Interdepartmental Committee on Canadian Handcrafts 1942-1944[157] included two NGC staff and the NGC Director, H.O.McCurry. That Committee concluded that there was

> "an unusual national-scale interest" in craft and "that it would prove of considerable national economic, cultural and social importance...to encourage wider practice and appreciation of useful Canadian hand arts and crafts for both our rural and urban populations."

It was suggested that this could be achieved through an extension of NGC's existing national service of exhibitions and tours of reproductions, lantern slides and lectures. The Committee added,

> "Art institutions, whether in Europe or North America, which have adopted the policy of displaying and encouraging the creative hand arts and crafts, have observed a rapid increase in the numbers of people who visit such institutions as compared with the numbers who visit art services offering only fine paintings and sculpture."[158]

It was recommended that NGC be responsible for conducting

> "[a] thorough national survey in order to arrive at a complete and comprehensive picture of present activities and potential interest, needs and capacities prevailing in all sections of Canada...[and] that, simultaneously with the conducting of the national survey, plans be laid for the holding of a national exhibition which will present to the general public a comprehensive review of typical Canadian hand arts and crafts."[159]

An Advisory Council on Canadian Hand Arts and Crafts was also recommended.

---

[155] Massey p.235

[156] P.Litt *The Muses, the Masses and the Massey Commission* (Toronto 1992) p.289 note 17

[157] chapter 4, 'Government Intervention'

[158] NAC Massey Commission C2005 8:13:126 CHG Annual Report 1946-7 p.6 The Winnipeg Art Gallery handcraft exhibition had over 7000 visitors, "a far larger number than it has been usual to record for any other exhibition in the gallery."

[159] Russell Interdepartmental Committee Report 1942-44 p.5
All underlinings appear in the report.

Museums and Craft Collections

The Committee had felt it necessary to issue a disclaimer early in its report underlining that it was to conduct a study only and had no official status. That the burden of the recommendations fell on NGC is perplexing given the lack of staff, facilities and finances under which the institution suffered at that time. The recommendation by the Committee that NGC work closely with the Department of Agriculture and "all rural services" and the statement that "it is the <u>homes of the common people</u> which determine a country's characteristic national culture"[160] would fit uncomfortably with Tippet's assertion that NGC was centralist in outlook, catered to one medium 'paint' and one style 'conservative modernism', and that

> "...none of it could have been sustained without the...support of the Canadian government, which was persuaded that painting and sculpture, more than any form of art, had a permanent, tangible character."[161]

No move to implement the recommendations appears to have been taken by NGC.

Past presidents of CHG had sat on the Committee (Bouchard, CHG President 1940-41 and Assistant Deputy Minister of Agriculture, sat on both the 1941 and 1944 committees) and past, present and future CHG presidents and staff from various branches 'visited' and corresponded with it. NGC's inaction and CHG's not altogether successful experience with MMFA may have influenced CHG's argument to the Massey Commission that craft collections should go to museums, particularly NMC.

The variety of craft activity presented by briefs is reflected in the Massy report,
> "We have had...some difficulty in determining what exactly is meant by "handicrafts", although we found this definition helpful: 'An individual product of usefulness and beauty, created by hand on a small scale, preferably by the same person from start to finish, employing primarily the raw materials of [his] own country and when possible of [his] own locality.' But it seems to us that the term is employed in Canada rather loosely to include the work of highly-skilled full-time professionals (notably in metal crafts, ceramics and textiles), of skilled amateurs who augment their normal income by part-time handicrafts, of invalids who find a therapeutic value in such work, of Indians or Eskimos, of cellar-workshop hobbyists who work for their own and their friend's pleasure, of employees in small "handicraft industries", of part-time workers who make at home to a fixed design what are essentially mass-produced goods for commercial markets, and no doubt of still other groups such as housewives who take pleasure in weaving their own curtains...However we define the term, there is no doubt that

---

[160] Russell 1942-43 p.30

[161] M.Tippett *Making Culture: English-Canadian Institutions and the Arts before the Massey Commission* (Toronto 1990) pp.89,90

handicrafts are an important activity of Canadian citizens."[162]

The briefs from craft organizations make little mention of existing museums or museum collections. C.T.Woodside, CHG:AB Calgary, said, "There is no museum in Alberta that I know of"[163] and Nora McCullough refers to the UWAC:UMC.[164] There is however an extraordinary concentration on the national institutions given the physical distance of Ottawa from many of the presenters.

The briefs themselves show a division about where craft should be positioned, locating them with decorative arts as a separate museum, remaining with the status quo at the national museum, associated with industrial design in an aesthetic context at the national gallery, and located with fine arts. CHG.ON[165] "believ[ing] that with proper direction and adequate incentive young men and women may make a living as full-time professional craftsmen" argued that,

> "Art in the three dimensional field or handicrafts tends to become subordinated. Recognition of its equal importance has been made by the establishment of separate museums in England (for example the Victoria and Albert, British Museum, the National Gallery and the Tate Gallery...)"

CHG:HQ said,

> "there is confusion between the duties of a National Gallery and National Museum...The Guild further thinks that the proper place for crafts is in a Museum rather than in a Fine Art Gallery and that the jurisdiction of the National Museum should be widened to include examples of Canadian crafts."[166]

The CMA also referred to the Victoria and Albert in their proposal to establish an Institute of Industrial Design.[167] It may have been because of the "department of Industrial Design now connected with the National Gallery" referred to in the Community Arts Council of Vancouver (CACV) brief[168] that Ivan Crowell of the Handicrafts Division, New Brunswick Department of

---

[162] Massey p.235

[163] NAC Massey Commission C2005 8:13:124

[164] NAC Massey Commission C2014 17:29:362

[165] Ruth Home who presented on behalf of CHG.ON was museum lecturer and guide at ROM c1928-46, from 1946 she lectured at OCA

[166] NAC Massey Commission C2005 8:13:128 CHG:ON brief

[167] NAC Massey Commission C2005 8:14:136a

[168] NAC Massey Commission C2006 9:16:161 CACV

Museums and Craft Collections

Industry and Reconstruction proposed, "Greater recognition of Handicrafts and our craftsmen by the National Gallery of Canada."[169] However MAG, who wished "to be recognised as artists in metal" recommended

> "Encouragement of Art Galleries and Museums to display permanently and in travelling exhibitions worthy examples of the Metal Arts on the same basis as painting and sculpture."[170]

The location of craft within a museum seems to mark a narrowing of focus by CHG. CHG:AB's definition "folk crafts or handicrafts"[171] is echoed by CHG:HQ "folk arts or handicrafts...the basic arts...the practical arts."[172] This position was expanded by Nora McCullough[173] on behalf of the Saskatchewan Arts Board. Acknowledging the UMC:UWAC she argued,

> "This province has in addition to its indigenous groups many cultural heritages which would be a great loss to the pattern of Canadian culture...a survey undertaken by the National Museum to investigate closely what exists in the way of handmade arts by indigenous and ethnic groups in Canada and to gather up fine and typical examples in the various traditions for a permanent collection...in this way, the traditional crafts would receive the care and appreciation they warrant, the craftsmen would be encouraged and the public would receive constant inspiration. Museums of handicraft as described could be part of the extension services of the National Museum with local collaborations. The collections would be more useful and integrated with the life of the people in the areas the work originated...[A] thorough investigation of handicraft...would undoubtedly disclose vast new fields of inspiring source material for those Canadian painters, designers, musicians and writers, in search of rich and fresh ways of expressing Canadian life."[174]

Although the topic of craft collections was raised on a number of occasions, CHG.HQ in its proposals requests only Grants-in-Aid for travelling exhibitions (as did CHG.AB, CACV and

---

[169] NAC Massey Commission C2013 16:26:299

[170] NAC Massey Commission C2010 13:22:276

[171] NAC Massey Commission C2005 8:13:124 CHG:AB Calgary

[172] NAC Massey Commission C2005 8:13:126

[173] Nora McCullough was SAB's only permanent full time employee, Vivian Morton was Chair of SAB Handicrafts Committee

[174] NAC Massey Commission C2014 17:29:362

others) and for purchases for permanent collections. The Massey Commission Report made no specific recommendations.

Summary

The history of museum practice in any substantial form during this period is bounded by the Miers-Markham survey in 1932 and the Massey Report 1949-51. By the time of the Miers-Markham report, three of the museums discussed (MMFA, NMC and NBM) were extant, the two former were involved with collecting handcrafted objects although not necessarily under that designation. Seven of the collecting organizations were also active. Within five years of the Miers-Markham report the remaining two museums and four collecting organizations were active. By the time of the Massey Report in 1949, at least six collections were dispersed (CHG:HQ 1908-CHG:HQ/MMFA 1916-1928; USKFM 1917-44) or in stasis (SACS, CHG:AB/UAB and NBM).

The Miers-Markham comparison between the condition of museums in Canada and in the United States and Britain is unfair given their greater wealth, population, stability and establishment. The first three decades of the twentieth century for Canada were ones of land settlement, immigration, industrialization, economic and political power shifts, and the establishment of an infrastructure for a 'civilized' country. Cultural activity, as part of civilized life, was initiated and largely continued by individuals, groups or corporate patrons. There was little secure commitment from municipal, provincial or Dominion governments. The Dominion government's support went to the fledging national archive, museum and art gallery in Ottawa, a small town on the Quebec Ontario border distanced from the metropolis of Montreal and the urban horseshoe of southern Ontario. The thirty years between the Miers-Markham survey and the Massey report covered the Depression and WWII so it is not surprising that the Massey Commission found little change in the situation of museums.

The Massey Commission reported that the number of museums had hardly changed;[175] the financial situation had, if possible, worsened; lack of funding and accommodation meant no purchased acquisitions and no capacity to accept donations, the Commission reiterates that in all parts of the country there was loss or destruction of museum material; and there was a lack of trained expertise. A decrease in Quebec museums (54>28) and an increase in Ontario (37>66) seems to parallel a shift in population, wealth and political power. Outside Central Canada, there was little growth except in Saskatchewan which doubled the number of museums, British

---

[175] Miers-Markham 1932/Massey 1951
BC 9; AB 6;   SK 6;   MB 3; ON 37; PQ 54; NB 7;   NS 11; PEI 0; (NFD 1) 134
     6   7   12   5   66   28   7   9   1   2   143

Columbia and Nova Scotia lost museums.[176] There was also a decrease in natural history museums (58>47) and an increase in regional history museums (51>68); art galleries/museums remained static (27>28). This state of affairs would impact negatively on craft collections through lack of facilities and/or inability to accept new collections, particularly at the closure of the originating organization. It might impact positively through craft articles coming into museums as regional history or pioneer artifacts.

I identified 13 craft collections, with starting dates from 1908 to 1937, 8 of these started during the Depression but from 1937 there is a gap of more than a decade when no new collections were started. Three of the 13 (PQ/l'EdAD; CHG:HQ/MMFA; and NBM) appear from the information available to deal largely with non-Canadian crafts.

The majority of these collections (10) are associated with craft organizations or institutions. Eight of these collections were started by organisations directly involved with craft production, only two (SACS and UWAC:U) were not closely involved with or branches of CHG. Of these 8 collections, one (CHG:HQ/MMFA) was made in conjunction with a museum, one (CHG:AB/UAB) in conjunction with a university extension department involved with craft through programs to rural women, and one through the WI in collaboration with CHG:MB. Two collections were associated with Quebec craft schools. Nine of these thirteen collections (and one collection museum) were initiated by a woman, Alice Webster at NBM, or by women's organizations (CHG and branches, WI, SACS, and UWAC), which reflects the extraordinarily high involvement of women with craft activity.

Only five were museum collections (NBM, NMC, CHG:HQ/MMFA, USKFM and UWAC:U). Of these only three were within established public museums, the fourth (USKFM) was a university museum and the fifth (UWAC:U) generated public display space within another related institution and later built their own museum. Even within the public museums activity was instigated by outsiders, at MMFA and NBM, rather than by the museum itself, resulting in conflict, and in the case of CHG:HQ/MMFA dispersal of the original collections and application of collecting funds to different artifacts (oriental, historical) than those customarily selected by the Guild (Native and Euro-Canadian, recent). At NMC, the collection was started by a museum employee, Barbeau, but was seen as a new and not very welcome departure.[177]

All of the collectors but one, Alice Webster, worked under institutional control, as a result

---

[176] Teather p.26 suggests approximately 400 museums by 1949, "These numbers are approximations based on my research." p.29

[177] McFeat in Ames 1976 p.156 Jenness, Barbeau's director, is reported to have told Barbeau that NMC was an "Indian" Museum, "meaning that research should be both ethnological and Indian-directed."

collectors were a series of committees rather than identifiable individuals. The obvious exception is Barbeau but even Barbeau operated within a government department, which for political reasons may have sanctioned his foray into Quebec culture, and perhaps A.S.Morton at USKFM as the museum seems to have collapsed on his death. In general, these institutions represented the dominant English culture in an increasingly multi-cultural nation. The three exceptions are Barbeau, a Québécois by birth and affiliation, and EdM, which with UWAC:UMC collected only within their own cultures. USKFM specifically collected the work of non-anglophone Canadian immigrants, SACS seems to have largely followed suit. CHG and its various branches were highly interested in non-anglophone producers but appear to have collected work from all Euro-Canadian craftsmakers. SACS certainly exhibited work belonging to Canadians of Chinese and Japanese ancestry, however the work of Canadians of Black, East Indian or Oriental ancestry is not profiled or identifiable in these collections.

All the craft organizations (and craft schools less directly) were involved with the exhibition, marketing, promotion, development and preservation through teaching and collecting, of craft skills and techniques. Given the quantity and quality of work which passed through their hands it is not surprising that they wished to save what they saw as often irreplaceable examples of fine craft works. Thus the salvaging of work which was seen as in danger of disappearing and/or as examples of high skill, specific techniques and/or ethnic authenticity underlies at least six of these collections (UWAC:UMC, CHG:HQ, NMC, SACS, USKFM, CHG:MB). Although these collections, particularly UWAC:UMC, CHG:HQ and SACS, were used as exemplars, five collections were set up specifically as educational collections (CHG:MB/WI, PQ/l'EdAD, l'EdM, NBM, MMFA). Technique, skill and/or aesthetics underlay their selection. The CHG:AB/UAB collection seems to have been put together purely to stimulate interest in craft.

The life of these collections in many cases paralleled the life of the collecting organization or initiator, within and without the museums system. Three (PQ/l'EdAD, CHG:AB/UAB, WI/CHG:MB) were put together relatively quickly for a specific purpose and, apparently, did not develop much beyond. The two former have not been traced beyond 1933 and 1949, the latter joined the CHG:MB collection in 1992. Seven collections have closed, four with the demise of the main collector or the organization (USKFM 1910-1941, SACS 1925-1956, CHG:HQ 1930-1974, l'EdM c1925-c1958), three within museums because of differing or changing priorities (CHG:HQ 1908-CHG:HQ:MMFA 1916-1928, NBM 1934-1955). The active life of these collections ranged from 20 to 44 years, averaging 27 years. Three of the thirteen still exist as identifiable collections, Barbeau/NMC within a museum complex as an identified collection and also in association with similar or related objects building on Barbeau's work, and CHG:MB/Manitoba Crafts Museum and UWAC:U as museums under their own jurisdiction.

From available information, there is little to chose between the treatment of organization and museum collections. Artifacts suffered damage from fire, water and neglect in storage. Collections were broken up as museums selected and reselected artifacts reflecting changing discipline categories, fashions and collecting foci none of which centred on the handcrafted object. In the transfer of collections to museums twentieth century handcrafted works, particularly work by studio craftspeople, disappears. Contemporary handcrafts were discarded - 'lost', appropriated for private purposes, given away or thrown out - by collecting organizations and museums. The Massey Report's picture of lack of museums, lack of museum capacity, funding and expertise, and loss of museum materials is in part reflected in the life history of these craft collections.

Only the three continuing collections have a catalogue of artifacts. McLeod says that there is no evidence of CHG:HQ having a register of works in their collections;[178] the confusion in 1928 between what was stored at MMFA, what was gifted to MMFA and what was bought by MMFA through CHG:HQ funding would support the lack of an inventory. Acquisitions registers in damaged condition remain from USKFM but it has not been possible to compare them with records from the Guilford textile collection currently in the USK Drama Department[179] to see whether textiles from USKFM became part of that collection. SACS files refer to an acquisitions register but it is not extant. It is not known whether PQ/l'EdBA, CHG:AB/UAB or l'EdM had acquisitions registers although the former were bought with public money. Nor is it clear whether the original Alice Webster collection, NBM, was catalogued at the time. As a result knowledge of precisely what was in the collections is very fragmentary.

In comparison to the rich range of craft production surveyed in chapters 4-6, collections from the available evidence reflected a limited selection. Collections were related to organization focus, and most obviously constrained by access to the field, available storage and purchase funding, other parameters are not known. Contact would have been primarily with makers marketing and exhibiting either as individuals or through marketing groups, which implies a particular orientation on the part of the maker and an ability to meet the organization (or school's) criteria. For all organizations, adequate storage was limited or non-existent which would make size, fragility and portability acquisitions constraints. These considerations combined with marketing strategies and the heavy involvement of women inclined collections heavily towards textiles, predominantly woven, embroidered and hooked. Pottery, small wood carvings and basketry were also collected. EdM, not surprisingly, concentrated on furniture, rural, reproduction and student work, the latter may also have included textiles, ironwork and ceramics, and Quebec traditional crafts. The second CHG collection was probably the most comprehensive including a wide range of media, except possibly glass and furniture, and production sources. Four collections contained

---

[178] McLeod personal communication 10 November 1997. It is possible that records were destroyed as artifacts were donated or sold to other museums, sold or gifted to members, and otherwise 'lost' or discarded.

[179] Until 6 June 1997, because computer discs cataloguing the collection were untranslatable, the collection was closed. In June a hard copy list was found. fax Rhoda Miko Department of Drama USK 6 June 1997

the work of 'studio' craftspeople: EdM,[180] CHG:HQ,[181] CHG:MB and NBM. The public museums, despite different agendas, did not contain substantially different collections although all were more limited ethnically and only one, NBM, contained studio craftspeople.

Discussion

The discussion centres on the two questions of why so few of the craft organization's collections were not, in the long term, viable and, arising from that, why contemporary Canadian craft was unwelcome in Canadian museums. The first question is answered briefly. With the exception of UWAC:U none of the other organizations was predicated on collecting. Collecting was for them part of ambitious programs priorizing marketing and exhibiting but for UWAC:U, in order to support the authenticity and retention of Ukrainian handcraft culture, it was necessary to have a collection. Collecting and education based on the contents of the collection formed the entire aim of the Association, the museum emerged naturally out of these concerns. The only other organization collection which has remained intact is that of the CHG:MB/Manitoba Guild of Crafts who set up the Manitoba Crafts Museum with money raised at the dissolution of the Guild in 1997.

Museums and Craft

It can be argued that nineteenth century intellectual concerns continued to dominate museum practice well into the twentieth century, priorizing the 'scientific' disciplines. Almost without exception executive and professional staff who controlled museums' activities throughout this period were men, thus the museum world view was positioned from a high status, academic, white, male, Eurocentric viewpoint.[182] It will be argued that this is a schema within which craft found it hard to position itself.

Handcraft, in the collections discussed above, was accepted, reluctantly, into public museums through two departments: the applied, decorative or industrial arts (MMFA and NBM) or

---

[180] This included student work.

[181] No studio work is indicated in the disposition of the two collections prior to and associated with MMFA. McLeod thinks that it is unlikely that studio craft was collected before the collection started in 1930. personal communication 12 November 1997. She has a reference to work by Paul Beau, metal smith, and a pottery vase by Addie Greenwood of Victoria, BC acquired for the permanent collection in 1933. In 1943 Mrs A. Greenwood was a member of The Pottery Club, Victoria (Gibbon SKAB SACS file). A batik by Winifred Fox was considered for the permanent collection in 1956.

[182] The author of the NBM brief to the Massey Commission, quoted earlier, typifies these attitudes in his discomfort with the expansion of a natural history museum into history and art and his gendered dismissal of a trained female Art Curator.

anthropology (NMC). Museums dealing with history, particularly regional or pioneer history, inside or more commonly outside the public system, also collected handcrafts occasionally as craft artifacts most frequently as social history artifacts.

Applied Arts

In *Contemporary Craft Collecting in Museums* I explored the location of recent craft collections in British museums. I argued that craft was located in applied arts collections by common media, function, and a presumed but not elucidated historical continuity.[183] These assignations are implicit in these early Canadian collections. Explicitly the applied arts were seen as exemplars to raise the standards of and give inspiration to designers and makers, as "good examples...objects of artistic merit...all objects tending to the education of the designer and the worker."[184] The emphasis is on art, "aesthetic merit", not technique. Ian Wolfenden notes that after the (British) Museum of Ornamental Art moved to South Kensington "the scientific, or material and technical, aspects of the applied arts came to be regarded as the province of the Science Museum",[185] it is likely that the same ideas prevailed in the Anglo-Montreal community. It is not known whether there was any attempt to illustrate specific design principles by the organization of artifacts or labels. The criteria for a "good example" and "artistic merit" in both museums (and other collections) was not articulated and was to be inferred from the authority of the selected object.[186]

Nobbs, who was associated with MMFA, in a 1908 article primarily about architectural education, argued that "a museum of arts, to be complete, should contain," as the second of six departments,[187] "handicraft." However in expanding on this department he renames it "industrial art",

> "Under the heading of industrial art, the collection should contain textiles and fabrics, glass and pottery, metal work, wood carving, stained glass, and furniture of all periods."[188]

This leaves in question whether this mix of media, techniques and products could be both

---

[183] Flood 1993 pp.39-40

[184] McLeod p.117 relating to MMFA

[185] Ian Wolfenden in S.M.Pearce *Museum Studies in Material Culture* (Leicester 1989) p.28

[186] Flood 1993 p.29

[187] The departments in order are architecture, handicraft, sculpture, painting, temporary exhibitions, art literature library.

[188] Nobbs 1908 p.46

manufactured and handcrafted, and added a historical dimension moving the concentration from the recent or current. In fact at NBM (and probably at MMFA[189]) the collection of "Industrial Art" consisted of "the arts and crafts of [ancient] Egypt, Greece and Rome...of China, Japan and the Near East" and historical "European ceramics, textiles and furniture."[190] These seem to have had more to do with fashionable archaeological and historical interests supported by "the globe-trotting dilettanti" and a connoisseurial market than with designer/maker education, craft history or technical development.[191] In a period of embryonic interest in Canadian buildings and crafts, Nobbs supported exposure to Greek, Roman, Celtic, Norman, French and Italian arts but protests that,

> "[W]ith characteristic British modesty and want of forethought...the average English [and by extension Canadian] student of design is apt to grow up in ignorance of the masterpieces of English design and to despise his national aesthetic traditions. He is thus encouraged to look to exotic styles and types for his inspiration, finding English art but little appreciated on the Continent, and less still by the officials of the science and art department at home."[192]

At NBM a temporary exhibition case was provided for the handicrafts of New Brunswick, pottery and "characteristic 'homespuns'", but it was "in the hope of encouraging production and promoting home industries."[193] Nobbs included among his museum departments, exhibition galleries,

> "for current works of art...It is very salutary to place the old and new in close relation."

Contemporary work was for temporary exhibition not for collection.[194]

Although much formal craft education was theoretically aimed at manufacturing, the degree to which manufacturers made use of art school trained designers and handcraft design prototypes is open to question. By extension manufacturers' input and apprehension of applied art collections

---

[189] This is largely true of current permanent exhibitions of decorative arts at MMFA

[190] *New Brunswick Museum Administrative Series* (a)1 pp.3, 5

[191] This is certainly how this collection is displayed at MMFA currently.

[192] Nobbs 1908 p.46

[193] NBM.A Art department, Alice Lusk Webster File F545 October 1936

[194] NGC under the Directorship of Eric Brown, 1911-1938, focused on Canadian artists because of its origins in the collection of works by Canadian Academicians and the work of the Group of Seven and others which explored in new ways a distinctively Canadian milieu but also because its budget did not allow it to purchase the more desirable European or American 'masterworks'. The Gallery was constantly under attack for this policy.

as relevant educational tools is problematic. Thus manufacturing did not form the third vital link in a museums/art schools/industry triangle. Without this limited *raison d'etre*, or sustainable connoisseurial, academic or archaeological (which precluded contemporary crafts) interests, applied arts collections were easily superseded by the more prestigious fine arts, as at MMFA and NBM.

Nobbs alluded to "national aesthetic traditions". Despite public discussion of the development of a distinctively Canadian national art, there was little consensus about what defined Canadian craft and much concern about traditional skills and motifs from certain clearly defined ethnic groups being replaced by techniques and motifs drawn from increasingly international, modern sources through popular publications. This lack of a distinctive Canadian style was not resolved for studio crafts.

The issues of 'Canadian' characteristics, contemporaneity, lack of status verified by market or academic interests and, in the light of Barbeau's activity probably most important, the lack of a proponent within the museum applied arts area excluded Canadian craft from collections.

Anthropology
Apparently opposed to the limited aesthetic and design education concerns of applied arts collections lay the wider scientific and cultural parameters of anthropology. The concerns of the applied art collections decontextualized the works; geographic, ethnic and period origin were universal and subordinate, there was no reference to the class of the maker, designer or client or to whether production was located in town or country. In Barbeau's anthropological collections the cultural contextualization was precise. The work was from the "ancient French colony of Quebec [city]" and related isolated areas, ethnically Québécois, folk, rural, traditional, and by implication for domestic consumption. Within this highly delineated selection of "arts and crafts", Barbeau was looking at "technological or artistic processes." In fact it is clear from Barbeau's field notes, from his choice of painters and architects as expedition associates, from many of the galleries he sold work to and from his exhibitions format that aesthetics, particularly linked with high art, were a principal criterium both in selection and display.

Barbeau's collections of Québécois craft linked craft with ethnicity and 'folk', and heightened the profile of material culture. Ethnicity, folk and rural in combination denoted 'peasant' cultures, raising theoretical questions of continuity, stability, authenticity, group mores and informal education. While many of the non-museum collections included work associated with specific ethnic or cultural groups, the questions which controlled ethnologists were of interest to only one, UWAC:UMC. These ethnological parameters excluded craft from: the formally educated, the middle-classes (non-folk) and urban makers, work not distinctively linked to geographic area, and work which was innovative or perceived as 'contemporary'. It reflected the museum professional's world view, the examination of the unfamiliar and exotic Other, sharply differentiated from the familiar and unquestioned Us. It is noticeable that no-one from the dominant anglophone community concurrently extended their anthropological studies to the *folk* technology and colonial arts and crafts of the ancient *British* colonial settlements, and that as late as 1960 "European culture in Canada"[195] had only temporary and intermittent exhibition space at NMC.

Despite the amassing of artifacts, it appears that Museum ethnologists (and later historians) had problems with material culture. McFeat says that, by the 1950s ethnologists had become unlike other museum scientists, including folklorists, who routinely collected, retrieved and analyzed specimens,

"Anyone who has experienced the life of an ethnologist in a Museum is aware of his traditionally embarrassing relationship to collections...material objects are pleasant (even beautiful) but productive of little interesting research...ethnologists have not been quite clear in their minds what should be done about material culture since one no longer charts the distributions of material items or endeavours to construct culture areas by assembling them."[196]

The same gap between "our studies of society and work on the artifacts themselves"[197] existed for the History department, whose staff were divided into "historians (documents men)"[198] and associate curators who applied connoisseurial skills to artifacts defined by media and product as in applied arts collections.[199] However the history museum was to be "not only a museum of beautiful furnishings and of arts and crafts...[it was] for the general public, not only for the collector."[200] Silent objects were relegated to mere beauty by ethnologists; 'beautiful' objects, with which arts and crafts were associated, were decontextualized within the ethnology and history museums. 'Art' and 'cultural' parameters appeared mutually exclusive.[201] In addition, from this

---

[195] Euro-Canadian material culture, following Barbeau, concentrated on French Quebec, then 'pre-industrial' rural peasant ethnic/cultural groups from Eastern Europe; Euro-Canadian history c.1967 looked at French and English pre-Confederation activity, predominantly in Central and Eastern Canada.

[196] Ames 1976 p.168

[197] CMC.A 'Newsletter: History Division' 1 1971 p.1

[198] NAC had been considered the national history museum, reinforcing the concentration on documents, although it had acquired a small collection of artifacts.

[199] CMC.A draft 'The History Division' 1967 p.1

[200] CMC.A 'Newsletter: History Division' 1 1971 p.1 The implication that the museum thought the general public was uninterested in arts and crafts is curious and as argued unfounded.

[201] Flood 1993 pp.37-8

positioning the history of materials, techniques and, implicitly, skill values, primary definitions of craft, dealt with in Anthropology, was ignored. Antiquarian interests in both areas excluded the contemporary.

Gendered museums

In view of the very high profile of women in organizations associated with crafts, and as craft teachers and makers in contrast to the male dominated museum milieu, the issue of gendered decision making by museums must be considered. There is a growing body of literature demonstrating that women, women's history and women's interpretations are lacking in museums.[202] This would not have been an issue for museums during the period under discussion as Martine Segalen, discussing French ethnography museums says,

> "Any acknowledgement of issues of gender was singularly absent from the ideological and social forces that shaped the first museums. Gender relationships were given, and thus were 'naturally' absent from the preoccupations of the turn-of-the-century folklorists and other regionalists who founded museums."[203]

Nancy Shoemaker in looking at representations of women in three American Natural History Museums concludes that natural history museums still use cultural constructions that put men and women, white and non-white, culture and nature into discrete, oppositional categories.[204] Moreover 'man' is pre-eminent and the gendered oppositional categories are man produced culture: woman, associated with nature, reproduced children; male is the norm: female the variation. Using these categories one could postulate elite male + culture = fine arts: female + variation + culture = crafts. Helen Knibb examining a particular community museum as a source of women's history[205] concludes that "women collectors, donors and curators are not a homogeneous group and their motives for collecting and donating are varied" and that more research is required on the subject of women as collectors, including the question of whether women collect differently from men.[206] The histories of the craft collections in this chapter show that women through special interest organizations were consciously and, by the standards of the

---

[202] including *Gender and History* 6:3 1994, *History News* 50:2 1995, *CRM* 20:3 US Department of the Interior 1997 which are dedicated to exploring these issues and include bibliographies.

[203] Segalen p.334

[204] N.Shoemaker 'The Natural History of Gender' *Gender and History* 6:3:331

[205] H.Knibb '"Present but Not Visible": Searching for Women's History in Museum Collections' *Gender and History* 6:3:352-69
Knibb defines community museums in Ontario as "small-to-medium sized institutions reflecting the natural history, white settlement and development of a community or region." p.368

[206] Knibb p.262

time, expertly putting together collections in a unique area, recent and contemporary craft, and that this was an area in which men as collectors and as museum curators were uninterested.

CHAPTER 7
CONCLUSION

The thesis set out to explore the relationship between two communities, the museum community and the craft community, in the context of Canada from 1900 to 1950. The results of this exploration determined a thesis which has charted the extensive activity of a diverse craft community. The thesis proposed to determine the degree of shared understanding of 'craft'. It also proposed to determine the extent of museums' recognition of contemporary craft activity and whether this recognition in turn affected the public concept of craft or the craft community's concept of its work.

The context

It was an underlying premise of the thesis that craft activity, is embedded in society and is affected by the changing parameters affecting the society. While the urge to make, the endowment and expression of a bodily-kinaesthetic intelligence,[1] may be a constant, the conditions of making and the products are societal and are as Peck said in 1934,

"in relation to the resources, climate and scenery of various localities in addition to reflecting, to some degree, social conditions and ideas."[2]

Canada during the period 1900-1950 presented a unique and unstable combination of conditions which, I have argued, affected all aspects of craft. The museum community, being a small, circumscribed institution in Canadian society, was exposed to a lesser range of variables but geography, economics and politics affected its development. It reacted to and reflected aspects of the Canadian context through the period. Neither craft nor museum activity can be detached from their context and period without damage to the veracity of the account.

The communities

Crafts emerge as the most widespread and democratic of the visual arts. The craft community, as demonstrated, was large, diverse and fragmented. Its diversity extended through ethnicity, class, craft education, production circumstances, products and reason for making. As a result it

---

[1] Gardner in Peter Dormer *The Culture of Craft* (Manchester 1997) p.75

[2] Peck 1934 p.204 I would give "social conditions and ideas" equality at least, and in the contemporary milieu, primacy.

can be seen as a group of communities, including isolates, distinguished by locale, culture, mode of craft education, purpose and media, each group operating independently but with areas of overlap, and with limited intercourse or desire for intercourse between groups.

In contrast, the museum community was small, more coherent but not necessarily cohesive, undeveloped, isolated and struggling for survival. The community was almost exclusively male, academically educated and belonging to the professional classes. Museums were, at their most developed, a hierarchical structure devoted to accumulating, categorizing and interpreting a selected range of objects based on and reflecting the interests of the elite of the dominant culture. These interests were informed by a scientific or classical education and by a colonial viewpoint.

The relationship between the communities

The relationship between the two communities, as recounted, was limited and lopsided. The museum community with one anomaly, Marius Barbeau at NMC, was not interested in handcrafts. The craft community, through the agency of national, local and media organizations, who were concerned with promoting and exhibiting craft as an integral part of Canadian culture or as an art form, lobbied for and initiated temporary exhibitions in major galleries and art museums. The national craft organization, CHG, in particular over three decades collected, donated and subsidized acquisitions at a major art museum. The evidence confirms that art museums were passive partners with no long term interest in craft.

The shared understanding of craft

- through publications
It was presumed that the communities' understanding of the concept 'craft' would emerge from their activities and more particularly from articulation. However the historiography shows that craftmakers, with very rare exceptions, did not write about the craft community, much less about their experience or philosophy as craftspeople. The vast majority of the very diverse craft community was voiceless as far as the public and relatively enduring printed text was concerned.

Writing about craft was done by government officials, academics, journalists, volunteer administrators of craft organizations and craft teachers, people of the same social background as the museum community. Given their role as activators, their concept of craft was basically pragmatic, a stance which predicated intervention and frequently gave rise to writing which verged on the didactic and the patronizing.

The museums' articulation of the concept 'craft' was through one person, Barbeau. That articulation arose from a focus on one region and one ethnic group; it posited an anthropological view in tracing the motifs and techniques of a limited group of objects to their place of origin;

Conclusion

it positioned crafts and craftspeople (within its limited focus) as the Other - rural, working class and picturesque. As an employee of the national museum, Barbeau had salaried support for collecting, research and publications, and attributed authority. The historiography shows Barbeau as one of the two major disseminators of ideas on craft, the other was CHG. Barbeau's area of interest coincided with CHG's province of origin and earliest area of interest, which gave Barbeau's ideas additional and extended currency.

The shared understanding of 'craft' which emerges from publications is representative of neither the general museum community nor the various sectors of the craft making community. It, to a great degree, represents circular thinking between people, many of whom were intimately involved with the craft community but not as craftspeople, and a museum anthropologist, who was the exception in the museums community.

- *through activity*

The diversity within the craft community was acknowledged by the community through the variety of activities, organizations, exhibitions and commercial locations or lack, and so on. This diversity was both acknowledged and brought together under the exhibiting and marketing auspices of various organizations, primarily CHG and its branches, who argued that the diversity was unified by integral craft attributes of materials and technical knowledge, skill and an appropriate aesthetic,

> "the Guild recognizes no set line between professional and amateur contestants...[a] worker is either a good or bad *craftsman.*"[3]

The diversity appears to have become more actively articulated in the 1940s by studio craftspeople working in major urban areas.

The activity of the museum community, in so far as it existed during this period, was directed into narrow channels based on distinct disciplines. These artificially imposed boundaries separated art and culture and science. Thus craft inextricably entwined with knowledge and manipulation of materials (science); with culturally embedded products, usages, materials, techniques, motifs and histories; and with aesthetics, either overlapped impermeable boundaries or aspects could be selected to fit particular categories to the negation of the whole. The study of the activity of Canadian peoples was restricted, particularly at national level, to Aboriginal Peoples and the early economic, political and martial history of Eastern Canada, the latter studied primarily through texts. The introduction into the museum by Barbeau of selected media, Québécois and traditional by attribution, relatively recent crafts required the creation of a classification 'folk'. The category 'folk' presented an arbitrary and partial aspect of craft and furthered the misconception of craft as rural, untutored, static and not part of modernity or the dominant culture. Barbeau's parameters

---

[3] Lighthall p.30 with reference to CHG Dominion exhibitions

explicitly excluded all but a small segment of craft activity leading a commentator to say in 1945, "Perhaps the handicrafts have passed their peak of creative quality. Marius Barbeau, our greatest writer on the crafts, says they have..."[4]

The ideology, aims and interests of the museum community precluded any shared comprehensive understand of 'craft'.

The extent of recognition of contemporary craft activity by museums

If "recognition of contemporary craft activity by museums" means the primary museum activities of collecting and study, leading to publications and exhibitions as secondary activities, my research shows that in relation to contemporary craft there was no such recognition by museum professionals, the one exception being through NBM in the late 1940s.

- the effect on the public concept of craft
The effect of museums' lack of recognition on the public's concept of contemporary craft is difficult to determine directly, however it may be extrapolated from two factors, the profile of the museum within the community and exposure to craft through other means. Outside the major cities of Eastern Canada there was relatively little development of permanent, public museums or galleries until the third or fourth decade. Museums were primarily initiated and funded through private rather than state institutions, even within the established areas of Canada, and as such maintained an isolated, precarious and under-funded existence. While museums attracted audiences within their immediate area, the scale of the country, the thinly scattered population and the state of transportation and the economy precluded the vast majority of the population from ever visiting a museum. Crafts were exhibited at agricultural/industrial fairs, from major regional to local events, through corporate patronage in department stores, some of whom had permanent art galleries, and hotels, and in other public or private buildings. Efforts were made to tour exhibitions nationally and inter-regionally throughout the period, principally by CHG, and in the 1930s and 1940s, craft exhibitions were circulated outside the principle cities notably in Alberta and Nova Scotia. The exposure to crafts appears as diverse as the makers, moreover accounts consistently report higher than average audiences for craft exhibitions.

Within the period the obvious impact of museums' lack of recognition of craft on the wider public may have been minimal. However the partial explication of 'craft' through Barbeau's work was to an extent internalized by influential craft organizations and by a wider public through publications to the detriment of 'craft' in its diversity.

---

[4] E.W.Wood address to National Arts Club, New York *Canadian* Art p.225 Summer 1945

Conclusion

- the effect on the craft community

The effect of museums' lack of recognition on the craft community's concept of 'craft' is also difficult to determine through the community's response. Where museums are considered an important component of the nation's public face, there were two far reaching effects of this lack of recognition. The first was to deprive craftspeople, unlike artists and Aboriginal Peoples, of official recognition of their activity and products as an intrinsic and valued part of Canadian cultural life. The second was to deprive the craft community in total, of material evidence of its history through museums' unwillingness (or inability) to accommodate collections put together by craft organizations. The astonishment of the 1950 Massey Commission on national development in the *arts*, letters and sciences to finding crafts presented for its consideration reflects an elitist, compartmentalized, official perspective.

Final comments

Before launching into this preliminary survey of pan-Canadian craft activity in the first half of the twentieth century, nothing in the current literature or in current studio craft community mythology had led me to suspect the wealth and diversity of activity I was to find. At this point I have not done a comparable survey of craft from 1950 on, however viewing the evidence in combination with such factors as fashions, education, continuing artisan practice, population size and lifestyles in the early period, it is conceivable that craft practice at a very high level was more widespread, that craft making and craft organizations were higher profile, and that organizational craft activity through exhibitions and marketing was less provincial than currently.

In addition, I did not anticipate the extra-ordinarily high level of women's involvement in all aspects of craft activity throughout the period, as presented in the literature and through archival records. There was no intent to write a gendered account. Further research may redress the gender balance of makers but not, I think, in other areas. Feminist re-evaluation of male-generated histories and practice lead me to speculate that the association of women and craft in the eyes of the male world of government and museums may have seriously undermined craft's status and credibility and distorted its history. This thesis aims to redress this distortion to some extent through a fresh look at data which recovers the dimensions and vitality of craft and its influence and importance in the first half of the twentieth century in Canada.

APPENDIX 1

date	author	occupation	sex	publication	type	audience	subject	region
1904	n/a [M.A.Peck]	cc/craftp	f	newspaper			organization	C
1907	n/a [Peck?]			journal	industry	business	organization	C
1923	n/a			journal	building	business	exhibition	PQ
1924	E.Z.Massicotte	historian	m	journal		academic	art/tec	PQ
1925	# W.Carless	architect	m	booklet			survey	C
	J.Tremblay		m	journal	architects	architects	craftperson	PQ
	# A.Y.Jackson	artist	m	journal	books		medium	PQ
1926	# F.B.Housser	n/k	m	book	fine art		general	PQ/ON
1927	# N.De Bertrand Lugrin	n/k	n/k	magazine	c.affairs		medium	BC
	G.Pearson	n/k	m	magazine	c.affairs		medium	NS
	n/a			newspaper		women	CHG/exhibit	C
1928	# H.Turcot	government	m	booklet	government		medium	PQ
	V.Hayward	n/k	f	newspapr			medium	PQ
	C.Holmes	journalist	f	magazine		rural	survey	SK
	A.E.Wilson	journalist	f	magazine		women	survey	C
1929	Peck			booklet			survey	C
1930	# Holmes			journal	CGJ		event	AB
	V.M [V.Morton?]	cc	f	newspaper		rural	craftperson	MB
	M.MacLaughlin	n/k	f	journal	CGJ		art/tec	PQ
1931	H.Dickson	n/k	f	magazine	c.affairs		education	BC
	M.C.Ringland	journalist	f	magazine		women	survey	PQ/ON
1932	# Ringland			magazine	organisation	women	survey	e.C
	C.Scott	educator	m	magazine	c.affairs		survey	BC
	B.Meredith	n\k	m	magazine			survey	PQ
1933	# O.Beriau	craftp/gov	m	journal	CGJ		survey	PQ
	# L.A.Cunningham	n/k	m	magazine		women	organisation	NB
	# A.MacKay	journalist	f	journal	CGJ		survey	PQ
	Beriau			manual			art/tec	PQ
	# E.Steele	craftp/cc	f	magazine		women	organisation	NS
	CHG bulletin							
1934	# Peck			journal	CGJ		organisation	C
1935	M.Barbeau	anthro/mus	m	journal	CGJ		medium	PQ
1936	Barbeau			journal	CGJ		general	PQ
	Barbeau			book	travel		general	PQ
	# Barbeau			book	travel		general	PQ
	Ringland			magazine	arts		organi/surv	ON
1937	# G.Bouchard	government	m	journal	agriculture	academic	survey	PQ
	n/a			magazine		women	organization	ON
	n/a			newspaper			CHG exhibit	C
1938	# W.Bovey	cc	m	booklet	CHG		survey	C
1939	Barbeau			journal	organisation	academic	art/tec	PQ
	Bovey			journal	finance	business	survey	C
1940	# A.McAnn	gov/cc	f	journal	CGJ		survey	NB
	H.G.Kettle		n\k	journal	c.affairs	business	critique	C
	J-M.Gavreau	craftp/tch	m	book			craftpeople	PQ*

Appendices

Year	Name	Occupation	Gender	Pub Type	Subject	Audience	Focus	Province
1941 #	D.H.Russell	government	m	report	government		survey	C
	W.G.Forster	n/k	f	newspaper			organization	BC
	Barbeau			journal	antiques	academic	medium	PQ
1942	Barbeau			journal	education		survey	PQ
#	Russel			report	government		survey	PQ
	Barbeau			journal	organisation	academic	art/tec	PQ
	Barbeau			book			survey	PQ*
	Barbeau			book			survey	PQ*
#	Anselm/Michael	craftp/cc	f, f	journal	fine arts		planning	NS
1943	Beriau			journal	CGJ		survey	PQ
#	I.H.Crowell	gov/tch/cc	m	journal	CGJ		education	C
#	J.M.Gibbon	adm/cc	m	journal	CGJ		survey	C
#	Gibbon			journal	CGJ		medium	C
	R.Traquair	architect	m	journal	CGJ		art/tec	eC
#	N.E.Vaughan	cc	f	magazine	c.affairs		planning	C
	M.G.Bonner	journalist	f	book	children	children	survey	C
	n/a			magazine			craftperson	ON
	K.Strange		f	magazine			medium	MB/SK/AB
#	W.Colgate	n/k	m	book			survey	C
1944 #	R.Home	t/mus	f	journal	CGJ		medium	C
	n/a			booklet	organization		medium	MB/SK/AB
	P.Nobbs	architect	m	journal	CGJ		medium	C
#	E.W.Wood	n/k	f	journal	CA		plan	C
#	D.G.W.McRae	n/k	m	book	fine art		survey	C
#	L.Harris	artist	m	journal	CA		plan	C
1945 #	Wood			journal	CA		survey	C
	R.Brooks	n/k	f	journal	c.affairs		craftperson	ON
	P.Brieger	n/k	m	journal	art		survey	C
	n/a	n/k	n/k	magazine	dec. arts	women	survey	C
1946	J.L.Shadbolt	artist	m	journal	CA		general	BC
	Barbeau			book			survey	PQ*
#	E.Gilbert	n/k	f	magazine		rural	medium	wC
1947 #	R.Ayre	n/k	m	journal	CA		craftperson	PQ
	McLeod, Bruce	journalist	m	book/chptr	reader	children	craftperson	ON
	Barbeau			journal	antiques		art/tec	PQ
1948 #	Barbeau			journal	CA		critique	C
	B.Davis	craftp/journa	f	magazine			organization	ON
	A. Lighthall	cc		magazine			organization	C
	P.McCarthy	journalist	f	newspaper			education	PQ
	M.Tanton		f	magazine	organization	women	medium	C
	K.Towers	craftperson	f	magazine	CH&G	women	medium	ON
1949	L.Harrington	n/k	m?	journal	CGJ		craftperson	AB
	M.Angus	n\k	f	newspaper	finance	business	craftperson	BC
	A.Leitch	n/k		magazine			medium	NFD
	L.D.Millar		f	magazine			organization	ON
	n/a			magazine			craftperson	ON[SK]
	D.Rosser	n/k	m	journal	CA		medium	C

Key: occupation: craftp-craftperson; cc-craft organization personnel; anthro-anthropologist; tch-craft teacher; mus-museum employee;   publication type: c.affairs-current affairs; dec arts- decorative arts; audience: unless indicated
subject: art/tec-specific artifact or technique
# indicates articles selected for analysis; PQ* indicates French language publication

APPENDIX 1:2a

date	author	loss of skills & traditions	national economy	craft: machine	industrial design	rural life	technical information
1924	~~~~~~						
1925	Carless	Carless	Carless	Carless		Carless	Carless
	Jackson	Jackson					
1926	Housser/Lismer	Housser/Lismer			Housser/Lismer		
1927	de Bertrand Lugin						
1928	Turcot	Turcot	Turcot	Turcot		Turcot	Turcot
1929	~~~~~~						
1930	Holmes	Holmes					
1931	~~~~~~						
1932	Ringland	Ringland	Ringland	Ringland		Ringland	Ringland
1933	Beriau	Beriau				Beriau	Beriau
	Cunningham					Cunningham	Cunningham
	MacKay	MacKay	MacKay	MacKay		MacKay	MacKay
	Steele					Steele	
1934	Peck	Peck					
1935	~~~~~~						
1936	Barbeau	Barbeau					
1937	Bouchard		Bouchard	Bouchard		Bouchard	Bouchard
1938	Bovey	Bovey	Bovey	Bovey		Bovey	
1939	~~~~~~						
1940	McAnn	McAnn	McAnn			McAnn	McAnn
1941	Russell		Russell		Russell		
1942	Michael	Michael		Michael		Michael	
1943	Crowell			Crowell			
	Gibbon	Gibbon	Gibbon				
	Gibbon						
	Vaughan	Vaughan	Vaughan	Vaughan	Vaughan	Vaughan	
	Colgate			Colgate	Colgate		
1944	Home		Home	Home			Home
	Russell		Russell			Russell	
	Wood		Wood	Wood		Wood	
	McRae						
	Harris						
1945	Wood		Wood		Wood		Wood
1946	Gilbert						
1947	Ayre						Ayre
1948	Barbeau			Barbeau		Barbeau	
1949	~~~~~~						
1950	~~~~~~						
		15	14	13	5	15	11

Appendices

Appendix 1:2b

date	national art	art:craft	benefits: social	cultural	racial unity	universality
	~~					
1924						
1925	Carless	Carless				Carless
	Jackson	Jackson				
1926						Housser/Lismer
1927						
1928		Turcot				
1929	~~~~~					
1930	Holmes					
1931						
1932	Ringland	Ringland		Ringland		Ringland
1933	Beriau					
	Cunningham					Cunningham
	MacKay					MacKay
1934	Peck					
1935	~~~~~					
1936						
1937	Bouchard	Bouchard				
1938		Bovey				Bovey
1939	~~~~~					
1940	McAnn					
1941	Russell		Russell	Russell	Russell	Russell
1942						
1943						Crowell
	Gibbon	Gibbon				
					Gibbon	Gibbon
	Vaughan		Vaughan	Vaughan	Vaughan	
	Colgate	Colgate	Colgate			Colgate
1944			Home			
	Russell		Russell	Russell	Russell	
			Wood			
					Harris	
1945						
1946						Gilbert
1947						
1948						
1949	~~~~~					
1950	~~~~~					
	15	8	6	4	5	11

Appendix 1:2c

date	personal benefits:				
	mental	emotional	physical	economic	spiritual
1924	~~~~~				
1925	Carless	Carless	Carless	Carless	
1926	Housser/Lismer	Housser/Lismer			
1927				de Bertrand Lugrin	
1928	Turcot	Turcot	Turcot	Turcot	
1929	~~~~~				
1930				Holmes	
1931	~~~~~				
1932		Ringland		Ringland	
1933		Beriau		Beriau	
	Cunningham	Cunningham	Cunningham		
			MacKay	MacKay	MacKay
				Steele	
1934		Peck	Peck	Peck	
1935	~~~~~				
1936		Barbeau			
1937				Bouchard	
1938				Bovey	
1939	~~~~~				
1940	McAnn	McAnn		McAnn	McAnn
1941	Russell	Russell	Russell	Russell	
1942				Michael	
1943	Crowell		Crowell	Crowell	
	Gibbon		Gibbon		
	Vaughan	Vaughan	Vaughan	Vaughan	Vaughan
				Colgate	
1944				Home	
		Russell		Russell	
	Wood				Wood
					McRae
					Harris
1945				Wood	
1946				Gilbert	
1947		Ayre			
1948					
1949	~~~~~				
1950	~~~~~				
	10	12	9	21	6

Appendices

Appendix 1:2d

	attributes of craft: beautiful	craft: useful	human hand	skill	patience	ingenuity
1924	~~~~~					
1925	Carless	Carless	Carless	Carless		Carless
1926			Housser/Lismer			
1927						
1928	Turcot					
1929	~~~~~					
1930	Holmes		Holmes	Holmes	Holmes	Holmes
1931	~~~~~					
1932	Ringland	Ringland		Ringland		
1933		Beriau				Beriau
	Cunningham		Cunningham	Cunningham		
	MacKay	MacKay			MacKay	
1934				Peck		
1935	~~~~~					
1936				Barbeau		
1937	Bouchard	Bouchard				
1938	Bovey			Bovey		
1939	~~~~~					
1940	McAnn	McAnn	McAnn	McAnn		
1941		Russell	Russell			
1942	Michael	Michael	Michael			
1943	Crowell	Crowell	Crowell	Crowell		
	Gibbon					
	Gibbon		Gibbon	Gibbon		
	Vaughan			Vaughan		
	Colgate	Colgate	Colgate	Colgate	Colgate	
1944			Home	Home		
					Russell	
			Wood			
1945		Wood		Wood		
1946	Gilbert	Gilbert	Gilbert			
1947						
1948	Barbeau	Barbeau		Barbeau		Barbeau
1949	~~~~~					
1950	~~~~~					
	17	13	13	15	4	4

Appendix 1:2e

	attributes cont.				27	
	art	personal expression	originality	quality		
1924	~~~~~					
1925	Carless	Carless		Carless	20	
					3	
1926	Housser/Lismer	Housser/Lismer			8	
1927					1	
1928				Turcot	12	
1929	~~~~~					
1930	Holmes			Holmes	10	
1931	~~~~~					
1932	Ringland	Ringland	Ringland	Ringland	18	
1933		Beriau		Beriau	10	
		Cunningham	Cunningham	Cunningham	13	
		MacKay	MacKay	MacKay	16	
				Steele	3	
1934				Peck	7	
1935	~~~~~					
1936	Barbeau	Barbeau	Barbeau		6	
1937			Bouchard	Bouchard	11	
1938	Bovey	Bovey	Bovey		12	
1939	~~~~~					
1940			McAnn	McAnn	15	
1941					13	17)
1942				Michael	8	
1943			Crowell	Crowell	11	
					7	(total
					5	11)
				Vaughan	17	
	Colgate		Colgate	Colgate	15	
1944		Home		Home	9	
		Russell		Russell	11	(total
					7	
		McRae		McRae	3	
					2	
1945	Wood			Wood	8	
1946	Gilbert	Gilbert		Gilbert	8	
1947	Ayre			Ayre	4	
1948			Barbeau		7	
1949	~~~~~					
1950	~~~~~					
	10	12	10	21	299	

Appendices 303

APPENDIX 1:3

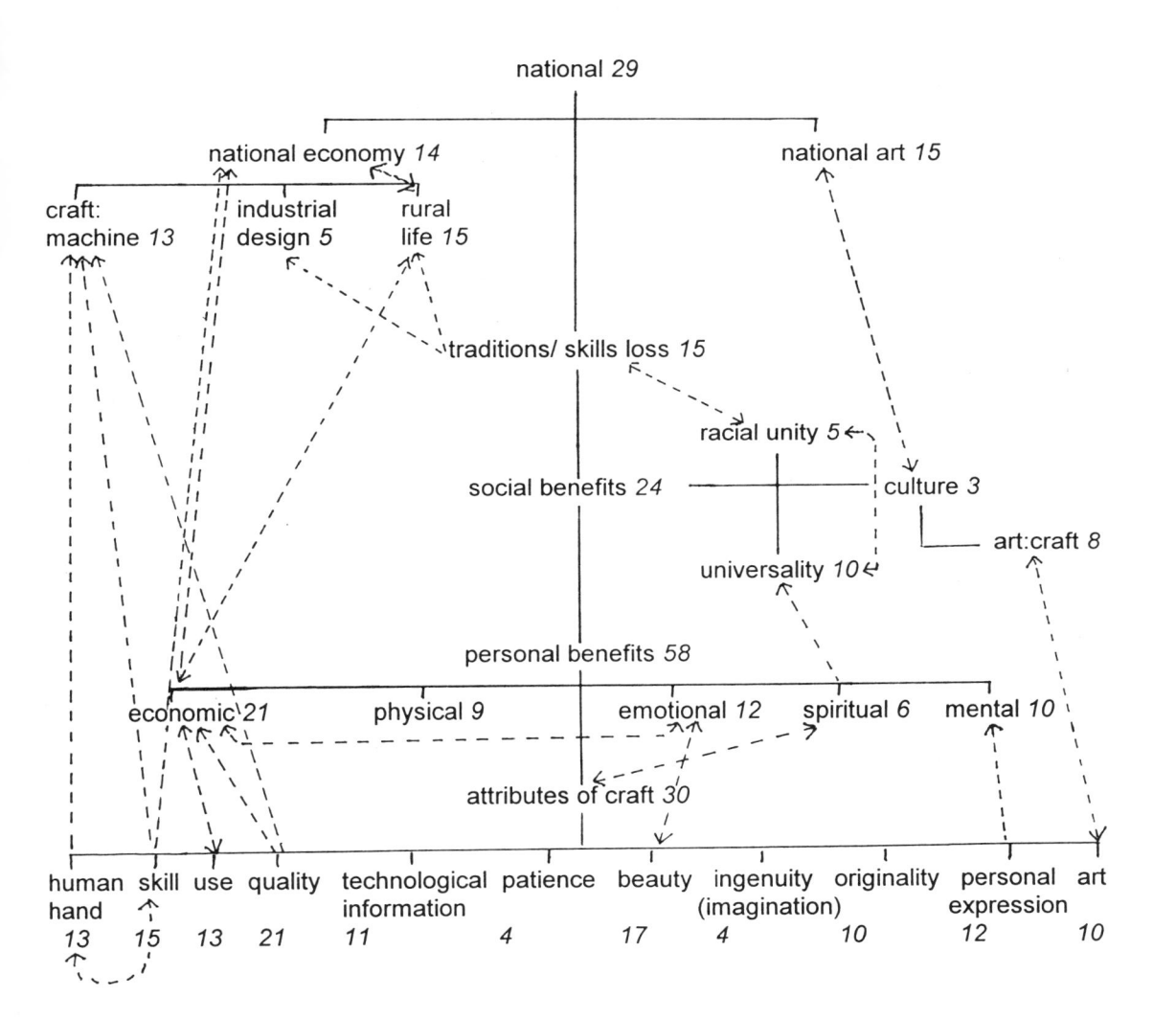

```
                                    national 29
         ┌──────────────────────────────┼──────────────────────────┐
              national economy 14                        national art 15
   ┌──────────────┬─────────────┬─────────────┐
  craft:         industrial    rural
  machine 13     design 5      life 15

                         traditions/ skills loss 15

                                          racial unity 5
                      social benefits 24 ──────┼────── culture 3
                                                              art:craft 8
                                          universality 10

                            personal benefits 58
        ┌──────────┬──────────┬──────────┬──────────┐
     economic 21  physical 9  emotional 12  spiritual 6  mental 10

                        attributes of craft 30

  human  skill  use  quality  technological  patience  beauty  ingenuity  originality  personal     art
  hand                        information                       (imagination)          expression
   13     15    13    21          11            4        17        4           10          12         10
```

Dotted lines indicate links made by various authors

APPENDIX 2a

PEI Provincial Exhibitions	P.E.I	Watson	P.E.I	Watson	P.E.I	Nkmis	P.E.I	Foam	P.E.I	P.E.I	P.E.I
woolen and cotton goods (handmade)											
weaving: 21											
7.5 yds black wool cloth dressed	1900		1910		1920		n/k				
7.5 yds grey wool cloth dressed	1900		1910				n/k				
ladies shawl	1900		1910				n/k				
pair horse rugs	1900		1910				1930				
10 yds twilled flannel	1900		1910		1920		1930		1939		
10 yds plain flannel	1900		1910								
20 yds carpet cotton w/wool	1900		1910								
10 yds fancy drugget	1900		1910				1930				
pair blankets wool	1900		1910		1920						
pair union blankets							1930		1939		
fancy counterpane all wool							1930				
fancy counterpane, cotton or linen					1920		1930				
6 yd draft weaving							1930		1939		
linen:											
island flaz made in last year	1900		1910								
ditto unbleached sheeting					1920						
ditto, tablecloth									1939		
best hank home made yarn					1920		1930		1939		
fancy bag, hand woven									1939		
any other piece of home woven material									1939		
rugs, all wool									1939		
weaving any article except carriage cover, place mats or shopping bag											1951
	10	0	10	0	6	0	8	0	8		1
TOTAL CLASSES BY YEAR	50	*24*	63	*26*	77	*56*	95	*31*	93	34	21

It is possible that some categories for PEI are not complete, these are indicated where suspected
PEI classifications were divided into 'woolen and cotton goods-handmade' and 'industrial', entrants from the former seem predominantly from outside Charlottetown – indicated by city.
PEI 1920 Handicraft Guild category includes: woven carpet 2.5 yds; basket rafia, dolls furniture; original toy; mechanical toy etc.
From 1939 PEI has categories for entrants over 70/75 years. Tracing women as their names change from single to married and from married (where husband's given name is used) to widowed is difficult. However some names repeat over 2 decades particularly in 1920, 1930.
PEI From 1900 small numbers of entrants from Nova Scotia and New Brunswick, in 1930 from Ontario and Vancouver, BC. In 1950 WI took over the women's work section, entrants are all local.
Watson, Nokomis, and *Foam Lake* are all small agricultural societies in Saskatchewan.

Totals: Techniques 62 approximately
Technique is defined as variation in tools or process/technique, occassionally materials are considered where they affect process.
Total number of classes over period 261
Specific object required 182 classes (70%). Of these 56 classes were garments

Appendices

Appendix 2b

PEI Provincial Exhibitions	P.E.I	Watson	P.E.I	Watson	P.E.I.	Nkmis	P.E.I	Foam Lake	P.E.I.	P.E.I.	P.E.I.
Woolen and cotton goods (handmade)											
knitting: 28 +15 43											
2 pr mens socks Island wool	1900	pr coarse	1910		1920		1930			1950	
2pr mens socks		fine wool	1910	pr hose	1920		1930	1 pair		fancy	
socks/stockings plain/ribbed						1937					
2pr womens stockings Island wool			1910		1920		1930				
ditto not black					1920		1930				
2 pr womens stockings	1900	fine wool	1910	pr hose	1920		1930				
ditto not black					1920		1930				
2 pr mens mitts Island wool			1910							1950	
2 pr mens mitts	1900		1910		1920		1930			fancy	
1 pr mens overalls	1900										
collection knitwork	1900		1910		1920		1930				
ditto cotton, wool, silk 3 categories			1910								
quilt white				quilt	1920	or afghan					
shawl white or coloured					1920		1930				
lace specimen		1908			1920		1930				
golf coat (mens)					1920		1930				
bedroom slippers					1920		1930				
ladies slip on sweater					1920						
ladies coat sweater							1930				
1 pr mens woolen gloves					1920		1930	gloves			
1 pr Ladies woolen golves					1920		1930				
gloves Island wool										1950	
gent's fancy knitted vest							1930				
petticoat any colour					1920	bloomers	1930				
boys golf hose, special prize					1920						
baby's knit leggings					1920						
felt mats					1920						
scarf						1927					
	5	4	7	4	20	4	17	2	0	5	
industrial: ladies fancy work NB. quilt, shawl and lace specimen are duplicate categories.											
knitting:											
silk socks or hose	1900										
lace specimen min. yd	1900		1910							1950	
cotton quilt	1900		1910								
bedspread										1950	
sweater			1910			1927				1950	
ladies slip on sweater					1920				1939	1950	
ditto, other than wool									1939		
fancy sweater							1930		1939		
ladies coat sweater							1930				
girls dress										1950	
child's dress/suit						1927		1937			
boys suit										1950	
sweater childs wool										1950	
shawl			1910								
afghan										1950	
	3	0	4	0	1	2	2	1	3	8	0
	8	4	11	4	21	6	19	3	3	13	

Appendix 2c

PEI Provincial Exhibitions	P.E.I.	Watson	P.E.I	Watson	P.E.I.	Nkmis	P.E.I.	Foam Lake	P.E.I	P.E.I	P.E.I
woolen and cotton goods (handmade)											
hooking: 28 +3 +3											
mat any material	1900		1910								
hooked door mat any material		door mat			1920		1930		1939		
hooked door mat yarn								1937	1939		
hooked door mat other									1939		
hooked square for a room					1920		1930		1939		
hooked rug any material						1927	1930		1939		
ditto, cotton rag											
hooked rug any materia lexcept yarn, floral									1939		
ditto, cotton rag											1951
ditto, conventional									1939		
ditto, animal									1939		1951
ditto, landscape or marine									1939		
hooked rug, wool rag conventional design 2 classes											1951
hooked rug wool rag vegetable dyes conventional design											1951
ditto, original design											1951
mat/rug all yarn	1900		1910		1920		1930				
hooked rug all yarn floral									1939		1951
ditto, landscape or marine, special									1939		
ditto, landscape or marine									1939		1951
ditto, conventional									1939		1951
ditto, animal design									1939		1951
ditto, original											1951
hooked rug any other [2 classes]									1939		
machine hooked rug, any material									1939		
mat best original design									1939		
wall hanging, hooked									1939		1951
hooked chair seats all yarn									1939		1951
hooked chair seats any material									1939		
subtotal		0	2	0	3	1	4	1	20		12
braided bathroom mats						braided rug		cotton	1939		rug
ditto, wool								1937			
bathroom mat crochet								mat	1939		
subtotal	2	0	2	0	3	2	4	4	22		13
afghan							1930				
quilt white							1930				
down or wool quilt with fancy							1930			1950	1951
	2	0	2	0	3	2	7	4	22	1	14

Appendix 2d

P.E.I provincial exhibiton	Watson	P.E.I	Watson	P.E.I	Nkmis	P.E.I	Foam	P.E.I	P.E.I	P.E.I
industrial: ladies fancy work etc	Total embroidery 63 + 7 sewing Total 70									
Honiton work on linen	1900									
Honiton Lace work	1900		1910				1930			
Point lace	1900		1910		1920					
Battenburg lace		*1908*	1910	*1910*	1920					
lace dessert d'oylies			1910				1930			
lace centre piece				*1910*			1930			
luncheon set in handmade lace							1930		1939	
subtotal lace	3	*1*	4	2	2	*0*	4	*0*	1	*0*	0
luncheon set any other									1939	
eyelet embroidery		*1908*	1910	*1910*	1920	*1927*	1930		1939	
Cambric embroidery large	1900									
Kensington embroidery	1900		1910							
Mount Mellick work			1910		1920					
Hardanger work			1910		1920				1939	
cut work or Roman work			1910		1920	or Italian	1930	*1937*	1939	
French embroidery					1920	*1927*	1930		1939	
French knot						*1927*				
Hedebo embroidery			1910							
drawn work (or Mexican work)	1900	*1908*	1910	*1910*	1920	*1927*				
Teneriffe			1910							
cross stitch					1920	*1927*	1930	fine	1939		1951
ditto wool								*1937*		
needle point									1939	
petti point									1939		1951
petit point framed											1951
crewel embroidery									1939	
sampler											1951
cover for bench or chair, tapestry stitch									1939	
Itallian hemstitch						hemstch	1930			
ditto, pr towels									1939	
ditto, table cover									1939	
six button holes on garment						*1927*				
bead work						*1927*				
Art Fancy work	1900		1910		1920		1930		1939	
embroidery, any other kind				silk on satin						
embroidered linen white s	1900	*1908*		1910				white		
embroidered linen coloured silk	1900	satin				*1927*		colord		
centre piece coloured silk	1900		1910	*1910*	1920	*1927*				
centre piece white silk			1910		1920					
centre piece white/colour on coloured linen or cotton		1910		1920		1930		1939		
centre piece colour linen/cotton							1930		1939	
centre piece, any other		*1908*							1939	
tea cloth white/colour linen/coton			1910		1920	no specs	1930		1939	
tea cloth coloured silk	1900		1910				1930		1939	1950	
table cover coloured cotton or linen		*1908*			1920		1930		1939	
table mats, any kind of work						dinner 3			1939	
embroidered bridge table cover							1930		1939	
embroidered bureeau cover							1930		1939	
embroidered d'oylies			1910				1930		1939	
collection dresser d'oylies	1900									
subtotals categories 49:	12	6	19	7	15	*13*	18	5	25	1	4

Appendix 2e

P.E.I provincial exhibition	P.E.I	Watson	P.E.I	Watson	P.E.I	Nkmis	P.E.I	Foam Lake	P.E.I	P.E.I	P.E.I
embroidery cont:											
sideboard cloth	1900		1910		1920				1939		
sideboard cloth white, in white									1939		
sideboard cloth, any other									1939		
ditto in white							1930				
ditto in colour							1930				
6 serviettes white					1920		1930		1939		
luncheon set all white						1927	1930		1939		
luncheon set in colours						no specs	1930	*1937*	1939		
buffet or vanity set						buffet	1930	buffet	1939		
buffet in white									1939		
vanity set in colours									1939		
scarf or runner embroidered						1927			1939		
ditto, any other kind									1939		
suit ladies plain underclothing	1900		1910			lingerie 2		pantie dress			
shirt waist			1910	any kind	1920						
fancy waist or smock				shadow			1930				
embroidered stocks and collars			1910								
3 pocket handkerchiefs	1900		1910		1920	1 fancy	1930				
with monogram/initial				*1910*	1920	*1927*	1930				
lace hankerchief	1900						1930				
childs handmade dress				*1910*		/rompers	1930				
childs dress machine made				*1910*							
girls dress smocked										1950	
hand made pillow slips	1900		1910		1920	embroid	1930	*1937*	1939	1950	
ditto worked in colours									1939	1950	
ditto any other kind								cutwork	1939	cut wk	1951
bedspread embroidered						1927					
pr towels embroidered						1927					
braiding			1910								
applique							1930	*1937*	1939		
embroidery total	15	6	23	9	9	23	28	8	39	4	5
NB. There are 5 classes of fine sewing, viz. plain underclothing, shirt waist, child's dress hand sewn and machine sewn , pillow slips handmade; one non-embroidery technique. Art Fancy work is probably shell work, hair work etc.											
class totals by year	17	6	27	12	11	24	31	11	41	5	5
leather work		1908				1927					

Appendix 2f

P.E.I provincial exhibition	P.E.I.	Watson	P.E.I.	Watson	P.E.I.	Nkmis	P.E.I.	Foam Lake	P.E.I.	P.E.I.	P.E.I.
crochet 21 + 9 T 30											
afghan	1900		1910			*or quilt*					
lace specimen	1900		1910				1930		1939	1950	
quilt	1900		1910	*1910*	1920		1930	*bedspread*		1950	
shawl			1910								
filet crochet					1920		1930		1939		
irish crochet							1930		1939		
tea cloth filet lace						*1927*	1930				
crochet trimmed article not filet						*1927*					
tea cloth crochet										1950	
luncheon set [crochet?]									1939		
table cover									1939		
centrepiece										1950	
d'oylies					1920		1930		1939	1950	
collars					1920						
girls dress											
pillow slips, crochet trimmed						*1927*					
crochet any article								*1937*			
towels, crochet trimmed						*1927*					
crochet bag of cotton or silk thread							1930		1939		
crochet in wool		1908				*1927*					
crochet in silk		1908				*1927*					
	3	2	4	1	4	7	7	2	7	5	
tattting	1900		1910		1920	*article/trimming*					
netting	1900		1910				1930			1950	
wax work						*1927*					
gesso work						*1927*					
candle or electric shade							1930				
Fancy Art work in crepe paper									1939		
pyrography on wood			*1910*								
painting on satin/silk		*1908*									
painting on velvet/plush		*1908*									
	5	4	7	1	5	10	9	2	8	6	

Appendix 2g

PEI Provincial Exhibitions	P.E.I	Watson	P.E.I	Watson	P.E.I	Nkmis	P.E.I	Foam Lake	P.E.I	P.E.I	P.E.I
miscellaneous: 54 [46 craft]											
best collection ladies work, 5 different designs, professional or amateur	1900										
ditto amateur	1900										
articles ladies handwork not listed							*3 doillies various*				
darned net	1900				1920						
punch work					1920	*1927*				1950	
ribbon work					1920						
sofa pillow	1900	*1908*	1910	*1910*	1920	*1927*	1930	*1937*	1939		
sofa cushion floral design					1920		1930		1939		
sofa cushion conventional design					1920		1930				
ditto worked coloured cotton, linen									1939		
ditto worked wool									1939		
ditto original design											1951
chesterfield set any kind									1939		
curtains pr any kind of work									1939		
patchwork quilt cotton	1900	*pieced*	1910	*1910*	1920	*1927*	1930	*1937 #*			
patchwork quilt silk		*crazy*	1910	*1910*	1920						
patchwork quilt any material							1930	*wool*		?	
quilt autographed made by a group										1950	
quilt appliqued crib size										1950	
tufted quilt							1930				
feather comforter, hand made						*1927*					
bedspread, any kind						*1927*		*cotton*			
bedspread chenille										1950	
set sheet, pair pillow slips fancy						*1927*					
pillow shams	1900	*1908*	1910	*1910*	1920		1930				
1 pr fancy towels					1920		1930		1939		
tea cosy	1900		1910	*1910*	1920						
ladies bedroom slippers	1900		1910						1939		
night robe					1920		1930				
camisoles					1920						
boudoir caps					1920						
fancy aprons		*1908*		*1910*	1920		1930	*1937*			
4 articles made from flour bags						*1927*		*pillows#*			
baby's bonnet							1930			1950	
baby's wool booties				*knt/crht*	1920		1930			1950	
baby's wool jacket white/coloured				*knt/crht*	1920		1930			1950	
baby's dress cotton/wool					1920		1930				
novelty for gift or Bazaar					1920		1930				
pin cushion		*1908*		*1910*	1920		1930				
darning on cotton, wool and silk 3		*1908*				*1927*		*2 materials #*			
patch on check or plaid		*1908*				*1927*		*patching*			
ladies work bag		*1908*				*1927*					
homespun bag							1930				
shopping bag woven										1950	
fancy crochet bag knitted/wool x stitch							1930		1939		
NB:man/boy's shirt, house dress, work apron, specimen patched garment, darned stockings; canvas bag, dish cloth bag, laundrey bag which are not decorated items are included in the numbers but not by row.											
Total classes	9	7	6	9	20	8	20	6	11	9	1
Total categories 252; Entries	51	*21*	63	*26*	66	*50*	94	*26*	93	34	21

Appendix 2h

Comparison of previous tables including Vancouver Opening Exhibition 1 [PNE]											
	PEI	Watson	PEI	Watson	PNE	PEI	Nokomis	PEI	Foam L.	PEI	PEI
	1900	1908	1910	1910	1910	1920	1927	1930	1937	1939	1950/1
weaving	10	0	10	0	n\k	6	0	8	0	8	9
crocket\knitting	13	8	18	5	18	26	16	28	5	11	19
rugs	2	1	2	0	12	3	2	4	4	22	13
lace	3	1	4	2	35	2	0	4	0	1	0
embroidery	14	5	23	10	n\k	19	24	31	11	40	10
baby clothes	0	0	0	2	16	4	11	4	0	0	3
quilts	1	2	2	2		2	1	3	2	0	3
sewing\quilts			9appr		10						
	41	17	66	21	86	62	44	82	22	82	57
					2 classes n\k						

BIBLIOGRAPHY

Achieving the Modern: Canadian Abstract Painting and Design in the 1950s Manitoba: Winnipeg Art Gallery 1993

Albers, Anni 'Handweaving Today: Textile Work at Black Mountain College' *The Weaver* 6:1 January 1941

Alice Hagen: Years in Mahone Bay 1930-1972 Mahone Bay, NS: Settlers' Museum 1989 (leaflet)

Allen, Catherine 'Paul Beau's Gift: Rediscovering a forgotten artist' *Canadian Heritage* 38 1982 pp.12,13,16

Alsop Joseph *The Rare Art Traditions: The History of Art Collecting and Its Related Phenomena* New York:Harper and Row 1982 1st ed.

Ames, Michael M. *The History of Canadian Anthropology* Canadian Ethnology Society 1976

Ames, Michael M. *Cannibal Tours and Glass Boxes: The Anthropology of Museums* Vancouver: UBC Press 1992

Anderson, Anne 'Painting on China' *Antique Dealer and Collectors Guide 51:6:52-57*

Anderson, Morna '25 Years with the Metal Arts Guild of Nova Scotia' typescript Metal Arts Guild of Nova Scotia 1976

Angus, Marion 'Beautiful Pottery from the Sea [Le Coq]' *Montreal Financial Times* 7 December 1949

Anselm, Sr. Mary 'Toward a Nova Scotia League of Arts and Crafts:Handcraft for Commercial Purposes, its Possibilities and Dangers' *Maritime Art* 2 pp.154,171 June 1942

Antonelli, Marylu, J.Forbes *Pottery in Alberta: the Long Tradition* Edmonton: University of Alberta Press 1978

Arthur, Eric; T.Richie *Iron: cast and wrought iron in Canada from the 17C to the present* University of Toronto Press 1982

Art of the Needle: Past and Present catalogue Edmonton Needlecraft Guild/Alberta Provincial Museum c1987

Atwater, M.M. '"It's Pretty - But Is It Art?"' *The Weaver* 6:?:13,14,26 1941

Ayre, Robert 'Introducing Valentin Shabaeff' *Canadian Art* 5:2:47-48 1947/48

Bibliography

Ayre, Robert 'Creative Craftsmanship in Jewellery [Georges Delrue]' *Canadian Art* 8:3:102-105 Spring 1951

Ayre, Robert 'The Saskatchewan Arts Board' *Canadian Art* 11:1 Autumn 1953

Ayre, Robert 'Enamels and Ceramics in Quebec' *Canadian Art* 11:3:95 Spring 1954 p.95

Baker, Marilyn *The Winnipeg School of Art: The Early Years* Winnipeg: University of Manitoba Press 1984

Baker, Marilyn, C.Majzels 'Women's Art/Women's Lives:Women Artists in Manitoba before 1955' exhibition leaflet Winnipeg Art Gallery 1995

Bamberger, Joan 'Revivals: Diverse Traditions' 1920-1945 *American Craft* Feb/Mar 1995

Barbeau, Marius 'Laurentian Wood Carvers' *CGJ* 11:4:181-190 October 1935

Barbeau, Marius *Quebec Where Ancient France Lingers* Toronto:Macmillan Canada 1936(a)

Barbeau, Marius *The Kingdom of the Saguenay* Toronto:Macmillan Canada 1936(b)

Barbeau, Marius 'Isle aux Coudres' *CGJ* 11:10:201 April 1936(c)
(repeated as 'Bright Yarn on the Loom' *The Kingdom of Saguenay*

Barbeau, Marius *Assomption Sash* NMC#93 Ottawa:NMC 1939

Barbeau, Marius 'Canadian Pottery' *Antiques* 39:6:296-299 June 1941

Barbeau, Marius *Maitres artisans de chez nous* Montreal:Les Editions du Zodiaque 1942(a)

Barbeau, Marius *Cahiers d'art: Les Brodeuses* Montreal:Editions Fides 1942(b)

Barbeau, Marius 'Folk Arts in French Canada' Montreal:*Educational Record* 58:1 1942(c)

Barbeau, Marius 'The Hooked Rug - Its Origin' *Royal Society of Canada* 3rd series, section 2, vol 36 pp.25-32 [and plates] 1942(d)

Barbeau, Marius *Cahiers d'art: Mille petites adresses* Montreal:Editions Fides 1946

Barbeau, Marius 'The Origin of the Hooked Rug' *Antiques* 52:2:110-113 1947

Barbeau, Marius 'Are the Real Folk Arts and Crafts Dying Out?' *Canadian Art* 5:3:128-133 Winter 1948

Barbeau, Marius, Price Arthur *I have Seen Quebec* Toronto: McMillan 1957

Barbeau, Marius, E.P.Richard *The Arts of French Canada 1613-1870* catalogue USA/The Detroit Institute of Arts 1946

Barnett, A. 'A Stitch out of Time' *Womens Art Magazine* March 1993

Barros, Anne 'The Metal Arts Guild of Ontario' *MAGazine* Summer 1994

Barros, Anne *Ornament and Object; Canadian Jewellery and Metal Art 1946-1996* Toronto: Boston Mills Press 1997

Barss, Peter, J.Gorden *Older Ways: Traditional Nova Scotian Craftsmen* Toronto: Van Nostrand Reinhold 1980

Becker, Howard S. *Art Worlds* Berkeley:University of California Press 1982

Behm, D; K.Leitch 'Spinning and Weaving on the Prairies' *The Craft Factor* Summer 1987

Bell, Andrew 'An Exhibition of Contemporary Canadian Arts' *Canadian Art* 7:4 Summer 1950

Bell, Michael ed. *The Kingston Conference Proceedings* Kingston:Queens University 1991

Beriau, O.A. *Home Weaving* Gardenvale, Quebec:The Institute of Industrial Arts 1933(a)

Beriau, Oscar A. 'The Handicraft Renaissance in Quebec' *CGJ* 7:3:143-149 September 1933(b)

Beriau, Oscar 'Home Weaving in Canada' *CGJ* 27:1:18-29 July 1943

Berlo, Janet C. *The Early Years of Native American Art History* University of British Columbia Press/University of Washington Press 1992

Bilash, Radomir, B.Wilber ed.s *Tkynyna: An Exhibit of Ukrainian Weaving* Toronto:Canadian Institute Ukrainian Studies et al/University of Toronto Press 1988

Billington, Dora *The Art of the Potter* Toronto:Oxford University Press 1937

Bird, Michael S. *A Splendid Harvest: Germanic Folk and Decorative Arts in Canada* Scarborough, Ontario:van Nostrand Reinhold 1981

Bird, Michael S. *Canadian Folk Art: Old Ways in a New Land* Toronto:Oxford University Press 1983

Bitner, Ruth 'Prairie Patchwork' *The Craft Factor* Summer 1993 pp.7,8,11

Black, Mary 'Weaving in Nova Scotia - Yesterday and Today' *Handweaver and Craftsman* Fall 1951 pp.5-8

Black, Mary 'Improving Design in Handcrafts' *Canadian Art* 9:4:158-162 Summer 1952

Blanchard, Paula *The Life of Emily Carr* Seattle:University of Washington Press 1987

Blaszezyk, R.L. 'The Aesthetic Moment: China Decorators, Consumer Demand and Technological Change in the American Pottery Industry 1865-1900' *Winterthur Portfolio* 29:2&3 Summer 1994

Bocking, R and L.Nowry *Heritage of MB* (Barbeau) CBC-TV (recording) 1984

Boggs, Jean Sutherland *The National Gallery of Canada* Toronto:Oxford University Press 1971

Bonner, Mary Graham *Made in Canada* 1st ed. New York:Knopf 1943

Boris, Eileen 'Crafts Shop or Sweatshop: The Uses and Abuses of Craftsmanship in Twentieth Century America' *Journal of Design History* 2:175-92 1989

Bouchard, Georges 'The Rennaisance of Rustic Crafts' *Scientific Agriculture* reprint Ottawa 1937

Bourgeois, C.A. 'International Exhibition, Paris, 1937' *CGJ* 15:2 August 1937

Boux, Rene 'New Directions in British Columbia Pottery' *Canadian Art* 11:3 Spring 1951

Bovey, Wilfrid *Canadian Handicrafts Survey of Domestic Art and Craft in Canadian Intellectual and Economic Life* Montreal:CHG 1938

Bovey, Wilfrid 'Canadian Handicrafts' *The Canadian Banker* 46:2:168-182 January 1939

Boyd, Cynthia 'Hooked Mats of Canada's Atlantic Provinces:Newfoundland and Labrador' *Piecework* VI:1:50-51 January 1998

Brieger, Peter 'Handicrafts and Industrial Design' *The Studio* 129:625:121-125 April 1945

British American Oil Company *B-A Canadiana: Canadian Crafts in Industry* Toronto: s.n. 1951 (4 booklets)

Broadfoot, B. *Six War Years 1939-1945* Toronto:Doubleday 1974

Broadfoot, B. *The Pioneer Years 1895-1914* Toronto:Doubleday 1976

Broadfoot, B. *Ten Lost Years 1929-39* Ontario:Paperjacks 1975

Broadfoot, B. *The Immigrant Years: From Europe to Canada 1945-1967* Vancouver/Toronto:Douglas & McIntyre 1986

Bronner, Simon J. *Grasping Things: Folk Material Culture and Mass Society in America* USA: University Press Kentucky 1986

Brooks, Reva 'Canadian Artists:Jarko Zavi' *World Affairs* May 1945

Brown, Margaret W. 'Never Worked Never Will' [Jim Bailey, woodcarver] *Gay Adventurers* Toronto: J.M.Dent & Sons (Canada Ltd) 1947 p.270

Brown, F. Maud *Breaking Barriers: Eric Brown and the National Gallery* Ottawa: The Society for Art Publications 1964

Brown, Rosemary A. *Katharine Emma Maltwood: Artist 1878-1961* Victoria BC: University of Victoria 1981

Bruce, Jean *After the War* Fitzhenry and Whiteside 1982

Bruce, J.E.M. 'Adult Education' *The Daily Colonist*: Victoria, BC 26 March 1939 Section 3 p.1

Burkhauser, Jude ed. *Glasgow Girls: Women in Art and Design 1880-1920* Glasgow: Red Ochre Press 1990

Burnham, Dorothy K. *The Comfortable Arts: Tradition Spinning and Weaving in Canada* Ottawa: National Museums of Canada 1981

Burnham, Dorothy K. *Unlike the Lilies: Doukhobor Textile Traditions in Canada* Toronto: Royal Ontario Museum 1986

Burt, S., L.Burt, L.Dorney *Changing Patterns: Women in Canada* Toronto:Toronto University Press 1988

Button, Billy *I Married an Artist* Toronto:Ryerson Press 1951

Calder, Eva 'A Song of Bohemia' *Canadian Home Journal* September 1932

Canadian Almanac Toronto:Copp Clark 1889, 1901, 1913, 1915, 1916, 1920, 1925, 1926

Canada Year Book 1994 Ottawa: Statistics Canada *Canada Year Book 1994* Ottawa: Statistics Canada 1993

'Canadian Folk Song and Handicraft Festival' program Quebec May 1927

'Canadian Folk Song and Handicraft Festival' progam Quebec May 1928

Canadian Parks Service: Classification System for Historical Collections Ottawa:Minister of Supply and Services Canada 1992

Carbone, Stanislao *The Streets Were Not Paved With Gold: A Social History of Italians in Winnipeg* Winnipeg: Manitoba Italian Heritage Committee 1993

Carless, William *The Arts and Crafts of Canada* McGill University Publications Series, Art and Architecture Montreal:McGill University Press 1925

Carney, Margaret *Alfred Teaches Ceramics 1900-1996* catalogue New York: Museum of Ceramic Art, Alfred University 1996

Carpenter, Carole H. *Many Voices: A Study of Folklore Activities in Canada and their Role in Canadian Culture* Canadian Centre for Folk Culture Studies Mercury 26   Ottawa:National Museums of Canada 1979

Carr, Emily *The Complete Writings of Emily Carr* Vancouver: Douglas & McIntyre 1997

Cash, Gwen 'Witch at the Wheel Performs White Magic With Her Touch [Daisy Swayne]' *Vancouver Sun* 18 July 1953 p.19

Celebration: 50th Anniversary of the Metal Arts Guild catalogue Toronto:Metal Arts Guild 1996

Charles, Evelyn 'Pottery in Canada' *Encyclopedia Canadiana* 1962 pp.279-282

Charles, Evelyn 'A History of the Guild: The Canadian Guild of Potters' *Tactile* August 1976

Chiasson, Anselme ed. *The History of Cheticamp Hooked Rugs and Their Artisans* Nova Scotia:Lescarbot Publications 1988

Clark, R.J. 'A History of the Department of Extension at the University of Alberta 1912-1956' Ph.D thesis Edmonton: University of Alberta 1985

Coady, M.M. *Masters of Their Own Destiny: Antigonish Movement of Adult Education through Economic Cooperation* Harper and Row/Formac Publishing, Antigonish 1939,1967

Cochrane, Grace *The Craft Movement in Australia: A History* New South Wales: University Press 1992

Colgate, William *Canadian Art: its origin and development* Toronto: Ryerson Press 1943

Collard, Elizabeth *Nineteenth Century Pottery and Porcelain in Canada* McGill/Queens University Press 1984 2nd edition

Conrad M., A.Finkel, C.Jaenen *History of the Canadian Peoples: Beginnings to 1876* Vol 1 Toronto:Copp Clark Pitman 1993

Continuity and Change: the Ukrainian Folk Heritage in Canada Ottawa: National Museums of Canada 1972

Cooper, Emmanuel *People's Art: Working Class Art from 1750 to the Present Day* Edinburgh:Mainstream 1994

Crafts Council [U.K.] *The context for Critical Studies in the crafts* London, UK:Crafts Council 1995

Crawford, Gail 'Guild Shop Marks Jubilee' *CraftNews* April-May 1992 Ontario Craft Council pp.1-3

Crawford, Gail M. book ms [*A Fine Line: Studio Crafts in Ontario from 1930 to the present* Ontario: Dundurn Press Fall 1998]

Crepeau, Pierre *Pointing at the Wind* catalogue Ottawa/Hull:CMC 1990

Crosby, Joni S. 'The History of the Evolution of the Teaching of Textiles and Weaving in Quebec since 1905' M.A. dissertation Montreal:Concordia University 1987

Crowell, I.H.. 'Teaching Handicrafts in Canada' *CGJ* 27:2:84-94 1943

Crowley, David *National style and nation-state: Design from Poland from the venacular revival to the international style* Manchester:Manchester University Press 1992

Csikszentmihalyi, Mihaly and E.Rochberg-Halton *The Meaning of Things: Domestic Symbols and the Self* UK:Cambridge University Press 1981

Cullum, Linda K. 'Under Construction: Women and the Jubilee Guild and the Commission of Government in Newfoundland and Labrador 1935-1941' M.A. dissertation Toronto: University of Toronto 1993

Cullum, Linda '"I was a Curiosity": Working for the Jubilee Guilds in the 1930s' *Newfoundland Quarterly* 88:1:25 Spring 1993(a)

Cumming, Elizabeth *Phoebe Anna Traquair: 1852-1936* catalogue Scotland:National Galleries of Scotland 1993

Cunningham, Louis Arthur 'Among the Cottage Crafters' *Canadian Home Journal* March 1933 pp.8,34,40d

Cushman, Karen 'Museum Studies: The Beginnings, 1900-1926' *Museum Studies Journal* 1:3:8-19 Spring 1984

Davis, Blodwen 'Generosity of Craftmen Too Long Exploited' *Saturday Night* 20 November 1948 pp.18-19

Daye, Vera L. 'Lady in Design [Violet Gillett]' *The Country Guide* April 1977 pp.72,78,80

De Bertrand Lugrin, N. 'Women Potters and Indian Themes' *MacLeans's Magazine* 15 March 1927

Dempsey, Hugh A. *Ethnic Furniture* catalogue Calgary:Glenbow-Alberta Institute 1970

Desmarais, L.and J-L.Bouchard 'Handicrafts in Quebec: A Short History' *Parlure-Craftsman* December 1979

Dexter, J. *Traditional Nova Scotian Double-Knitting Patterns* Nova Scotia Museum

Dickenson, Victoria 'A History of the National Museums from their Founding to the Present Day' *Muse* Summer 1992 pp.56-63

Dickson, Helen 'The Vancouver School of Decorative and Applied Art' *The Canadian Forum* 12:142:102-103 Dececember 1931

Dickson, Lovat *The Museum Makers: The Story of the Royal Ontario Museum* Toronto: Royal Ontario Museum 1986

Dormer, Peter ed. *The Culture of Craft* Manchester UK: Manchester University Press 1997

Dorson, Richard M. ed. *Folklore and Folklife: An Introduction* Chicago:University of Chicago Press 1972

Dragan, Rose *Ukrainian Embroidery Designs and Stitches* SK:UWAC.UMC 1957

Ducie, Rose 'Old-time Crafts Still Live' *Western Producer* 8 February 1951

Dunn, Josephine Hambleton 'The Woodcarver of St-Jean-Port-Joli' *CGJ* 65:6:234-241 December 1952

Duval, Paul *Glorious Visions, Peter Haworth, Studies for Stained Glass Windows* catalogue Ontario: The Art Gallery of Windsor 1985

Eaton, Allen H. *Handicrafts of the Southern Highlands* New York:Dover 1973 [reissue 1937 edition]

Eaton, Allen H. *Handicrafts of New England* New York:Harper & Bros. 1949 1st ed.

Eaton, Allen, Lucinda Crile *Rural Handicrafts in the United States* Washington, D.C.:United States Printing Office 1946

Eggleston, Wilfrid 'Canadian Geography and National Culture' *CGJ* 63:6:254 December 1951

Einarsson, Magnus; H.Benndorf Taylor ed.s *Just for Nice: German-Canadian Folk Art* Ottawa/Hull:CMC 1993

Elinor, Gillian ed. *Women and Craft* London:Virago Press 1987

Elwood, Marie *Potters of Our Past* exhibition leaflet Halifax: Art Gallery of Nova Scotia/Nova Scotia Potters Guild 1996

Evans, Jane Turnbull 'Championing the Crafts: The Role of the Saskatchewan arts Board in the Development of Crafts - The First Ten Years [1948-57]' *The Craft Factor* Saskatchewan Fall 1988 pp.2-6

Eyland, Cliff et al *Atque Ars: Art from Mount Allison University 1854-1989* catalogue New Brunswick:Owens Art Gallery, Mount Allison University 1989

Fallis, Donna 'World War I Knitting' Alberta Museums *Review* 9:2:8-10 Fall 1984

Fedorak, Rose Marie 'A Continuing Heritage' *The Craft Factor* Summer 1993 pp.9-11

Finlayson, Margot 'Womens's Activities at the Canadian National Exhibition During the Years 1928-1937' essay Toronto:Canadian National Exhibition Archives 1976

Finnie, Richard 'Filming Rural French Canada' *CGJ* 14:4 April 1937

Finkel A., M.Conrad, V. Strong-Boag *History of the Canadian Peoples:1867 to the Present* Vol 2 Toronto:Copp Clark Pitman 1993

Fitzpatrick, Deanne 'Hooked Mats of Canada's Atlantic Provinces: Hooking Traditions Together' *Piecework* VI:1:52-53 January/February 1998

Flood, Sandra 'Contemporary Craft Collecting in Museums' M.A. dissertation Manchester UK:University of Manchester 1993

Flood, Sandra *Made for a Cause* exhibition catalogue Saskatchewan Craft Council 1994

Foam Lake Agricultural Fair prize list 1937 Saskatchewan: WDM.A

Foster, W. Garland 'Murray Tweeds' *Family Herald and Weekly Star* December 24 1941

Fox, Ross *Presentation Pieces and Trophies: From the Henry Birks Collection of Canadian Silver 1790-1930* Ottawa:National Gallery of Canada 1985

Frame, Fredette *Mount Allison Ladies' College 1854-1937* catalogue New Brunswick:Owens Art Gallery, Mount Allison University 1994

Friesen, Gerald *The Canadian Prairies: A History* Toronto:University of Toronto Press 1987 (student edition)

From, Dot 'The Crafts Guild of Manitoba Celebrates Sixty-Five Years' *Manitoba History* 25 Spring 1993 pp.28-32

Galipeau, Pascale et al. *Les Paradis du monde: Quebec Folk Art* Ottawa/Hull:CMC CCFC Mercury Series 68 1996

Gauvreau, Jean-Marie *Artisans du Quebec* Les editions du bien public 1940

Gell, Alfred 'Vogel's Net: Traps as Artworks and Artworks as Traps' *Journal of Material Culture* 1:1 Sage Publications 1996

Gender and History 6:3 (Special Issue on Public History) Oxford: Blackwell Publishers November 1994

Gibbon, John Murray *Canadian Mosaic: The Making of a Northern Nation* Toronto: McClelland and Stewart 1938

Gibbon, J.M. 'Canadian Handicraft Old and New' *CGJ* 26:3:130-141 March 1943

Gibbon, J.M. 'Canada's Million and More Needlecraft Workers' *CGJ* 26:3:144-155 March 1943(b)

Gilbert, Evelyn 'Weaving in the West' *Country Guide* October 1946 p.74

Giovine, C.M. 'Jean-Marie Gavreau: Art, Handicrafts and National Culture in Quebec from the 1920s until the 1950s' *Design Issues* 10:3 Autumn 1994

Gould, Richard and M.B.Schiffer ed.s *Modern Material Culture: The Archaeology of Us* New York/London:Academic Press Inc 1981

Gowans, Alan *The Unchanging Arts* USA:J.B. Lippencott Co. 1971

Granatstein, J.L. 'Culture and Scholarship: The First Ten Years of the Canada Council' *Canadian Historical Review* 1984

Green, Henry G. ed. *A Heritage of Canadian Handicrafts* Montreal: McClelland and Stewart 1967

Green, Lydian 'Ayreshire Whitework' *Piecework* March/April 1995

Greenfield, Valerie *Founders of the Alberta College of Art* catalogue Calgary: Alberta College of Art 1986

Greg, Andrew ed. *Primavera: Pioneering Craft and Design 1945-1995* catalogue U.K.: Tyne and Wear Museums 1995

Gregor, Helen F. *The Fabric of My Life: Reflections of Helen Frances Gregor RCA* Toronto:Dreadnought 1987

Hadjinicolaou, Nicos *Art History and Class Struggle* Pluto Press 1978

Hafter, Daryl M. ed. *European Women and Preindustrial Craft* Bloomington: Indiana University Press 1995

Hall, M.D., E.W.Metcalf ed.s *The Artist Outsider: Creativity and the Boundaries of Culture* Washington: Smithsonian Institute 1994

Hamilton, Alice *Manitoban Stained Glass* Winnipeg: University of Winnipeg Press 1970

Handbook of Canadian Universities, Colleges and Private Schools for Use in Other Countries Ottawa: King's Printer 1944

Handicraft News 1:1 CHG May 1933

Hand Loom Weaving: The Story of the Searle Effort to Sponsor Hand-Loom Weaving in the Prairie Provinces Winnipeg:Searle Grain Company Ltd July 1944

Harrington, Lyn 'Sculptor of Wood - W.G.Hodgson' *CGJ* 39:5 November 1949

Harrington, Lyn 'Czechs and Spaniards, Glass Blowers of Medicine Hat' *Canadian Scene* issue 782 July 1969

Harris, Jennifer ed. *Textiles 5000 Years* UK: British Museum Press 1993

Harris, Jennifer et al *William Morris Revisited: Questioning the Legacy* catalogue Manchester UK: Whitworth Gallery 1996

Harris, Lawren 'Reconstruction through the Arts' *Canadian Art* 1:185 June 1944

Harrison, Charles and P.Wood *Art in Theory 1900-1990* Blackwell 1992

Haydon, Michael ed. *So Much To Do, So Little Time: The Writings of Hilda Neatby* Vancouver:University of British Columbia Press 1983

Hayward, Victoria 'Rug Hunting in Habitant Quebec' *Toronto Star Weekly* 30 June 1928

Henning-Rees 'Texture Identity in Weaving' *The Weaver* 6:1:8-9 January 1941

Hickey, Gloria A. ed. *Making and Metaphor* Ottawa/Hull:CMC Mercury Series 66 1994

Hobsbawm, E., T.Ranger *The Invention of Tradition* UK:Cambridge University Press 1983

Holmes, Clara L. 'The Great West Festival at Calgary' *CGJ* 1:3:269-275 1930

Holmes, Clara L. 'Old Crafts in a New Land' *The Country Guide* p.4 1 May 1928

Home, Ruth 'Pottery' *CGJ* 28:2:64-77 1944

Hoskins, Janet A. 'Weaving Education in Manitoba in the 1940s' M.A. dissertation Winnipeg:University of Manitoba 1982

Hoskins, Janet A. 'The Searle grain Company and Manitoba handweaving: A Programme of Imaginative Philanthropy' *Manitoba History* 6:10-14 Fall 1983

Housser, F.B. *A Canadian Art Movement* Toronto:Macmillan 1926/1974

100 Years: Evolution of the Ontario College of Art catalogue Toronto: Art Gallery of Ontario 1977

150 Years of Art in Manitoba: Struggle for a Visual Civilization catalogue Winnipeg: Winnipeg Art Gallery 1970

Ina D.D.Uhthoff catalogue BC: Art Gallery of Greater Victoria 1972

Inglis, Stephen 'Creators and Consecrators: A Potter Community of South India' Ph.D thesis Vancouver: University of British Columbia 1984

Inglis, Stephen 'A Company of Travellers: Some Early Studio Potters in Canada' in Mayer C. ed. *The Potter's Art: Contributions to the Study of the Koerner Collection of European Ceramics* Vancouver: UBC Museum of Anthropology 1997

Inglis, Stephen *The Turning Point: The Deichmann Pottery, 1935-1965* catalogue Ottawa/Hull: CMC 1991

Ioannou, Noris *Ceramics in South Australia 1836-1986: From Folk to Studio Pottery* South Australia: Wakefield Press 1986

Ioannou, Noris ed. *Craft in Society: An Anthology of Perspectives* Australia:Fremantle Arts Centre Press 1992

Jackson, A.Y. 'Early Wood Carving in Quebec' *The Canadian Bookman* p.186 November 1925

Jackson, A.Y. *A Painter's Country* Canada:Clarke, Irwin and Co. 1958

Janzen, R.K., J.M.Janzen *Mennonite Furniture: A Migrant Tradition (1766-1910)* Pennsylvania USA:Good Books 1991

Jarvis, Alan ed. *Douglas Duncan: A Memorial Portrait* Toronto: University of Toronto Press 1974

Johnson, Pamela 'Naming of Parts' *Crafts* UK:Crafts Council May 1995 pp.42-45

Johnson, Paul *The Offshore Islanders: A History of the English People* Phoenix 1992

Jones, David C., I.MacPherson *Building Beyond the Homestead* Calgary:University of Calgary Press 1985

Jones, Michael Owen *The Hand Made Object and Its Maker* USA: University of California 1978

Jukes, Mary 'New Pottery Designed to Suit Modern House' Toronto: *Globe and Mail* 27 December 1937

Kaplan, E.S. ed. *Museums and the Making of "Ourselves": The Role of Objects in National Identity* UK:Leicester University Press 1994

Kardon, Janet *A Neglected History: 20th century American craft* New York: American Craft Museum 1990

Kardon, Janet ed. *The Ideal Home: The History of Twentieth Century American Craft 1900-1920* New York:Harry N. Abrams/American Craft Museum 1993

Kardon, Janet ed. *Revivals! Diverse Traditions 1920-1945* New York:Harry N. Abrams/American Craft Museum 1994

Kardon, Janet ed. *Craft in the Machine Age 1920-1945* New York:Harry N. Abrams/American Craft Museum 1995

Kenneley, Frances 'A Tale of Two Champions' *Piecework* 6:1:22-24

Kettle, H.G. 'The Canadian Handicraft Movement' *The Canadian Forum* XX:234:112,114 July 1940

Kerr, et al. *Historical Atlas of Canada 1891-1961* University of Toronto Press 1990

Key, Archie F. *Beyond Four Walls: The Origins and Development of Canadian Museums* Toronto:McClelland and Stewart 1973

Kingsmill, Bob *A Catalogue of British Columbian Potters* n/p 1977

Klymasz, R. B. *Art and Ethnicity: The Ukrainian Tradition in Canada* catalogue Ottawa/Hull:CMC 1991

Knibb, Helen 'Present but Not Visible: Searching for Women's History in Museum Collections' *Gender and History* 6:3:352-369 Blackwell 1994

Kohuska, N *A Half-Century of Service to the Community: An outline of the Ukrainian Womens' Association of Canada 1926-1976* Winnipeg: UWCA 1986

Komendant, Kristina 'Stephan Horpynka' *The Craft Factor* Saskatchewan Crafts Council 1994 p.11

Kuper, Adam *Anthropology and Anthropologists* Routledge 1983

L.L.J. 'the tapestries of Krystyna Sadowski' *Craft Horizons* Spring 1957 pp.36,37

Lackey, Thomas 'Image Sources for Bluenose Hooked Rugs' *Canadian Antiques and Art Review* April 1980

Lambert, Barbara 'A wonderfully-accurate restoration' Ottawa:*The Saturday Citizen* 8 September 1973

Landon, John E. *Canadian Silversmiths 1700-1900* U.S.A.:Stinehour Press 1966

Layton, Robert *The Anthropology of Art* UK:Cambridge University Press 2nd edition 1991

Lazarowich, Linda A. 'A Social History of Ukrainian Cottage Weaving in Alberta 1900-1940' M.A. dissertation Winnipeg:University of Manitoba 1983

Leach, Bernard *A Potter's Book* Faber and Faber 3rd edition 1976

Leighton, David *Artists, Builders and Dreamers: Fifty Years at the Banff School* Toronto: McClelland and Stewart 1982

Leitch, Adelaide 'Newfoundland's Looms' *Saturday Night* 64 17 May 1949 p.29

Leitch, Adelaide 'Where Handicrafts Build Homes' *CGJ* 62:5 May 1951

Leitch, Adelaide 'Handicrafts under the Midday Moon' *CGJ* 52:3 March 1956

Leitch, Adelaide 'Pictures on Brin - The Grenfell Hooked Mats' *CGJ* 56:2:75 February 1958(a)

Leitch, Adelaide 'The Tartan Weavers of Cape Breton' *CGJ* 56:5:176 May 1958(b)

Lesser, Gloria 'Biography and bibliography of the writings of Donald William Buchanan (1908-1966)' *The Journal of Canadian Art History* 2:129-137 1981

Lesser, Gloria 'Le design au Canada de 1940 a 1980 (Design in Canada: 1940-80)' *Cahiers des arts visuels au Quebec* 24:7-16 Winter 1984

Lesser, Gloria *Ecole du Meuble 1930-1950* catalogue Montreal:Chateau Dufresne Inc, Montreal Museum of Decorative Arts, 1989

Lesser, Gloria 'Karen Bulow: Masterweaver' *Canadian Society of Decorative Arts Bulletin* 8:2:8 Winter 1990

Lesser, Gloria 'Carl Poul Petersen: Master Danish-Canadian Silversmith' *Material History Review 43* Spring 1996 pp.47-54

Lighthall, Alice 'Handicraft Guild Program Encourages and Instructs' *Saturday Night* 64 11 December 1948 pp.30-31

Litt, Paul *The Muses, the Masses and the Massey Commission* Toronto: University of Toronto Press 1992

Lochnan, Katharine A. ed. *The Earthly Paradise: Arts and Crafts by William Morris and His Circle from Canadian Collections* catalogue Art Gallery of Ontario/Key Porter Books Ltd 1993

Lord, Barry *The History of Painting in Canada: Towards a People's Art* Toronto:NC Press 1974

Lotz, Jim *Head, Heart and Hands: Craftspeople in Nova Scotia* Halifax, N.S: Braemar Publicaions 1986

Lucie-Smith, Edward *The Story of Craft: The Craftsman's Role in Society* Oxford:Phaidon 1981

Lynch, Coleen *The Fabric of their Lives: hooked and poked mats of Newfoundland and Labrador* catalogue NFD: The Art Gallery, Memorial University 1980

Lynch, Colleen/Newfoundland Museum *Helping Ourselves: Crafts of the Grenfell Mission* catalogue St. John's, NFD: The Museum c1985

Lynch, Colleen 'A Handle on the Past: A Compilation of Research on Craft Design in Newfoundland and Labrador' typescript Craft Development Division, Department of Tourism and Culture, Newfoundland and Labrador 1994

McAnn, Aida 'Busy Hands in New Brunswick' *CGJ* 20:3:127-138 March 1940

McCarthy, Pearl 'Ecole du Meuble Joins Carpentry and Culture' Toronto: *Globe and Mail* 3 July 1948 p.8

McCausland, M.B. [Robert McCausland Ltd] *On The Making of Stained Glass Windows* Toronto:n/p 1913

McCormick, Heather J. *The Alice Hagen Collection* Halifax: Mount Saint Vincent University 1994

Macdonald, Stuart *The History and Philosophy of Art Education* UK:University of London Press Ltd 1970

McFall, Tom 'Prairie Folk Furniture' *The Craft Factor* Winter 1989/90 pp.22-24

Macfarlane, Fiona C., E.F. Arthur *Glascow School of Art Embroidery 1894-1920* Glascow:Glascow Museums and Art Galleries 1980

McInnes, Graham 'The Allied Arts Council' *Saturday Night* 54:16:24 18 February 1939

MacKay, Alice 'French-Canadian Handicrafts' *CGJ* 6:1:27-34 January 1933

McKay, Ian *The Quest of the Folk: Antimodernism and cultural selection in twentieth-century Nova Scotia* Canada:McGill-Queen's U.P. 1994

McKenzie, Karen; Larry Pfaff 'The Art Gallery of Ontario: Sixty Years of Exhibitions, 1906-1966 *RACAR* VII:1-2

Mackley, Florence MacDonald *Handweaving in Cape Breton* Sydney, NS:privately printed 1967

MacLaughlin, Marjorie 'Landscape Rugs in Quebec' *CGJ* 1:8:671-680 December 1930

McLeod, Bruce 'Petrik the Potter' *Gay Adventurers* Toronto: J.M.Dent & Sons (Canada Ltd) 1947 p.167

McLeod, Ellen M.E 'Enterprising Women and the Early Years of the Canadian Handicraft Guild 1905-1936' M.A. dissertation Ottawa:Carlton University 1994

MacNutt, Dawn A conversation with Mary Black c1980 tape [Dawn MacNutt]

McRae, D.G.W. *The Arts and Crafts of Canada* Toronto: MacMillan and Co. 1944

Mainzer, Janet C. 'The relation between the crafts and the fine arts in the United States from 1876 to 1980' Ph.D thesis New York: New York University 1989

Major, Marjorie 'History of the the Nova Scotia Tartan' *Nova Scotia Historical Quarterly* 2:2 June 1972

Majzels, Claudine 'Constructing the Woman Artist: Marie Hewson Guest in Winnipeg' *Manitoba History* 29 spring 1995 pp.2-10

Manhart, Marcia and T.Manhart ed.s *The Eloquent Object: The Evolution of American Art in Craft Media Since 1945* Seattle USA: University of Washington Press 1987

Massy V. et al *Report: National Development in the Arts, Letters and Sciences* Ottawa: King's Printer 1951

Meikle, Margaret *Cowichan Indian Knitting* Vancouver:UBC Museum of Anthopology 1987

Melnyk, Steve 'Leo Mol Western Canada's Only Stained Glass Artist' *Winnipeg Tribune* 21 March 1959

Melvin, Grace W. *Teacher's Manual* Victoria: Department of Education, Government of B.C. 1941

Meredith, Brian 'The handicrafts of New France' *The Seigneur* January 1932 pp.19-25,31

Michael, Sr. Marie 'Toward a Nova Scotia League of Arts and Crafts:The Objectives of a Handicraft Movement' *Maritime Art 2* June 1942 pp.150-153

Miers, Sir Henry A., S.F. Markham *Directory of Museums and Art Galleries* London: The Museums Association 1932

Millar, L.D., 'Guild Community Programs for Richer Recreation' *Saturday Night* 64 29 March 1949 p.16

Moogk, Peter N 'In the Darkness of a Basement: Craftsmen's Associations in Early French Canada' *Canadian Historical Review* LVII:4 Toronto: University of Toronto Press 1976

Morgan, Wayne 'Early Saskatchewan Pottery' *The Craft Factor* 2:1:17 Saskatchewan: Saskatchewan Craft Council

Morrison, Rosalyn *Canadian Glassworks 1970-1990* catalogue Toronto:Ontario Crafts Council 1990

Morton Weizman, Sandra; E.Eliot-Los *Alberta Quilts* catalogue Edmonton: Alberta Art Foundation[?] 1984

Muir, N.P. 'What do Canadian Women Lack?' *Canadian Home Journal* June 1932 p.13

Murchie, John 'Here and There, Now and Agin, Regions End Where Countries Begin' *Art Libraries Journal* 22:4:16-23 1997

Murray, Joan *Daffodils in Winter: the Life and Letters of Pegi Nicol MacLeod, 1904-1949* Ontario: Penumbra Press 1984

n/a 'A Handicrafts Exhibition: Cottage Industries of Canadian-Born and Immigrant Settlers' *Family Herald and Weekly Star* Montreal 26 October 1927 p.31

n/a 'Beginning Anew/Jarko Zavi/ Ceramic Pioneer' *Bulletin of the Canadian National Committee on Refugees, No.1* January 1945 [first printed *Saturday Night* 1943/44]

n/a 'Canadian Industries in the Home' *Industrial Canada* VII:8:645-647 March 1907

n/a 'Canadian Metalsmith Creates Unique Beauty [Harold Stacey]' *Mayfair* XXV:4:54-56 April 1951

n/a 'Craftsmen at Work' *Handcrafts* Nova Scotia 5:1:4 January 1948 p.

n/a 'Does "Contemporary Design" Mean Anything to You?' *Canadian Homes and Gardens* June 1945

n/a 'Folk Art for Petroleum Executives' *Mayfair* XXV:2:37-42 February 1951

n/a 'Grace Annie Lockhart - A Shining Model for Women of the 90s' *Mount Allison Record* Spring 1994 pp.37-38

n/a 'Guild of All Arts' *Canadian Magazine* 88 November 1937

n/a 'Pewter is Her Medium [Marjorie Stokes]' *Saturday Night* 65 8 November 1949 p.44

n/a 'Stained Glass [Marius Plamondon]' *The Standard, Montreal* 23 September 1944 p.13

n/a 'The Arts and Crafts Exhibit, Montreal' *Construction* XVL:11:391-393 November 1923

n/a 'The Canadian Handicraft' *The Argus* [Montreal ?] 22 October 1904 pp.15-16

n/a 'The Canadian Handicraft Guild: Manitoba Branch' *The Manitoba School Journal* April 1957 18:8:12-16

n/a 'The Romance of Handicrafts' *Family Herald and Weekly Star* 20 October 1937 pp.32, 36

Newfoundland Royal Commission 1933 (Amulree Report) UK:HMSO 1933

National Film Board *The Story of Peter and the Potter* (Deichmans) film c1950 CMC 113C 0153 018

National Film Board *Artisans du Nouveau Brunswick* film c1950 CMC 113C 0246 041

Nobbs, Percy 'State Aid to Art Education in Canada' *Construction* 1:44-47 April 1908

Nobbs, Percy E. 'Metalcraft' *CGJ* 28:5:212 May 1944

Norris, J.A. 'The Book of Giving: A History of the Ontario Handweavers and Spinners 1956-1979' Toronto: Ontario Handweavers and Spinners c1980

Nowry, Laurence *Marius Barbeau* Toronto:NC Press Ltd 1995

Nylen, Anna-Maja *Swedish Handcraft* Toronto: Van Nostrand Reinhold Co. 1977

Ostrom, Walter (transcript) interview with Mr and Mrs Ernest Lorenzen April 1979 CMC Research Dept File

Panton, L.A.C. 'The Sadowskis - Artists and Craftsmen' *Canadian Art* 11:3:100 Spring 1954

Parker, Roszita *The Subversive Stitch: Embroidery and the Making of the Feminine* New York:Routledge 1989

Parry, Linda *Textiles of the the Arts and Crafts Movement* UK:V&A/Thames & Hudson 1988

Patterson, Nancy-Lou/Kitchener Waterloo Art Gallery *Mennonite Traditional Arts of the Waterloo Region and Southern Ontario* catalogue Kitchener: The Gallery 1974

Pearce, Susan M. ed. *Museum Studies in Material Culture* London: Leicester University Press 1989

Pearce, Susan M. *Museums, Objects and Collections: A Cultural Study* London: Leicester University Press 1992

Pearson, George 'The Art of Rug Hooking' *MacLean's Magazine* 40 pp.59-62 15 June 1927

Peck, M.A. *Sketch of the Activities of the Canadian Handicraft Guild and of the Dawn of the Handicraft Movement in the Dominion* booklet n/p 1929

Peck, M.A. 'Handicrafts from Coast to Coast' *CGJ* 9:4:204-216 October 1934

Peddle, Walter E. *The Traditional Furniture of Outport Newfoundland* St. John's: Harry Cuff Publications 1983

Pepall, Rosalind 'Montreal Metalsmith Paul Beau' *Canadian Collector* September/October 1979 pp.32-36

Pepall, Rosalind M. *Building a Beaux-Arts Museum: Montreal 1912* catalogue Montreal: Montreal Museum of Fine Arts 1986

Perry, Hattie A. *Old Days, Old Ways* Tantallon, NS: Four East Publications 1989

Perry, P. *Traditional-Functional Weaving in Saskatchewan* catalogue Regina: Dunlop Art Gallery/ Regina Public Library 1976

Petryshyn, W.R. ed *Changing Realities: Social Trends Among Ukrainian Canadians* Edmonton:Canadian Institute of Ukrainain Studies 1980

Phillips, Charles E. *The Development of Education in Canada* Toronto:Gage 1957

Pinneo, Paige G. 'High School Students Design Textiles' *Canadian Art* 6:1:19 Autumn 1948

Pocius, Gerald L. *Textile Traditions of Eastern Newfoundland* Mercury Series CCFCS 29 Ottawa:NMC 1979

Pocius, Gerald L. ed. *Living in a Material World: Canadian and American Approaches to Material Culture* NFD: ISER Memorial University of Newfoundland 1991

Pocius, Gerald L. 'Material Culture Research: Authentic Things, Authentic Values' *Material History Review 45* Spring 1997 pp.5-15

Pointon, Marcia ed. *Art Apart: Art Institutions and Ideology Across England and North America* UK:Manchester University Press 1994

Popular Mechanics Company *Mission Furniture: How to Make It* Parts I,II & III (orig. pub 1909, 1910, 1912) NY: Dover Publications 1980

Posen, I. Sheldon 'Reminiscent of a Tree: A Canadian Rustic Album' book ms. CMC 1997

'Prize List 1927 Nokomis Agricultural Fair' Saskatchewan:WDM.A DOC PA 291

Quimby, Ian M.C. and T.S.Scott ed.s *Perspectives On American Folk Art* N.Y.: W.W. Norton & Co 1980

Rasmussen, Linda *A Harvest Yet to Reap: a History of Prairie Women* Toronto:Women's Press c1975

Reid, J.G. *Mount Allison University: A History, to 1963* Toronto: University of Toronto Press 1984

Reynolds, Nila *Dream of Excellence* Haliburton ON: Haliburton Highlands Guild of Fine arts/ Haliburton School of Fine Arts c1976

Rider, Peter E. *Studies in History and Museums* Mercury Series 47 Ottawa/Hull: CMC 1994

Ringland, Mabel Crews 'The Work of Canadian Hands' *The Canadian Magazine* May 1931 pp.11,36,37

Ringland, Mabel Crews 'Encouraging Canadian Handicrafts' *Echoes* (I.O.D.E.) December 1932

Ringland, Mabel Crews 'Indian Handicrafts of Algoma' *CGJ* 6:4 April 1933

Ringland, Mabel Crews 'Canadian Handicrafts in Paris' *The Curtain Call* December 1936 pp.5-6

Robertson, Heather *The Salt of the Earth* Toronto:J.Lorimer 1974

Robinson, Carolyn; Ken Carpenter *Caricature and Conscience: The Ceramic Sculpture of Dora Wechsler* catalogue York: The Koffler Gallery 1992

Robson, Scott; S.MacDonald *Old Nova Scotian Quilts* catalogue Nova Scotia Museum: Nimbus Publishing Ltd 1995

Robson, Scott 'Hooked Mats of Canada's Atlantic Provinces: Nova Scotia' *Piecework* VI:1:48-49 January/February 1998

Rompkey, Ronald ed *Labrador Odyssey: The Journal and Photographs of Eliot Curwen on the Second Voyage of Wilfred Grenfell, 1893* Montreal: McGill Press 1996

Rosaldo, Michelle Z, L. Lampere ed.s *Women, Culture, and Society* California: Stanford University Press 1974

Rose, Muriel 'Crafts in Contemporary Life' *Canadian Art* 1:1:21 October 1943

Ross, Malcolm ed. *The Arts in Canada: A Stock-taking at Mid-century* Canada: Macmillan 1958

Rossbach, E. 'Mary Atwater and the Revival of American Traditional Weaving' *American Craft* 42:2:21-26 April 1983

Rosser, David 'Who Designs Canadian Textiles' *Canadian Art* 7:2:50 1949/50

Rossi, Sara 'Omar Ramsden Me Fecit' *Antique Dealer and Collectors Guide 51:6:*44-46

Rowan, Michael; J.Fleming *Ukrainian Pioneer Furniture* catalogue Ontario:Ukrainian Museum of Canada, Ontario Branch 1992

Royal Commission Studies: A Selection of Essays Prepared for the Royal Commission on National Development in the Arts, Letters and Sciences Ottawa:Government Publications 1951

Russell, Deane H. 'Composite Report to the Minister of Agriculture concerning some values to be derived from the development of a National Handcraft Programme' Ottawa:Ministry of Agriculture April 1941

Russell, Deane H. 'Review Statement outlining the Work and Recommendations of the Provisional Interdepartmental Committee on Canadian Hand Arts and Craft January 1942-January 1944' Ottawa:Ministry of Agriculture 1944

Russell, Loris S. *The National Museum of Canada 1910 to 1960* Ottawa: Department of Northern Affairs and National Resources 1961

Rutt, Richard *A History of Hand Knitting* Colorado:Interweave Press 1987

Ruryk, N. *Ukrainian Embroidery Design and Stitches* Winnipeg:UWAC 1956

Sabbath, Lawrence 'Mystery shrouds life of Montreal's master artist [Paul Beau]' *Montreal Gazette* 15 May 1982

'Saskatchewan Arts Board Handicraft Survey' *Saskatchewan Community* 2:3 Adult Education Division, Department of Education & Saskatchewan Arts Board September 1950

Saskatchewan Community 6: Handicraft and the Saskatchewan Arts Board Adult Education Division, Department of Education & Saskatchewan Arts Board July 1954

Saskatchewan Municipal Government Visual Arts and Crafts Economic Impact Assessment Final Report Anderson/Fast and Associates for Government of Saskatchewan, Regina 1996

Schamis, Elsa 'David Lambert, Vancouver's First Potter' paper 1984

Schlereth, Thomas J. ed. *Material Culture: A Research Guide* USA:University Press of Kansas 1985

Schroeder, Fred E.H. *Outlaw Aesthetics: Arts and the Public Mind* Ohio: Bowling Green University Popular Press 1977

Scott, Charles H. 'Art in British Columbia' *The Canadian Forum* 12:142:382-383 July 1932

Scott, Charles H. 'A Short Art History of British Columbia' *Behind the Palette* BC:Vancouver School of Art 1947/48 n/p

Scott, Charles H. *100 Years of B.C. Art* catalogue Vancouver: Vancouver Art Gallery 1958

Scott, Shirley A. *Canada Knits: Craft and Comfort in a Northern Land* Toronto:McGraw-Hill Ryerson 1990

Segalen, Martine 'Here but Invisible: The Presentation of Women in French Ethnography Museums' *Gender and History* 6:3:334-344 Blackwell 1994

Shackleton, M and P 'They Play with Mud [Lorenzens]' *Saturday Night* 25 July 1950 p.26

Shadbolt, J.L. 'A Report on Art Today in British Columbia' *Canadian Art* 4:1:4 November 1946

Shaw-Rimmington, Marie; D. Rickard *The Arts and Crafts Tradition in Vancouver* catalogue Vancouver: Cartwright Gallery 1986

Shenstone, Douglas A. *For the love of Pewter* Toronto:Metal Arts Guild 1990

Shoemaker, Nancy 'The Natural History of Gender' *Gender and History* 6:3:320-333 Blackwell 1994

Shrigley, Ruth, J.Davis *Inspired by Design: The Arts and Crafts Collection of the Manchester Metropolitan University* catalogue Manchester: City Art Gallery 1994

Sibyl Laubental: Pottery catalogue Edmonton Art Gallery/Winnipeg Art Gallery Winnipeg:the gallery 1962

Silverman, Elaine Leslau *The Last Best West: Women on the Alberta Frontier 1880-1930* Montreal: Eden Press 1984

Silverthorne, Judith *Made in Saskatchewan: Peter Rupchan* Saskatoon: Prairie Lily Co-operative 1991

Silverthorne, Judith 'Prairie Harvest: Saskatchewan Woodworkers and Furniture Makers, 1870-1930' book ms 1996

Simon, Frank 'History of the Alberta Provincial Institute of Technology and Art' M.A. dissertation Calgary:University of Alberta 1962

Bibliography

Simpson, Valerie 'Our Gracious Lady' *Journal New Brunswick Museum* 1978 pp.10-16

Smith, David E. ed. *Building a Province: A History of Saskatchewan in Documents* Saskatoon:Fifth House 1992

Soucy, Donald; H.Pearse *The First Hundred Years: A History of the Nova Scotia College of Art and Design* Halifax: Nova Scotia College of Art and Design/University of New Brunswick 1993

Southern Arts and Crafts 1890-1940 catalogue North Carolina USA: Mint Museum of Art, Charlotte 1996

Spencer Clark Collection of Historic Architecture catalogue Scarborough, ON: The Guild, n/d

Stacey, Robert 'Stacey Sterling: Master Metalsmith Harold Stacey' *Metalsmith* Spring 1985 pp.11-15

Stechishin, Savella *[Art Treasures of the Ukrainain Embroidery]* Winnipeg:UWAC 1950 (Ukrainian language publication)

Steele, Eloise 'Acadian Handicrafts' *The American Home* October 1933 p.250

Stevens, Gerald *Early Canadian Glass* Toronto: Ryerson Press 1960

Stevens, Gerald *Canadian Glass c.1825-1925* Toronto: Ryerson Press 1967

Stephenson, H.J.M. *A Few Words on the Making of Canadian Hooked Rugs/Tapis Canadiens au Crochet* booklet Montreal:CHG n/d

Strange, Kathleen 'Weaving a Girl's Hobby' *The Country Guide* February 1946

Strange, Kathleen 'Will Profitable Hearthside Industry Develop From Revival of Handloom Weaving in West?' *Saturday Night* reprint n/d [c.1943/34]

Studio Ceramics in Alberta 1947-1952 catalogue Alberta Art Foundation c1981

Tabachek, Jo-Anne 'Our Weaving History: for the 50th Anniversary of the Guild of Canadian Weavers, Manitoba Branch' Winnipeg:Guild of Canadian Weavers, Manitoba Branch 1997

Taft, Michael *Discovering Saskatchewan Folklore: Three Case Studies* Edmonton: NeWest Press 1983

Tanton, Margaret 'The Potter's Wheel Turns in Canada' *Echoes* Summer 1948 pp.6,7,46

Teather, J.Lynne 'Museum-Making in Canada (to 1972)' *Muse* Summer/Fall 1992 pp.21-29

Tennerhouse, Esther 'Fifty Years of Creative Friendship [Yellowknife Guild of Arts and Crafts 50th anniversary]' *Up Here Magazine* July 1996 p.70 (and unedited ms)

The Diversions of Keramos: 1925-1950 American Clay Sculpture catalogue Syracuse, NY:Everson Museum of Art 1983*The End of an Era/ La fin d'une epoque: Montreal 1880-1914* catalogue Montreal:McCord Museum, McGill University 1977

The Vancouver School of Decorative and Applied Arts prospectus for 1925/26, 1926/27, 1927/28, 1928/29 BC: Vancouver School of Decorative and Applied Arts

Thomas, Peter 'One Voice: Erica and Kjeld Deichmann' *ArtsAtlantic 30* Winter 1988 pp.26-29

Thompson, Allison 'A Worthy Place in the Art of Our Country: The Women's Art Association of Canada 1887-1987' M.A. dissertation Ottawa: Carleton University 1989

Tippett, Maria *Making Culture: English-Canadian Institutions and the Arts before the Massey Commission* Toronto: University of Toronto Press 1990

Todd, Irene 'Ottawa Children Know Their Museum' *CJG* 32:4 April 1951

Towers, Kathleen 'Pottery...a Canadian Handicraft' *Canadian Homes and Gardens* June 1948 pp.44,45,94

Townshend, Nancy/ Edmonton Art Gallery/ Alberta College of Art *The History of Ceramics in Alberta* catalogue Edmonton: the Gallery 1975

Traquair, Ramsay 'Hooked Rugs in Canada' *CGJ* 26:5:240-248 May 1943

Tremblay, Jules 'Paul Beau Revives a Lost Art' *Journal of the Royal Architectural Institute of Canada* 2:3:101-5 May/June 1925

Turcot, Henri *The French-Canadian Homespun Industry* Ottawa: Federal Department of Trade and Commerce 1928

Tweedie, R.A. et al *Arts in New Brunswick* NB:Brunswick Press 1967

Vancouver School of Art: the Growth Years 1939-1965 catalogue Vancouver:VSA 1983

V.M.[probably Vivian Morton] 'A Norwegian Woman Who Weaves Pictures [Mitzi Dahl]' *The Western Producer* 27 February 1930

Vaughan, Nora E. 'The Future of Handcraft in Canada' *Public Affairs* Autumn 1943 pp.10-14

Wagg, Susan *Percy Erskine Nobbs: Architect, Artist, Craftsman* Montreal:McGill-Queen's University Press 1982

'Watson Agricultural Society Second Annual Fair' prize list 1908 Saskatoon:Saskatchewan Western Development Museum, Curatorial Center Library [WDMCC]

'Watson Agricultural Society Annual Fair' prize list 1910 WDMCC

Bibliography

Watt, Robert D. *Rainbows on our walls: art and stained glass in Vancouver 1890 -1940* catalogue Vancouver: Vancouver Museums and Planetarium Association c1980 (with additional notes)

'Weaving Our Way Through 50 Years: Greater Vancouver Weavers' and Spinners' Guild' booklet Vancouver: Greater Vancouver Weavers' and Spinners' Guild c1985

Weiner, Annette B., J.Schneider ed.s *Cloth and Human Experience* USA:Smithsonian Institution Press 1989

Weltge, Sigrid W. *Women's Work: Textile Art from the Bauhaus* San Francisco: Chronicle Books 1993

Wetherell, Donald, I.Kmet *Useful Pleasures: The Shaping of Leisure in Alberta 1896-1945* Regina: Alberta Culture and Multiculturalism/Canadian Plains Research Centre 1990

Where to Buy Crafts in Nova Scotia NS: Handcraft Division, Nova Scotia Department of Trade and Industry 1947

Wickens, Keith 'Ecanada Art Pottery: a profile' *CMA Gazette* 12:3:38-42 Summer 1979

Wilks, Connie *PNE Arts and Crafts Program: historical overview* Vancouver:Pacific National Exhibition 1994

Wilson, Anne Elizabeth 'Creating a Nation's Handicrafts: The Pastime Work of the Nations in Canada' *The Chatelaine* October 1928 pp.8-9,40

Wilson, Anne Elizabeth 'The Day of Canadian Craftswomen' *The Chatelaine* October 1928 p.16

Withrow, Oswald *The Romance of the Canadian National Exhibition* Toronto: Reginald Saunders 1936

Wolff, Janet *The Social Production of Art* MacMillan 1981

Wood, Elizabeth Wyn 'A National Program for the Arts in Canada' *Canadian Art* 1:3:93 March 1944

Wood, Elizabeth Wyn 'Canadian Handicrafts' *Canadian Art* 2:5:186 1945

Wright, Virginia 'Craft Education in Canada: A History of Confusion' in Hickey ed. *Making and Metaphor* Ottawa/Hull:CMC Mercury Series 66 1994 pp.79-85

Wright, Virginia *Modern Furniture in Canada 1920 to 1970* Toronto: University of Toronto Press 1997